150 Best Jobs® for the Military-to-Civilian Transition

Part of JIST's Best Jobs® Series

Laurence Shatkin, Ph.D.

Also in JIST's *Best Jobs* Series

- ❋ *Best Jobs for the 21st Century*
- ❋ *50 Best Jobs for Your Personality*
- ❋ *150 Best Jobs for a Secure Future*
- ❋ *200 Best Jobs for College Graduates*
- ❋ *300 Best Jobs Without a Four-Year Degree*
- ❋ *225 Best Jobs for Baby Boomers*
- ❋ *250 Best-Paying Jobs*
- ❋ *10 Best College Majors for Your Personality*

- ❋ *150 Best Jobs for Your Skills*
- ❋ *175 Best Jobs Not Behind a Desk*
- ❋ *250 Best Jobs Through Apprenticeships*
- ❋ *150 Best Jobs for a Better World*
- ❋ *200 Best Jobs for Renewing America*
- ❋ *200 Best Jobs for Introverts*
- ❋ *150 Best Low-Stress Jobs*

JIST Works
America's Career Publisher®

150 Best Jobs for the Military-to-Civilian Transition

© 2013 by JIST Publishing

Published by JIST Works, an imprint of JIST Publishing
875 Montreal Way
St. Paul, MN 55102

E-mail: info@jist.com   Website: www.jist.com

Some Other Books by the Author

The Sequel

Panicked Student's Guide to Choosing a College Major

Your $100,000 Career Plan

90-Minute College Major Matcher

Quick Guide to College Majors and Careers

Visit www.jist.com for information on JIST, free job search tips, tables of contents, sample pages, and ordering information on our many products.

Acquisitions Editor: Susan Pines
Development Editor: Jeanne Clark
Cover Designer: Julie Johnston
Interior Layout: PerfecType, Nashville, TN
Proofreader: Chuck Hutchinson
Indexer: Cheryl Ann Lenser

Printed in the United States of America
18 17 16 15 14 13   9 8 7 6 5 4 3 2

Library of Congress Cataloging-in-Publication data is on file with the Library of Congress.

Print ISBN 978-1-59357-929-6

E-book ISBN 978-1-59357-936-4

This Is a Big Book, But It Is Very Easy to Use

After serving your country, you're now ready to take your skills into the civilian job market. But what are the best civilian jobs that your military experience has prepared you for? That's what this book is about. It identifies civilian jobs actually held by recent veterans of enlisted service and orders these jobs to emphasize those with the highest earnings and the highest demand for workers. Specialized lists arrange the jobs by personality types, educational levels, and demographic groups such as workers who are self-employed, female, male, urban, or rural.

Every job is described in detail later in the book, so you can explore the jobs that interest you most. You'll learn the major work tasks, all the important skills, the work conditions, the related military jobs, and many other informative facts.

You'll also find extensive references to resources to help with the transition to civilian employment, plus detailed suggestions for how to get college credit for your military experience; how to find job openings; and how to represent your military experience effectively in resumes, cover letters, and interviews.

Using this book, you'll be surprised how quickly you'll get new ideas for civilian career goals that can benefit from your military service and can suit you in many other ways.

Some Things You Can Do with This Book

- ❀ Identify interesting or good-paying jobs that recent veterans tend to hold.
- ❀ Develop plans for jobs that require a small amount of additional training, education, or experience.
- ❀ Explore and select a training or educational program that relates to a career objective.
- ❀ Prepare for the job search by learning the most effective strategies and resources for veterans.
- ❀ Prepare for interviews by learning how to connect your military-acquired skills to your career goal.

These are a few of the many ways you can use this book. I hope you find it as interesting to browse as I did to put together. I have tried to make it easy to use and as interesting as occupational information can be.

When you are done with this book, pass it along or tell someone else about it. I wish you well in your career and in your life.

Credits and Acknowledgments: While the author created this book, it is based on the work of many others. The occupational information is based on data obtained from the U.S. Department of Labor and the U.S. Census Bureau. These sources provide the most authoritative occupational information available. The noneconomic job-related information is from the O*NET database, which was developed by researchers and developers under the direction of the U.S. Department of Labor. They, in turn, were assisted by thousands of employers who provided details on the nature of work in the many thousands of job samplings used in the database's development. The author used the most recent version of the O*NET database, release 16. The author appreciates and thanks the staff of the U.S. Department of Labor for their efforts and expertise in providing such a rich source of data. The taxonomy of educational and training programs (the Classification of Instructional Programs) is from the U.S. Department of Education.

Table of Contents

Summary of Major Sections

Introduction. A short overview to help you better understand and use the book. *Starts on page 1.*

Part I. Making the Transition. Explains the career advantages of military service. Using a question-and-answer format, it identifies dozens of resources that you can use to get help with choosing a career goal, finding funds for education and training, getting college credit for military training, finding job leads, writing resumes, and starting a business. *Starts on page 17.*

Part II. The Best Jobs Lists. Very useful for exploring career options! Lists are arranged into easy-to-use groups. The first group of lists presents the 150 jobs that many recent veterans hold and that have the highest rankings based on earnings, projected growth, and number of openings. More-specialized lists follow, presenting the best jobs by demographic group, level of education or training, personality type, career cluster, and more. The column starting at right presents all the list titles. *Starts on page 29.*

Part III. Descriptions of the Best Jobs for the Military-to-Civilian Transition. Provides complete descriptions of the jobs that are held by recent veterans and that met my criteria for a combination of high pay, fast growth, and large number of openings. Each description contains information on earnings, projected growth, job duties, skills, related military job titles, education and training required, related knowledge and courses, and many other details. *Starts on page 99.*

Appendix. Definitions of Skills and Knowledge/Courses. Defines some of the terms that are used in the job descriptions. *Starts on page 321.*

Detailed Table of Contents

Introduction

After Military Service, What Next?

The training and work experience you gained in the military can qualify you to enter a good-paying, high-growth civilian job. This book is designed to help you make that transition.

I decided to write this book for enlisted personnel rather than for officers, because enlisted personnel make up four-fifths of the armed forces, are less likely than officers to make a career of military service, and are less likely to have a college degree that narrows down career goals. As a result of the book's focus on enlisted personnel, you won't find jobs such as medical doctor or college professor listed here. As I explain in a later section of this introduction, the jobs I selected for this book are those that enlisted personnel can transition into without many years of additional education and training.

So look at the jobs covered by this book and understand that they are selected to reflect the actual experiences of recent veterans. The chances are good that you'll find one or more jobs that will appeal to you.

Where the Information Came From

To develop the occupational information in this book, I relied mostly on databases created by the U.S. Department of Labor, the U.S. Census Bureau, and the U.S. Department of Defense:

❋ I started with data from the Census Bureau's American Community Survey for the years 2005–2009, describing 1.5 million recent veterans: 1.3 million men and 200,000 women. I was able to identify the occupational titles they hold, their employment status, their earnings, their level of education, and what segment of the economy they work in.

✸ For information about skills, personality types, and other characteristics of the civilian jobs held by these veterans, I used the Department of Labor's O*NET (Occupational Information Network) database, which is now the primary source of detailed information on occupations. The Labor Department updates the O*NET on a regular basis, and I used the most recent update available—O*NET release 16. I matched the job titles listed in the O*NET database, including some job specializations, to the slightly different job titles used by the Census Bureau and by other Labor Department databases.

✸ Although the data from the Census Bureau provided earnings data about the veterans, data from the Bureau of Labor Statistics (BLS) gave me the best estimates of the average earnings of *all* workers in each occupation. From the BLS, I also obtained information about future prospects in the different occupations: projected job growth and number of job openings. In addition, the BLS provided data about the percentage of urban and rural workers in each occupation and about the typical entry requirements for education, work experience, and on-the-job training.

✸ For information about the career clusters and pathways linked to each occupation, I used materials published by the National Association of State Directors of Career Technical Education Consortium.

✸ I used the Classification of Instructional Programs, a system developed by the U.S. Department of Education, for the names of the educational and training programs related to each job. I linked programs to jobs by following the crosswalk developed jointly by the BLS and the National Center for Education Statistics.

✸ For information about licensing and certification requirements, I relied partly on the Career OneStop website (www.careerinfonet.org) and partly on the *Occupational Outlook Handbook,* a Department of Labor website published in book form by JIST.

✸ For information about military specializations related to civilian jobs, I used a crosswalk developed by the Defense Manpower Data Center.

Of course, information in a database format can be boring and even confusing, so I did many things to help make the data useful and present it to you in a form that is easy to understand.

How the Best Jobs for the Military-to-Civilian Transition Were Selected

This book is based on the real experiences of veterans, not on some ideal notions of what veterans might do. To identify the actual jobs held by veterans, I used data from the Census Bureau's American Community Survey (ACS) and limited my sample to people who have been on active duty, not just training for the Reserves or National Guard, and who have served in September 2001 or later. By setting this cutoff date, I excluded people who have had more than a decade for postmilitary career development. This allowed me to keep the focus on the jobs veterans hold in the first years of transition from the military.

The 1.2 million recent veterans in my ACS survey sample held 459 unique occupations. I eliminated 235 jobs held by fewer than 1,000 vets. Of the 224 remaining occupations, many were groups of occupations, such as Diagnostic Related Technologists and Technicians, and when these were expanded to identify the detailed occupations included within them, the total came to 446.

From this list of detailed occupations, I removed 27 because my databases lacked important information about them, such as employment outlook, annual earnings, or work tasks. To keep the focus of the book on good jobs, I removed another 16 occupations that are projected to shrink in size and to offer fewer than 500 job openings per year, plus another 29 occupations with average annual earnings of less than $22,380. (Three-quarters of workers earn more than that.) This left 374 occupations.

I also removed an additional 74 jobs for which a bachelor's (or higher) degree is usually required and where work experience is rarely accepted as a substitute for the degree. For example, most civil engineers need to be licensed, and that in turn requires at least a bachelor's degree from a college program accredited by the industry organization. The engineering curriculum involves a lot of highly theoretical subject matter that is too extensive to be covered in a military training program and that cannot be learned through work experience in a military occupation. Although it is possible for you to get the appropriate college degree for this career after leaving the military, it is not very likely. The ACS found only 5,170 veterans (out of a total of 1.3 million) who were civil engineers, and although the ACS database doesn't tell me what rank vets had held in the service, it's likely that many or most of these engineers were former officers. So I eliminated civil engineers, judges, physicians, pharmacists, political scientists, and many other jobs like these so I could maintain the focus of the book on careers that enlisted personnel can transition into without many years of additional education or training. I gave the benefit of the doubt to several bachelor's-level managerial occupations, but I eliminated those focusing on business functions that enlisted personnel rarely are trained for, such as marketing.

After this sifting process, only a few of the 300 remaining occupations were equivalent to officer-level military jobs. Although this book is aimed at transitioning enlisted service members, I retained a few officer-level occupations that an appropriately experienced veteran could transition into without many years of postmilitary education or training—for example, Registered Nurses, Food Service Managers, and Accountants and Auditors.

Next, I followed these procedures to create the list of best jobs:

1. I compiled three lists that ranked the remaining 300 jobs based on three major criteria: median annual earnings, projected growth through 2020, and number of job openings projected per year.

2. I then added the numerical ranks for each job from all three lists to calculate its overall score.

3. To emphasize jobs that tend to pay more, are likely to grow more rapidly, and have more job openings, I selected the 150 job titles with the best numerical scores for my final list. These civilian jobs are the focus of this book.

For example, Software Developers, Systems Software, has the best combined score for earnings, growth, and number of job openings, so this occupation ranks first in my "150 Best Civilian Jobs Overall Through Military Training" list, even though it is neither the best-paying job (which is Air Traffic Controllers), the fastest-growing job (Veterinary Technologists and Technicians), nor the job with the most job openings (Registered Nurses). In fact, the best-paying job, Air Traffic Controllers, actually did not make it to the list of 150 best because it ranked very low on the other two economic factors.

Understand the Limits of the Data in This Book

In this book I use the most reliable and up-to-date information available on earnings, projected growth, number of openings, and other topics. The earnings data came partly from the Census Bureau's American Community Survey (the figures for veterans) and partly from the U.S. Department of Labor's Bureau of Labor Statistics (the figures for all workers). The job outlook information comes from the Office of Occupational Statistics and Employment Projections, a program within the Bureau of Labor Statistics that develops information about projected trends in the nation's labor market for the next 10 years. As you look at the figures, keep in mind that they are estimates. They give you a general idea about the annual earnings, rate of job growth, and annual job openings.

Understand that a problem with such data is that it describes an average. Just as there is no precisely average person, there is no such thing as a statistically average example of a particular job. I say this because data, while helpful, can also be misleading.

Take, for example, this book's figures for the yearly earnings of all workers in an occupation. This is highly reliable data obtained from a very large U.S. working population sample by the Bureau of Labor Statistics. It tells us the average annual pay received in May 2011 by people in various job titles (actually, it is the median annual pay, which means that half earned more and half less).

This sounds great, except that half of all people in that occupation earned less than that amount. For example, people who are new to the occupation or with only a few years of work experience often earn much less than the median amount. People who live in rural areas or who work for smaller employers typically earn less than those who do similar work in cities (where the cost of living is higher) or for bigger employers. People in certain areas of the country earn less than those in others. Other factors also influence how much you are likely to earn in a given job in your area. For example, some industries cluster in certain metropolitan areas (think of Detroit's automobile industry), causing workers there to be more productive and more often unionized, thus earning more.

Also keep in mind that the figures for job growth and number of openings are projections by labor economists—their best estimates of what our nation can expect between now and 2020. They are not guarantees. A major economic downturn, war, or technological breakthrough could change the actual outcome.

Finally, don't forget that the job market consists of both job openings and job *seekers*. The figures on job growth and openings don't tell you how many people will be competing with you to be hired. At best, in Part III I can provide a general, non-numerical statement regarding competition in an information topic called "Considerations for Job Outlook." Like earnings, however, competition can vary greatly from one community to another, so you need to research this issue locally for any career goal you're considering. You should speak to people in your community who educate or train tomorrow's workers; they probably have a good idea of how many local people with a background like yours find rewarding employment and how quickly. People in the local workforce, especially other veterans, also can provide insights into this issue. Use your critical thinking skills to evaluate what people tell you. For example, recruiters at schools are highly motivated to get you to sign up, whereas people in the workforce may be trying to discourage you from competing. Get a variety of opinions to balance out possible biases.

So, in reviewing the information in this book, please understand the limitations of the data. You need to use common sense in career decision making as in most other things in life. I hope that, using that approach, you find the information helpful and interesting.

The Data Complexities

For those of you who like details, I present here some of the complexities inherent in my sources of information and what I did to make sense of them for you. You don't need to know these things to use the book, so jump to the next section of the introduction if details bore you.

I selected the jobs partly on the basis of economic data, and I include information on earnings, projected growth, and number of job openings for each job throughout this book. I think this information is important to most veterans, but getting it for each job is not a simple task.

Earnings

I include two earnings figures for the 150 jobs in this book: earnings for all workers and earnings for recent veterans. Understand that the figures for all workers are based on a more comprehensive survey and are therefore more accurate estimates. That's why I used these figures in sorting the lists of the best jobs.

The earnings figures for all workers are derived from a BLS program called Occupational Employment Statistics, or OES. The employment security agency of each state gathers information on earnings for various jobs and forwards it to the BLS, where the OES organizes and reports the information in standardized ways. To keep the earnings for the various jobs and regions comparable, the OES screens out certain types of earnings and includes others, so the OES earnings I use in this book represent straight-time gross pay exclusive of premium pay. More specifically, the OES earnings include each job's base rate; cost-of-living allowances; guaranteed pay; hazardous-duty pay; incentive pay, including commissions and production bonuses; on-call pay; and tips. The OES earnings do not include back pay, jury duty pay, overtime pay, severance pay, shift differentials, nonproduction bonuses, or tuition reimbursements. Also, self-employed workers are not included in the estimates, whereas part-time workers are included; these are significant segments of the workforce in certain occupations. When data on annual earnings for an occupation is highly unreliable, OES does not report a figure, which meant that I reluctantly had to exclude a few occupations, such as Actors, from this book. The median earnings for all workers in all occupations were $34,460 in May 2011. The jobs in this book were chosen partly on the basis of their earnings, so they average $45,656.

The earnings figures for recent veterans that I report in this book are based on the Census Bureau's American Community Survey (ACS) for the years 2005–2009, describing 1.3 million recent veterans. People surveyed by the ACS were asked to report their earnings over the past 12 months. For each occupation held by recent veterans, I computed the median earnings figure—that is, half earned more and half earned less. Understand that this figure is more reliable for some occupations than for others because of great variations in the number of veterans working in each occupation. For Police and Sheriff's Patrol Officers, the sample represents 200,000 workers; for Roofers, only 1,007. Because the veterans were surveyed several years ago, I brought the earnings figures up to date by inflating them at the same rate as the overall wage trends in the working population. The median earnings for recent veterans in all occupations are $38,140. Because the jobs in this book were chosen partly on the basis of earnings, the median earnings of vets in these 150 occupations are $40,380. This compares favorably with the median of $34,870 earned by nonvets in these same jobs.

In addition to these two figures for median earnings, I include a statement called Earnings Growth Potential. This represents the gap between the 10th percentile and the median. This information answers the question, "If I compared the wages of the low earners to the median, how much of a pay difference (as a percentage of the median) would I find?" If the difference is large, the job has great potential for increasing your earnings as you gain experience and skills. If the difference is small, you probably will need to move on to another occupation to improve your earnings substantially. Because a percentage figure, by itself, might be hard to interpret, I put the figure in parentheses and precede it with an easy-to-understand verbal tag that expresses the Earnings Growth Potential: "very low" when the percentage is less than 25%, "low" for 25%–35%, "medium" for 35%–40%, "high" for 40%–50%, and "very high" for any figure higher than 50%.

Projected Growth and Number of Job Openings

The most recent job outlook projections available cover the years from 2010 to 2020. The projections are based on information about people moving into and out of occupations. The BLS uses data from various sources in projecting the growth and number of openings for each job title—some data comes from the Census Bureau's Current Population Survey and some comes from an OES survey. In making the projections, the BLS economists assumed that there will be no major war, depression, or other economic upheaval. They also assumed that recessions may occur during the decade covered by these projections, as would be consistent with the pattern of business cycles the United States has experienced for several decades. However, because their projections cover 10 years, the figures for job growth and openings are intended to provide an average of both the good times and the bad times.

While salary figures are fairly straightforward, you may not know what to make of job-growth figures. For example, is projected growth of 15% good or bad? You should keep in mind that the average (mean) growth projected for all occupations by the Bureau of Labor Statistics is 14.3%. One-quarter of the occupations have a growth projection of 4.9% or lower. Growth of 11.5% is the median, meaning that half of the occupations have more growth, half less. Only one-quarter of the occupations have growth projected at 19.0% or higher.

Remember, however, that the jobs in this book were selected as "best" partly on the basis of high growth, so their median growth is better than the median for all jobs: 17.2%.

Among these 150 outstanding jobs, the job ranked 38th by projected growth has a figure of 23.6%, and the job ranked 113th has a projected growth of 12.6%.

The average number of job openings for the 150 best jobs—15,029—is twice as high as the national average of 7,510 openings for all occupations. Among the jobs in this book, the job ranked 38th for job openings has a figure of about 16,600 annual openings projected, the job ranked 75th (the median) has about 8,000 openings, and the job ranked 113th has about 3,200 openings.

Perhaps you're wondering why I present figures on both job growth *and* number of openings. Aren't these two ways of saying the same thing? Actually, you need to know both. Consider the occupation Athletic Trainers, which is projected to grow at the astounding rate of 30.0%. There should be lots of opportunities in such a fast-growing job, right? Not exactly. This is a very small occupation, with only about 18,200 people currently employed, so even though it is growing rapidly, it is expected to create only 1,190 job openings per year. Now consider First-Line Supervisors of Non-Retail Sales Workers. This occupation is growing at the sluggish rate of 4.0%. Nevertheless, this is a large occupation that employs 422,900 workers, so even though its growth rate is well below average, it is expected to take on 12,350 new workers each year. That's why I base my selection of the best jobs on both of these economic indicators and why you should pay attention to both when you scan the lists of best jobs.

Other Job Characteristics

In some of the lists in this book, two or more occupations have identical figures for a certain characteristic. Usually these are unrelated occupations and the tie is a coincidence. For example, 23.2% growth is projected for Electricians and also for Health Technologists and Technicians, All Other. On the other hand, in lists based on figures derived from the Census Bureau, ties sometimes occur when the Census Bureau lumps two or more occupations together, reporting them under a single title. For example, the Census Bureau reports data about a single occupation called Diagnostic Related Technologists and Technicians rather than separately for the various specializations, such as Diagnostic Medical Sonographers, Nuclear Medicine Technologists, Radiologic Technologists, and several related jobs. As a result, in Part II you'll find these separate occupations ordered alphabetically but otherwise tied in the list of jobs with the highest percentage of female veterans. You may notice similar figure-sharing among related jobs where I list the percentages of self-employed veterans.

Information in the Job Descriptions

For the job descriptions in Part III, I used the same government sources as for the lists in Part II. I explain how I interpreted the data from these various sources later in this introduction, in the section "Part III: Descriptions of the Best Jobs for the Military-to-Civilian Transition."

How This Book Is Organized

The information in this book about job options for the military-to-civilian transition moves from the general to the highly specific.

Part I. Making the Transition

Part I answers key questions about the transition from military service to a civilian job. It's particularly rich in references to resources that you can turn to for help with getting veteran benefits, getting education or training, and finding jobs. There are tips for veterans with disabilities and for those who are interested in self-employment.

Part II. The Best Jobs Lists

For many people, the 46 lists in Part II are the most interesting section of the book. Here you can see titles of civilian jobs that are commonly entered by recent veterans and that have the best combination of high salaries, fast growth, and plentiful job openings. You can see which jobs are best in terms of each of these factors combined or considered separately. The list of high-performing jobs is broken out further according to personality types and several other features of the jobs and of the people in them. Look in the table of contents for a complete list of lists. Although there are a lot of lists, they are not difficult to understand because they have clear titles and are organized into groupings of related lists.

People who prefer to think about careers in terms of personality types will want to browse the lists that show the best jobs for Realistic, Investigative, Artistic, Social, Enterprising, and Conventional personality types. I have also created lists for people who think first in terms of career clusters.

I suggest that you use the lists that make the most sense for you. Following are the names of each group of lists along with short comments on each group. You will find additional information in a brief introduction provided at the beginning of each group of lists in Part II.

Best Jobs Overall: Lists of Jobs for the Military-to-Civilian Transition with the Highest Pay, Fastest Growth, and Most Openings

This group has four lists, and they are the ones that most people want to see first. The first list presents all 150 jobs that are included in this book in order of their combined scores for earnings, growth, and number of job openings. These jobs are used in the more-specialized lists that follow and in the descriptions in Part III. Three more lists in this group present specialized lists of jobs for the military-to-civilian transition: the 50 best-paying jobs, the 50 fastest-growing jobs, and the 50 jobs with the most openings.

Best Jobs Lists for the Military-to-Civilian Transition by Demographic

This group of lists recognizes the diversity of civilian jobs where recent veterans work by presenting interesting information for a variety of types of workers based on data from the U.S. Census Bureau. The lists highlight jobs with large concentrations of recent veterans of all kinds and recent veterans who are self-employed, part-timers, women, and men. Additional lists identify jobs with high percentages of urban and rural workers (based on the general population, not just vets). For each group, I created two lists: one showing the jobs with a high percentage of people of each type, ordered by percentage; and one ordering these jobs by their combined scores for earnings, growth, and number of openings.

Best Jobs Lists Based on Educational Attainment of Recent Veterans

These four lists divide the 150 best jobs according to the median level of education attained by the recent veterans holding the jobs. The levels range from a high school diploma or less to a bachelor's degree or higher. Within each list, jobs are ordered by their combined scores for earnings, growth, and number of openings.

Best Jobs Lists Based on Career Clusters

These lists organize the 150 jobs into the 16 career clusters that were originally developed by the U.S. Department of Education in 1999. These clusters have since been modified by the National Association of State Directors of Career Technical Education Consortium and are used by many educational institutions and career information resources to divide up the world of work and the educational and training programs that prepare for careers. Some jobs are assigned to more than one cluster and thus appear on multiple lists. Here are the 16 interest career clusters used in these lists: Agriculture, Food, and Natural Resources; Architecture and Construction; Arts, Audio/ Video Technology, and Communications; Business, Management, and Administration; Education and Training; Finance; Government and Public Administration; Health Science; Hospitality and Tourism; Human Services; Information Technology; Law, Public Safety, Corrections, and Security; Manufacturing; Marketing, Sales, and Service; Science, Technology, Engineering, and Mathematics; and Transportation, Distribution, and Logistics. Some career resources use slightly different names for some of these clusters; I used the same titles as the online O*NET database (www.onetonline.org/

find/career). Within each cluster's list, the jobs are ranked by their combined scores for earnings, growth, and number of openings.

Best Jobs Lists Based on Personality Types

These lists organize the 150 civilian jobs into six personality types, which are described in the introduction to the lists: Realistic, Investigative, Artistic, Social, Enterprising, and Conventional. (If those terms don't mean a lot to you, you can find their definitions in the introduction to the lists.) The jobs within each list are presented in order of their combined scores for earnings, growth, and number of openings.

Bonus List: Best Jobs with the Greatest Earnings Advantage for Recent Veterans

This list shows the 33 jobs in which the earnings of recent veterans exceed the earnings of all other workers by the greatest percentage. It is based on earnings data from the American Community Survey.

Bonus List: Best-Paying Industries for Recent Veterans

This list shows the 25 industries in which recent veterans have the highest earnings. It is based on earnings data from the American Community Survey.

Part III: Descriptions of the Best Jobs for the Military-to-Civilian Transition

This part describes each of the 150 best jobs, using a format that is informative yet compact and easy to read. The descriptions contain statistics such as earnings and projected growth; lists such as major work tasks, skills, and work environment; and key descriptors such as personality type and career cluster. Because the jobs in this section are arranged in alphabetical order, you can easily find a job that you've identified from Part II and that you want to learn more about.

I used the most current information from a variety of government sources to create the descriptions. Although I've tried to make the descriptions easy to understand, the sample that follows—with an explanation of each of its parts—may help you better understand and use the descriptions.

Here are some details on each of the major parts of the job descriptions you will find in Part III:

❋ **Job Title:** This is the title for the job as defined by the U.S. Department of Labor within the Standard Occupational Classification scheme that is used in all government databases with information about occupations.

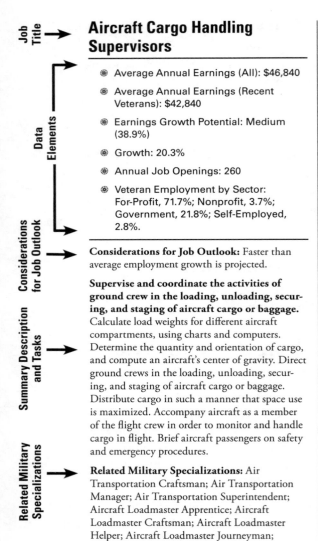

Job Title →

Aircraft Cargo Handling Supervisors

Data Elements →

- ❋ Average Annual Earnings (All): $46,840
- ❋ Average Annual Earnings (Recent Veterans): $42,840
- ❋ Earnings Growth Potential: Medium (38.9%)
- ❋ Growth: 20.3%
- ❋ Annual Job Openings: 260
- ❋ Veteran Employment by Sector: For-Profit, 71.7%; Nonprofit, 3.7%; Government, 21.8%; Self-Employed, 2.8%.

Considerations for Job Outlook →

Considerations for Job Outlook: Faster than average employment growth is projected.

Summary Description and Tasks →

Supervise and coordinate the activities of ground crew in the loading, unloading, securing, and staging of aircraft cargo or baggage. Calculate load weights for different aircraft compartments, using charts and computers. Determine the quantity and orientation of cargo, and compute an aircraft's center of gravity. Direct ground crews in the loading, unloading, securing, and staging of aircraft cargo or baggage. Distribute cargo in such a manner that space use is maximized. Accompany aircraft as a member of the flight crew in order to monitor and handle cargo in flight. Brief aircraft passengers on safety and emergency procedures.

Related Military Specializations →

Related Military Specializations: Air Transportation Craftsman; Air Transportation Manager; Air Transportation Superintendent; Aircraft Loadmaster Apprentice; Aircraft Loadmaster Craftsman; Aircraft Loadmaster Helper; Aircraft Loadmaster Journeyman; C-130 Loadmaster; C-130 Second Loadmaster;

Education, Knowledge, Experience, Training, Certification, Licensure

Loadmaster; Parachute Rigger. **Average Educational Level of Vets:** One or more years of college, no degree. **Usual Educational Requirement:** High school diploma or equivalent. **Relevant Educational Program:** Aviation/Airway Management and Operations. **Related Knowledge/Courses:** Transportation; Public Safety and Security; Geography; Personnel and Human Resources; Psychology; Customer and Personal Service. **Work Experience Needed:** 1 to 5 years. **On-the-Job Training Needed:** None. **Certification/Licensure:** None.

Personality Types, Career Cluster, Career Pathway, Top Industries ←

Personality Types: Enterprising-Realistic. **Key Career Cluster:** 16 Transportation, Distribution, and Logistics. **Key Career Pathway:** 16.1 Transportation Operations. **Top Industries for Vets:** National Security and International Affairs; Couriers and Messengers; Services Incidental to Transportation; Truck Transportation; Rail Transportation.

Skills ←

Skills: Management of Personnel Resources; Repairing; Learning Strategies; Equipment Maintenance; Operation and Control; Management of Material Resources; Equipment Selection; Troubleshooting.

Work Environment ←

Work Environment: Outdoors; standing; walking and running; using hands; repetitive motions; noise; very hot or cold; bright or inadequate lighting; contaminants; hazardous equipment.

❋ **Data Elements:** These bulleted information topics tell you some important economic characteristics of the workers and of the occupation. The information comes from various U.S. Department of Labor and Census Bureau databases, as explained elsewhere in this introduction.

❋ **Considerations for Job Outlook:** This information explains some factors that are expected to affect opportunities for job seekers. The content is derived from the Employment Projections Office of the Bureau of Labor Statistics.

❋ **Job Specializations:** Thirty-nine of the jobs described in Part III contain specializations within the larger job category being described. These specialized titles are based on the classification scheme used in the O*NET database. When specializations exist, some information topics (such as personality types and skills) are available only for the specializations and not for the "parent" occupation.

❋ **Summary Description and Tasks:** The bold sentence provides a summary description of the occupation. It is followed by a listing of tasks that are generally performed by people who work in this job. This information comes from the O*NET database but where necessary has been edited to avoid exceeding 2,200 characters.

❋ **Related Military Specializations**: These military jobs commonly serve as training routes for the civilian job or involve similar work tasks. A crosswalk from the Defense Manpower Data Center identified the appropriate military job titles. Where necessary, the list has been edited to avoid exceeding 500 characters.

❋ **Average Educational Level of Vets**: I derived this information from the responses of recent veterans polled by the American Community Survey. For each job, I found the median level of educational attainment of the recent veterans holding the job.

❋ **Usual Educational Requirement**: This is the level of education that the BLS identifies as the common civilian entry route to this occupation. You'll notice many instances where this level is higher than the level that is typical of recent veterans. That happens when veterans' military training and experience are able to compensate for a lower level of formal education, and it demonstrates some of the advantages that you bring to the job market as a veteran.

❋ **Relevant Educational Programs:** These are the college majors or other postsecondary programs that are the most frequent civilian entry routes to this occupation. Keep in mind that your military training and work experience, if it is relevant to this career goal and taught you a high level of skill, may substitute for one of these programs.

❋ **Related Knowledge/Courses:** This entry can help you understand the most important knowledge areas that are required for the job. As you read each item on this list, decide whether you will need to learn it by taking a course or program that teaches it or whether you already are well informed about it because of your military training and experience. For each job, I identified the highest-rated knowledge area in the O*NET database, so every job for which data is available has at least one listed. I identified any additional knowledge area that had a rating that was higher than the average rating for that knowledge area for all jobs. I listed as many as five knowledge areas in descending order. For definitions of the knowledge areas, see the appendix.

✱ **Work Experience Needed:** This is the amount of experience in a related job that is usually required to enter the occupation. For example, many managerial positions require experience in the kind of work being supervised.

✱ **On-the-Job Training Needed:** This is the amount of training that new workers need to get before they attain competency in the occupation. Short-term on-the-job training takes one month or less. Moderate-term training takes between one month and one year. Long-term training takes more than a year. For some occupations, an apprenticeship is the normal route; these usually take several years and include night classes.

✱ **Certification/Licensure:** This statement indicates whether a certificate or license is required or helpful for entry to the occupation (or perhaps a specialization) in most states. I don't bother to note when an ordinary driver's license is needed or when certification is the usual outcome of an apprenticeship. Keep in mind that this information is a generalization that describes the whole nation and the full range of specializations within the occupation. Some states may be exceptions, and sometimes licensure is required or waived for a highly specialized niche within the occupation.

✱ **Personality Types:** Each job description includes the name of the personality types that the O*NET links to the job. You'll find a primary personality type and as many as two secondary types. You can find more information on the personality types as well as a brief definition of each type in the introduction to the lists of jobs based on personality types in Part II.

✱ **Key Career Cluster** and **Key Career Pathway:** This information cross-references the 16 career clusters developed by the U.S. Department of Education and used in a variety of educational institutions and career information systems. I identify the single cluster and pathway that the job best fits into. This information will help you discover other job titles that have similar interests, require similar skills, or need similar secondary school preparation.

✱ **Top Industries for Vets:** This list is based on the responses to the American Community Survey. For the occupation being described, it shows the five industries (taken from the North American Industry Classification System) employing the largest number of recent veterans. The industries with the largest percentages of vets are listed first. A few occupations, such as Postal Service Mail Carriers, are found in fewer than five industries.

❋ **Skills:** The O*NET database provides data on many skills; I decided to list only those that were most important for each job rather than list pages of unhelpful details. For each job, I identified any skill that had a rating at a level higher than the average rating for that skill for all jobs, and that also is not rated as an unimportant skill. If there were more than eight, I included only those eight with the highest ratings, and I present them from highest to lowest score (that is, in terms of by how much its score exceeds the average score). If any of the skill names are not familiar to you, turn to the appendix to read the definitions.

❋ **Work Environment:** I include any work condition with a rating that exceeds the midpoint of the rating scale. The order does not indicate any condition's frequency on the job. Consider whether you like these conditions and whether any of these conditions would make you uncomfortable. Keep in mind that when hazards are present (for example, contaminants), protective equipment and procedures are provided to keep you safe.

Getting all the information I used in the job descriptions was not a simple process, and it is not always perfect. For some information topics, data is not available. However, I used the best and most recent sources of data I could find, and I think that the results will be helpful to many people.

PART I

Making the Transition

Leaving military service and finding a civilian job can mean a big adjustment. This part of the book answers several important questions about the military-to-civilian transition—including some that you might not have thought to ask. What you learn here can help you find a job faster.

What Career Advantages Do I Have as a Veteran?

Many employers prefer to hire veterans rather than recent high school graduates. They understand that the military teaches more than just how to march in time and throw a salute. Veterans have learned many technical and managerial skills through their military training and experience. In addition to skills that apply to a particular job, veterans have learned certain fundamental skills and work-related attitudes that the wet-behind-the-ears job candidates don't bring to the workplace: teamwork, a sense of responsibility, a positive attitude toward authority, initiative, and experience with diversity—to name only a few. Many veterans have a security clearance, which is necessary for some jobs.

One employer gives special recognition for military service: the federal government. If you get a federal civil service job after you leave the military, your time in uniform will count toward your seniority on the job. This will boost your pay and allow you to take retirement earlier. Some states also have this rule for their civil service jobs. Even better, if you served during an armed conflict, your score on the federal civil service exam will be awarded additional points, giving you an edge over other job candidates.

One measure of the payoff of military service is the relative earnings of veterans versus nonveterans. Using data from the Census Bureau's American Community Survey, I was able to compare the median earnings of recent veterans and nonveterans. (The median is the point at which half earned more, half earned less.) I found that the vets had median earnings of $38,142 (in 2010 dollars), compared to $30,503 for the nonvets. That's a 25 percent advantage.

Of course, veterans tend to cluster more in certain occupations than the general population does, so I also compared the median earnings of recent vets and nonvets who work in the same occupations. To determine the overall average difference between the two groups, I computed the weighted average earnings, meaning that occupations with a larger number of workers had extra weight in the calculations. I found that recent veterans had an earnings advantage of 21 percent compared to nonvets in the same occupations. This wage advantage is all the more impressive considering that the veterans in these occupations were considerably younger than the nonveterans, with a median age of 36 compared to 42 for the nonvets.

Another measure of the work-related value of military service is the unemployment rate reported by the Bureau of Labor Statistics. In January 2012, the unemployment rate for male veterans of the Second Gulf War era was 7.7 percent, compared to 9.3 percent for the male nonveteran population.

What's disturbing is the fact that female vets don't share this advantage: The unemployment rate for female vets of the same era was a whopping 13.5 percent. This figure is even more alarming when you consider that among women who were *not* veterans, the unemployment rate was only 8.1 percent.

It's not fully clear why female veterans are having more trouble finding jobs. In some cases, it may be that the military has trained them for a nontraditional job—truck mechanic, for example—but in civilian life, they either are uninterested in the equivalent job or are not welcome in it. Some female vets have child-care responsibilities that complicate their efforts to find suitable work.

Probably the main reason for the high unemployment of female veterans is that many civilian employers still are not used to the idea of women in the military and therefore don't readily perceive that female vets possess the skills and work attitudes that military service teaches. If you're a female vet, you will probably have to put more effort into your resume, cover letter, and job interviews so that they clearly communicate your qualifications to employers.

Actually, this advice applies to all vets, male and female. The skills and work habits you acquired in the military may not be immediately obvious to employers, so you need to find ways to express them effectively in terms that civilians will understand. See the "What Makes an Effective Transitional Resume?" section later in this chapter.

Where Can I Get Help with My Transition to a Civilian Career?

Each service branch provides a Transition Assistance Office, although the name varies; for example, the Army calls it an Army Career and Alumni Program (ACAP) office. If you have already left the service and didn't visit this office beforehand, be sure to go there now. This office can advise you about your benefits for health and education and can help you with your career planning. Independent research has found that, on average, service members participating in the Transition Assistance Program find their first postmilitary job three weeks sooner than those who do not participate in TAP.

An extremely valuable resource that's part of TAP is the Department of Defense's TurboTap.org website (www.turbotap.org). It includes printable transition guides and an interactive course with voiceover narration to inform you about important issues related to the transition. The course is so rich in content that you can spend several hours within it. It covers these topics:

* Career exploration (including advice about relocation and options for education)
* Financial planning
* Job search success
* Effective resumes and cover letters
* Interviewing excellence
* Negotiating your ideal compensation

The Military OneSource website (www.militaryonesource.mil) offers links to counseling and many pages of advice for the transition to civilian life. At the home page, choose "Military Life" under the "Military Life & Deployment" tab and then click the options under the "Separation and Transition" heading.

Another valuable source of help is your local One-Stop Career Center. Find its location at www.careeronestop.org. As a recent veteran, you're eligible for a Gold Card (www.dol.gov/vets/goldcard.html) that entitles you to receive enhanced intensive services at your local one-stop, including up to six months of follow-up. The enhanced in-person services available for Gold Card holders at local one-stop career centers may include the following:

* Job-readiness assessment, including interviews and testing
* Development of an Individual Development Plan (IDP)
* Career guidance through group or individual counseling to help you make decisions about training and a career
* Information about the labor market, careers, and transferable skills to help with decisions about education, training, and career goals
* Referral to job banks, job portals, and job openings
* Referral to employers and sponsors of registered apprenticeships

⁕ Referral to training by Workforce Investment Act–funded or third-party service providers

⁕ Monthly follow-up by an assigned case manager for as long as six months

The National Resource Directory (www.nationalresourcedirectory.gov) is a website for connecting wounded warriors, service members, veterans, their families, and caregivers with those who support them. It provides access to services and resources at the national, state, and local levels to support recovery, rehabilitation and community reintegration. The site covers topics such as benefits and compensation, education and training, employment, family and caregiver support, health, homeless assistance, housing, transportation and travel, volunteer opportunities, and other services and resources. The site is a partnership among the Departments of Defense, Labor, and Veterans Affairs.

To learn about all the benefits that are available to you and to take advantage of them, use the eBenefits site (www.ebenefits.va.gov) as a launch pad. Once you have registered at this site, you can apply for benefits, download your DD 214 (Certificate of Release or Discharge from Active Duty), view your benefits status, and accomplish several other tasks related to benefits.

As this book goes to press, the Veterans Job Bank (www.nationalresourcedirectory.gov/jobSearch) is still in beta testing and is part of the National Resource Directory. Using either keywords or the MOS or MOC code, you tell the website your military job plus your present location, and it retrieves job listings that are the closest match. For any job listed, note the date of posting, because some job listings are much more current than others.

The Army Reserve and the National Guard jointly operate a site (www.employerpartnership.org) with job search capability, plus suggestions for how to find and apply for jobs.

If you're thinking about finding a job with the federal government, USAJOBS (www.usajobs.gov) is the central place for retrieving job postings. But first visit the Feds Hire Vets site (www.fedshirevets.gov), where you can get detailed information about how your status as a veteran can help you get a federal job. (This website is particularly valuable for transition from the National Guard or Reserves.) Another valuable site is Mil2FedJobs (www.dllr.state.md.us/mil2fedjobs). Although this site is hosted by the State of Maryland, the federal jobs it links to may be in other states or even overseas.

Here are some privately sponsored websites, all of which include job searches plus links to other helpful content. These services are not all alike, so I suggest you look at several and decide which site or sites better serve your needs. Some of them offer (or advertise) paid services such as resume writing and job-hunt coaching. Before you sign up for any such services, find out whether you can get the same help free of charge at your local one-stop career center. I have tried to exclude sites that are dominated by advertising:

❋ Monster.com, as part of its Military.com site, has created the Veteran Job Search (www.veteranemployment.com).

❋ Militaryhire.com is a similar site.

❋ More and more employers are using Twitter to post their job openings. The TweetMyJobs For Veterans site (www.veterans.tweetmyjobs.com) helps you identify Twitter channels to follow for news about relevant job openings.

❋ Many of the jobs listed in this book are in construction, and the Helmets to Hardhats program (www.helmetstohardhats.org) is specifically designed to help you make the transition to this career field.

❋ For transition to jobs in health care, try the Heroes to Healthcare site (www. heroes2healthcare.org).

❋ TAOnline (www.taonline.com) has links to a site with a resume-writing utility.

❋ VetJobs (http://vetjobs.com) is sponsored by the Veterans for Foreign Wars and specializes in jobs for which security clearance is required.

For information about occupations that may be related to your military training, My Next Move for Veterans (www.mynextmove.org/vets) is a site that uses some of the same databases I used for the job descriptions in this book. You can also search for occupations by specifying keywords or by choosing an industry. If you're not sure what job might suit you, follow the link to the O*NET Interest Profiler. The Interest Profiler produces a score report based on the personality types that I used to create one set of lists of best jobs in Part II.

I Signed Up for G.I. Bill Benefits. How Can I Use Them Now?

You can use your G.I. Bill benefits to pay for a wide variety of programs: college, business school, vocational courses, correspondence courses (partial payment), degree-related independent study, and apprenticeships. The funding can be particularly helpful if your military training doesn't provide all the qualifications you need for the career you want or if you decide to pursue a career different from your military job. It also can be useful to help you advance in a career once you are employed—for example, to get a college degree that boosts you from an entry-level job to the management track. Employers sometimes pay for employees to get additional education or training, but they certainly will appreciate letting the G.I. Bill pick up the tab for you.

You are eligible to use G.I. Bill benefits at any time during the 10 years after honorable discharge. The funding will cover a specified amount that may exceed tuition costs and thus also can function as a stipend. If you served in the selected reserve—that is, reservists in jobs of highest priority at times of mobilization—the benefits are available for the 14 years after boot camp and military job training. However, this program pays only about one-third as much as the program for veterans of active duty.

Before you sign up for an educational or training program, make sure that the program is respected by employers. Some shady educational institutions are offering bogus degrees, and others offer degrees that are legitimate but are of little interest to employers. For any degree program you're considering, check the Database of Accredited Postsecondary Institutions and Programs (http://ope.ed.gov/accreditation) to make sure that the institution is recognized by a regional accrediting commission. If you need certification for your career goal, be sure that the training program prepares you for the exam and for all other requirements for certification. Is the exam you're being prepared for the one that is most widely recognized in the industry? Does the externship provide the required number of hours? Ideally, you should talk to the people who hire the kind of worker you want to be; find out what qualifications these employers value.

Can I Get College Credit for My Military Training?

One way to help your military training boost your career is to get college credit for what you've learned. Having these credits on your resume can convince employers that the military taught you skills at the college level. It also means that if you enter (or re-enter) college now, some of your course requirements may already be completed. That can save a lot of tuition money and time.

Even if you don't apply for official recognition in the form of college credits, understanding what you *would* qualify for can help you make a more convincing case for your job-related skills on your resume and in interviews.

The American Council on Education (ACE) has determined the course credits that are appropriate for various training programs, and most colleges grant at least some of this credit. (You may need to shop around to find the most military-friendly college.) To see how to get these credits, go to www.acenet.edu and click "Military Programs" on the "Programs & Services" pull-down menu. From there, click "Military Guide Online" to go to a webpage where you can specify a military training program or occupation and retrieve information about the kinds of credits that it usually earns at colleges. Or you can get an official transcript of your military training by clicking a link under the "Military Registries" heading that takes you to the appropriate webpage for your service branch. Note that for the Army, Navy, or Marine Corps, this transcript shows the ACE's recommendations for equivalent college credits.

You may also get college credit by demonstrating your knowledge through a testing program. If you are planning to attend a particular college, you should find out which of the following widely accepted programs they favor:

* CLEP (College Level Examination Program—www.collegeboard.com/clep)
* DSST (DANTES Subject Standardized Tests, formerly called DANTES, for Defense Activity for Non-Traditional Education Support—www.getcollegecredit.com)
* Excelsior College Examinations (www.excelsior.edu/military)
* TECEP (Thomas Edison State College Examination Program—www.tesc.edu/degree-completion/Testing.cfm)

Finally, several "colleges without walls" specialize in granting credit for experiential learning. You can get credit, even a degree, without visiting the college. You don't even have to live in the same state. But to prove that you have learned at college level, you need to assemble a portfolio of your work. That requires more work than just stating your experience on a resume. You also need to write a statement explaining how the items in your portfolio indicate that you used college-level knowledge and skills.

You may think that only artists use a portfolio to show their work. Actually, almost any kind of work can be shown in a portfolio. Work that's done on paper can go in easily. With many other kinds of work, you can take photos and include them. Or you can include letters from people who can vouch for your output. If the portfolio is Web-based, you also can include videos, sound recordings, or computer programs.

A "college without walls" explains the guidelines for creating the portfolio and assigns you a mentor. This person decides whether your work is college-level and, if so, how much credit to give for the work.

The following colleges offer credit for portfolios:

* Thomas Edison State College (www.tesc.edu)
* Charter Oak State College (www.charteroak.edu)
* Excelsior College (www.excelsior.edu)

Will I Need a License, Certificate, or Other Credential for the Job I Have in Mind?

Many jobs require a specific credential, such as a license or certificate. (The Part III job descriptions identify many of these.) For these jobs, completion of a college major or training program may teach you the skills required, but you'll still need to get the appropriate credential before you can do the work. Often this means sitting for an exam or passing a work performance test; it's very much like getting your driver's license, only the level of skill is usually higher.

To see what credentialed occupations are related to your military service, explore the Credentialing Opportunities On-Line (COOL) site for your service branch. Find links under "Military Resources" at www.careeronestop.org/CREDENTIALING/CredentialingHome.asp. The COOL sites also have information about resources that can help you qualify for the credentials.

Which Businesses Hire Veterans?

This book focuses on the careers where veterans work, but you may be wondering which particular businesses and organizations employ veterans. In fact, all kinds of businesses hire veterans, and some vets start their own businesses and work for themselves.

But if you'd like to see the names of the top 100 employers of veterans, you can download a list at the Today's Military website (www.todaysmilitary.com/military-careers/life-after-the-military).

Another valuable site is ClearedJobs.net, which has brief profiles of companies that hire people with security clearances.

I Have a Disability Related to My Military Service. How Will This Affect My Career Opportunities?

The most important thing for you to remember is that employers are not allowed to discriminate against people with disabilities if it is reasonably possible to make accommodations in the workplace.

You do not need to reveal your disability when you apply for a job unless there is no way that accommodations can allow you to perform the work tasks. Nevertheless, you may want to discuss your disability with the employer because many employers recognize the skills that veterans bring to the job, and in fact workplace accommodations typically cost them $500 or less. Larger employers are usually more willing and able to make these accommodations and to have a policy in place to encourage the hiring of veterans with disabilities. The federal government is particularly welcoming. For example, in some cases veterans with a disability can submit an application for a federal job after the deadline that applies to other applicants. You can read more about this at the USAJOBS website (www.usajobs.gov/IndividualsWithDisabilities).

For help with getting rehabilitation services and with understanding the workplace accommodations that are appropriate for you, the place to start is the Department of Veterans Affairs, especially the new eBenefits website (www.ebenefits.va.gov). Another useful government site is Disability.gov (www.disability.gov/employment).

Understand that the VA is a complex bureaucracy and is understaffed, so sometimes you can use help navigating it to get the benefits you need. Several veterans' advocacy organizations have corps of volunteers who specialize in offering this help: Blinded Veterans Association (www.bva.org), Disabled American Veterans (www.dav.org), Military Order of the Purple Heart (www.purpleheart.org), Paralyzed Veterans of America (www.pva.org), Veterans of Foreign Wars (www.vfw.org), Vietnam Veterans of America (www.vva.org), and Wounded Warrior Project (www.woundedwarriorproject.org). These organizations generally do not require you to become a member to qualify for their services.

What Makes an Effective Transitional Resume?

Resume-writing deserves a book in its own right, and in fact JIST has one, *Expert Resumes for Military-to-Civilian Transitions,* by Wendy S. Enelow and Louise M. Kursmark. But I can identify some of the key points you should consider for writing an effective resume.

First, keep the resume short. The purpose of the resume is not to get you the job, so it doesn't need enormous detail. Its purpose is to get you the interview.

Second, use wording that civilians will understand and that has relevance for civilian work. Keep in mind that employers are looking for workers who can jump right into the job without a lot of retraining, so you need to make your experience sound comparable to a civilian job. A tank is "heavy mobile equipment." Establishing a new FOB is a "construction project." Instead of saying what you were "responsible for," say what actions you took and what your successes were.

Third, emphasize your transferable knowledge, skills, and abilities (KSAs). A good place to get ideas is My Next Move for Veterans (www.mynextmove.org/vets). Use the function called "Find careers like your military job" and review the information about the related civilian careers, especially those that are closest to the jobs you're considering now. Jot down the KSAs that appear here, and note those that repeat across several related careers. Think about your specific tasks and accomplishments that have used these KSAs so you can identify them on your resume.

Any good book about resumes discusses the difference between a chronological resume, which lists all your work experiences in the order they happened, and a skills-based resume. The skills-based approach probably will be more effective at communicating the strengths you acquired in the military and in any previous civilian jobs.

Many employers scan resumes into a database so they can search for keywords that indicate which applicants have the right skills. To make your resume easy to scan, avoid complicated layouts or fancy fonts. Keeping the resume visually simple will help with human readers, too.

What Makes an Effective Transitional Cover Letter?

Just as the resume is meant to get you the interview, the cover letter is meant to entice the employer to look at your resume. It should be short, get to the point quickly, and make reference to the enclosed resume. It should focus on the fact that your skills are a good match for what the job requires. Unless you know the employer has a preference for veterans, it should be even more "demilitarized" than the resume. It should end with a suggested action item—for example, that the employer should call you to talk about your qualifications in greater detail—rather than a statement of what you *hope* the employer will do.

Ask someone else to read over your resume and cover letter to catch any little mistakes and to make sure you convey the right tone.

What's the Best Way to Find Out About Job Openings?

Research has shown that most jobs open and are filled without being advertised. Although online job banks can be a useful part of your job-hunting efforts, they should not be the major part. Instead, aim most of your efforts at *networking*.

Make a list of everyone you know. You may want to organize the list into different groups, depending on the kind of connection you have to each person (military, family, social, school, and so forth). Let all of these people know what kind of work you are looking for and a very brief idea of why your background is relevant. Research shows that these people usually don't know any more about job openings than you do, but the people *they* know can have valuable leads to jobs. That's why networking is so powerful.

The LinkedIn.com website is designed to help people network about work. If you import your address book to LinkedIn, the site will tell you which contacts have a LinkedIn profile and will alert you later when others sign up. LinkedIn also has a People You May Know page that shows you the contacts of your contacts. Some of them may know you well enough to be willing to join your network; in other cases, you can ask one of your contacts to introduce you. LinkedIn has many helpful features for job seekers, but they work only if you use them *actively*. Simply adding people to your network is only the first step; it will not make your contacts aware of your goal and what you have to offer.

Purely social sites such as Facebook and MySpace can also be useful, as long as you don't have anything on your page that employers would object to. As with LinkedIn, expand your network by looking for the contacts of your contacts. For specific strategies to use with these sites, see *Find a Job Through Social Networking,* by Diane Crompton and Ellen Sautter (JIST).

By joining the Veteran Career Network (http://benefits.military.com/vcn/search.do), you can identify vets working in occupations, industries, or locations that interest you.

Twitter is becoming a lively place for learning about job openings and building your network. By "following" people in your targeted industry, you can learn a lot about trends and perhaps about actual job openings. By "tweeting" about what you're doing and about industry news, you can help establish your reputation for knowledge of the field. Remember that Twitter can help with your career only as long as you restrict your "tweets" to topics of professional interest. For lots of useful suggestions, see *The Twitter Job Search Guide,* by Susan Britton Whitcomb, Chandlee Bryan, and Deb Dib (JIST).

Cold calling is another way to learn about job openings. To identify likely employers, browse through business directories such as the Yellow Pages—or, on the Web, Yellowbook.com. Browse magazines or websites aimed at your targeted industry, and note businesses that advertise there.

Avoid the employer's human resources office. Instead, research to identify a person who is in charge of the kind of work you want to do. Network contacts can be very handy for this. The LinkedIn database can also be useful. (Google the terms "X-ray search" for tips on how to use LinkedIn in this way. By using your service branch as one of your search terms, you can identify fellow veterans.) In a small business, the owner is the appropriate person.

Call the person you've identified, ideally early in the day, and ask if the company expects to do any hiring. If the person says yes, ask for an interview. If not, offer to send your resume and make that person one more connection in your network. Expect lots of rejection, but don't take it personally. Even though the odds of success are low for each call you make, you can make a lot of calls very quickly compared to other ways of making contacts. If your timing is lucky, you may be the first person to learn about a job opening.

Self-Employment

You may decide to be your own boss if you have an idea for a product or service that people will pay you for. Veterans often make good entrepreneurs because they have been trained to understand risk. Of course, starting up a new business is a complex process and requires a lot of dedication and sometimes some seed money. The Small Business Administration site (www.sba.gov) offers extensive guidance on the essentials for getting a business up and running, such as what belongs in a business plan, important business laws and regulations, and marketing techniques.

PART II

The Best Jobs Lists

This part contains a lot of interesting lists, and it's a good place for you to start using the book. Here are some suggestions for using the lists to explore career options:

❋ The table of contents at the beginning of this book presents a complete listing of the list titles in this section. You can browse the lists or use the table of contents to find those that interest you most.

❋ I gave the lists clear titles, so most require little explanation. I provide comments for each group of lists.

❋ As you review the lists of jobs, one or more of the jobs may appeal to you enough that you want to seek additional information. As this happens, mark that job (or, if someone else will be using this book, write it on a separate sheet of paper) so that you can look up the description of the job in Part III.

❋ Keep in mind that all jobs in these lists meet my basic criteria for being included in this book, as explained in the introduction. All lists, therefore, contain jobs that are held by many recent enlisted veterans; do not require long years of education or postmilitary training; and have high pay, high growth, or large numbers of openings. These economic measures are easily quantified and are often presented in lists of best jobs in the newspapers and other media. Although earnings, growth, and openings are important, you also should consider other factors in your career planning, such as location, liking the people you work with, amount of stress, and having opportunities to be creative. Many other factors that may help define the ideal job for you are difficult or impossible to quantify and thus aren't used in this book, so you will need to consider the importance of these issues yourself.

❋ All data used to create these lists comes from the U.S. Department of Labor, the Census Bureau, and the Department of Defense. The earnings figures are based on the average annual pay received by *all* full-time salaried workers, not just veterans (except in the two bonus lists). Because the earnings represent the national averages, actual pay rates can vary greatly by location, amount of previous work experience, and other factors. Even lists that focus on a particular type of worker (for example, rural workers) use earnings figures based on the national averages.

Some Details on the Lists

The sources of the information I used in constructing these lists are presented in this book's introduction. Here are some additional details on how to interpret the lists:

❋ Some jobs have the same scores for one or more data elements. For example, in the category of fastest-growing, two jobs (Nuclear Medicine Technologists and Surgical Technologists) are listed with the same projected growth, 18.9 percent. Therefore, I ordered these two jobs alphabetically, and their order in relation to each other has no other significance.

❋ In many cases, jobs are not tied, but their differences are too small to be important. For example, Mechanical Drafters are projected to have 2,050 job openings per year, whereas 2,070 openings are projected for Captains, Mates, and Pilots of Water Vessels. This is a difference of only 20 jobs spread over the entire United States, and of course, it is only a projection. So keep in mind that small differences of position on a list aren't very significant.

Best Jobs Overall: Lists of Jobs with the Highest Pay, Fastest Growth, and Most Openings

The four lists that follow are this book's premier lists. They are the lists that are most often mentioned in the media and the ones that most readers want to see.

To create these lists, I started with a database of 459 jobs held by a reasonably large number of recent veterans; expanded those that were families of occupations; eliminated those that were inappropriate for various reasons (as the introduction explains in detail); and ranked the remaining 300 jobs according to a combination of their earnings, growth, and number of openings. I then selected the 150 jobs with the best total scores for use in this book.

The first list presents all 150 best jobs. Three additional lists present the 50 jobs with the top scores on each of three measures: annual earnings, projected percentage growth through 2020, and number of annual openings. Descriptions for all the jobs in these lists are included in Part III.

The Best Jobs Overall—Jobs with the Best Combination of Pay, Growth, and Openings

This list arranges all 150 jobs that were selected for this book in order of their overall scores for pay, growth, and number of openings, as explained in the introduction. The job with the best overall score was Software Developers, Systems Software. Other jobs follow in order of their combined scores for pay, growth, and number of openings. These 150 jobs are the ones I use throughout this book: in the other lists in Part II and in the descriptions found in Part III.

As you look over the list, remember that jobs near the top of the list are not necessarily "good" jobs for you to consider—nor are jobs toward the end of the list necessarily "bad" jobs for you to ignore. Their positions in the list are simply a result of each one's total score based on pay, growth, and number of openings. This means, for example, that some jobs with low pay and modest growth but a high number of openings appear higher on the list than some jobs with higher pay and modest growth but a low number of openings. A "right" job for you could be anywhere on this list.

The Best Jobs Overall for the Military-to-Civilian Transition

Job	Annual Earnings	Percent Growth	Annual Openings
1. Software Developers, Systems Software	$96,600	32.4%	16,800
2. Registered Nurses	$65,950	26.0%	120,740
3. Network and Computer Systems Administrators	$70,970	27.8%	15,530
4. Computer Systems Analysts	$78,770	22.1%	22,250
5. Supervisors of Construction and Extraction Workers	$59,150	23.5%	25,970
6. Personal Financial Advisors	$66,580	32.1%	9,020
7. Database Administrators	$75,190	30.6%	5,270
8. Accountants and Auditors	$62,850	15.7%	45,210
9. Training and Development Specialists	$55,150	28.3%	9,830
10. Electricians	$49,320	23.2%	28,920
11. Sales Representatives, Wholesale and Manufacturing, Technical and Scientific Products	$74,750	16.4%	15,970
12. Radiologic Technologists	$55,120	27.8%	9,510
13. Logisticians	$71,910	25.5%	4,870
14. Plumbers, Pipefitters, and Steamfitters	$47,750	25.6%	22,880
15. Construction Managers	$84,240	16.6%	12,040
16. Public Relations Specialists	$53,190	22.5%	12,720
17. Social and Community Service Managers	$58,660	26.7%	6,480
18. Sales Representatives, Wholesale and Manufacturing, Except Technical and Scientific Products	$53,540	15.6%	55,990
19. Diagnostic Medical Sonographers	$65,210	43.5%	3,170
20. Securities, Commodities, and Financial Services Sales Agents	$72,060	15.2%	13,370
21. Sales Representatives, Services, All Other	$50,630	18.8%	27,010

(continued)

(continued)

The Best Jobs Overall for the Military-to-Civilian Transition

Job	Annual Earnings	Percent Growth	Annual Openings
22. Heating, Air Conditioning, and Refrigeration Mechanics and Installers	$43,380	33.7%	13,760
23. Insurance Sales Agents	$47,450	21.9%	18,440
24. Administrative Services Managers	$79,540	14.5%	9,980
25. Licensed Practical and Licensed Vocational Nurses	$41,150	22.4%	36,920
26. Business Operations Specialists, All Other	$64,030	11.6%	32,720
27. First-Line Supervisors of Office and Administrative Support Workers	$48,810	14.3%	58,440
28. Computer Programmers	$72,630	12.0%	12,800
29. Industrial Machinery Mechanics	$46,270	21.6%	11,710
30. Operating Engineers and Other Construction Equipment Operators	$41,510	23.5%	16,280
31. Meeting, Convention, and Event Planners	$46,020	43.7%	4,500
32. Health Educators	$47,940	36.5%	3,690
33. Carpenters	$40,010	19.6%	40,830
34. Heavy and Tractor-Trailer Truck Drivers	$37,930	20.6%	64,940
35. Managers, All Other	$99,540	7.9%	24,940
36. First-Line Supervisors of Helpers, Laborers, and Material Movers, Hand	$44,580	27.2%	8,000
37. First-Line Supervisors of Mechanics, Installers, and Repairers	$59,850	11.9%	16,490
38. Loan Officers	$58,030	14.2%	11,520
39. Compliance Officers	$60,740	15.0%	5,860
40. Commercial Pilots	$70,000	21.2%	1,930
41. General and Operations Managers	$95,150	4.6%	41,010
42. Cardiovascular Technologists and Technicians	$51,020	29.3%	2,210
43. Construction and Building Inspectors	$53,180	17.9%	4,860
44. Captains, Mates, and Pilots of Water Vessels	$63,920	20.4%	2,070
45. Medical Secretaries	$31,060	41.3%	27,840
46. Paralegals and Legal Assistants	$46,730	18.3%	8,340
47. Dental Assistants	$34,140	30.8%	15,400
48. Executive Secretaries and Executive Administrative Assistants	$45,580	12.6%	32,180
49. Electrical Power-Line Installers and Repairers	$60,190	13.2%	5,270
50. Police and Sheriff's Patrol Officers	$54,230	8.2%	24,940
51. First-Line Supervisors of Transportation and Material-Moving Machine and Vehicle Operators	$52,950	14.3%	6,930

The Best Jobs Overall for the Military-to-Civilian Transition

Job	Annual Earnings	Percent Growth	Annual Openings
52. Medical Equipment Repairers	$44,870	31.5%	2,230
53. Automotive Service Technicians and Mechanics	$36,180	17.2%	31,170
54. Clergy	$44,140	17.5%	7,990
55. Security and Fire Alarm Systems Installers	$39,540	33.0%	3,670
56. Technical Writers	$64,610	17.2%	1,830
57. Medical Assistants	$29,100	30.9%	24,380
58. Probation Officers and Correctional Treatment Specialists	$47,840	18.4%	3,730
59. Pharmacy Technicians	$28,940	32.4%	16,630
60. Structural Iron and Steel Workers	$45,690	21.9%	2,540
61. Substance Abuse and Behavioral Disorder Counselors	$38,560	27.3%	4,170
62. Emergency Medical Technicians and Paramedics	$30,710	33.3%	12,080
63. Interior Designers	$47,620	19.3%	2,840
64. Mobile Heavy Equipment Mechanics, Except Engines	$45,600	16.2%	5,250
65. Telecommunications Line Installers and Repairers	$51,720	13.6%	5,140
66. Transportation, Storage, and Distribution Managers	$80,860	10.0%	3,370
67. Painters, Construction and Maintenance	$35,430	18.5%	15,730
68. Receptionists and Information Clerks	$25,690	23.7%	56,560
69. Medical and Clinical Laboratory Technologists	$57,010	11.3%	5,210
70. Self-Enrichment Education Teachers	$36,100	20.9%	9,150
71. Graphic Designers	$44,010	13.4%	12,380
72. Social and Human Service Assistants	$28,740	27.6%	18,910
73. Billing and Posting Clerks	$32,880	19.7%	18,760
74. First-Line Supervisors of Non-Retail Sales Workers	$70,520	4.0%	12,350
75. Nuclear Medicine Technologists	$69,450	18.9%	750
76. Construction Laborers	$29,730	21.3%	29,240
77. Sheet Metal Workers	$42,730	17.5%	4,700
78. Health Technologists and Technicians, All Other	$38,080	23.2%	4,040
79. Coaches and Scouts	$28,470	29.4%	13,300
80. Bus and Truck Mechanics and Diesel Engine Specialists	$41,640	14.5%	8,780
81. Fitness Trainers and Aerobics Instructors	$31,030	24.0%	10,060
82. First-Line Supervisors of Landscaping, Lawn Service, and Groundskeeping Workers	$42,050	15.1%	6,010
83. Ship Engineers	$70,840	18.0%	620
84. Environmental Science and Protection Technicians, Including Health	$42,270	23.6%	1,950
85. Bookkeeping, Accounting, and Auditing Clerks	$34,740	13.6%	46,780

(continued)

(continued)

The Best Jobs Overall for the Military-to-Civilian Transition

Job	Annual Earnings	Percent Growth	Annual Openings
86. Customer Service Representatives	$30,610	15.5%	95,960
87. Advertising Sales Agents	$45,250	13.0%	6,990
88. Veterinary Technologists and Technicians	$30,140	52.0%	5,570
89. Welders, Cutters, Solderers, and Brazers	$35,920	15.0%	14,070
90. Surgical Technologists	$40,950	18.9%	3,390
91. First-Line Supervisors of Fire Fighting and Prevention Workers	$69,510	8.2%	3,310
92. Tile and Marble Setters	$37,080	25.4%	2,770
93. Purchasing Agents, Except Wholesale, Retail, and Farm Products	$57,580	5.3%	9,120
94. Landscaping and Groundskeeping Workers	$23,410	20.9%	44,440
95. Athletic Trainers	$42,400	30.0%	1,190
96. Budget Analysts	$69,090	10.4%	1,960
97. Office Clerks, General	$27,190	16.6%	101,150
98. Occupational Health and Safety Specialists	$66,270	8.5%	2,570
99. Real Estate Sales Agents	$39,070	12.2%	12,760
100. Firefighters	$45,420	8.6%	11,230
101. Transportation Inspectors	$62,230	14.4%	1,070
102. Pipelayers	$35,900	25.3%	2,880
103. Security Guards	$23,900	18.8%	35,950
104. Property, Real Estate, and Community Association Managers	$52,510	6.0%	8,230
105. Forensic Science Technicians	$52,180	18.6%	790
106. Private Detectives and Investigators	$43,710	20.5%	1,490
107. Environmental Engineering Technicians	$44,850	24.3%	820
108. First-Line Supervisors of Retail Sales Workers	$36,480	8.4%	51,370
109. Claims Adjusters, Examiners, and Investigators	$59,320	3.0%	7,990
110. Payroll and Timekeeping Clerks	$37,160	14.6%	6,570
111. Pest Control Workers	$30,220	26.1%	4,850
112. Maintenance and Repair Workers, General	$35,030	11.0%	37,910
113. Wholesale and Retail Buyers, Except Farm Products	$50,490	9.0%	4,170
114. Roofers	$35,280	17.8%	5,250
115. Commercial and Industrial Designers	$60,760	10.5%	1,690
116. Real Estate Brokers	$59,340	7.6%	2,970
117. Aircraft Mechanics and Service Technicians	$54,590	6.3%	4,520
118. Laborers and Freight, Stock, and Material Movers, Hand	$23,750	15.4%	98,020
119. Medical and Clinical Laboratory Technicians	$36,950	14.7%	5,510

The Best Jobs Overall for the Military-to-Civilian Transition

Job	Annual Earnings	Percent Growth	Annual Openings
120. Sailors and Marine Oilers	$36,800	21.3%	2,150
121. Light Truck or Delivery Services Drivers	$29,080	14.7%	29,590
122. First-Line Supervisors of Police and Detectives	$77,890	2.1%	3,870
123. Pile-Driver Operators	$45,500	36.0%	230
124. Bus Drivers, Transit and Intercity	$35,720	14.8%	6,350
125. First-Line Supervisors of Production and Operating Workers	$53,670	1.9%	8,790
126. Paving, Surfacing, and Tamping Equipment Operators	$35,270	22.1%	2,200
127. Civil Engineering Technicians	$46,900	12.0%	2,460
128. Rail Car Repairers	$47,740	16.9%	930
129. Bill and Account Collectors	$31,920	14.2%	13,550
130. Teacher Assistants	$23,580	14.8%	48,160
131. Music Directors and Composers	$47,410	10.2%	3,220
132. Detectives and Criminal Investigators	$71,770	2.9%	3,010
133. Radio, Cellular, and Tower Equipment Installers and Repairers	$42,160	29.4%	450
134. Postal Service Mail Carriers	$55,160	−12.0%	10,340
135. Life, Physical, and Social Science Technicians, All Other	$43,120	11.8%	3,350
136. Production, Planning, and Expediting Clerks	$43,100	6.6%	8,880
137. Mechanical Drafters	$49,200	11.1%	2,050
138. Biological Technicians	$39,480	13.5%	3,790
139. Credit Counselors	$38,430	20.3%	1,520
140. Machinists	$39,220	8.5%	9,950
141. Water and Wastewater Treatment Plant and System Operators	$41,780	11.6%	4,150
142. Nuclear Technicians	$68,030	13.5%	330
143. Surveying and Mapping Technicians	$39,350	15.9%	2,000
144. Audio and Video Equipment Technicians	$41,630	13.4%	2,560
145. Human Resources Assistants, Except Payroll and Timekeeping	$37,250	11.2%	6,160
146. Athletes and Sports Competitors	$39,670	21.6%	780
147. Compensation, Benefits, and Job Analysis Specialists	$57,960	5.0%	2,400
148. Geological and Petroleum Technicians	$49,690	14.7%	700
149. Industrial Truck and Tractor Operators	$30,010	11.8%	20,950
150. Aircraft Cargo Handling Supervisors	$46,840	20.3%	260

The 50 Best-Paying Jobs for the Military-to-Civilian Transition

I sorted all 150 jobs based on their annual median earnings from highest to lowest. *Median earnings* means that half of all workers in each of these jobs earn more than that amount and half earn less. I then selected the 50 jobs with the highest earnings to create the list that follows.

It shouldn't be a big surprise to learn that most of the highest-paying jobs require advanced levels of education, training, or experience. For example, 9 of the 20 jobs with the highest earnings normally require a bachelor's degree, although military training and experience sometimes may be suitable substitutes. Although the top 20 jobs may not appeal to you for various reasons, you are likely to find others that will among the top 50 jobs with the highest earnings.

Keep in mind that the earnings reflect the national average for *all* civilian workers in the occupation. This is an important consideration, because starting pay in the job is usually much less than the pay that workers can earn with several years of work experience. (To get an idea of how much difference this might make, see the statement about earnings growth potential in the Part III description of the job.) Earnings also vary significantly by region of the country, so actual pay in your area could be substantially different.

The 50 Best-Paying Jobs for the Military-to-Civilian Transition

Job	Annual Earnings
1. Managers, All Other	$99,540
2. Software Developers, Systems Software	$96,600
3. General and Operations Managers	$95,150
4. Construction Managers	$84,240
5. Transportation, Storage, and Distribution Managers	$80,860
6. Administrative Services Managers	$79,540
7. Computer Systems Analysts	$78,770
8. First-Line Supervisors of Police and Detectives	$77,890
9. Database Administrators	$75,190
10. Sales Representatives, Wholesale and Manufacturing, Technical and Scientific Products	$74,750
11. Computer Programmers	$72,630
12. Securities, Commodities, and Financial Services Sales Agents	$72,060
13. Logisticians	$71,910
14. Detectives and Criminal Investigators	$71,770

The 50 Best-Paying Jobs for the Military-to-Civilian Transition

Job	Annual Earnings
15. Network and Computer Systems Administrators	$70,970
16. Ship Engineers	$70,840
17. First-Line Supervisors of Non-Retail Sales Workers	$70,520
18. Commercial Pilots	$70,000
19. First-Line Supervisors of Fire Fighting and Prevention Workers	$69,510
20. Nuclear Medicine Technologists	$69,450
21. Budget Analysts	$69,090
22. Nuclear Technicians	$68,030
23. Personal Financial Advisors	$66,580
24. Occupational Health and Safety Specialists	$66,270
25. Registered Nurses	$65,950
26. Diagnostic Medical Sonographers	$65,210
27. Technical Writers	$64,610
28. Business Operations Specialists, All Other	$64,030
29. Captains, Mates, and Pilots of Water Vessels	$63,920
30. Accountants and Auditors	$62,850
31. Transportation Inspectors	$62,230
32. Commercial and Industrial Designers	$60,760
33. Compliance Officers	$60,740
34. Electrical Power-Line Installers and Repairers	$60,190
35. First-Line Supervisors of Mechanics, Installers, and Repairers	$59,850
36. Real Estate Brokers	$59,340
37. Claims Adjusters, Examiners, and Investigators	$59,320
38. Supervisors of Construction and Extraction Workers	$59,150
39. Social and Community Service Managers	$58,660
40. Loan Officers	$58,030
41. Compensation, Benefits, and Job Analysis Specialists	$57,960
42. Purchasing Agents, Except Wholesale, Retail, and Farm Products	$57,580
43. Medical and Clinical Laboratory Technologists	$57,010
44. Postal Service Mail Carriers	$55,160
45. Training and Development Specialists	$55,150
46. Radiologic Technologists	$55,120
47. Aircraft Mechanics and Service Technicians	$54,590
48. Police and Sheriff's Patrol Officers	$54,230
49. First-Line Supervisors of Production and Operating Workers	$53,670
50. Sales Representatives, Wholesale and Manufacturing, Except Technical and Scientific Products	$53,540

The 50 Fastest-Growing Jobs for the Military-to-Civilian Transition

I created this list by sorting all 150 best jobs by their projected growth over the 10-year period from 2010 to 2020. Growth rates are one measure to consider in exploring career options, as jobs with higher growth rates tend to provide more job opportunities.

Jobs in the health-care field dominate the top 20 positions on the list. Veterinary Technologists and Technicians is the job with the highest growth rate—the number employed is projected to grow by more than half from 2010 to 2020. You can find a wide range of rapidly growing jobs in a variety of fields and at different levels of training and education among the jobs in this list.

The 50 Fastest-Growing Jobs for the Military-to-Civilian Transition

Job	Percent Growth
1. Veterinary Technologists and Technicians	52.0%
2. Meeting, Convention, and Event Planners	43.7%
3. Diagnostic Medical Sonographers	43.5%
4. Medical Secretaries	41.3%
5. Health Educators	36.5%
6. Pile-Driver Operators	36.0%
7. Heating, Air Conditioning, and Refrigeration Mechanics and Installers	33.7%
8. Emergency Medical Technicians and Paramedics	33.3%
9. Security and Fire Alarm Systems Installers	33.0%
10. Pharmacy Technicians	32.4%
11. Software Developers, Systems Software	32.4%
12. Personal Financial Advisors	32.1%
13. Medical Equipment Repairers	31.5%
14. Medical Assistants	30.9%
15. Dental Assistants	30.8%
16. Database Administrators	30.6%
17. Athletic Trainers	30.0%
18. Coaches and Scouts	29.4%
19. Radio, Cellular, and Tower Equipment Installers and Repairers	29.4%
20. Cardiovascular Technologists and Technicians	29.3%
21. Training and Development Specialists	28.3%
22. Network and Computer Systems Administrators	27.8%
23. Radiologic Technologists	27.8%
24. Social and Human Service Assistants	27.6%
25. Substance Abuse and Behavioral Disorder Counselors	27.3%

The 50 Fastest-Growing Jobs for the Military-to-Civilian Transition

Job	Percent Growth
26. First-Line Supervisors of Helpers, Laborers, and Material Movers, Hand	27.2%
27. Social and Community Service Managers	26.7%
28. Pest Control Workers	26.1%
29. Registered Nurses	26.0%
30. Plumbers, Pipefitters, and Steamfitters	25.6%
31. Logisticians	25.5%
32. Tile and Marble Setters	25.4%
33. Pipelayers	25.3%
34. Environmental Engineering Technicians	24.3%
35. Fitness Trainers and Aerobics Instructors	24.0%
36. Receptionists and Information Clerks	23.7%
37. Environmental Science and Protection Technicians, Including Health	23.6%
38. Operating Engineers and Other Construction Equipment Operators	23.5%
39. Supervisors of Construction and Extraction Workers	23.5%
40. Electricians	23.2%
41. Health Technologists and Technicians, All Other	23.2%
42. Public Relations Specialists	22.5%
43. Licensed Practical and Licensed Vocational Nurses	22.4%
44. Computer Systems Analysts	22.1%
45. Paving, Surfacing, and Tamping Equipment Operators	22.1%
46. Insurance Sales Agents	21.9%
47. Structural Iron and Steel Workers	21.9%
48. Athletes and Sports Competitors	21.6%
49. Industrial Machinery Mechanics	21.6%
50. Construction Laborers	21.3%

The 50 Jobs with the Most Openings for the Military-to-Civilian Transition

I created this list by sorting all 150 best jobs by the number of job openings that each is expected to have per year. These job openings occur either when the workforce expands or when replacement workers are needed. Many of these occupations, such as Customer Service Representatives, are not among the highest-paying jobs. But jobs with large numbers of openings often provide easier entry for new workers, make it easier to move from one position to another, or are attractive for other reasons. Some of these jobs may also appeal to veterans who want to work part-time or move easily from one employer to another. And some of these jobs pay quite well, offer good benefits, or have other advantages.

The 50 Jobs with the Most Openings for the Military-to-Civilian Transition

Job	Annual Openings
1. Registered Nurses	120,740
2. Office Clerks, General	101,150
3. Laborers and Freight, Stock, and Material Movers, Hand	98,020
4. Customer Service Representatives	95,960
5. Heavy and Tractor-Trailer Truck Drivers	64,940
6. First-Line Supervisors of Office and Administrative Support Workers	58,440
7. Receptionists and Information Clerks	56,560
8. Sales Representatives, Wholesale and Manufacturing, Except Technical and Scientific Products	55,990
9. First-Line Supervisors of Retail Sales Workers	51,370
10. Teacher Assistants	48,160
11. Bookkeeping, Accounting, and Auditing Clerks	46,780
12. Accountants and Auditors	45,210
13. Landscaping and Groundskeeping Workers	44,440
14. General and Operations Managers	41,010
15. Carpenters	40,830
16. Maintenance and Repair Workers, General	37,910
17. Licensed Practical and Licensed Vocational Nurses	36,920
18. Security Guards	35,950
19. Business Operations Specialists, All Other	32,720
20. Executive Secretaries and Executive Administrative Assistants	32,180
21. Automotive Service Technicians and Mechanics	31,170
22. Light Truck or Delivery Services Drivers	29,590
23. Construction Laborers	29,240
24. Electricians	28,920
25. Medical Secretaries	27,840
26. Sales Representatives, Services, All Other	27,010
27. Supervisors of Construction and Extraction Workers	25,970
28. Managers, All Other	24,940
29. Police and Sheriff's Patrol Officers	24,940
30. Medical Assistants	24,380
31. Plumbers, Pipefitters, and Steamfitters	22,880
32. Computer Systems Analysts	22,250
33. Industrial Truck and Tractor Operators	20,950
34. Social and Human Service Assistants	18,910
35. Billing and Posting Clerks	18,760
36. Insurance Sales Agents	18,440

The 50 Jobs with the Most Openings for the Military-to-Civilian Transition

Job	Annual Openings
37. Software Developers, Systems Software	16,800
38. Pharmacy Technicians	16,630
39. First-Line Supervisors of Mechanics, Installers, and Repairers	16,490
40. Operating Engineers and Other Construction Equipment Operators	16,280
41. Sales Representatives, Wholesale and Manufacturing, Technical and Scientific Products	15,970
42. Painters, Construction and Maintenance	15,730
43. Network and Computer Systems Administrators	15,530
44. Dental Assistants	15,400
45. Welders, Cutters, Solderers, and Brazers	14,070
46. Heating, Air Conditioning, and Refrigeration Mechanics and Installers	13,760
47. Bill and Account Collectors	13,550
48. Securities, Commodities, and Financial Services Sales Agents	13,370
49. Coaches and Scouts	13,300
50. Computer Programmers	12,800

Best Jobs Lists for the Military-to-Civilian Transition by Demographic

Different types of jobs attract different types of workers. For example, it's interesting to consider which jobs have the highest percentage of female veterans or rural workers. I'm not saying that female veterans or people living in rural areas should consider these jobs over others based solely on this information, but it is useful information to know. And this is information you're not likely to find anywhere else.

The lists may help you identify jobs that work well for others like you—for example, jobs that tend to attract recent veterans. In some cases, these lists can give you ideas for jobs to consider that you might otherwise overlook. For example, perhaps women should consider some jobs that traditionally have high percentages of men in them. Or rural workers might consider some jobs typically held by urban people. Although these aren't obvious ways of using these lists, the lists may give you some good ideas for jobs to consider.

All lists in this section were created through a similar process. I began with the 150 best jobs and sorted those jobs in order of the primary criterion for each set of lists. I eliminated jobs that scored low on the primary criterion and created an initial list of jobs ordered from highest to lowest percentage of the criterion. For example, when I sorted the 150 jobs based on the percentage of female vets, I set the cutoff point at 25 percent and produced a list of 30 jobs, ranging from a high of 78.5 percent women to a low of 26.6 percent. For other criteria, such as percentage of recent veterans or rural workers, I used other cutoff levels. All the demographic statistics I used are derived from the Census Bureau and describe recent veterans in the workforce. The exception is the figures for percentages of urban and rural workers, which are based on data from the Occupational Employment Statistics program of the BLS and describe the general population.

From the initial list of jobs with a high percentage of each type of worker, I then created a list ordered to show the best jobs overall. That is, the jobs that have the highest combined scores for earnings, growth rate, and number of openings are to be found highest on this list. I decided not to limit this "best-of" list to the top 25 or 50 jobs because the number of jobs meeting the cutoff varies widely.

The economic figures I used to sort the jobs in these lists are based on the averages for *all* civilian workers, not just workers who match the particular demographic group and not just recent veterans. For example, it was not possible to obtain earnings figures that applied specifically to people in rural areas, although it is known that they tend to earn less. It also was not possible to get projections of the number of job openings for self-employed workers because they create their own jobs.

Best Jobs with a High Percentage of Recent Veterans

To find the subset of the 150 best occupations where recent veterans are concentrated, I analyzed data from the American Community Survey for the years 2005–2009. For each job, I calculated the percentage of recent veterans employed and created a list of those jobs with 2 percent or more recent veterans. Two percent may not seem like a high concentration, but consider that recent veterans made up only 1.1 percent of the people surveyed by the ACS.

As you might expect, the veteran-friendly occupations tend to involve skills that are most likely to be learned through military training. The formal entry requirements for these jobs typically are undemanding.

One reason this list can be useful is that you probably have much in common with these other veterans. Whatever the reasons that recent veterans are concentrated in these jobs, these same reasons may work in your favor, improving your odds of getting hired.

On the other hand, remember that the list is based on data from a few years ago; the list reflects the hiring patterns of that time, and these can change. It's helpful to look also at the next list—the *best* jobs with a high percentage of recent veterans—and consider each occupation's figures for projected job growth and job openings over the years ahead.

Jobs with the Highest Percentage of Recent Veterans

Job	Percent Recent Veterans
1. Aircraft Mechanics and Service Technicians	22.9%
2. Commercial Pilots	15.2%
3. Logisticians	15.1%
4. Police and Sheriff's Patrol Officers	8.3%
5. Sailors and Marine Oilers	7.5%
6. Ship Engineers	7.5%
7. Security Guards	5.5%
8. Detectives and Criminal Investigators	5.4%
9. Firefighters	5.3%
10. Private Detectives and Investigators	5.2%
11. Transportation Inspectors	5.2%
12. Captains, Mates, and Pilots of Water Vessels	4.8%
13. Radio, Cellular, and Tower Equipment Installers and Repairers	4.6%
14. Emergency Medical Technicians and Paramedics	4.2%
15. Bus and Truck Mechanics and Diesel Engine Specialists	4.1%
16. First-Line Supervisors of Mechanics, Installers, and Repairers	3.7%
17. Network and Computer Systems Administrators	3.7%
18. Medical Equipment Repairers	3.4%
19. Civil Engineering Technicians	3.3%
20. Compliance Officers	3.3%
21. Environmental Engineering Technicians	3.3%
22. Telecommunications Line Installers and Repairers	3.3%
23. Transportation, Storage, and Distribution Managers	3.3%
24. First-Line Supervisors of Police and Detectives	3.2%
25. Maintenance and Repair Workers, General	3.0%
26. Mobile Heavy Equipment Mechanics, Except Engines	3.0%
27. Rail Car Repairers	3.0%
28. Athletic Trainers	2.9%
29. Occupational Health and Safety Specialists	2.9%
30. Security and Fire Alarm Systems Installers	2.8%
31. Water and Wastewater Treatment Plant and System Operators	2.7%
32. Budget Analysts	2.6%
33. First-Line Supervisors of Fire Fighting and Prevention Workers	2.5%
34. Human Resources Assistants, Except Payroll and Timekeeping	2.5%

(continued)

(continued)

Jobs with the Highest Percentage of Recent Veterans

Job	Percent Recent Veterans
35. Postal Service Mail Carriers	2.5%
36. Self-Enrichment Education Teachers	2.5%
37. Electricians	2.4%
38. Audio and Video Equipment Technicians	2.3%
39. Computer Systems Analysts	2.3%
40. Electrical Power-Line Installers and Repairers	2.3%
41. Industrial Machinery Mechanics	2.3%
42. Pest Control Workers	2.3%
43. Administrative Services Managers	2.1%
44. Surveying and Mapping Technicians	2.0%
45. Technical Writers	2.0%

The jobs in the following list are derived from the preceding list of jobs with the highest percentage of recent veterans.

Best Jobs Overall with a High Percentage of Recent Veterans

Job	Percent Recent Veterans	Annual Earnings	Percent Growth	Annual Openings
1. Computer Systems Analysts	2.3%	$78,770	22.1%	22,250
2. Network and Computer Systems Administrators	3.7%	$70,970	27.8%	15,530
3. Logisticians	15.1%	$71,910	25.5%	4,870
4. Electricians	2.4%	$49,320	23.2%	28,920
5. Administrative Services Managers	2.1%	$79,540	14.5%	9,980
6. Industrial Machinery Mechanics	2.3%	$46,270	21.6%	11,710
7. Emergency Medical Technicians and Paramedics	4.2%	$30,710	33.3%	12,080
8. Compliance Officers	3.3%	$60,740	15.0%	5,860
9. First-Line Supervisors of Mechanics, Installers, and Repairers	3.7%	$59,850	11.9%	16,490
10. Commercial Pilots	15.2%	$70,000	21.2%	1,930
11. Electrical Power-Line Installers and Repairers	2.3%	$60,190	13.2%	5,270

Best Jobs Overall with a High Percentage of Recent Veterans

Job	Percent Recent Veterans	Annual Earnings	Percent Growth	Annual Openings
12. Medical Equipment Repairers	3.4%	$44,870	31.5%	2,230
13. Security and Fire Alarm Systems Installers	2.8%	$39,540	33.0%	3,670
14. Transportation, Storage, and Distribution Managers	3.3%	$80,860	10.0%	3,370
15. Captains, Mates, and Pilots of Water Vessels	4.8%	$63,920	20.4%	2,070
16. Police and Sheriff's Patrol Officers	8.3%	$54,230	8.2%	24,940
17. Security Guards	5.5%	$23,900	18.8%	35,950
18. Mobile Heavy Equipment Mechanics, Except Engines	3.0%	$45,600	16.2%	5,250
19. Self-Enrichment Education Teachers	2.5%	$36,100	20.9%	9,150
20. Telecommunications Line Installers and Repairers	3.3%	$51,720	13.6%	5,140
21. Ship Engineers	7.5%	$70,840	18.0%	620
22. Technical Writers	2.0%	$64,610	17.2%	1,830
23. First-Line Supervisors of Police and Detectives	3.2%	$77,890	2.1%	3,870
24. Pest Control Workers	2.3%	$30,220	26.1%	4,850
25. Bus and Truck Mechanics and Diesel Engine Specialists	4.1%	$41,640	14.5%	8,780
26. Postal Service Mail Carriers	2.5%	$55,160	−12.0%	10,340
27. Athletic Trainers	2.9%	$42,400	30.0%	1,190
28. Firefighters	5.3%	$45,420	8.6%	11,230
29. Detectives and Criminal Investigators	5.4%	$71,770	2.9%	3,010
30. First-Line Supervisors of Fire Fighting and Prevention Workers	2.5%	$69,510	8.2%	3,310
31. Maintenance and Repair Workers, General	3.0%	$35,030	11.0%	37,910
32. Occupational Health and Safety Specialists	2.9%	$66,270	8.5%	2,570
33. Environmental Engineering Technicians	3.3%	$44,850	24.3%	820
34. Budget Analysts	2.6%	$69,090	10.4%	1,960
35. Radio, Cellular, and Tower Equipment Installers and Repairers	4.6%	$42,160	29.4%	450
36. Transportation Inspectors	5.2%	$62,230	14.4%	1,070
37. Aircraft Mechanics and Service Technicians	22.9%	$54,590	6.3%	4,520
38. Private Detectives and Investigators	5.2%	$43,710	20.5%	1,490
39. Sailors and Marine Oilers	7.5%	$36,800	21.3%	2,150
40. Civil Engineering Technicians	3.3%	$46,900	12.0%	2,460

(continued)

(continued)

Best Jobs Overall with a High Percentage of Recent Veterans

Job	Percent Recent Veterans	Annual Earnings	Percent Growth	Annual Openings
41. Rail Car Repairers	3.0%	$47,740	16.9%	930
42. Human Resources Assistants, Except Payroll and Timekeeping	2.5%	$37,250	11.2%	6,160
43. Water and Wastewater Treatment Plant and System Operators	2.7%	$41,780	11.6%	4,150
44. Audio and Video Equipment Technicians	2.3%	$41,630	13.4%	2,560
45. Surveying and Mapping Technicians	2.0%	$39,350	15.9%	2,000

Best Jobs with a High Percentage of Self-Employed Recent Veterans

Currently, 7.8 percent of all working people and 3.4 percent of recent veterans are self-employed. Although you may think of the self-employed as having similar jobs, they actually work in an enormous range of situations, fields, and work environments that you may not have considered.

Among the self-employed are people who own small or large businesses, as many Real Estate Brokers and Public Relations Specialists do; people working on a contract basis for one or more employers, as many Public Relations Specialists do; people running home consulting or other businesses, as many Personal Financial Advisors do; and people in many other situations. The point is that people are self-employed in many different ways, and one of these arrangements could make sense for you now or in the future.

The following list contains jobs in which 5 percent or more of the recent veterans are self-employed.

Jobs with the Highest Percentage of Self-Employed Recent Veterans

Job	Percent Self-Employed Recent Veterans
1. Music Directors and Composers	55.2%
2. First-Line Supervisors of Landscaping, Lawn Service, and Groundskeeping Workers	31.5%
3. Real Estate Brokers	31.0%
4. Real Estate Sales Agents	31.0%

Jobs with the Highest Percentage of Self-Employed Recent Veterans

Job	Percent Self-Employed Recent Veterans
5. Painters, Construction and Maintenance	23.7%
6. Personal Financial Advisors	21.7%
7. Insurance Sales Agents	20.7%
8. Construction Managers	19.5%
9. Tile and Marble Setters	18.7%
10. Carpenters	17.4%
11. Supervisors of Construction and Extraction Workers	15.6%
12. Property, Real Estate, and Community Association Managers	14.7%
13. Fitness Trainers and Aerobics Instructors	13.2%
14. Landscaping and Groundskeeping Workers	12.1%
15. Construction and Building Inspectors	11.9%
16. Construction Laborers	10.8%
17. Budget Analysts	10.7%
18. First-Line Supervisors of Fire Fighting and Prevention Workers	10.7%
19. Securities, Commodities, and Financial Services Sales Agents	9.1%
20. Clergy	8.5%
21. Commercial and Industrial Designers	8.0%
22. Graphic Designers	8.0%
23. Interior Designers	8.0%
24. Social and Community Service Managers	7.9%
25. Mechanical Drafters	7.7%
26. Roofers	7.6%
27. Sailors and Marine Oilers	7.4%
28. Ship Engineers	7.4%
29. Credit Counselors	6.8%
30. Loan Officers	6.8%
31. Accountants and Auditors	6.5%
32. First-Line Supervisors of Non-Retail Sales Workers	6.5%
33. First-Line Supervisors of Retail Sales Workers	6.4%
34. Pipelayers	6.1%
35. Plumbers, Pipefitters, and Steamfitters	6.1%
36. Public Relations Specialists	6.0%
37. Private Detectives and Investigators	5.4%
38. Security and Fire Alarm Systems Installers	5.4%
39. Network and Computer Systems Administrators	5.3%

(continued)

(continued)

Jobs with the Highest Percentage of Self-Employed Recent Veterans

Job	Percent Self-Employed Recent Veterans
40. Structural Iron and Steel Workers	5.3%
41. Sales Representatives, Wholesale and Manufacturing, Except Technical and Scientific Products	5.2%
42. Sales Representatives, Wholesale and Manufacturing, Technical and Scientific Products	5.2%
43. Sales Representatives, Services, All Other	5.1%

The jobs in the following list are derived from the preceding list of jobs with the highest percentage of self-employed veterans. Where the following list gives earnings estimates, keep in mind that these figures are based on a survey that *doesn't include self-employed workers*. The median earnings for self-employed workers in these occupations may be significantly higher or lower.

Best Jobs Overall with a High Percentage of Self-Employed Recent Veterans

Job	Percent Self-Employed Recent Veterans	Annual Earnings	Percent Growth	Annual Openings
1. Network and Computer Systems Administrators	5.3%	$70,970	27.8%	15,530
2. Supervisors of Construction and Extraction Workers	15.6%	$59,150	23.5%	25,970
3. Personal Financial Advisors	21.7%	$66,580	32.1%	9,020
4. Plumbers, Pipefitters, and Steamfitters	6.1%	$47,750	25.6%	22,880
5. Sales Representatives, Wholesale and Manufacturing, Technical and Scientific Products	5.2%	$74,750	16.4%	15,970
6. Accountants and Auditors	6.5%	$62,850	15.7%	45,210
7. Public Relations Specialists	6.0%	$53,190	22.5%	12,720
8. Social and Community Service Managers	7.9%	$58,660	26.7%	6,480
9. Insurance Sales Agents	20.7%	$47,450	21.9%	18,440
10. Construction Managers	19.5%	$84,240	16.6%	12,040

Best Jobs Overall with a High Percentage of Self-Employed Recent Veterans

Job	Percent Self-Employed Recent Veterans	Annual Earnings	Percent Growth	Annual Openings
11. Sales Representatives, Wholesale and Manufacturing, Except Technical and Scientific Products	5.2%	$53,540	15.6%	55,990
12. Sales Representatives, Services, All Other	5.1%	$50,630	18.8%	27,010
13. Securities, Commodities, and Financial Services Sales Agents	9.1%	$72,060	15.2%	13,370
14. Carpenters	17.4%	$40,010	19.6%	40,830
15. Construction Laborers	10.8%	$29,730	21.3%	29,240
16. Landscaping and Groundskeeping Workers	12.1%	$23,410	20.9%	44,440
17. Security and Fire Alarm Systems Installers	5.4%	$39,540	33.0%	3,670
18. First-Line Supervisors of Non-Retail Sales Workers	6.5%	$70,520	4.0%	12,350
19. Loan Officers	6.8%	$58,030	14.2%	11,520
20. Construction and Building Inspectors	11.9%	$53,180	17.9%	4,860
21. Fitness Trainers and Aerobics Instructors	13.2%	$31,030	24.0%	10,060
22. Ship Engineers	7.4%	$70,840	18.0%	620
23. Painters, Construction and Maintenance	23.7%	$35,430	18.5%	15,730
24. Structural Iron and Steel Workers	5.3%	$45,690	21.9%	2,540
25. Clergy	8.5%	$44,140	17.5%	7,990
26. Interior Designers	8.0%	$47,620	19.3%	2,840
27. Tile and Marble Setters	18.7%	$37,080	25.4%	2,770
28. First-Line Supervisors of Fire Fighting and Prevention Workers	10.7%	$69,510	8.2%	3,310
29. First-Line Supervisors of Retail Sales Workers	6.4%	$36,480	8.4%	51,370
30. Graphic Designers	8.0%	$44,010	13.4%	12,380
31. Pipelayers	6.1%	$35,900	25.3%	2,880
32. Real Estate Sales Agents	31.0%	$39,070	12.2%	12,760
33. Budget Analysts	10.7%	$69,090	10.4%	1,960
34. Property, Real Estate, and Community Association Managers	14.7%	$52,510	6.0%	8,230
35. Real Estate Brokers	31.0%	$59,340	7.6%	2,970
36. Sailors and Marine Oilers	7.4%	$36,800	21.3%	2,150

(continued)

(continued)

Best Jobs Overall with a High Percentage of Self-Employed Recent Veterans				
Job	Percent Self-Employed Recent Veterans	Annual Earnings	Percent Growth	Annual Openings
37. Commercial and Industrial Designers	8.0%	$60,760	10.5%	1,690
38. First-Line Supervisors of Landscaping, Lawn Service, and Groundskeeping Workers	31.5%	$42,050	15.1%	6,010
39. Private Detectives and Investigators	5.4%	$43,710	20.5%	1,490
40. Roofers	7.6%	$35,280	17.8%	5,250
41. Credit Counselors	6.8%	$38,430	20.3%	1,520
42. Mechanical Drafters	7.7%	$49,200	11.1%	2,050
43. Music Directors and Composers	55.2%	$47,410	10.2%	3,220

Best Jobs with a High Percentage of Part-Time Recent Veterans

Part-time workers are defined as those whose workweek averages less than 35 hours. About one-quarter of all workers fit this definition, but only about 10 percent of recent vets do. Various reasons may explain this. Recent vets are of prime working age, whereas teenagers and retirees tend to work part-time. Vets are more heavily male than the general population, and men are more likely than women to work full-time. And let's not forget the skills and work habits that vets have acquired in the military, which probably help their chances of landing a full-time job.

But maybe you would prefer to work a part-time schedule because you want the freedom of time that this work arrangement can provide. Or perhaps you're considering adding a part-time job to your full-time workweek to help make ends meet. Whatever your reason is, look over the list of the jobs with high percentages (more than 15 percent) of part-time recent veterans and you will find some interesting things. For example, many of the jobs on the list involve providing services at times when most other people are not working. Some are in the field of health care.

Note: The earnings estimates in the following lists are based on a survey of both part-time and full-time workers. On average, part-time workers earn about 10 percent less per hour than full-time workers, although in a few highly skilled jobs they actually earn more per hour.

Jobs with the Highest Percentage of Part-Time Recent Veterans

Job	Percent Part-Time Recent Veterans
1. Athletes and Sports Competitors	48.7%
2. Coaches and Scouts	48.7%
3. Music Directors and Composers	47.2%
4. Fitness Trainers and Aerobics Instructors	34.8%
5. Bus Drivers, Transit and Intercity	31.4%
6. Receptionists and Information Clerks	26.3%
7. Teacher Assistants	22.9%
8. Roofers	20.8%
9. Public Relations Specialists	20.7%
10. Laborers and Freight, Stock, and Material Movers, Hand	18.0%
11. Landscaping and Groundskeeping Workers	17.5%
12. Wholesale and Retail Buyers, Except Farm Products	17.3%
13. Painters, Construction and Maintenance	17.2%
14. Medical Assistants	17.1%
15. Cardiovascular Technologists and Technicians	16.9%
16. Diagnostic Medical Sonographers	16.9%
17. Nuclear Medicine Technologists	16.9%
18. Radiologic Technologists	16.9%
19. Environmental Science and Protection Technicians, Including Health	16.1%
20. Forensic Science Technicians	16.1%
21. Life, Physical, and Social Science Technicians, All Other	16.1%
22. Nuclear Technicians	16.1%
23. Dental Assistants	15.8%
24. Geological and Petroleum Technicians	15.7%
25. Health Educators	15.6%
26. Probation Officers and Correctional Treatment Specialists	15.6%
27. Social and Human Service Assistants	15.6%
28. Real Estate Brokers	15.5%
29. Real Estate Sales Agents	15.5%
30. Advertising Sales Agents	15.1%
31. Customer Service Representatives	15.1%

The jobs in the following list are derived from the preceding list of the jobs with the highest percentages of part-time recent veterans.

Best Jobs Overall with a High Percentage of Part-Time Recent Veterans

Job	Percent Part-Time Recent Veterans	Annual Earnings	Percent Growth	Annual Openings
1. Radiologic Technologists	16.9%	$55,120	27.8%	9,510
2. Diagnostic Medical Sonographers	16.9%	$65,210	43.5%	3,170
3. Public Relations Specialists	20.7%	$53,190	22.5%	12,720
4. Health Educators	15.6%	$47,940	36.5%	3,690
5. Medical Assistants	17.1%	$29,100	30.9%	24,380
6. Dental Assistants	15.8%	$34,140	30.8%	15,400
7. Cardiovascular Technologists and Technicians	16.9%	$51,020	29.3%	2,210
8. Receptionists and Information Clerks	26.3%	$25,690	23.7%	56,560
9. Social and Human Service Assistants	15.6%	$28,740	27.6%	18,910
10. Coaches and Scouts	48.7%	$28,470	29.4%	13,300
11. Fitness Trainers and Aerobics Instructors	34.8%	$31,030	24.0%	10,060
12. Nuclear Medicine Technologists	16.9%	$69,450	18.9%	750
13. Painters, Construction and Maintenance	17.2%	$35,430	18.5%	15,730
14. Customer Service Representatives	15.1%	$30,610	15.5%	95,960
15. Probation Officers and Correctional Treatment Specialists	15.6%	$47,840	18.4%	3,730
16. Forensic Science Technicians	16.1%	$52,180	18.6%	790
17. Landscaping and Groundskeeping Workers	17.5%	$23,410	20.9%	44,440
18. Laborers and Freight, Stock, and Material Movers, Hand	18.0%	$23,750	15.4%	98,020
19. Environmental Science and Protection Technicians, Including Health	16.1%	$42,270	23.6%	1,950
20. Advertising Sales Agents	15.1%	$45,250	13.0%	6,990
21. Real Estate Sales Agents	15.5%	$39,070	12.2%	12,760
22. Teacher Assistants	22.9%	$23,580	14.8%	48,160
23. Bus Drivers, Transit and Intercity	31.4%	$35,720	14.8%	6,350
24. Roofers	20.8%	$35,280	17.8%	5,250
25. Wholesale and Retail Buyers, Except Farm Products	17.3%	$50,490	9.0%	4,170
26. Athletes and Sports Competitors	48.7%	$39,670	21.6%	780
27. Nuclear Technicians	16.1%	$68,030	13.5%	330
28. Real Estate Brokers	15.5%	$59,340	7.6%	2,970
29. Geological and Petroleum Technicians	15.7%	$49,690	14.7%	700
30. Life, Physical, and Social Science Technicians, All Other	16.1%	$43,120	11.8%	3,350
31. Music Directors and Composers	47.2%	$47,410	10.2%	3,220

Best Jobs with a High Percentage of Recent Female Veterans

To create the lists that follow, I sorted the 150 best jobs according to the percentages of female and male recent veterans in the workforce, setting the cutoff level at 90 percent for men and 25 percent for women. I used different cutoff levels because 87 percent of all recent vets are men, and only 13 percent are women.

Similar lists of the best jobs with high percentages of men and women are included in all the books in the *Best Jobs* series. It's important to understand that these lists aren't meant to restrict women or men from considering job options. Actually, my reasoning for including them is exactly the opposite: I hope the lists help people see possibilities that they might not otherwise have considered. In fact, economists have found a recent uptick of men moving into jobs traditionally dominated by women.

The fact is that jobs with high percentages of women or high percentages of men offer good opportunities for both men and women if they want to do one of these jobs. So I suggest that women browse the lists of jobs that employ high percentages of men and that men browse the lists of jobs with high percentages of women. There are jobs in both sets of lists that pay well, and women or men who are interested in them and who have or can obtain the necessary education and training should consider them. You may already have the necessary skills to enter one of these nontraditional occupations, because the armed forces have an excellent reputation for encouraging men and women to serve in nontraditional roles.

An interesting and unfortunate tidbit to bring up at your next party is that the average earnings for the jobs in this book with the highest percentage of female vets is $40,072, compared to average earnings of $46,611 for the jobs with the highest percentage of male vets. But earnings don't tell the whole story. I computed the average growth and job openings of the jobs with the highest percentage of female vets and found statistics of an average of 19.5% growth and 25,798 openings, compared to an average of 16.0% growth and 15,030 openings for the jobs with the highest percentage of men. This discrepancy reinforces the idea that men have had more problems than women in adapting to an economy dominated by service and information-based jobs. Many women may simply be better prepared, possessing more appropriate skills for the jobs that are now growing rapidly and have more job openings. On the other hand, keep in mind that these job outlook figures apply to *all* workers in these occupations. As Part I notes, recent female veterans have a high unemployment rate. So perhaps the lesson to take from these figures is that male veterans should consider taking jobs that defy traditional gender roles.

Jobs with the Highest Percentage of Recent Female Veterans

Job	Percent Recent Female Veterans
1. Executive Secretaries and Executive Administrative Assistants	78.5%
2. Medical Secretaries	78.5%
3. Dental Assistants	69.8%
4. Receptionists and Information Clerks	64.9%
5. Registered Nurses	61.8%
6. Billing and Posting Clerks	61.0%
7. Licensed Practical and Licensed Vocational Nurses	54.4%
8. Medical Assistants	50.3%
9. Pharmacy Technicians	47.3%
10. Surgical Technologists	47.3%
11. Veterinary Technologists and Technicians	47.3%
12. Teacher Assistants	47.3%
13. Paralegals and Legal Assistants	47.0%
14. Medical and Clinical Laboratory Technicians	45.7%
15. Medical and Clinical Laboratory Technologists	45.7%
16. Payroll and Timekeeping Clerks	44.0%
17. Bookkeeping, Accounting, and Auditing Clerks	44.0%
18. Office Clerks, General	43.5%
19. Human Resources Assistants, Except Payroll and Timekeeping	42.4%
20. Cardiovascular Technologists and Technicians	38.4%
21. Diagnostic Medical Sonographers	38.4%
22. Nuclear Medicine Technologists	38.4%
23. Radiologic Technologists	38.4%
24. Health Technologists and Technicians, All Other	38.4%
25. Claims Adjusters, Examiners, and Investigators	32.8%
26. Customer Service Representatives	27.5%
27. Accountants and Auditors	27.4%
28. Substance Abuse and Behavioral Disorder Counselors	26.9%
29. Budget Analysts	26.8%
30. Public Relations Specialists	26.6%

The jobs in the following list are derived from the preceding list of the jobs with the highest percentage of female veterans.

Best Jobs Overall with a High Percentage of Recent Female Veterans

Job	Percent Recent Female Veterans	Annual Earnings	Percent Growth	Annual Openings
1. Registered Nurses	61.8%	$65,950	26.0%	120,740
2. Accountants and Auditors	27.4%	$62,850	15.7%	45,210
3. Radiologic Technologists	38.4%	$55,120	27.8%	9,510
4. Diagnostic Medical Sonographers	38.4%	$65,210	43.5%	3,170
5. Licensed Practical and Licensed Vocational Nurses	54.4%	$41,150	22.4%	36,920
6. Medical Secretaries	78.5%	$31,060	41.3%	27,840
7. Public Relations Specialists	26.6%	$53,190	22.5%	12,720
8. Dental Assistants	69.8%	$34,140	30.8%	15,400
9. Medical Assistants	50.3%	$29,100	30.9%	24,380
10. Pharmacy Technicians	47.3%	$28,940	32.4%	16,630
11. Receptionists and Information Clerks	64.9%	$25,690	23.7%	56,560
12. Cardiovascular Technologists and Technicians	38.4%	$51,020	29.3%	2,210
13. Paralegals and Legal Assistants	47.0%	$46,730	18.3%	8,340
14. Executive Secretaries and Executive Administrative Assistants	78.5%	$45,580	12.6%	32,180
15. Nuclear Medicine Technologists	38.4%	$69,450	18.9%	750
16. Veterinary Technologists and Technicians	47.3%	$30,140	52.0%	5,570
17. Customer Service Representatives	27.5%	$30,610	15.5%	95,960
18. Substance Abuse and Behavioral Disorder Counselors	26.9%	$38,560	27.3%	4,170
19. Billing and Posting Clerks	61.0%	$32,880	19.7%	18,760
20. Office Clerks, General	43.5%	$27,190	16.6%	101,150
21. Bookkeeping, Accounting, and Auditing Clerks	44.0%	$34,740	13.6%	46,780
22. Health Technologists and Technicians, All Other	38.4%	$38,080	23.2%	4,040
23. Claims Adjusters, Examiners, and Investigators	32.8%	$59,320	3.0%	7,990
24. Surgical Technologists	47.3%	$40,950	18.9%	3,390
25. Medical and Clinical Laboratory Technologists	45.7%	$57,010	11.3%	5,210
26. Teacher Assistants	47.3%	$23,580	14.8%	48,160
27. Budget Analysts	26.8%	$69,090	10.4%	1,960
28. Payroll and Timekeeping Clerks	44.0%	$37,160	14.6%	6,570
29. Medical and Clinical Laboratory Technicians	45.7%	$36,950	14.7%	5,510
30. Human Resources Assistants, Except Payroll and Timekeeping	42.4%	$37,250	11.2%	6,160

Best Jobs with a High Percentage of Male Veterans

If you haven't already read the intro to the previous group of lists, "Best Jobs with a High Percentage of Recent Female Veterans," consider doing so. Much of the content there applies to these lists as well.

I didn't include these groups of lists with the assumption that men should consider only jobs with high percentages of men or that women should consider only jobs with high percentages of women. Instead, these lists are here because I think they are interesting and perhaps helpful in considering nontraditional career options. For example, some men would do very well in and enjoy some of the jobs with high percentages of women but may not have considered them seriously. Similarly, some women would very much enjoy and do well in some jobs that traditionally have been held by high percentages of men. I hope that these lists help you consider options that you didn't seriously consider simply because of gender stereotypes.

In the jobs on the following lists, more than 90 percent of the recent veterans are men, but increasing numbers of women are entering many of these jobs. Note that some of the jobs listed as having 100 percent men probably include a few women but have such a small total workforce that the sample queried by the Census Bureau did not include any female workers.

Jobs with the Highest Percentage of Recent Male Veterans	
Job	Percent Recent Male Veterans
1. Roofers	100.0%
2. Security and Fire Alarm Systems Installers	100.0%
3. Structural Iron and Steel Workers	100.0%
4. Water and Wastewater Treatment Plant and System Operators	100.0%
5. Heating, Air Conditioning, and Refrigeration Mechanics and Installers	99.6%
6. Industrial Machinery Mechanics	99.5%
7. Bus and Truck Mechanics and Diesel Engine Specialists	99.3%
8. Mobile Heavy Equipment Mechanics, Except Engines	99.3%
9. Rail Car Repairers	99.3%
10. Captains, Mates, and Pilots of Water Vessels	99.2%
11. Tile and Marble Setters	99.1%
12. Pipelayers	99.0%
13. Plumbers, Pipefitters, and Steamfitters	99.0%
14. Construction Laborers	98.7%

Jobs with the Highest Percentage of Recent Male Veterans

Job	Percent Recent Male Veterans
15. First-Line Supervisors of Fire Fighting and Prevention Workers	98.7%
16. Automotive Service Technicians and Mechanics	98.6%
17. Supervisors of Construction and Extraction Workers	98.6%
18. Carpenters	98.4%
19. Firefighters	98.1%
20. Industrial Truck and Tractor Operators	98.1%
21. Landscaping and Groundskeeping Workers	98.0%
22. Paving, Surfacing, and Tamping Equipment Operators	98.0%
23. Operating Engineers and Other Construction Equipment Operators	97.9%
24. Pile-Driver Operators	97.9%
25. Commercial Pilots	97.8%
26. Medical Equipment Repairers	97.8%
27. Heavy and Tractor-Trailer Truck Drivers	97.6%
28. Light Truck or Delivery Services Drivers	97.6%
29. Painters, Construction and Maintenance	97.6%
30. First-Line Supervisors of Mechanics, Installers, and Repairers	97.5%
31. Sheet Metal Workers	97.5%
32. Electricians	97.4%
33. Machinists	97.0%
34. Welders, Cutters, Solderers, and Brazers	96.9%
35. Telecommunications Line Installers and Repairers	96.8%
36. Maintenance and Repair Workers, General	96.7%
37. Pest Control Workers	96.3%
38. Construction and Building Inspectors	96.0%
39. Construction Managers	96.0%
40. First-Line Supervisors of Police and Detectives	95.8%
41. Aircraft Mechanics and Service Technicians	95.5%
42. Securities, Commodities, and Financial Services Sales Agents	95.3%
43. First-Line Supervisors of Production and Operating Workers	94.9%
44. Laborers and Freight, Stock, and Material Movers, Hand	94.8%
45. Sailors and Marine Oilers	94.3%
46. Ship Engineers	94.3%
47. Electrical Power-Line Installers and Repairers	94.1%
48. First-Line Supervisors of Landscaping, Lawn Service, and Groundskeeping Workers	94.0%
49. Radio, Cellular, and Tower Equipment Installers and Repairers	93.8%
50. Transportation Inspectors	93.6%

(continued)

(continued)

Jobs with the Highest Percentage of Recent Male Veterans

Job	Percent Recent Male Veterans
51. Police and Sheriff's Patrol Officers	93.5%
52. Detectives and Criminal Investigators	93.0%
53. Sales Representatives, Wholesale and Manufacturing, Except Technical and Scientific Products	92.5%
54. Sales Representatives, Wholesale and Manufacturing, Technical and Scientific Products	92.5%
55. Surveying and Mapping Technicians	92.5%
56. Clergy	92.0%
57. Civil Engineering Technicians	91.9%
58. Environmental Engineering Technicians	91.9%
59. General and Operations Managers	91.5%
60. Software Developers, Systems Software	91.4%
61. Security Guards	91.3%
62. Computer Programmers	91.2%
63. Audio and Video Equipment Technicians	90.9%
64. Aircraft Cargo Handling Supervisors	90.1%
65. First-Line Supervisors of Helpers, Laborers, and Material Movers, Hand	90.1%
66. First-Line Supervisors of Transportation and Material-Moving Machine and Vehicle Operators	90.1%

The jobs in the following list are derived from the preceding list of the jobs with the highest percentage of recent male veterans.

Best Jobs Overall with a High Percentage of Recent Male Veterans

Job	Percent Recent Male Veterans	Annual Earnings	Percent Growth	Annual Openings
1. Software Developers, Systems Software	91.4%	$96,600	32.4%	16,800
2. Supervisors of Construction and Extraction Workers	98.6%	$59,150	23.5%	25,970
3. Plumbers, Pipefitters, and Steamfitters	99.0%	$47,750	25.6%	22,880
4. Electricians	97.4%	$49,320	23.2%	28,920
5. Sales Representatives, Wholesale and Manufacturing, Technical and Scientific Products	92.5%	$74,750	16.4%	15,970

Best Jobs Overall with a High Percentage of Recent Male Veterans

Job	Percent Recent Male Veterans	Annual Earnings	Percent Growth	Annual Openings
6. Heating, Air Conditioning, and Refrigeration Mechanics and Installers	99.6%	$43,380	33.7%	13,760
7. Sales Representatives, Wholesale and Manufacturing, Except Technical and Scientific Products	92.5%	$53,540	15.6%	55,990
8. Construction Managers	96.0%	$84,240	16.6%	12,040
9. General and Operations Managers	91.5%	$95,150	4.6%	41,010
10. Securities, Commodities, and Financial Services Sales Agents	95.3%	$72,060	15.2%	13,370
11. Industrial Machinery Mechanics	99.5%	$46,270	21.6%	11,710
12. First-Line Supervisors of Helpers, Laborers, and Material Movers, Hand	90.1%	$44,580	27.2%	8,000
13. Heavy and Tractor-Trailer Truck Drivers	97.6%	$37,930	20.6%	64,940
14. Operating Engineers and Other Construction Equipment Operators	97.9%	$41,510	23.5%	16,280
15. Carpenters	98.4%	$40,010	19.6%	40,830
16. Computer Programmers	91.2%	$72,630	12.0%	12,800
17. First-Line Supervisors of Mechanics, Installers, and Repairers	97.5%	$59,850	11.9%	16,490
18. Commercial Pilots	97.8%	$70,000	21.2%	1,930
19. Construction and Building Inspectors	96.0%	$53,180	17.9%	4,860
20. Construction Laborers	98.7%	$29,730	21.3%	29,240
21. Landscaping and Groundskeeping Workers	98.0%	$23,410	20.9%	44,440
22. Police and Sheriff's Patrol Officers	93.5%	$54,230	8.2%	24,940
23. Captains, Mates, and Pilots of Water Vessels	99.2%	$63,920	20.4%	2,070
24. Medical Equipment Repairers	97.8%	$44,870	31.5%	2,230
25. Automotive Service Technicians and Mechanics	98.6%	$36,180	17.2%	31,170
26. Security and Fire Alarm Systems Installers	100.0%	$39,540	33.0%	3,670
27. Pile-Driver Operators	97.9%	$45,500	36.0%	230
28. Security Guards	91.3%	$23,900	18.8%	35,950
29. Structural Iron and Steel Workers	100.0%	$45,690	21.9%	2,540
30. Electrical Power-Line Installers and Repairers	94.1%	$60,190	13.2%	5,270
31. Ship Engineers	94.3%	$70,840	18.0%	620
32. Clergy	92.0%	$44,140	17.5%	7,990

(continued)

(continued)

Best Jobs Overall with a High Percentage of Recent Male Veterans

Job	Percent Recent Male Veterans	Annual Earnings	Percent Growth	Annual Openings
33. First-Line Supervisors of Transportation and Material-Moving Machine and Vehicle Operators	90.1%	$52,950	14.3%	6,930
34. Painters, Construction and Maintenance	97.6%	$35,430	18.5%	15,730
35. Mobile Heavy Equipment Mechanics, Except Engines	99.3%	$45,600	16.2%	5,250
36. Laborers and Freight, Stock, and Material Movers, Hand	94.8%	$23,750	15.4%	98,020
37. Environmental Engineering Technicians	91.9%	$44,850	24.3%	820
38. Pest Control Workers	96.3%	$30,220	26.1%	4,850
39. Radio, Cellular, and Tower Equipment Installers and Repairers	93.8%	$42,160	29.4%	450
40. Telecommunications Line Installers and Repairers	96.8%	$51,720	13.6%	5,140
41. Tile and Marble Setters	99.1%	$37,080	25.4%	2,770
42. Sheet Metal Workers	97.5%	$42,730	17.5%	4,700
43. First-Line Supervisors of Police and Detectives	95.8%	$77,890	2.1%	3,870
44. First-Line Supervisors of Production and Operating Workers	94.9%	$53,670	1.9%	8,790
45. Pipelayers	99.0%	$35,900	25.3%	2,880
46. Aircraft Cargo Handling Supervisors	90.1%	$46,840	20.3%	260
47. First-Line Supervisors of Fire Fighting and Prevention Workers	98.7%	$69,510	8.2%	3,310
48. Light Truck or Delivery Services Drivers	97.6%	$29,080	14.7%	29,590
49. Firefighters	98.1%	$45,420	8.6%	11,230
50. First-Line Supervisors of Landscaping, Lawn Service, and Groundskeeping Workers	94.0%	$42,050	15.1%	6,010
51. Bus and Truck Mechanics and Diesel Engine Specialists	99.3%	$41,640	14.5%	8,780
52. Detectives and Criminal Investigators	93.0%	$71,770	2.9%	3,010
53. Transportation Inspectors	93.6%	$62,230	14.4%	1,070
54. Welders, Cutters, Solderers, and Brazers	96.9%	$35,920	15.0%	14,070
55. Aircraft Mechanics and Service Technicians	95.5%	$54,590	6.3%	4,520
56. Rail Car Repairers	99.3%	$47,740	16.9%	930
57. Maintenance and Repair Workers, General	96.7%	$35,030	11.0%	37,910

Best Jobs Overall with a High Percentage of Recent Male Veterans

Job	Percent Recent Male Veterans	Annual Earnings	Percent Growth	Annual Openings
58. Roofers	100.0%	$35,280	17.8%	5,250
59. Sailors and Marine Oilers	94.3%	$36,800	21.3%	2,150
60. Paving, Surfacing, and Tamping Equipment Operators	98.0%	$35,270	22.1%	2,200
61. Civil Engineering Technicians	91.9%	$46,900	12.0%	2,460
62. Industrial Truck and Tractor Operators	98.1%	$30,010	11.8%	20,950
63. Machinists	97.0%	$39,220	8.5%	9,950
64. Water and Wastewater Treatment Plant and System Operators	100.0%	$41,780	11.6%	4,150
65. Audio and Video Equipment Technicians	90.9%	$41,630	13.4%	2,560
66. Surveying and Mapping Technicians	92.5%	$39,350	15.9%	2,000

Best Jobs with a High Percentage of Urban or Rural Workers

Some people have a strong preference for an urban setting. They want to live and work where there's more energy and excitement, more access to the arts, more diversity, more really good restaurants, and better public transportation. On the other hand, some prefer the open spaces, closeness to nature, quiet, and inexpensive housing of rural locations. If you are strongly attracted to either setting, you'll be interested in the following lists.

I identified urban jobs as those for which 20 percent or more of the workforce is located in the 38 most populous metropolitan areas of the United States. These 38 metro areas—the most populous 10 percent of all U.S. metro areas, according to the Census Bureau—consist primarily of built-up communities, unlike smaller metro areas, which consist of a core city surrounded by a lot of countryside. In the following lists of urban jobs, you'll see a figure called the "urban ratio" for each job that represents the percentage of the total U.S. workforce for the job that is located in those 38 populous metro areas.

The Census Bureau also identifies 173 nonmetropolitan areas—areas that have no city of 50,000 people and a total population of less than 100,000. I identified rural jobs as those for which 15 percent or more of the total U.S. workforce is located in these nonmetropolitan areas. In the following lists of rural jobs, you'll see a figure called the "rural ratio" that represents the percentage of the total U.S. workforce for the job that is located in nonmetropolitan areas.

The "best-of" lists of both urban and rural jobs are ordered by the usual three economic measures: earnings, growth, and number of openings.

Jobs with the Highest Percentage of Urban Workers

Job	Urban Ratio
1. Sales Representatives, Wholesale and Manufacturing, Technical and Scientific Products	25.1%
2. Computer Systems Analysts	24.9%
3. Bill and Account Collectors	24.4%
4. Claims Adjusters, Examiners, and Investigators	23.2%
5. Medical Equipment Repairers	22.9%
6. Technical Writers	22.8%
7. Security and Fire Alarm Systems Installers	22.7%
8. Security Guards	22.7%
9. Training and Development Specialists	22.5%
10. Database Administrators	22.4%
11. Customer Service Representatives	22.2%
12. Insurance Sales Agents	22.1%
13. Construction Managers	22.0%
14. First-Line Supervisors of Non-Retail Sales Workers	22.0%
15. Audio and Video Equipment Technicians	21.8%
16. Computer Programmers	21.8%
17. Property, Real Estate, and Community Association Managers	21.7%
18. Software Developers, Systems Software	21.5%
19. Clergy	21.4%
20. Sales Representatives, Services, All Other	21.4%
21. Sheet Metal Workers	21.4%
22. Purchasing Agents, Except Wholesale, Retail, and Farm Products	21.2%
23. First-Line Supervisors of Helpers, Laborers, and Material Movers, Hand	21.1%
24. Production, Planning, and Expediting Clerks	21.1%
25. Accountants and Auditors	21.0%
26. Civil Engineering Technicians	21.0%
27. Network and Computer Systems Administrators	21.0%
28. Occupational Health and Safety Specialists	21.0%
29. Laborers and Freight, Stock, and Material Movers, Hand	20.9%
30. Loan Officers	20.9%
31. Surgical Technologists	20.9%
32. First-Line Supervisors of Office and Administrative Support Workers	20.8%
33. Health Technologists and Technicians, All Other	20.8%
34. Paralegals and Legal Assistants	20.8%

Jobs with the Highest Percentage of Urban Workers

Job	Urban Ratio
35. Budget Analysts	20.7%
36. Medical Secretaries	20.6%
37. Transportation, Storage, and Distribution Managers	20.6%
38. Cardiovascular Technologists and Technicians	20.5%
39. Compensation, Benefits, and Job Analysis Specialists	20.5%
40. Firefighters	20.4%
41. Pest Control Workers	20.4%
42. Tile and Marble Setters	20.4%
43. Human Resources Assistants, Except Payroll and Timekeeping	20.3%
44. Medical and Clinical Laboratory Technicians	20.2%
45. Real Estate Brokers	20.2%
46. Billing and Posting Clerks	20.1%
47. Plumbers, Pipefitters, and Steamfitters	20.1%
48. First-Line Supervisors of Landscaping, Lawn Service, and Groundskeeping Workers	20.0%
49. Sales Representatives, Wholesale and Manufacturing, Except Technical and Scientific Products	20.0%

Best Jobs Overall with a High Percentage of Urban Workers

Job	Urban Ratio	Annual Earnings	Percent Growth	Annual Openings
1. Software Developers, Systems Software	21.5%	$96,600	32.4%	16,800
2. Computer Systems Analysts	24.9%	$78,770	22.1%	22,250
3. Network and Computer Systems Administrators	21.0%	$70,970	27.8%	15,530
4. Database Administrators	22.4%	$75,190	30.6%	5,270
5. Accountants and Auditors	21.0%	$62,850	15.7%	45,210
6. Construction Managers	22.0%	$84,240	16.6%	12,040
7. Plumbers, Pipefitters, and Steamfitters	20.1%	$47,750	25.6%	22,880
8. Sales Representatives, Wholesale and Manufacturing, Technical and Scientific Products	25.1%	$74,750	16.4%	15,970
9. Training and Development Specialists	22.5%	$55,150	28.3%	9,830
10. Sales Representatives, Services, All Other	21.4%	$50,630	18.8%	27,010
11. Sales Representatives, Wholesale and Manufacturing, Except Technical and Scientific Products	20.0%	$53,540	15.6%	55,990

(continued)

(continued)

Best Jobs Overall with a High Percentage of Urban Workers

Job	Urban Ratio	Annual Earnings	Percent Growth	Annual Openings
12. Insurance Sales Agents	22.1%	$47,450	21.9%	18,440
13. Medical Secretaries	20.6%	$31,060	41.3%	27,840
14. First-Line Supervisors of Office and Administrative Support Workers	20.8%	$48,810	14.3%	58,440
15. Computer Programmers	21.8%	$72,630	12.0%	12,800
16. First-Line Supervisors of Helpers, Laborers, and Material Movers, Hand	21.1%	$44,580	27.2%	8,000
17. Loan Officers	20.9%	$58,030	14.2%	11,520
18. Billing and Posting Clerks	20.1%	$32,880	19.7%	18,760
19. Security Guards	22.7%	$23,900	18.8%	35,950
20. Paralegals and Legal Assistants	20.8%	$46,730	18.3%	8,340
21. Cardiovascular Technologists and Technicians	20.5%	$51,020	29.3%	2,210
22. First-Line Supervisors of Non-Retail Sales Workers	22.0%	$70,520	4.0%	12,350
23. Customer Service Representatives	22.2%	$30,610	15.5%	95,960
24. Security and Fire Alarm Systems Installers	22.7%	$39,540	33.0%	3,670
25. Laborers and Freight, Stock, and Material Movers, Hand	20.9%	$23,750	15.4%	98,020
26. Medical Equipment Repairers	22.9%	$44,870	31.5%	2,230
27. Clergy	21.4%	$44,140	17.5%	7,990
28. Transportation, Storage, and Distribution Managers	20.6%	$80,860	10.0%	3,370
29. Technical Writers	22.8%	$64,610	17.2%	1,830
30. Purchasing Agents, Except Wholesale, Retail, and Farm Products	21.2%	$57,580	5.3%	9,120
31. Health Technologists and Technicians, All Other	20.8%	$38,080	23.2%	4,040
32. Sheet Metal Workers	21.4%	$42,730	17.5%	4,700
33. Firefighters	20.4%	$45,420	8.6%	11,230
34. Pest Control Workers	20.4%	$30,220	26.1%	4,850
35. Claims Adjusters, Examiners, and Investigators	23.2%	$59,320	3.0%	7,990
36. Property, Real Estate, and Community Association Managers	21.7%	$52,510	6.0%	8,230
37. Surgical Technologists	20.9%	$40,950	18.9%	3,390
38. Bill and Account Collectors	24.4%	$31,920	14.2%	13,550

Best Jobs Overall with a High Percentage of Urban Workers

Job	Urban Ratio	Annual Earnings	Percent Growth	Annual Openings
39. Tile and Marble Setters	20.4%	$37,080	25.4%	2,770
40. Occupational Health and Safety Specialists	21.0%	$66,270	8.5%	2,570
41. First-Line Supervisors of Landscaping, Lawn Service, and Groundskeeping Workers	20.0%	$42,050	15.1%	6,010
42. Budget Analysts	20.7%	$69,090	10.4%	1,960
43. Real Estate Brokers	20.2%	$59,340	7.6%	2,970
44. Production, Planning, and Expediting Clerks	21.1%	$43,100	6.6%	8,880
45. Medical and Clinical Laboratory Technicians	20.2%	$36,950	14.7%	5,510
46. Civil Engineering Technicians	21.0%	$46,900	12.0%	2,460
47. Human Resources Assistants, Except Payroll and Timekeeping	20.3%	$37,250	11.2%	6,160
48. Compensation, Benefits, and Job Analysis Specialists	20.5%	$57,960	5.0%	2,400
49. Audio and Video Equipment Technicians	21.8%	$41,630	13.4%	2,560

Jobs with the Highest Percentage of Rural Workers

Job	Rural Ratio
1. Water and Wastewater Treatment Plant and System Operators	28.8%
2. Operating Engineers and Other Construction Equipment Operators	27.1%
3. Electrical Power-Line Installers and Repairers	26.9%
4. Welders, Cutters, Solderers, and Brazers	24.7%
5. Emergency Medical Technicians and Paramedics	22.7%
6. Industrial Machinery Mechanics	21.7%
7. Heavy and Tractor-Trailer Truck Drivers	21.7%
8. First-Line Supervisors of Production and Operating Workers	20.4%
9. Licensed Practical and Licensed Vocational Nurses	19.4%
10. Mobile Heavy Equipment Mechanics, Except Engines	19.0%
11. Teacher Assistants	18.0%
12. Bus and Truck Mechanics and Diesel Engine Specialists	17.9%
13. Industrial Truck and Tractor Operators	17.8%
14. Postal Service Mail Carriers	17.2%
15. Paving, Surfacing, and Tamping Equipment Operators	16.9%
16. Maintenance and Repair Workers, General	16.9%
17. Supervisors of Construction and Extraction Workers	16.1%

(continued)

(continued)

Jobs with the Highest Percentage of Rural Workers

Job	Rural Ratio
18. Machinists	16.0%
19. Carpenters	16.0%
20. First-Line Supervisors of Mechanics, Installers, and Repairers	15.9%
21. Social and Human Service Assistants	15.9%
22. Pharmacy Technicians	15.8%
23. First-Line Supervisors of Retail Sales Workers	15.7%
24. Music Directors and Composers	15.6%
25. Surveying and Mapping Technicians	15.5%
26. Construction Laborers	15.5%
27. First-Line Supervisors of Transportation and Material-Moving Machine and Vehicle Operators	15.3%
28. Automotive Service Technicians and Mechanics	15.1%
29. Bookkeeping, Accounting, and Auditing Clerks	15.0%

Best Jobs Overall with a High Percentage of Rural Workers

Job	Rural Ratio	Annual Earnings	Percent Growth	Annual Openings
1. Supervisors of Construction and Extraction Workers	16.1%	$59,150	23.5%	25,970
2. Licensed Practical and Licensed Vocational Nurses	19.4%	$41,150	22.4%	36,920
3. Heavy and Tractor-Trailer Truck Drivers	21.7%	$37,930	20.6%	64,940
4. Carpenters	16.0%	$40,010	19.6%	40,830
5. Operating Engineers and Other Construction Equipment Operators	27.1%	$41,510	23.5%	16,280
6. Industrial Machinery Mechanics	21.7%	$46,270	21.6%	11,710
7. First-Line Supervisors of Mechanics, Installers, and Repairers	15.9%	$59,850	11.9%	16,490
8. Automotive Service Technicians and Mechanics	15.1%	$36,180	17.2%	31,170
9. Emergency Medical Technicians and Paramedics	22.7%	$30,710	33.3%	12,080
10. Pharmacy Technicians	15.8%	$28,940	32.4%	16,630
11. Social and Human Service Assistants	15.9%	$28,740	27.6%	18,910
12. Construction Laborers	15.5%	$29,730	21.3%	29,240

Best Jobs Overall with a High Percentage of Rural Workers

Job	Rural Ratio	Annual Earnings	Percent Growth	Annual Openings
13. Electrical Power-Line Installers and Repairers	26.9%	$60,190	13.2%	5,270
14. Bookkeeping, Accounting, and Auditing Clerks	15.0%	$34,740	13.6%	46,780
15. First-Line Supervisors of Retail Sales Workers	15.7%	$36,480	8.4%	51,370
16. First-Line Supervisors of Transportation and Material-Moving Machine and Vehicle Operators	15.3%	$52,950	14.3%	6,930
17. Mobile Heavy Equipment Mechanics, Except Engines	19.0%	$45,600	16.2%	5,250
18. Teacher Assistants	18.0%	$23,580	14.8%	48,160
19. Bus and Truck Mechanics and Diesel Engine Specialists	17.9%	$41,640	14.5%	8,780
20. Welders, Cutters, Solderers, and Brazers	24.7%	$35,920	15.0%	14,070
21. Maintenance and Repair Workers, General	16.9%	$35,030	11.0%	37,910
22. Postal Service Mail Carriers	17.2%	$55,160	−12.0%	10,340
23. First-Line Supervisors of Production and Operating Workers	20.4%	$53,670	1.9%	8,790
24. Paving, Surfacing, and Tamping Equipment Operators	16.9%	$35,270	22.1%	2,200
25. Industrial Truck and Tractor Operators	17.8%	$30,010	11.8%	20,950
26. Surveying and Mapping Technicians	15.5%	$39,350	15.9%	2,000
27. Music Directors and Composers	15.6%	$47,410	10.2%	3,220
28. Water and Wastewater Treatment Plant and System Operators	28.8%	$41,780	11.6%	4,150
29. Machinists	16.0%	$39,220	8.5%	9,950

Best Jobs Lists Based on Educational Attainment of Recent Veterans

In most of the books in the *Best Jobs* series, you'll find a set of lists that organize the best jobs into groups based on the level of education or training usually required for career entry. However, the usual entry requirements often don't apply to veterans. Many employers are willing to hire veterans who have less formal education than would be required of nonveterans. These employers recognize that military training and work experience equip veterans with many valuable skills and work-related attitudes.

Using data from the Census Bureau's American Community Survey, I analyzed the actual educational attainments of the recent veterans who hold each of the jobs in this book. For each job, I calculated the median level of educational attainment—that is, half of the vets had more education, half had less. Then I created the following set of lists, in which the jobs at each level are sorted by their total combined score for earnings, growth, and number of openings.

Keep in mind that the veterans who were surveyed by the Census Bureau were not all freshly out of uniform. They had served sometime following September 2001 and were surveyed between 2005 and 2009. That means that some of these vets had time to take classes after leaving the service, perhaps taking advantage of benefits from the GI Bill of Rights. Others may have received academic credit for their military training. (Part I explains how to get this credit.)

My point is that these lists are not intended to suggest only jobs to consider entering now, with your present level of education. You also may want to look at jobs that would be options if you were to get additional education or training.

Don't assume that your military record will speak for itself and will automatically substitute for the formal educational credentials that are the usual entry route to the job. To get hired, you will need to find ways to convince employers of your skills and work attitudes—in your resume, in your cover letter, and by statements you make at job interviews.

Best Jobs Held by Recent Vets with a High School Diploma or Less

Job	Annual Earnings	Percent Growth	Annual Openings
1. Supervisors of Construction and Extraction Workers	$59,150	23.5%	25,970
2. Plumbers, Pipefitters, and Steamfitters	$47,750	25.6%	22,880
3. Electricians	$49,320	23.2%	28,920
4. Heating, Air Conditioning, and Refrigeration Mechanics and Installers	$43,380	33.7%	13,760
5. Industrial Machinery Mechanics	$46,270	21.6%	11,710
6. Operating Engineers and Other Construction Equipment Operators	$41,510	23.5%	16,280
7. Carpenters	$40,010	19.6%	40,830
8. Heavy and Tractor-Trailer Truck Drivers	$37,930	20.6%	64,940
9. Receptionists and Information Clerks	$25,690	23.7%	56,560
10. Security and Fire Alarm Systems Installers	$39,540	33.0%	3,670
11. Pile-Driver Operators	$45,500	36.0%	230
12. Captains, Mates, and Pilots of Water Vessels	$63,920	20.4%	2,070

Best Jobs Held by Recent Vets with a High School Diploma or Less

Job	Annual Earnings	Percent Growth	Annual Openings
13. Coaches and Scouts	$28,470	29.4%	13,300
14. Structural Iron and Steel Workers	$45,690	21.9%	2,540
15. Automotive Service Technicians and Mechanics	$36,180	17.2%	31,170
16. Radio, Cellular, and Tower Equipment Installers and Repairers	$42,160	29.4%	450
17. Construction Laborers	$29,730	21.3%	29,240
18. Electrical Power-Line Installers and Repairers	$60,190	13.2%	5,270
19. Mobile Heavy Equipment Mechanics, Except Engines	$45,600	16.2%	5,250
20. Landscaping and Groundskeeping Workers	$23,410	20.9%	44,440
21. Ship Engineers	$70,840	18.0%	620
22. Postal Service Mail Carriers	$55,160	–12.0%	10,340
23. Sheet Metal Workers	$42,730	17.5%	4,700
24. Telecommunications Line Installers and Repairers	$51,720	13.6%	5,140
25. Tile and Marble Setters	$37,080	25.4%	2,770
26. Painters, Construction and Maintenance	$35,430	18.5%	15,730
27. Pest Control Workers	$30,220	26.1%	4,850
28. First-Line Supervisors of Landscaping, Lawn Service, and Groundskeeping Workers	$42,050	15.1%	6,010
29. Pipelayers	$35,900	25.3%	2,880
30. Laborers and Freight, Stock, and Material Movers, Hand	$23,750	15.4%	98,020
31. Transportation, Storage, and Distribution Managers	$80,860	10.0%	3,370
32. Bus and Truck Mechanics and Diesel Engine Specialists	$41,640	14.5%	8,780
33. Rail Car Repairers	$47,740	16.9%	930
34. Welders, Cutters, Solderers, and Brazers	$35,920	15.0%	14,070
35. Aircraft Mechanics and Service Technicians	$54,590	6.3%	4,520
36. Athletes and Sports Competitors	$39,670	21.6%	780
37. Light Truck or Delivery Services Drivers	$29,080	14.7%	29,590
38. Maintenance and Repair Workers, General	$35,030	11.0%	37,910
39. Roofers	$35,280	17.8%	5,250
40. Sailors and Marine Oilers	$36,800	21.3%	2,150
41. Paving, Surfacing, and Tamping Equipment Operators	$35,270	22.1%	2,200
42. Bus Drivers, Transit and Intercity	$35,720	14.8%	6,350
43. Machinists	$39,220	8.5%	9,950
44. Water and Wastewater Treatment Plant and System Operators	$41,780	11.6%	4,150
45. Industrial Truck and Tractor Operators	$30,010	11.8%	20,950
46. Audio and Video Equipment Technicians	$41,630	13.4%	2,560
47. Surveying and Mapping Technicians	$39,350	15.9%	2,000

Best Jobs Held by Recent Vets with One Year or More of College, No Degree

Job	Annual Earnings	Percent Growth	Annual Openings
1. Network and Computer Systems Administrators	$70,970	27.8%	15,530
2. Sales Representatives, Services, All Other	$50,630	18.8%	27,010
3. First-Line Supervisors of Office and Administrative Support Workers	$48,810	14.3%	58,440
4. Licensed Practical and Licensed Vocational Nurses	$41,150	22.4%	36,920
5. Administrative Services Managers	$79,540	14.5%	9,980
6. Medical Secretaries	$31,060	41.3%	27,840
7. First-Line Supervisors of Mechanics, Installers, and Repairers	$59,850	11.9%	16,490
8. First-Line Supervisors of Helpers, Laborers, and Material Movers, Hand	$44,580	27.2%	8,000
9. Dental Assistants	$34,140	30.8%	15,400
10. Executive Secretaries and Executive Administrative Assistants	$45,580	12.6%	32,180
11. Medical Assistants	$29,100	30.9%	24,380
12. Pharmacy Technicians	$28,940	32.4%	16,630
13. Police and Sheriff's Patrol Officers	$54,230	8.2%	24,940
14. Construction and Building Inspectors	$53,180	17.9%	4,860
15. Emergency Medical Technicians and Paramedics	$30,710	33.3%	12,080
16. Billing and Posting Clerks	$32,880	19.7%	18,760
17. Customer Service Representatives	$30,610	15.5%	95,960
18. First-Line Supervisors of Transportation and Material-Moving Machine and Vehicle Operators	$52,950	14.3%	6,930
19. First-Line Supervisors of Non-Retail Sales Workers	$70,520	4.0%	12,350
20. Office Clerks, General	$27,190	16.6%	101,150
21. Medical Equipment Repairers	$44,870	31.5%	2,230
22. Technical Writers	$64,610	17.2%	1,830
23. Security Guards	$23,900	18.8%	35,950
24. Bookkeeping, Accounting, and Auditing Clerks	$34,740	13.6%	46,780
25. Fitness Trainers and Aerobics Instructors	$31,030	24.0%	10,060
26. Self-Enrichment Education Teachers	$36,100	20.9%	9,150
27. Teacher Assistants	$23,580	14.8%	48,160
28. Veterinary Technologists and Technicians	$30,140	52.0%	5,570
29. Environmental Engineering Technicians	$44,850	24.3%	820
30. Forensic Science Technicians	$52,180	18.6%	790
31. Health Technologists and Technicians, All Other	$38,080	23.2%	4,040

Best Jobs Held by Recent Vets with One Year or More of College, No Degree

Job	Annual Earnings	Percent Growth	Annual Openings
32. Purchasing Agents, Except Wholesale, Retail, and Farm Products	$57,580	5.3%	9,120
33. Medical and Clinical Laboratory Technologists	$57,010	11.3%	5,210
34. Environmental Science and Protection Technicians, Including Health	$42,270	23.6%	1,950
35. First-Line Supervisors of Retail Sales Workers	$36,480	8.4%	51,370
36. Advertising Sales Agents	$45,250	13.0%	6,990
37. Aircraft Cargo Handling Supervisors	$46,840	20.3%	260
38. Surgical Technologists	$40,950	18.9%	3,390
39. Firefighters	$45,420	8.6%	11,230
40. Nuclear Technicians	$68,030	13.5%	330
41. Real Estate Sales Agents	$39,070	12.2%	12,760
42. First-Line Supervisors of Production and Operating Workers	$53,670	1.9%	8,790
43. Bill and Account Collectors	$31,920	14.2%	13,550
44. First-Line Supervisors of Fire Fighting and Prevention Workers	$69,510	8.2%	3,310
45. Geological and Petroleum Technicians	$49,690	14.7%	700
46. Payroll and Timekeeping Clerks	$37,160	14.6%	6,570
47. Medical and Clinical Laboratory Technicians	$36,950	14.7%	5,510
48. Wholesale and Retail Buyers, Except Farm Products	$50,490	9.0%	4,170
49. Real Estate Brokers	$59,340	7.6%	2,970
50. Civil Engineering Technicians	$46,900	12.0%	2,460
51. Biological Technicians	$39,480	13.5%	3,790
52. Music Directors and Composers	$47,410	10.2%	3,220
53. Production, Planning, and Expediting Clerks	$43,100	6.6%	8,880
54. Life, Physical, and Social Science Technicians, All Other	$43,120	11.8%	3,350
55. Human Resources Assistants, Except Payroll and Timekeeping	$37,250	11.2%	6,160

Best Jobs Held by Recent Vets with an Associate Degree

Job	Annual Earnings	Percent Growth	Annual Openings
1. Diagnostic Medical Sonographers	$65,210	43.5%	3,170
2. Radiologic Technologists	$55,120	27.8%	9,510
3. Cardiovascular Technologists and Technicians	$51,020	29.3%	2,210
4. Nuclear Medicine Technologists	$69,450	18.9%	750
5. Transportation Inspectors	$62,230	14.4%	1,070
6. Mechanical Drafters	$49,200	11.1%	2,050

Best Jobs Held by Recent Vets with a Bachelor's Degree or Higher

Job	Annual Earnings	Percent Growth	Annual Openings
1. Software Developers, Systems Software	$96,600	32.4%	16,800
2. Computer Systems Analysts	$78,770	22.1%	22,250
3. Registered Nurses	$65,950	26.0%	120,740
4. Database Administrators	$75,190	30.6%	5,270
5. Personal Financial Advisors	$66,580	32.1%	9,020
6. Construction Managers	$84,240	16.6%	12,040
7. Managers, All Other	$99,540	7.9%	24,940
8. Sales Representatives, Wholesale and Manufacturing, Technical and Scientific Products	$74,750	16.4%	15,970
9. General and Operations Managers	$95,150	4.6%	41,010
10. Accountants and Auditors	$62,850	15.7%	45,210
11. Securities, Commodities, and Financial Services Sales Agents	$72,060	15.2%	13,370
12. Logisticians	$71,910	25.5%	4,870
13. Training and Development Specialists	$55,150	28.3%	9,830
14. Computer Programmers	$72,630	12.0%	12,800
15. Business Operations Specialists, All Other	$64,030	11.6%	32,720
16. Public Relations Specialists	$53,190	22.5%	12,720
17. Sales Representatives, Wholesale and Manufacturing, Except Technical and Scientific Products	$53,540	15.6%	55,990
18. Insurance Sales Agents	$47,450	21.9%	18,440
19. Social and Community Service Managers	$58,660	26.7%	6,480
20. Social and Human Service Assistants	$28,740	27.6%	18,910
21. Health Educators	$47,940	36.5%	3,690
22. Meeting, Convention, and Event Planners	$46,020	43.7%	4,500

Best Jobs Held by Recent Vets with a Bachelor's Degree or Higher

Job	Annual Earnings	Percent Growth	Annual Openings
23. Commercial Pilots	$70,000	21.2%	1,930
24. Loan Officers	$58,030	14.2%	11,520
25. Compliance Officers	$60,740	15.0%	5,860
26. Paralegals and Legal Assistants	$46,730	18.3%	8,340
27. First-Line Supervisors of Police and Detectives	$77,890	2.1%	3,870
28. Substance Abuse and Behavioral Disorder Counselors	$38,560	27.3%	4,170
29. Clergy	$44,140	17.5%	7,990
30. Graphic Designers	$44,010	13.4%	12,380
31. Probation Officers and Correctional Treatment Specialists	$47,840	18.4%	3,730
32. Claims Adjusters, Examiners, and Investigators	$59,320	3.0%	7,990
33. Budget Analysts	$69,090	10.4%	1,960
34. Interior Designers	$47,620	19.3%	2,840
35. Detectives and Criminal Investigators	$71,770	2.9%	3,010
36. Occupational Health and Safety Specialists	$66,270	8.5%	2,570
37. Athletic Trainers	$42,400	30.0%	1,190
38. Property, Real Estate, and Community Association Managers	$52,510	6.0%	8,230
39. Commercial and Industrial Designers	$60,760	10.5%	1,690
40. Private Detectives and Investigators	$43,710	20.5%	1,490
41. Compensation, Benefits, and Job Analysis Specialists	$57,960	5.0%	2,400
42. Credit Counselors	$38,430	20.3%	1,520

Best Jobs Lists Based on Career Clusters

To make it easy for you to identify jobs quickly based on your interests, I organized the 150 best jobs into 16 career clusters, and they form the basis of the following set of lists. The U.S. Department of Education's Office of Vocational and Adult Education developed this system of 16 career clusters in 1999, and many states now use it to organize their career-oriented programs and career information. When you find jobs on these lists that you want to explore in more detail, look up their descriptions in Part III. You can also review clusters that represent areas in which you've had past experience, education, or training to see whether jobs in those areas would meet your current requirements.

In this set of lists, you may notice that some occupations appear on multiple lists. This happens when two or more industries commonly employ workers with the same occupational title. For example, Accountants and Auditors may work in the private sector (and thus belong in the Business, Management, and Administration cluster) or in the public sector (Government and Public Administration). If you decide to pursue one of these multiple-cluster occupations, you may need to choose one of these industries to specialize in, but it may be possible for you to jump between industries after you have worked for several years. In the job descriptions in Part III, I link each job to only *one* key cluster to save space and to focus on the chief industry employing the workers.

Within each cluster-based list, jobs are ranked by their combined scores for earnings, job growth, and number of job openings, from highest to lowest.

Descriptions of the 16 Career Clusters

Brief descriptions follow for the 16 career clusters, defining them in terms of interests. Some of them refer to jobs (as examples) that aren't included in this book.

❋ **Agriculture, Food, and Natural Resources:** *An interest in working with plants, animals, forests, or mineral resources for agriculture, horticulture, conservation, extraction, and other purposes.* You can satisfy this interest by working in farming, landscaping, forestry, fishing, mining, and related fields. You may like doing physical work outdoors, such as on a farm or ranch, in a forest, or on a drilling rig. If you have a scientific curiosity, you could study plants and animals or analyze biological or rock samples in a lab. If you have management ability, you could own, operate, or manage a fish hatchery, a landscaping business, or a greenhouse.

❋ **Architecture and Construction:** *An interest in designing, assembling, and maintaining components of buildings and other structures.* You may want to be part of the team of architects, drafters, and others who design buildings and render plans. If construction interests you, you might find fulfillment in the many building projects that are being undertaken at all times. If you like to organize and plan, you can find careers in managing these projects. Or you can play a more direct role in putting up and finishing buildings by doing jobs such as plumbing, carpentry, masonry, painting, or roofing, either as a skilled craftsworker or as a helper. You can prepare the building site by operating heavy equipment or installing, maintaining, and repairing vital building equipment and systems such as electricity and heating.

❋ **Arts, Audio/Visual Technology, and Communications:** *An interest in creatively expressing feelings or ideas, in communicating news or information, or in performing.* You can satisfy this interest in creative, verbal, or performing activities. For example, if you enjoy literature, perhaps writing or editing would appeal to you. Journalism and public relations are other fields for people who like to use their writing or speaking skills. Do you prefer to work in the performing arts? If so, you could direct or perform in drama, music, or dance. If you especially enjoy the visual arts, you could create paintings, sculpture, or ceramics or design products or visual displays. A flair for technology might lead you to specialize in photography, broadcast production, or dispatching.

❇ **Business, Management, and Administration:** *An interest in making a business organization or function run smoothly.* You can satisfy this interest by working in a position of leadership or by specializing in a function that contributes to the overall effort in a business, a nonprofit organization, or a government agency. If you especially enjoy working with people, you may find fulfillment from working in human resources. An interest in numbers may lead you to consider accounting, finance, budgeting, billing, or financial record-keeping. A job as an administrative assistant may interest you if you like a variety of tasks in a busy environment. If you are good with details and word processing, you may enjoy a job as a secretary or data-entry clerk. Or perhaps you would do well as the manager of a business.

❇ **Education and Training:** *An interest in helping people learn.* You can satisfy this interest by teaching students, who may be preschoolers, retirees, or any age in between. You may specialize in a particular academic field or work with learners of a particular age, with a particular interest, or with a particular learning problem. Working in a library or museum may give you an opportunity to expand people's understanding of the world.

❇ **Finance:** *An interest in helping businesses and people be assured of a financially secure future.* You can satisfy this interest by working in a financial or insurance business in a leadership or support role. If you like gathering and analyzing information, you may find fulfillment as an insurance adjuster or financial analyst. Or you may deal with information at the clerical level as a banking or insurance clerk or in person-to-person situations providing customer service. Another way to interact with people is to sell financial or insurance services that will meet their needs.

❇ **Government and Public Administration:** *An interest in helping a government agency serve the needs of the public.* You can satisfy this interest by working in a position of leadership or by specializing in a function that contributes to the role of government. You may help protect the public by working as an inspector or examiner to enforce standards. If you enjoy using clerical skills, you could work as a clerk in a law court or government office. Or perhaps you prefer the top-down perspective of a government executive or urban planner.

❇ **Health Science:** *An interest in helping people and animals be healthy.* You can satisfy this interest by working on a health-care team as a doctor, therapist, or nurse. You might specialize in one of the many different parts of the body (such as the teeth or eyes) or in one of the many different types of care. Or you may want to be a generalist who deals with the whole patient. If you like technology, you might find satisfaction working with X-rays or new diagnostic methods. You might work with relatively healthy people, helping them to eat better. If you enjoy working with animals, you might care for them and keep them healthy.

❋ **Hospitality and Tourism:** *An interest in catering to the personal wishes and needs of others so that they can enjoy a clean environment, good food and drink, comfortable lodging away from home, and recreation.* You can satisfy this interest by providing services for the convenience, care, and pampering of others in hotels, restaurants, airplanes, beauty parlors, and so on. You may want to use your love of cooking as a chef. If you like working with people, you may want to provide personal services by being a travel guide, a flight attendant, a concierge, a hairdresser, or a waiter. You may want to work in cleaning and building services if you like a clean environment. If you enjoy sports or games, you could work for an athletic team or casino.

❋ **Human Services:** *An interest in improving people's social, mental, emotional, or spiritual well-being.* You can satisfy this interest as a counselor, social worker, or religious worker who helps people sort out their complicated lives or solve personal problems. You may work as a caretaker for very young people or the elderly. Or you may interview people to help identify the social services they need.

❋ **Information Technology:** *An interest in designing, developing, managing, and supporting information systems.* You can satisfy this interest by working with hardware, software, multimedia, or integrated systems. If you like to use your organizational skills, you might work as a systems or database administrator. Or you can solve complex problems as a software engineer or systems analyst. If you enjoy getting your hands on hardware, you might find work servicing computers, peripherals, and information-intense machines such as cash registers and ATMs.

❋ **Law, Public Safety, Corrections, and Security:** *An interest in upholding people's rights or in protecting people and property by using authority, inspecting, or investigating.* You can satisfy this interest by working in law, law enforcement, firefighting, the military, or related fields. For example, if you enjoy mental challenge and intrigue, you could investigate crimes or fires for a living. If you enjoy working with verbal skills and research skills, you may want to defend citizens in court or research deeds, wills, and other legal documents. If you want to help people in critical situations, you may want to fight fires, work as a police officer, or become a paramedic. Or, if you want more routine work in public safety, perhaps a job in guarding, patrolling, or inspecting would appeal to you. If you have management ability, you could seek a leadership position in law enforcement and the protective services. Work in the military gives you a chance to use technical and leadership skills while serving your country.

❋ **Manufacturing:** *An interest in processing materials into intermediate or final products or maintaining and repairing products by using machines or hand tools.* You can satisfy this interest by working in one of many industries that mass-produce goods or by working for a utility that distributes electrical power or other resources. You might enjoy manual work, using your hands or hand tools in highly skilled jobs such as assembling engines or electronic equipment. If you enjoy making machines run efficiently or fixing them when they break down, you could seek a job installing or repairing such devices as copiers, aircraft engines, cars, or watches. Perhaps you prefer to set up or operate machines that are used to manufacture products made of food, glass, or paper. You could enjoy cutting and grinding metal and plastic parts to desired shapes and measurements. Or you may want to operate equipment in systems that provide water and process wastewater. You may like inspecting, sorting, counting, or weighing products. Another option is to work with your hands and machinery to move boxes and freight in a warehouse. If leadership appeals to you, you could manage people engaged in production and repair.

✴ **Marketing, Sales, and Service:** *An interest in bringing others to a particular point of view by personal persuasion and by sales and promotional techniques.* You can satisfy this interest in various jobs that involve persuasion and selling. If you like using knowledge of science, you may enjoy selling pharmaceutical, medical, or electronic products or services. Real estate offers several kinds of sales jobs as well. If you like speaking on the phone, you could work as a telemarketer. Or you may enjoy selling apparel and other merchandise in a retail setting. If you prefer to help people, you may want a job in customer service.

✴ **Science, Technology, Engineering, and Mathematics:** *An interest in discovering, collecting, and analyzing information about the natural world; in applying scientific research findings to problems in medicine, the life sciences, human behavior, and the natural sciences; in imagining and manipulating quantitative data; and in applying technology to manufacturing, transportation, and other economic activities.* You can satisfy this interest by working with the knowledge and processes of the sciences. You may enjoy researching and developing new knowledge in mathematics, or perhaps solving problems in the physical, life, or social sciences would appeal to you. You may want to study engineering and help create new machines, processes, and structures. If you want to work with scientific equipment and procedures, you could seek a job in a research or testing laboratory.

✴ **Transportation, Distribution, and Logistics:** *An interest in operations that move people or materials.* You can satisfy this interest by managing a transportation service, by helping vehicles keep on their assigned schedules and routes, or by driving or piloting a vehicle. If you enjoy taking responsibility, perhaps managing a rail line would appeal to you. If you work well with details and can take pressure on the job, you might consider being an air traffic controller. Or would you rather get out on the highway, on the water, or up in the air? If so, you could drive a truck from state to state, be employed on a ship, or fly a crop duster over a cornfield. If you prefer to stay closer to home, you could drive a delivery van, taxi, or school bus. You could use your physical strength to load freight and arrange it so that it gets to its destination in one piece.

Best Jobs for People Interested in Agriculture, Food, and Natural Resources

Job	Annual Earnings	Percent Growth	Annual Openings
1. First-Line Supervisors of Office and Administrative Support Workers	$48,810	14.3%	58,440
2. Mobile Heavy Equipment Mechanics, Except Engines	$45,600	16.2%	5,250
3. Environmental Engineering Technicians	$44,850	24.3%	820
4. Graphic Designers	$44,010	13.4%	12,380
5. First-Line Supervisors of Landscaping, Lawn Service, and Groundskeeping Workers	$42,050	15.1%	6,010
6. Landscaping and Groundskeeping Workers	$23,410	20.9%	44,440
7. Pest Control Workers	$30,220	26.1%	4,850
8. Environmental Science and Protection Technicians, Including Health	$42,270	23.6%	1,950
9. Geological and Petroleum Technicians	$49,690	14.7%	700
10. Occupational Health and Safety Specialists	$66,270	8.5%	2,570
11. First-Line Supervisors of Retail Sales Workers	$36,480	8.4%	51,370
12. Industrial Truck and Tractor Operators	$30,010	11.8%	20,950
13. Life, Physical, and Social Science Technicians, All Other	$43,120	11.8%	3,350
14. Water and Wastewater Treatment Plant and System Operators	$41,780	11.6%	4,150

Best Jobs for People Interested in Architecture and Construction

Job	Annual Earnings	Percent Growth	Annual Openings
1. Supervisors of Construction and Extraction Workers	$59,150	23.5%	25,970
2. Plumbers, Pipefitters, and Steamfitters	$47,750	25.6%	22,880
3. Electricians	$49,320	23.2%	28,920
4. Heating, Air Conditioning, and Refrigeration Mechanics and Installers	$43,380	33.7%	13,760
5. Operating Engineers and Other Construction Equipment Operators	$41,510	23.5%	16,280
6. Carpenters	$40,010	19.6%	40,830
7. Construction Managers	$84,240	16.6%	12,040
8. Security and Fire Alarm Systems Installers	$39,540	33.0%	3,670
9. Construction and Building Inspectors	$53,180	17.9%	4,860
10. Electrical Power-Line Installers and Repairers	$60,190	13.2%	5,270
11. Pile-Driver Operators	$45,500	36.0%	230

Best Jobs for People Interested in Architecture and Construction

Job	Annual Earnings	Percent Growth	Annual Openings
12. Construction Laborers	$29,730	21.3%	29,240
13. Interior Designers	$47,620	19.3%	2,840
14. Pipelayers	$35,900	25.3%	2,880
15. Structural Iron and Steel Workers	$45,690	21.9%	2,540
16. Tile and Marble Setters	$37,080	25.4%	2,770
17. Painters, Construction and Maintenance	$35,430	18.5%	15,730
18. Civil Engineering Technicians	$46,900	12.0%	2,460
19. Mechanical Drafters	$49,200	11.1%	2,050
20. Roofers	$35,280	17.8%	5,250
21. Paving, Surfacing, and Tamping Equipment Operators	$35,270	22.1%	2,200
22. Surveying and Mapping Technicians	$39,350	15.9%	2,000

Best Jobs for People Interested in Arts, Audio/Visual Technology, and Communications

Job	Annual Earnings	Percent Growth	Annual Openings
1. Public Relations Specialists	$53,190	22.5%	12,720
2. Managers, All Other	$99,540	7.9%	24,940
3. Interior Designers	$47,620	19.3%	2,840
4. Technical Writers	$64,610	17.2%	1,830
5. Graphic Designers	$44,010	13.4%	12,380
6. Commercial and Industrial Designers	$60,760	10.5%	1,690
7. Music Directors and Composers	$47,410	10.2%	3,220
8. Radio, Cellular, and Tower Equipment Installers and Repairers	$42,160	29.4%	450
9. Audio and Video Equipment Technicians	$41,630	13.4%	2,560

Best Jobs for People Interested in Business, Management, and Administration

Job	Annual Earnings	Percent Growth	Annual Openings
1. Construction Managers	$84,240	16.6%	12,040
2. Accountants and Auditors	$62,850	15.7%	45,210
3. Logisticians	$71,910	25.5%	4,870
4. Training and Development Specialists	$55,150	28.3%	9,830
5. Public Relations Specialists	$53,190	22.5%	12,720
6. Social and Community Service Managers	$58,660	26.7%	6,480
7. Administrative Services Managers	$79,540	14.5%	9,980
8. First-Line Supervisors of Office and Administrative Support Workers	$48,810	14.3%	58,440
9. General and Operations Managers	$95,150	4.6%	41,010
10. Managers, All Other	$99,540	7.9%	24,940
11. Office Clerks, General	$27,190	16.6%	101,150
12. Receptionists and Information Clerks	$25,690	23.7%	56,560
13. Business Operations Specialists, All Other	$64,030	11.6%	32,720
14. Customer Service Representatives	$30,610	15.5%	95,960
15. Billing and Posting Clerks	$32,880	19.7%	18,760
16. Technical Writers	$64,610	17.2%	1,830
17. Bookkeeping, Accounting, and Auditing Clerks	$34,740	13.6%	46,780
18. Executive Secretaries and Executive Administrative Assistants	$45,580	12.6%	32,180
19. Transportation, Storage, and Distribution Managers	$80,860	10.0%	3,370
20. Payroll and Timekeeping Clerks	$37,160	14.6%	6,570
21. Advertising Sales Agents	$45,250	13.0%	6,990
22. Budget Analysts	$69,090	10.4%	1,960
23. Postal Service Mail Carriers	$55,160	–12.0%	10,340
24. Compensation, Benefits, and Job Analysis Specialists	$57,960	5.0%	2,400
25. Human Resources Assistants, Except Payroll and Timekeeping	$37,250	11.2%	6,160

Best Jobs for People Interested in Education and Training

Job	Annual Earnings	Percent Growth	Annual Openings
1. Training and Development Specialists	$55,150	28.3%	9,830
2. Coaches and Scouts	$28,470	29.4%	13,300
3. Fitness Trainers and Aerobics Instructors	$31,030	24.0%	10,060
4. Athletes and Sports Competitors	$39,670	21.6%	780
5. Self-Enrichment Education Teachers	$36,100	20.9%	9,150
6. Teacher Assistants	$23,580	14.8%	48,160

Best Jobs for People Interested in Finance

Job	Annual Earnings	Percent Growth	Annual Openings
1. Securities, Commodities, and Financial Services Sales Agents	$72,060	15.2%	13,370
2. Insurance Sales Agents	$47,450	21.9%	18,440
3. Personal Financial Advisors	$66,580	32.1%	9,020
4. Loan Officers	$58,030	14.2%	11,520
5. Bill and Account Collectors	$31,920	14.2%	13,550
6. Budget Analysts	$69,090	10.4%	1,960
7. Claims Adjusters, Examiners, and Investigators	$59,320	3.0%	7,990
8. Credit Counselors	$38,430	20.3%	1,520

Best Jobs for People Interested in Government and Public Administration

Job	Annual Earnings	Percent Growth	Annual Openings
1. Accountants and Auditors	$62,850	15.7%	45,210
2. Managers, All Other	$99,540	7.9%	24,940
3. General and Operations Managers	$95,150	4.6%	41,010
4. Administrative Services Managers	$79,540	14.5%	9,980
5. Social and Community Service Managers	$58,660	26.7%	6,480
6. Compliance Officers	$60,740	15.0%	5,860
7. Transportation, Storage, and Distribution Managers	$80,860	10.0%	3,370
8. Surveying and Mapping Technicians	$39,350	15.9%	2,000

Best Jobs for People Interested in Health Science

Job	Annual Earnings	Percent Growth	Annual Openings
1. Registered Nurses	$65,950	26.0%	120,740
2. Computer Systems Analysts	$78,770	22.1%	22,250
3. Diagnostic Medical Sonographers	$65,210	43.5%	3,170
4. Medical Secretaries	$31,060	41.3%	27,840
5. Radiologic Technologists	$55,120	27.8%	9,510
6. First-Line Supervisors of Office and Administrative Support Workers	$48,810	14.3%	58,440
7. Health Educators	$47,940	36.5%	3,690
8. Licensed Practical and Licensed Vocational Nurses	$41,150	22.4%	36,920
9. Public Relations Specialists	$53,190	22.5%	12,720
10. Medical Assistants	$29,100	30.9%	24,380
11. Dental Assistants	$34,140	30.8%	15,400
12. Veterinary Technologists and Technicians	$30,140	52.0%	5,570
13. Emergency Medical Technicians and Paramedics	$30,710	33.3%	12,080
14. Pharmacy Technicians	$28,940	32.4%	16,630
15. Executive Secretaries and Executive Administrative Assistants	$45,580	12.6%	32,180
16. Cardiovascular Technologists and Technicians	$51,020	29.3%	2,210
17. Receptionists and Information Clerks	$25,690	23.7%	56,560
18. Social and Human Service Assistants	$28,740	27.6%	18,910
19. Nuclear Medicine Technologists	$69,450	18.9%	750
20. Substance Abuse and Behavioral Disorder Counselors	$38,560	27.3%	4,170
21. Athletic Trainers	$42,400	30.0%	1,190
22. Medical and Clinical Laboratory Technologists	$57,010	11.3%	5,210
23. Health Technologists and Technicians, All Other	$38,080	23.2%	4,040
24. Nuclear Technicians	$68,030	13.5%	330
25. Occupational Health and Safety Specialists	$66,270	8.5%	2,570
26. Medical and Clinical Laboratory Technicians	$36,950	14.7%	5,510
27. Surgical Technologists	$40,950	18.9%	3,390
28. Life, Physical, and Social Science Technicians, All Other	$43,120	11.8%	3,350

Best Jobs for People Interested in Hospitality and Tourism

Job	Annual Earnings	Percent Growth	Annual Openings
1. Managers, All Other	$99,540	7.9%	24,940

Best Jobs for People Interested in Human Services

Job	Annual Earnings	Percent Growth	Annual Openings
1. Public Relations Specialists	$53,190	22.5%	12,720
2. Social and Community Service Managers	$58,660	26.7%	6,480
3. Managers, All Other	$99,540	7.9%	24,940
4. Health Educators	$47,940	36.5%	3,690
5. Substance Abuse and Behavioral Disorder Counselors	$38,560	27.3%	4,170
6. Clergy	$44,140	17.5%	7,990
7. First-Line Supervisors of Retail Sales Workers	$36,480	8.4%	51,370
8. Probation Officers and Correctional Treatment Specialists	$47,840	18.4%	3,730

Best Jobs for People Interested in Information Technology

Job	Annual Earnings	Percent Growth	Annual Openings
1. Software Developers, Systems Software	$96,600	32.4%	16,800
2. Computer Systems Analysts	$78,770	22.1%	22,250
3. Database Administrators	$75,190	30.6%	5,270
4. Network and Computer Systems Administrators	$70,970	27.8%	15,530
5. Computer Programmers	$72,630	12.0%	12,800
6. Graphic Designers	$44,010	13.4%	12,380
7. Life, Physical, and Social Science Technicians, All Other	$43,120	11.8%	3,350

Best Jobs for People Interested in Law, Public Safety, Corrections, and Security

Job	Annual Earnings	Percent Growth	Annual Openings
1. Security Guards	$23,900	18.8%	35,950
2. Compliance Officers	$60,740	15.0%	5,860
3. Police and Sheriff's Patrol Officers	$54,230	8.2%	24,940
4. Paralegals and Legal Assistants	$46,730	18.3%	8,340
5. Firefighters	$45,420	8.6%	11,230
6. First-Line Supervisors of Fire Fighting and Prevention Workers	$69,510	8.2%	3,310
7. First-Line Supervisors of Police and Detectives	$77,890	2.1%	3,870
8. Detectives and Criminal Investigators	$71,770	2.9%	3,010
9. Forensic Science Technicians	$52,180	18.6%	790
10. Private Detectives and Investigators	$43,710	20.5%	1,490

Best Jobs for People Interested in Manufacturing

Job	Annual Earnings	Percent Growth	Annual Openings
1. Industrial Machinery Mechanics	$46,270	21.6%	11,710
2. First-Line Supervisors of Mechanics, Installers, and Repairers	$59,850	11.9%	16,490
3. First-Line Supervisors of Helpers, Laborers, and Material Movers, Hand	$44,580	27.2%	8,000
4. Telecommunications Line Installers and Repairers	$51,720	13.6%	5,140
5. Interior Designers	$47,620	19.3%	2,840
6. Medical Equipment Repairers	$44,870	31.5%	2,230
7. Mobile Heavy Equipment Mechanics, Except Engines	$45,600	16.2%	5,250
8. Automotive Service Technicians and Mechanics	$36,180	17.2%	31,170
9. First-Line Supervisors of Production and Operating Workers	$53,670	1.9%	8,790
10. Sheet Metal Workers	$42,730	17.5%	4,700
11. Rail Car Repairers	$47,740	16.9%	930
12. Aircraft Mechanics and Service Technicians	$54,590	6.3%	4,520
13. Environmental Engineering Technicians	$44,850	24.3%	820
14. Nuclear Technicians	$68,030	13.5%	330
15. Occupational Health and Safety Specialists	$66,270	8.5%	2,570
16. Welders, Cutters, Solderers, and Brazers	$35,920	15.0%	14,070
17. Environmental Science and Protection Technicians, Including Health	$42,270	23.6%	1,950
18. Civil Engineering Technicians	$46,900	12.0%	2,460
19. Radio, Cellular, and Tower Equipment Installers and Repairers	$42,160	29.4%	450
20. Maintenance and Repair Workers, General	$35,030	11.0%	37,910
21. Biological Technicians	$39,480	13.5%	3,790
22. Machinists	$39,220	8.5%	9,950
23. Life, Physical, and Social Science Technicians, All Other	$43,120	11.8%	3,350

Best Jobs for People Interested in Marketing, Sales, and Service

Job	Annual Earnings	Percent Growth	Annual Openings
1. Sales Representatives, Wholesale and Manufacturing, Technical and Scientific Products	$74,750	16.4%	15,970
2. Sales Representatives, Wholesale and Manufacturing, Except Technical and Scientific Products	$53,540	15.6%	55,990
3. Business Operations Specialists, All Other	$64,030	11.6%	32,720
4. Sales Representatives, Services, All Other	$50,630	18.8%	27,010
5. First-Line Supervisors of Non-Retail Sales Workers	$70,520	4.0%	12,350

Best Jobs for People Interested in Marketing, Sales, and Service

Job	Annual Earnings	Percent Growth	Annual Openings
6. Meeting, Convention, and Event Planners	$46,020	43.7%	4,500
7. First-Line Supervisors of Retail Sales Workers	$36,480	8.4%	51,370
8. Real Estate Sales Agents	$39,070	12.2%	12,760
9. Interior Designers	$47,620	19.3%	2,840
10. Purchasing Agents, Except Wholesale, Retail, and Farm Products	$57,580	5.3%	9,120
11. Real Estate Brokers	$59,340	7.6%	2,970
12. Property, Real Estate, and Community Association Managers	$52,510	6.0%	8,230
13. Wholesale and Retail Buyers, Except Farm Products	$50,490	9.0%	4,170

Best Jobs for People Interested in Science, Technology, Engineering, and Mathematics

Job	Annual Earnings	Percent Growth	Annual Openings
1. Nuclear Technicians	$68,030	13.5%	330

Best Jobs for People Interested in Transportation, Distribution, and Logistics

Job	Annual Earnings	Percent Growth	Annual Openings
1. Logisticians	$71,910	25.5%	4,870
2. First-Line Supervisors of Helpers, Laborers, and Material Movers, Hand	$44,580	27.2%	8,000
3. Heavy and Tractor-Trailer Truck Drivers	$37,930	20.6%	64,940
4. Managers, All Other	$99,540	7.9%	24,940
5. Operating Engineers and Other Construction Equipment Operators	$41,510	23.5%	16,280
6. Commercial Pilots	$70,000	21.2%	1,930
7. Captains, Mates, and Pilots of Water Vessels	$63,920	20.4%	2,070
8. Automotive Service Technicians and Mechanics	$36,180	17.2%	31,170
9. Compliance Officers	$60,740	15.0%	5,860
10. Environmental Science and Protection Technicians, Including Health	$42,270	23.6%	1,950

(continued)

(continued)

Best Jobs for People Interested in Transportation, Distribution, and Logistics			
Job	Annual Earnings	Percent Growth	Annual Openings
11. Laborers and Freight, Stock, and Material Movers, Hand	$23,750	15.4%	98,020
12. Ship Engineers	$70,840	18.0%	620
13. Transportation, Storage, and Distribution Managers	$80,860	10.0%	3,370
14. First-Line Supervisors of Transportation and Material-Moving Machine and Vehicle Operators	$52,950	14.3%	6,930
15. Bus and Truck Mechanics and Diesel Engine Specialists	$41,640	14.5%	8,780
16. Sailors and Marine Oilers	$36,800	21.3%	2,150
17. Light Truck or Delivery Services Drivers	$29,080	14.7%	29,590
18. Production, Planning, and Expediting Clerks	$43,100	6.6%	8,880
19. Aircraft Cargo Handling Supervisors	$46,840	20.3%	260
20. Transportation Inspectors	$62,230	14.4%	1,070
21. Aircraft Mechanics and Service Technicians	$54,590	6.3%	4,520
22. Bus Drivers, Transit and Intercity	$35,720	14.8%	6,350

Best Jobs Lists Based on Personality Types

These lists organize the 150 best jobs into groups matching six personality types. Within each personality type, I ranked the jobs based on each one's total combined score for earnings, growth, and number of annual job openings.

The personality types are Realistic, Investigative, Artistic, Social, Enterprising, and Conventional. This system was developed by John L. Holland and is used in the *Self-Directed Search (SDS)* and other career assessment inventories and information systems. When you took the ASVAB test, you may have seen these personality types discussed in the score-interpretation materials.

The following set of lists will help you identify jobs that most closely match these personality types. Even if you have not used one of the tests or interest inventories that use these personality types, you may find these six types useful for identifying jobs that suit the type of person you are.

Like the set of lists for the career clusters, this set assigns some of the jobs to more than one list in order to match the differing characteristics of job specializations. For example, you will find the job Geological and Petroleum Technicians on two lists because it is linked to the specializations Geophysical Data Technicians (Conventional) and Geological Sample Test Technicians (Realistic). Some of the list assignments may surprise you. For example, Registered Nurses appears on the Enterprising list (as well as the Social list) because it is linked to Clinical Nurse Specialists, a job that is primarily managerial.

In addition, you should be aware that these lists are based on the primary personality type that describes the job, but most jobs are also linked to one or two secondary personality types. The job descriptions in Part III indicate all significant personality types. Consider reviewing the jobs for more than one personality type so you don't overlook possible jobs that would suit you.

Descriptions of the Six Personality Types

Following are brief descriptions for each of the six personality types used in the lists. Select the two or three descriptions that most closely describe you and then use the lists to identify jobs that best fit these personality types.

* **Realistic:** These occupations frequently involve work activities that include practical, hands-on problems and solutions. They often deal with plants; animals; and real-world materials such as wood, tools, and machinery. Many of the occupations require working outside and don't involve a lot of paperwork or working closely with others.

* **Investigative:** These occupations frequently involve working with ideas and require an extensive amount of thinking. These occupations can involve searching for facts and figuring out problems mentally.

* **Artistic:** These occupations frequently involve working with forms, designs, and patterns. They often require self-expression, and the work can be done without following a clear set of rules.

* **Social:** These occupations frequently involve working with, communicating with, and teaching people. These occupations often involve helping or providing service to others.

* **Enterprising:** These occupations frequently involve starting up and carrying out projects. These occupations can involve leading people and making many decisions. They sometimes require risk taking and often deal with business.

* **Conventional:** These occupations frequently involve following set procedures and routines. These occupations can include working with data and details more than with ideas. Usually there is a clear line of authority to follow.

Best Jobs for People with a Realistic Personality Type

Job	Annual Earnings	Percent Growth	Annual Openings
1. Radiologic Technologists	$55,120	27.8%	9,510
2. Plumbers, Pipefitters, and Steamfitters	$47,750	25.6%	22,880
3. Electricians	$49,320	23.2%	28,920
4. Heating, Air Conditioning, and Refrigeration Mechanics and Installers	$43,380	33.7%	13,760
5. Industrial Machinery Mechanics	$46,270	21.6%	11,710
6. Operating Engineers and Other Construction Equipment Operators	$41,510	23.5%	16,280
7. Business Operations Specialists, All Other	$64,030	11.6%	32,720
8. Carpenters	$40,010	19.6%	40,830
9. Cardiovascular Technologists and Technicians	$51,020	29.3%	2,210
10. Heavy and Tractor-Trailer Truck Drivers	$37,930	20.6%	64,940
11. Construction and Building Inspectors	$53,180	17.9%	4,860
12. Medical Equipment Repairers	$44,870	31.5%	2,230
13. Commercial Pilots	$70,000	21.2%	1,930
14. Captains, Mates, and Pilots of Water Vessels	$63,920	20.4%	2,070
15. Security and Fire Alarm Systems Installers	$39,540	33.0%	3,670
16. Veterinary Technologists and Technicians	$30,140	52.0%	5,570
17. Electrical Power-Line Installers and Repairers	$60,190	13.2%	5,270
18. Police and Sheriff's Patrol Officers	$54,230	8.2%	24,940
19. Structural Iron and Steel Workers	$45,690	21.9%	2,540
20. Mobile Heavy Equipment Mechanics, Except Engines	$45,600	16.2%	5,250
21. Pile-Driver Operators	$45,500	36.0%	230
22. Construction Laborers	$29,730	21.3%	29,240
23. Landscaping and Groundskeeping Workers	$23,410	20.9%	44,440
24. Automotive Service Technicians and Mechanics	$36,180	17.2%	31,170
25. Telecommunications Line Installers and Repairers	$51,720	13.6%	5,140
26. Ship Engineers	$70,840	18.0%	620
27. Health Technologists and Technicians, All Other	$38,080	23.2%	4,040
28. Medical and Clinical Laboratory Technologists	$57,010	11.3%	5,210
29. Security Guards	$23,900	18.8%	35,950
30. Environmental Engineering Technicians	$44,850	24.3%	820
31. Painters, Construction and Maintenance	$35,430	18.5%	15,730
32. Pest Control Workers	$30,220	26.1%	4,850
33. Radio, Cellular, and Tower Equipment Installers and Repairers	$42,160	29.4%	450
34. Sheet Metal Workers	$42,730	17.5%	4,700
35. Tile and Marble Setters	$37,080	25.4%	2,770

Best Jobs for People with a Realistic Personality Type

Job	Annual Earnings	Percent Growth	Annual Openings
36. Bus and Truck Mechanics and Diesel Engine Specialists	$41,640	14.5%	8,780
37. Laborers and Freight, Stock, and Material Movers, Hand	$23,750	15.4%	98,020
38. Pipelayers	$35,900	25.3%	2,880
39. Surgical Technologists	$40,950	18.9%	3,390
40. Firefighters	$45,420	8.6%	11,230
41. Welders, Cutters, Solderers, and Brazers	$35,920	15.0%	14,070
42. Transportation Inspectors	$62,230	14.4%	1,070
43. Aircraft Mechanics and Service Technicians	$54,590	6.3%	4,520
44. Light Truck or Delivery Services Drivers	$29,080	14.7%	29,590
45. Rail Car Repairers	$47,740	16.9%	930
46. Nuclear Technicians	$68,030	13.5%	330
47. Medical and Clinical Laboratory Technicians	$36,950	14.7%	5,510
48. Roofers	$35,280	17.8%	5,250
49. Athletes and Sports Competitors	$39,670	21.6%	780
50. Bus Drivers, Transit and Intercity	$35,720	14.8%	6,350
51. Geological and Petroleum Technicians	$49,690	14.7%	700
52. Civil Engineering Technicians	$46,900	12.0%	2,460
53. Sailors and Marine Oilers	$36,800	21.3%	2,150
54. Maintenance and Repair Workers, General	$35,030	11.0%	37,910
55. Paving, Surfacing, and Tamping Equipment Operators	$35,270	22.1%	2,200
56. Life, Physical, and Social Science Technicians, All Other	$43,120	11.8%	3,350
57. Water and Wastewater Treatment Plant and System Operators	$41,780	11.6%	4,150
58. Machinists	$39,220	8.5%	9,950
59. Industrial Truck and Tractor Operators	$30,010	11.8%	20,950
60. Biological Technicians	$39,480	13.5%	3,790
61. Mechanical Drafters	$49,200	11.1%	2,050
62. Audio and Video Equipment Technicians	$41,630	13.4%	2,560
63. Surveying and Mapping Technicians	$39,350	15.9%	2,000

Best Jobs for People with an Investigative Personality Type

Job	Annual Earnings	Percent Growth	Annual Openings
1. Software Developers, Systems Software	$96,600	32.4%	16,800
2. Computer Systems Analysts	$78,770	22.1%	22,250
3. Network and Computer Systems Administrators	$70,970	27.8%	15,530
4. Logisticians	$71,910	25.5%	4,870
5. Computer Programmers	$72,630	12.0%	12,800
6. Diagnostic Medical Sonographers	$65,210	43.5%	3,170
7. Compliance Officers	$60,740	15.0%	5,860
8. Nuclear Medicine Technologists	$69,450	18.9%	750
9. Environmental Science and Protection Technicians, Including Health	$42,270	23.6%	1,950
10. Medical and Clinical Laboratory Technologists	$57,010	11.3%	5,210
11. Occupational Health and Safety Specialists	$66,270	8.5%	2,570
12. Forensic Science Technicians	$52,180	18.6%	790

Best Jobs for People with an Artistic Personality Type

Job	Annual Earnings	Percent Growth	Annual Openings
1. Interior Designers	$47,620	19.3%	2,840
2. Technical Writers	$64,610	17.2%	1,830
3. Graphic Designers	$44,010	13.4%	12,380
4. Commercial and Industrial Designers	$60,760	10.5%	1,690
5. Music Directors and Composers	$47,410	10.2%	3,220

Best Jobs for People with a Social Personality Type

Job	Annual Earnings	Percent Growth	Annual Openings
1. Registered Nurses	$65,950	26.0%	120,740
2. Computer Systems Analysts	$78,770	22.1%	22,250
3. Training and Development Specialists	$55,150	28.3%	9,830
4. Health Educators	$47,940	36.5%	3,690
5. Emergency Medical Technicians and Paramedics	$30,710	33.3%	12,080
6. Licensed Practical and Licensed Vocational Nurses	$41,150	22.4%	36,920
7. Medical Assistants	$29,100	30.9%	24,380

Best Jobs for People with a Social Personality Type

Job	Annual Earnings	Percent Growth	Annual Openings
8. Coaches and Scouts	$28,470	29.4%	13,300
9. Athletic Trainers	$42,400	30.0%	1,190
10. Fitness Trainers and Aerobics Instructors	$31,030	24.0%	10,060
11. Customer Service Representatives	$30,610	15.5%	95,960
12. Substance Abuse and Behavioral Disorder Counselors	$38,560	27.3%	4,170
13. Compliance Officers	$60,740	15.0%	5,860
14. Clergy	$44,140	17.5%	7,990
15. Probation Officers and Correctional Treatment Specialists	$47,840	18.4%	3,730
16. Self-Enrichment Education Teachers	$36,100	20.9%	9,150
17. Teacher Assistants	$23,580	14.8%	48,160

Best Jobs for People with an Enterprising Personality Type

Job	Annual Earnings	Percent Growth	Annual Openings
1. Registered Nurses	$65,950	26.0%	120,740
2. Supervisors of Construction and Extraction Workers	$59,150	23.5%	25,970
3. Personal Financial Advisors	$66,580	32.1%	9,020
4. Construction Managers	$84,240	16.6%	12,040
5. Sales Representatives, Wholesale and Manufacturing, Technical and Scientific Products	$74,750	16.4%	15,970
6. Securities, Commodities, and Financial Services Sales Agents	$72,060	15.2%	13,370
7. General and Operations Managers	$95,150	4.6%	41,010
8. Managers, All Other	$99,540	7.9%	24,940
9. Logisticians	$71,910	25.5%	4,870
10. Administrative Services Managers	$79,540	14.5%	9,980
11. Business Operations Specialists, All Other	$64,030	11.6%	32,720
12. Public Relations Specialists	$53,190	22.5%	12,720
13. Sales Representatives, Services, All Other	$50,630	18.8%	27,010
14. Insurance Sales Agents	$47,450	21.9%	18,440
15. Social and Community Service Managers	$58,660	26.7%	6,480
16. First-Line Supervisors of Office and Administrative Support Workers	$48,810	14.3%	58,440
17. First-Line Supervisors of Mechanics, Installers, and Repairers	$59,850	11.9%	16,490
18. Customer Service Representatives	$30,610	15.5%	95,960

(continued)

(continued)

Best Jobs for People with an Enterprising Personality Type

Job	Annual Earnings	Percent Growth	Annual Openings
19. First-Line Supervisors of Helpers, Laborers, and Material Movers, Hand	$44,580	27.2%	8,000
20. Police and Sheriff's Patrol Officers	$54,230	8.2%	24,940
21. Meeting, Convention, and Event Planners	$46,020	43.7%	4,500
22. Captains, Mates, and Pilots of Water Vessels	$63,920	20.4%	2,070
23. Transportation, Storage, and Distribution Managers	$80,860	10.0%	3,370
24. First-Line Supervisors of Non-Retail Sales Workers	$70,520	4.0%	12,350
25. First-Line Supervisors of Transportation and Material-Moving Machine and Vehicle Operators	$52,950	14.3%	6,930
26. First-Line Supervisors of Retail Sales Workers	$36,480	8.4%	51,370
27. First-Line Supervisors of Fire Fighting and Prevention Workers	$69,510	8.2%	3,310
28. First-Line Supervisors of Police and Detectives	$77,890	2.1%	3,870
29. Real Estate Sales Agents	$39,070	12.2%	12,760
30. Advertising Sales Agents	$45,250	13.0%	6,990
31. Aircraft Cargo Handling Supervisors	$46,840	20.3%	260
32. Detectives and Criminal Investigators	$71,770	2.9%	3,010
33. First-Line Supervisors of Landscaping, Lawn Service, and Groundskeeping Workers	$42,050	15.1%	6,010
34. Property, Real Estate, and Community Association Managers	$52,510	6.0%	8,230
35. First-Line Supervisors of Production and Operating Workers	$53,670	1.9%	8,790
36. Private Detectives and Investigators	$43,710	20.5%	1,490
37. Wholesale and Retail Buyers, Except Farm Products	$50,490	9.0%	4,170
38. Credit Counselors	$38,430	20.3%	1,520
39. Real Estate Brokers	$59,340	7.6%	2,970

Best Jobs for People with a Conventional Personality Type

Job	Annual Earnings	Percent Growth	Annual Openings
1. Accountants and Auditors	$62,850	15.7%	45,210
2. Database Administrators	$75,190	30.6%	5,270
3. Sales Representatives, Wholesale and Manufacturing, Except Technical and Scientific Products	$53,540	15.6%	55,990
4. Business Operations Specialists, All Other	$64,030	11.6%	32,720
5. Logisticians	$71,910	25.5%	4,870

Best Jobs for People with a Conventional Personality Type

Job	Annual Earnings	Percent Growth	Annual Openings
6. Managers, All Other	$99,540	7.9%	24,940
7. Medical Secretaries	$31,060	41.3%	27,840
8. Dental Assistants	$34,140	30.8%	15,400
9. Receptionists and Information Clerks	$25,690	23.7%	56,560
10. Office Clerks, General	$27,190	16.6%	101,150
11. Loan Officers	$58,030	14.2%	11,520
12. Pharmacy Technicians	$28,940	32.4%	16,630
13. Billing and Posting Clerks	$32,880	19.7%	18,760
14. Executive Secretaries and Executive Administrative Assistants	$45,580	12.6%	32,180
15. Paralegals and Legal Assistants	$46,730	18.3%	8,340
16. Social and Human Service Assistants	$28,740	27.6%	18,910
17. Compliance Officers	$60,740	15.0%	5,860
18. Bookkeeping, Accounting, and Auditing Clerks	$34,740	13.6%	46,780
19. Purchasing Agents, Except Wholesale, Retail, and Farm Products	$57,580	5.3%	9,120
20. Bill and Account Collectors	$31,920	14.2%	13,550
21. Claims Adjusters, Examiners, and Investigators	$59,320	3.0%	7,990
22. Budget Analysts	$69,090	10.4%	1,960
23. Payroll and Timekeeping Clerks	$37,160	14.6%	6,570
24. Postal Service Mail Carriers	$55,160	–12.0%	10,340
25. Surveying and Mapping Technicians	$39,350	15.9%	2,000
26. Detectives and Criminal Investigators	$71,770	2.9%	3,010
27. Geological and Petroleum Technicians	$49,690	14.7%	700
28. Production, Planning, and Expediting Clerks	$43,100	6.6%	8,880
29. Life, Physical, and Social Science Technicians, All Other	$43,120	11.8%	3,350
30. Human Resources Assistants, Except Payroll and Timekeeping	$37,250	11.2%	6,160
31. Compensation, Benefits, and Job Analysis Specialists	$57,960	5.0%	2,400

Bonus List: Best Jobs with the Greatest Earnings Advantage for Recent Veterans

In the job descriptions in Part III, you'll notice I report earnings figures for both recent veterans and all workers. In many of these jobs, recent veterans earn more than the average for all workers.

I thought you might be interested in seeing which of the 150 best jobs give recent veterans the greatest earnings advantage over other workers. To create this list, I found the median earnings figures within each occupation for recent veterans and for all other workers, based on responses to the American Community Survey. (In the job descriptions, the earnings of all workers are based on the more comprehensive OES Survey.) To keep the focus on pay, I eliminated occupations in which more than one-third of the workers keep part-time hours (fewer than 34 hours per week). Then, for the occupations in which recent vets earn more than other workers, I calculated the percentage of that earnings advantage and ordered the occupations by that percentage. The following list shows all the jobs in which the earnings advantage was greater than 10 percent.

With some exceptions, the jobs on this list tend to be those that do not require college education. In these jobs, military training and experience must be particularly valuable, outweighing the earning power of civilian experience and civilian on-the-job training.

Jobs with the Greatest Earnings Advantage for Recent Veterans	
Job	Earnings Advantage for Recent Veterans
1. Private Detectives and Investigators	49.0%
2. Landscaping and Groundskeeping Workers	36.3%
3. Carpenters	34.5%
4. Security Guards	32.4%
5. Business Operations Specialists, All Other	30.3%
6. Compensation, Benefits, and Job Analysis Specialists	30.3%
7. Training and Development Specialists	30.3%
8. Commercial and Industrial Designers	26.7%
9. Graphic Designers	26.7%
10. Interior Designers	26.7%
11. Meeting, Convention, and Event Planners	25.3%
12. Real Estate Brokers	25.0%

Jobs with the Greatest Earnings Advantage for Recent Veterans

Job	Earnings Advantage for Recent Veterans
13. Real Estate Sales Agents	25.0%
14. Biological Technicians	24.1%
15. Environmental Science and Protection Technicians, Including Health	23.6%
16. Forensic Science Technicians	23.6%
17. Life, Physical, and Social Science Technicians, All Other	23.6%
18. Nuclear Technicians	23.6%
19. Logisticians	23.2%
20. Tile and Marble Setters	22.8%
21. Office Clerks, General	22.3%
22. Laborers and Freight, Stock, and Material Movers, Hand	21.1%
23. Painters, Construction and Maintenance	20.0%
24. Pharmacy Technicians	19.1%
25. Surgical Technologists	19.1%
26. Veterinary Technologists and Technicians	19.1%
27. Athletic Trainers	17.5%
28. Occupational Health and Safety Specialists	17.5%
29. Geological and Petroleum Technicians	17.3%
30. Medical Equipment Repairers	17.1%
31. First-Line Supervisors of Office and Administrative Support Workers	16.9%
32. Production, Planning, and Expediting Clerks	16.6%
33. Purchasing Agents, Except Wholesale, Retail, and Farm Products	16.3%
34. Construction Laborers	14.5%
35. Payroll and Timekeeping Clerks	14.4%
36. Commercial Pilots	14.3%
37. Executive Secretaries and Executive Administrative Assistants	14.2%
38. Medical Secretaries	14.2%
39. Registered Nurses	14.0%
40. Wholesale and Retail Buyers, Except Farm Products	13.3%
41. Medical Assistants	12.2%

Bonus List: Best-Paying Industries for Recent Vets

Unlike all the other lists in this book, the following list deals with industries instead of jobs. It identifies the best-paying industries where large numbers of recent vets are working.

When you see the word "industry," don't limit your thinking to manufacturing and other smokestack enterprises. Education is an industry. So is health care.

Why should you care about what industry you work in? People often change occupations, but much of the time they are only moving to a different occupation in the same industry. For example, they may move from doing a certain kind of work to supervising the workers who do it. Or they may move from a technical role to a sales role. That's why the industry where you find your next job may be even more important than the particular job you fill, because it may be where you continue to earn your living even when your specific work role changes.

To create the following list, I analyzed the data that the American Community Survey collected about recent veterans. I limited the sample to vets working in the original pool of occupations that I sorted for this book; that allowed me to exclude most former officers from the calculations. I also discarded all industries with a sample of fewer than 1,000 recent vets. For each of the remaining industries, I computed the median earnings—half of the vets earn more, half earn less, inflated to represent 2010 dollars. Then I sorted the industries to create the following list of the 25 in which recent vets earn the highest pay.

Best-Paying Industries for Recent Veterans	
Job	Median Earnings of Recent Veterans
1. Drugs, Sundries, and Chemical and Allied Products Merchant Wholesalers	$70,940
2. Computer Systems Design and Related Services	$69,850
3. Pharmaceuticals and Medicines	$67,660
4. Air Transportation	$65,480
5. Architectural, Engineering, and Related Services	$64,390
6. Aerospace Products and Parts	$63,300
7. Electric Power Generation, Transmission, and Distribution	$62,210
8. Medical Equipment and Supplies	$61,120
9. Management, Scientific, and Technical Consulting Services	$60,020
10. Electric and Gas, and Other Combinations	$57,840
11. Aircraft and Parts	$56,750
12. Administration of Environmental Quality and Housing Programs	$54,570
13. Navigational, Measuring, Electromedical, and Control Instruments	$54,570
14. Petroleum Refining	$54,570
15. Administration of Economic Programs and Space Research	$54,020
16. Electronic Components and Products, Not Elsewhere Classified	$53,480
17. Rail Transportation	$52,380

Best-Paying Industries for Recent Veterans

Job	Median Earnings of Recent Veterans
18. Postal Service	$51,290
19. Ship and Boat Building	$51,290
20. Industrial and Miscellaneous Chemicals	$50,200
21. Justice, Public Order, and Safety Activities	$50,200
22. Natural Gas Distribution	$50,200
23. Communications, and Audio and Video Equipment	$49,110
24. Iron and Steel Mills and Steel Products	$49,110
25. Other Administrative and Other Support Services	$49,110

PART III

Descriptions of the Best Jobs for the Military-to-Civilian Transition

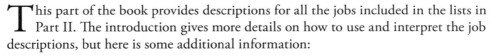

This part of the book provides descriptions for all the jobs included in the lists in Part II. The introduction gives more details on how to use and interpret the job descriptions, but here is some additional information:

❋ Job descriptions are arranged in alphabetical order by job title. This approach allows you to quickly find a description if you know its correct title from one of the lists in Part II.

❋ To save space, I use "vets" in some of the information headings as an abbreviated way of referring to *recent* veterans.

❋ As another space-saving measure, the skills and related knowledge/courses are listed here by name only. For definitions of these terms, see the appendix.

❋ If you are using this section to browse for interesting options, I suggest you begin with the table of contents. Part II features many interesting lists that will help you identify job titles to explore in more detail. If you have not browsed the lists in Part II, consider spending some time there. The lists are interesting and will help you identify job titles you can find described in the material that follows. The job titles and job specializations in Part III are also listed in the table of contents.

Accountants and Auditors

- ❋ Average Annual Earnings (All): $62,850

- ❋ Average Annual Earnings (Recent Veterans): $49,330

- ❋ Earnings Growth Potential: Medium (36.9%)

- ❋ Growth: 15.7%

- ❋ Annual Job Openings: 45,210

- ❋ Veteran Employment by Sector: For-Profit, 55.5%; Nonprofit, 4.7%; Government, 35.6%; Self-Employed, 4.2%.

Considerations for Job Outlook: Accountants and auditors who have earned professional recognition, especially as a Certified Public Accountants (CPA), should have the best prospects. Job applicants who have a master's degree in accounting or a master's degree in business with a concentration in accounting also may have an advantage. However, competition should be strong for jobs with the most prestigious accounting and business firms.

Examine, analyze, and interpret accounting records to prepare financial statements, give advice, or audit and evaluate statements prepared by others. For task data, see Job Specializations.

Related Military Specializations: Accounting Specialist; Aviation Storekeeper; Disbursing Afloat Automated Systems Specialist; Financial Management Resource Analyst; Financial Management Technician; Machine Accountant; NAF Audit Technician; Relational Supply Force Advanced Technical Specialist; Relational Supply Force Technical Specialist; Storekeeper; Supply and Accounting (SUADPS R/T) Advanced Technical Specialist. **Average Educational Level of Vets:** Bachelor's degree. **Usual Educational Requirement:** Bachelor's degree. **Relevant Educational Programs**: Accounting; Accounting and Business/Management; Accounting and Computer Science; Accounting and Finance; Auditing; Financial Forensics and Fraud Investigation; Taxation. **Work Experience Needed:** None. **On-the-Job Training Needed:** None. **Certification/Licensure:** Licensure for most specializations; voluntary certification by association.

Key Career Cluster: 04 Business, Management, and Administration. **Key Career Pathway:** 4.2 w Financial Management and Accounting. **Top Industries for Vets:** National Security and International Affairs; Accounting, Tax Preparation, Bookkeeping and Payroll Services; Public Finance Activities; Traveler Accommodation; Securities, Commodities, Funds, Trusts, and Other Financial Investments.

Job Specialization: Accountants

Analyze financial information and prepare financial reports to determine or maintain record of assets, liabilities, profit and loss, tax liability, or other financial activities within an organization. Prepare, examine, or analyze accounting records, financial statements, or other financial reports to assess accuracy, completeness, and conformance to reporting and procedural standards. Compute taxes owed and prepare tax returns, ensuring compliance with payment, reporting, or other tax requirements. Analyze business operations, trends, costs, revenues, financial commitments, and obligations to project future revenues and expenses or to provide advice. Report to management regarding the finances of establishment. Establish tables of accounts and assign entries to proper accounts. Develop, maintain, and analyze budgets, preparing periodic reports that compare budgeted costs to actual costs. Develop, implement, modify, and document recordkeeping and accounting systems, making use of current computer technology. Prepare forms and manuals for accounting and bookkeeping personnel, directing their work activities. Survey operations to ascertain accounting needs and to recommend, develop, or maintain solutions to business and financial problems. Work as Internal Revenue Service (IRS) agents. Advise management about issues such as resource utilization, tax strategies, and the assumptions underlying budget forecasts. Provide internal and external auditing services for businesses or individuals. Advise clients in areas such as compensation, employee health-care benefits, the design of accounting or data processing systems, or long-range tax or estate plans.

Related Knowledge/Courses: Economics and Accounting; Clerical Practices; Mathematics; Computers and Electronics; Personnel and Human Resources; Administration and Management.

Personality Types: Conventional-Enterprising.

Skills: Operations Analysis; Mathematics; Systems Analysis; Management of Financial Resources; Systems Evaluation; Critical Thinking; Judgment and Decision Making; Negotiation.

Work Environment: Indoors; sitting; repetitive motions.

Job Specialization: Auditors

Examine and analyze accounting records to determine financial status of establishment and prepare financial reports concerning operating procedures. Collect and analyze data to detect deficient controls; duplicated effort; extravagance; fraud; or noncompliance with laws, regulations, and management policies. Prepare detailed reports on audit findings. Supervise auditing of establishments, and determine scope

of investigation required. Report to management about asset utilization and audit results, and recommend changes in operations and financial activities. Inspect account books and accounting systems for efficiency, effectiveness, and use of accepted accounting procedures to record transactions. Examine records and interview workers to ensure recording of transactions and compliance with laws and regulations. Examine and evaluate financial and information systems, recommending controls to ensure system reliability and data integrity. Review data about material assets, net worth, liabilities, capital stock, surplus, income, and expenditures. Confer with company officials about financial and regulatory matters. Examine whether the organization's objectives are reflected in its management activities and whether employees understand the objectives. Prepare, analyze, and verify annual reports, financial statements, and other records, using accepted accounting and statistical procedures to assess financial condition and facilitate financial planning. Inspect cash on hand, notes receivable and payable, negotiable securities, and canceled checks to confirm records are accurate.

Related Knowledge/Courses: Economics and Accounting; Administration and Management; Personnel and Human Resources; Law and Government; Computers and Electronics; Mathematics.

Personality Types: Conventional-Enterprising-Investigative.

Skills: Systems Evaluation; Systems Analysis; Management of Financial Resources; Mathematics; Programming; Writing; Operations Analysis; Management of Personnel Resources.

Work Environment: Indoors; sitting.

Administrative Services Managers

- ❀ Average Annual Earnings (All): $79,540
- ❀ Average Annual Earnings (Recent Veterans): $46,930
- ❀ Earnings Growth Potential: High (45.8%)
- ❀ Growth: 14.5%
- ❀ Annual Job Openings: 9,980
- ❀ Veteran Employment by Sector: For-Profit, 39.5%; Nonprofit, 11.4%; Government, 49.1%; Self-Employed, 0.0%.

Considerations for Job Outlook: Applicants will likely face strong competition for the limited number of higher-level administrative services management jobs. Competition should be less severe for lower-level management jobs. Job prospects also are expected to be better for those who can manage a wide range of responsibilities than for those who specialize in particular functions.

Plan, direct, or coordinate one or more administrative services of an organization. Monitor the facility to ensure that it remains safe, secure, and well-maintained. Direct or coordinate the supportive services department of a business, agency, or organization. Set goals and deadlines for the department. Prepare and review operational reports and schedules to ensure accuracy and efficiency. Analyze internal processes, recommending and implementing procedural or policy changes to improve operations such as supply changes or the disposal of records. Acquire, distribute, and store supplies. Plan, administer, and control budgets for contracts, equipment, and supplies. Oversee construction and renovation projects to improve efficiency and to ensure that facilities meet environmental, health, and security standards and comply with government regulations. Hire and terminate clerical and administrative personnel. Oversee the maintenance and repair of machinery, equipment, and electrical and mechanical systems. Manage leasing of facility space. Participate in architectural and engineering planning and design, including space and installation management. Conduct classes to teach procedures to staff. Dispose of, or oversee the disposal of, surplus or unclaimed property.

Related Military Specializations: Adjutant; Administrative Assistant; Administrative Officer; Administrative Systems Management; Aide; Aide-de-Camp; Executive Assistant; Facilities Construction/Facilities Services Officer; Facilities Management Officer; Facilities Manager; Flag Lieutenant; Flag Secretary; Legal Administrative Officer; Management Officer; Personnel Administration; Personnel Officer; Records Management Officer; Ship's Secretary; Special Aides/Assistants/Liaison; Staff Administration Officer. **Average Educational Level of Vets:** One or more years of college, no degree. **Usual Educational Requirement:** High school diploma or equivalent. **Relevant Educational Programs:** Business Administration and Management, General; Business/Commerce, General; Medical/Health Management and Clinical Assistant/Specialist Training; Purchasing, Procurement/Acquisitions and Contracts Management. **Related Knowledge/Courses:** Clerical Practices; Economics and Accounting; Personnel and Human Resources; Customer and Personal Service; Sales and Marketing; Administration and Management. **Work Experience Needed:** 1 to 5 years. **On-the-Job Training Needed:** None. **Certification/Licensure:** Licensure for some specializations.

Personality Types: Enterprising-Conventional. **Key Career Cluster:** 04 Business, Management, and Administration. **Key Career Pathway:** 4.1 Management. **Top Industries for Vets:** National

Security and International Affairs; Religious Organizations; Restaurants and Other Food Services; Colleges and Universities, Including Junior Colleges; Administration of Economic Programs and Space Research.

Skills: Management of Financial Resources; Management of Material Resources; Management of Personnel Resources; Negotiation; Coordination; Time Management; Social Perceptiveness; Service Orientation.

Work Environment: Indoors; sitting.

Advertising Sales Agents

* Average Annual Earnings (All): $45,250

* Average Annual Earnings (Recent Veterans): $39,290

* Earnings Growth Potential: High (50.4%)

* Growth: 13.0%

* Annual Job Openings: 6,990

* Veteran Employment by Sector: For-Profit, 96.1%; Nonprofit, 1.9%; Government, 0.0%; Self-Employed, 2.1%.

Considerations for Job Outlook: Competition is expected to be strong for advertising sales agents. Applicants with experience in sales or a bachelor's degree should have the best opportunities.

Sell or solicit advertising space, time, or media in publications, signage, TV, radio, or Internet establishments or public spaces. Maintain assigned account bases while developing new accounts. Explain to customers how specific types of advertising will help promote their products or services in the most effective way possible. Provide clients with estimates of the costs of advertising products or services. Locate and contact potential clients to offer advertising services. Process all correspondence and paperwork related to accounts. Inform customers of available options for advertisement artwork and provide samples. Prepare and deliver sales presentations to new and existing customers to sell new advertising programs and to protect and increase existing advertising. Deliver advertising or illustration proofs to customers for approval. Prepare promotional plans, sales literature, media kits, and sales contracts, using computer. Recommend appropriate sizes and formats for advertising, depending on medium being used. Draw up contracts for advertising work and collect payments due.

Related Military Specializations: None. **Average Educational Level of Vets:** One or more years of college, no degree. **Usual Educational Requirement:** High school diploma or equivalent. **Relevant Educational Program:** Selling Skills and Sales Operations. **Related Knowledge/ Courses:** Sales and Marketing; Communications and Media; Clerical Practices; Customer and Personal Service; Economics and Accounting; Telecommunications. **Work Experience Needed:** None. **On-the-Job Training Needed:** Moderate-term on-the-job training. **Certification/ Licensure:** None.

Personality Types: Enterprising-Conventional-Artistic. **Key Career Cluster:** 04 Business, Management, and Administration. **Key Career Pathway:** 4.5 Marketing. **Top Industries for Vets:** Broadcasting, Including Internet Publishing and Web Search Portals; Advertising and Related Services; Newspaper Publishers; Periodical, Book, and Directory Publishers; Architectural, Engineering, and Related Services.

Skills: Persuasion; Negotiation; Service Orientation; Speaking; Management of Financial Resources; Social Perceptiveness; Mathematics; Systems Evaluation.

Work Environment: More often indoors than outdoors; sitting; noise.

Aircraft Cargo Handling Supervisors

* Average Annual Earnings (All): $46,840
* Average Annual Earnings (Recent Veterans): $42,840
* Earnings Growth Potential: Medium (38.9%)
* Growth: 20.3%
* Annual Job Openings: 260
* Veteran Employment by Sector: For-Profit, 71.7%; Nonprofit, 3.7%; Government, 21.8%; Self-Employed, 2.8%.

Considerations for Job Outlook: Faster than average employment growth is projected.

Supervise and coordinate the activities of ground crew in the loading, unloading, securing, and staging of aircraft cargo or baggage. Calculate load weights for different aircraft compartments, using charts and computers. Determine the quantity and orientation of cargo, and compute an aircraft's center of gravity. Direct ground crews in the loading, unloading, securing, and staging of aircraft cargo or baggage. Distribute cargo in such a manner that space use is maximized. Accompany aircraft as a member of the flight crew in order to monitor and handle cargo in flight. Brief aircraft passengers on safety and emergency procedures.

Related Military Specializations: Air Transportation Craftsman; Air Transportation Manager; Air Transportation Superintendent; Aircraft Loadmaster Apprentice; Aircraft Loadmaster Craftsman; Aircraft Loadmaster Helper; Aircraft Loadmaster Journeyman; C-130 Loadmaster; C-130 Second Loadmaster; Loadmaster; Parachute Rigger. **Average Educational Level of Vets:** One or more years of college, no degree. **Usual Educational Requirement:** High school diploma or equivalent. **Relevant Educational Program:** Aviation/Airway Management and Operations. **Related Knowledge/Courses:** Transportation; Public Safety and Security; Geography; Personnel and Human Resources; Psychology; Customer and Personal Service. **Work Experience Needed:** 1 to 5 years. **On-the-Job Training Needed:** None. **Certification/Licensure:** None.

Personality Types: Enterprising-Realistic. **Key Career Cluster:** 16 Transportation, Distribution, and Logistics. **Key Career Pathway:** 16.1 Transportation Operations. **Top Industries for Vets:** National Security and International Affairs; Couriers and Messengers; Services Incidental to Transportation; Truck Transportation; Rail Transportation.

Skills: Management of Personnel Resources; Repairing; Learning Strategies; Equipment Maintenance; Operation and Control; Management of Material Resources; Equipment Selection; Troubleshooting.

Work Environment: Outdoors; standing; walking and running; using hands; repetitive motions; noise; very hot or cold; bright or inadequate lighting; contaminants; hazardous equipment.

Aircraft Mechanics and Service Technicians

- ❀ Average Annual Earnings (All): $54,590
- ❀ Average Annual Earnings (Recent Veterans): $42,560
- ❀ Earnings Growth Potential: Medium (36.6%)
- ❀ Growth: 6.3%
- ❀ Annual Job Openings: 4,520
- ❀ Veteran Employment by Sector: For-Profit, 25.6%; Nonprofit, 0.3%; Government, 74.1%; Self-Employed, 0.0%.

Considerations for Job Outlook: Job prospects should be best for mechanics and technicians who hold an Airframe and Powerplant (A&P) certificate and a bachelor's degree in aircraft maintenance. Job prospects also will be better for those who keep up with technical advances in aircraft electronics and composite materials. Job opportunities may arise from the need to replace mechanics who leave the workforce. Over the next decade, many aircraft mechanics are expected to retire. As older mechanics retire and younger mechanics advance, entry-level positions may open up. However, if airlines continue to send maintenance work to other countries, competition for new jobs will remain strong.

Diagnose, adjust, repair, or overhaul aircraft engines and assemblies, such as hydraulic and pneumatic systems. Read and interpret maintenance manuals, service bulletins, and other specifications to determine the feasibility and method of repairing or replacing malfunctioning or damaged components. Inspect completed work to certify that maintenance meets standards and that aircraft are ready for operation. Maintain repair logs, documenting all preventive and corrective aircraft maintenance. Conduct routine and special inspections as required by regulations. Examine and inspect aircraft components, including landing gear, hydraulic systems, and de-icers to locate cracks, breaks, leaks, or other problems. Inspect airframes for wear or other defects. Maintain, repair, and rebuild aircraft structures, functional components, and parts such as wings and fuselage, rigging, hydraulic units, oxygen systems, fuel systems, electrical systems, gaskets, and seals. Measure the tension of control cables. Replace or repair worn, defective, or damaged components, using hand tools, gauges, and testing equipment. Measure parts for wear, using precision instruments. Assemble and install electrical, plumbing, mechanical, hydraulic, and structural components and accessories, using hand tools and power tools. Test operation of engines and other systems, using test equipment such as ignition analyzers, compression checkers, distributor timers, and ammeters. Obtain fuel and oil samples, and check them for contamination. Reassemble engines following repair or inspection, and re-install engines in aircraft. Read and interpret pilots' descriptions of problems in order to diagnose causes. Modify aircraft structures, space vehicles, systems, or components, following drawings, schematics, charts, engineering orders, and technical publications. Install and align repaired or replacement parts for subsequent riveting or welding, using clamps and wrenches. Locate and mark dimensions and reference lines on defective or replacement parts, using templates, scribes, compasses, and steel rules.

Related Military Specializations: A-4 Systems Organizational Maintenance Technician; Advanced Composite Structural Repair IMA Technician; Aerial Target System Maintenance Technician; Aerospace Maintenance Apprentice, B-1/B-2; Aerospace Maintenance Apprentice, B-52; Aerospace Maintenance Apprentice, C-12/C-26/C-27/C-130; Aerospace Maintenance

Apprentice, C-17; Aerospace Maintenance Apprentice, C-18/C-135/E-3/VC-25/VC-137; Aerospace Maintenance Apprentice, C-5; Aerospace Maintenance Apprentice, C-9/C-20/C-21/C-22/T-39/T-43; others. **Average Educational Level of Vets:** High school diploma or equivalent. **Usual Educational Requirement:** Postsecondary vocational training. **Relevant Educational Programs:** Agricultural Mechanics and Equipment/Machine Technology; Aircraft Powerplant Technology/Technician; Airframe Mechanics and Aircraft Maintenance Technology/Technician. **Related Knowledge/ Courses:** Mechanical Devices; Design; Physics; Engineering and Technology; Chemistry; Transportation. **Work Experience Needed:** None. **On-the-Job Training Needed:** None. **Certification/Licensure:** Licensure based on FAA certification.

Personality Types: Realistic-Conventional-Investigative. **Key Career Cluster:** 16 Transportation, Distribution, and Logistics. **Key Career Pathway:** 16.4 Facility and Mobile Equipment Maintenance. **Top Industries for Vets:** National Security and International Affairs; Services Incidental to Transportation; Air Transportation; Aircraft and Parts; Aerospace Products and Parts.

Skills: Equipment Maintenance; Repairing; Troubleshooting; Equipment Selection; Quality Control Analysis; Operation Monitoring; Operation and Control; Installation.

Work Environment: Indoors; standing; walking and running; using hands; bending or twisting the body; noise; contaminants; cramped work space; hazardous conditions; hazardous equipment.

Athletes and Sports Competitors

- ❋ Average Annual Earnings (All): $39,670
- ❋ Average Annual Earnings (Recent Veterans): $23,570
- ❋ Earnings Growth Potential: Very high (54.7%)
- ❋ Growth: 21.6%
- ❋ Annual Job Openings: 780
- ❋ Veteran Employment by Sector: For-Profit, 59.8%; Nonprofit, 17.9%; Government, 19.6%; Self-Employed, 2.7%.

Considerations for Job Outlook: Competition for professional athlete jobs will continue to be extremely intense, with progressively more favorable opportunities in lower levels of competition. In major sports, such as basketball and football, only about 1 in 5,000 high school athletes become professionals in these sports. The expansion of nontraditional sports may create some additional job opportunities. Most professional athletes' careers last only a few years because of debilitating injuries. Therefore, yearly replacement needs for these jobs is high, creating some job opportunities. However, the talented young men and women who dream of becoming sports superstars greatly outnumber the number of openings.

Compete in athletic events. Assess performance following athletic competition, identifying strengths and weaknesses, and making adjustments to improve future performance. Receive instructions from coaches and other sports staff prior to events, and discuss their performance afterwards. Lead teams by serving as captains. Maintain equipment used in a particular sport. Represent teams or professional sports clubs, performing such activities as meeting with members of the media, making speeches, or participating in charity events. Participate in athletic events and competitive sports, according to established rules and regulations. Attend scheduled practice and training sessions. Exercise and practice under the direction of athletic trainers or professional coaches, in order to develop skills, improve physical condition, and prepare for competitions. Maintain optimum physical fitness levels by training regularly, following nutrition plans, and consulting with health professionals.

Related Military Specialization: Physical Activities Specialist. **Average Educational Level of Vets:** High school diploma or equivalent. **Usual Educational Requirement:** High school diploma or equivalent. **Relevant Educational Program:** Health and Physical Education, General. **Related Knowledge/Courses:** Therapy and Counseling; Communications and Media; Psychology; Sales and Marketing. **Work Experience Needed:** None. **On-the-Job Training Needed:** Long-term on-the-job training. **Certification/Licensure:** Licensure for some specializations and in some localities.

Personality Types: Realistic-Enterprising. **Key Career Cluster:** 09 Hospitality and Tourism. **Key Career Pathway:** 9.4 Recreation, Amusements and Attractions. **Top Industries for Vets:** Other Amusement, Gambling, and Recreation Industries; Elementary and Secondary Schools; Independent Artists, Performing Arts, Spectator Sports and Related Industries; Other Schools and Instruction, and Educational Support Services; Colleges and Universities, Including Junior Colleges.

Skills: Coordination; Operations Analysis.

Work Environment: Indoors; standing; balancing; using hands; bending or twisting the body; repetitive motions; noise; very hot or cold.

Athletic Trainers

- ❋ Average Annual Earnings (All): $42,400
- ❋ Average Annual Earnings (Recent Veterans): $51,290
- ❋ Earnings Growth Potential: Medium (38.3%)
- ❋ Growth: 30.0%
- ❋ Annual Job Openings: 1,190
- ❋ Veteran Employment by Sector: For-Profit, 29.3%; Nonprofit, 2.3%; Government, 67.2%; Self-Employed, 1.1%.

Considerations for Job Outlook: As people become more aware of sports-related injuries at a young age, demand for athletic trainers is expected to increase, most significantly in schools and youth leagues. Because athletic trainers are usually on site with athletes and are often the first line of defense when injuries occur, the demand for trainers should continue to increase. Additionally, advances in injury prevention and detection and more sophisticated treatments are projected to increase the demand for athletic trainers. Growth in an increasingly active middle-aged and elderly population will likely lead to an increased incidence of athletic-related injuries, such as sprains. Sports programs at all ages and for all experience levels will continue to create demand for athletic trainers.

Evaluate and advise individuals to assist recovery from or avoid athletic-related injuries or illnesses, or maintain peak physical fitness. Conduct an initial assessment of an athlete's injury or illness to provide emergency or continued care and to determine whether he or she should be referred to physicians for definitive diagnosis and treatment. Care for athletic injuries, using physical therapy equipment, techniques, and medication. Evaluate athletes' readiness to play, and provide participation clearances when necessary and warranted. Apply protective or injury-preventive devices such as tape, bandages, or braces to body parts such as ankles, fingers, or wrists. Assess and report the progress of recovering athletes to coaches and physicians. Collaborate with physicians to develop and implement comprehensive rehabilitation programs for athletic injuries. Advise athletes on the proper use of equipment. Plan and implement comprehensive athletic-injury and illness-prevention programs. Develop training programs and routines designed to improve athletic performance. Travel with athletic teams to be available at sporting events. Instruct coaches, athletes, parents, medical personnel, and community members in the care and prevention of athletic injuries. Inspect playing fields to locate any items that could injure players. Conduct research and provide instruction on subject matter related to athletic training or sports medicine. Recommend special diets to improve athletes' health, increase their stamina, or alter their weight. Massage body parts to relieve soreness, strains, and bruises.

Related Military Specializations: None. **Average Educational Level of Vets:** Bachelor's degree. **Usual Educational Requirement:** Bachelor's degree. **Relevant Educational Programs:** Athletic Training/Trainer; Physical Fitness Technician Training. **Related Knowledge/Courses:** Medicine and Dentistry; Therapy and Counseling; Biology; Psychology; Customer and Personal Service; Clerical Practices. **Work Experience Needed:** None. **On-the-Job Training Needed:** None. **Certification/Licensure:** Licensure or registration in most states.

Personality Types: Social-Realistic-Investigative. **Key Career Cluster:** 08 Health Science. **Key Career Pathway:** 8.1 Therapeutic Services. **Top Industries for Vets:** National Security and International Affairs; Construction; Hospitals; Administration of Human Resource Programs; Administration of Environmental Quality and Housing Programs.

Skills: Learning Strategies; Quality Control Analysis; Service Orientation; Instructing; Social Perceptiveness; Science; Monitoring; Systems Evaluation.

Work Environment: More often indoors than outdoors; standing; using hands; exposed to disease or infections.

Audio and Video Equipment Technicians

- Average Annual Earnings (All): $41,630
- Average Annual Earnings (Recent Veterans): $34,920
- Earnings Growth Potential: High (44.1%)
- Growth: 13.4%
- Annual Job Openings: 2,560
- Veteran Employment by Sector: For-Profit, 51.6%; Nonprofit, 3.4%; Government, 42.2%; Self-Employed, 2.8%.

Considerations for Job Outlook: Competition for jobs will be strong. This occupation attracts many applicants who are interested in working with the latest technology and electronic equipment. Many applicants also are attracted to working in the radio and television industry. Those looking for work in this industry will have the most job opportunities in smaller markets or stations. Those with hands-on experience with electronics or with work experience at a radio or television station will have the best job prospects. In addition, technicians are expected to be versatile and contribute to the setup, operation, and maintenance of equipment, whereas previously technicians typically specialized in one area.

Set up, or set up and operate audio and video equipment. Notify supervisors when major equipment repairs are needed. Monitor incoming and outgoing pictures and sound feeds to ensure quality; notify directors of any possible problems. Mix and regulate sound inputs and feeds or coordinate audio feeds with television pictures. Install, adjust, and operate electronic equipment used to record, edit, and transmit radio and television programs, cable programs, and motion pictures. Design layouts of audio and video equipment and perform upgrades and maintenance. Perform minor repairs and routine cleaning of audio and video equipment. Diagnose and resolve media system problems in classrooms. Switch sources of video input from one camera or studio to another, from film to live programming, or from network to local programming. Meet with directors and senior members of camera crews to discuss assignments and determine filming sequences, camera movements, and picture composition. Construct and position properties, sets, lighting equipment, and other equipment. Compress, digitize, duplicate, and store audio and video data. Obtain, set up, and load videotapes for scheduled productions or broadcasts. Edit videotapes by erasing and removing portions of programs and adding video or sound as required. Direct and coordinate activities of assistants and other personnel during production. Plan and develop preproduction ideas into outlines, scripts, storyboards, and graphics, using own ideas or specifications of assignments.

Related Military Specializations: Regional Band Apprentice, Audio and Lighting Engineer; Regional Band Craftsman, Audio and Lighting Engineer; Regional Band Helper, Audio and Lighting Engineer; Regional Band Journeyman, Audio and Lighting Engineer;

Sound Reinforcement Technician; Visual Information Equipment Operator-Maintainer. **Average Educational Level of Vets:** High school diploma or equivalent. **Usual Educational Requirement:** Postsecondary vocational training. **Relevant Educational Programs:** Agricultural Communication/Journalism; Photographic and Film/Video Technology/Technician and Assistant; Recording Arts Technology/Technician. **Related Knowledge/Courses:** Telecommunications; Communications and Media; Fine Arts; Computers and Electronics; Engineering and Technology; Production and Processing. **Work Experience Needed:** None. **On-the-Job Training Needed:** Moderate-term on-the-job training. **Certification/Licensure:** Voluntary certification for some specializations.

Personality Types: Realistic-Investigative-Conventional. **Key Career Cluster:** 03 Arts, Audiovisual Technology, and Communications. **Key Career Pathway:** 3.1 Audio and Video Technologies. **Top Industries for Vets:** National Security and International Affairs; Broadcasting, Including Internet Publishing and Web Search Portals; Motion Picture and Video Industries; Architectural, Engineering, and Related Services; Executive Offices and Legislative Bodies.

Skills: Installation; Troubleshooting; Equipment Selection; Operation and Control; Repairing; Operation Monitoring; Equipment Maintenance; Quality Control Analysis.

Work Environment: Indoors; sitting; using hands; repetitive motions.

Automotive Service Technicians and Mechanics

❋ Average Annual Earnings (All): $36,180

❋ Average Annual Earnings (Recent Veterans): $31,650

❋ Earnings Growth Potential: High (43.0%)

❋ Growth: 17.2%

❋ Annual Job Openings: 31,170

❋ Veteran Employment by Sector: For-Profit, 69.3%; Nonprofit, 1.2%; Government, 24.5%; Self-Employed, 5.1%.

Considerations for Job Outlook: Job opportunities should be very good for job seekers with industry certification and formal training in automotive body repair and refinishing and in collision repair. Furthermore, demand for qualified workers with knowledge of specific technologies, materials, and makes and models of cars should create new job opportunities. Those without any training or experience will face strong competition for jobs. The need to replace experienced repair technicians who retire, change occupations, or stop working for other reasons also will provide some job opportunities.

Diagnose, adjust, repair, or overhaul automotive vehicles. For task data, see Job Specializations.

Related Military Specializations: Automotive Intermediate Maintenance Technician; Automotive Maintenance Technician; Basic Motor Transport Marine; Construction Mechanic; Construction Mechanic—Automotive; Crash/Fire/Rescue Vehicle Mechanic; Crash/Fire/Rescue Vehicle Technician; Expeditionary Fighting Vehicle (EFV) Repairer/Technician; Fuel and Electrical Systems Mechanic; General Purpose Vehicle Maintenance Apprentice; General Purpose Vehicle Maintenance Helper; General Purpose Vehicle Maintenance Journeyman; others. **Average Educational Level of Vets:** High school diploma or equivalent. **Usual Educational Requirement:** High school diploma or equivalent. **Relevant Educational Programs:** Alternative Fuel Vehicle Technology/Technician; Automobile/Automotive Mechanics Technology/Technician; Automotive Engineering Technology/Technician; High Performance and Custom Engine Technician/Mechanic Training; Medium/Heavy Vehicle and Truck Technology/Technician; Vehicle Emissions Inspection and Maintenance Technology/Technician; Vehicle Maintenance and Repair Technologies, General. **Work Experience Needed:** None. **On-the-Job Training Needed:** Long-term on-the-job training. **Certification/Licensure:** Voluntary certification by association.

Key Career Cluster: 16 Transportation, Distribution, and Logistics. **Key Career Pathway:** 16.4 Facility and Mobile Equipment Maintenance. **Top Industries for Vets:** Automotive Repair and Maintenance; Automobile Dealers; National Security and International Affairs; Auto Parts, Accessories, and Tire Stores; Motor Vehicles and Motor Vehicle Equipment.

Job Specialization: Automotive Master Mechanics

Repair automobiles, trucks, buses, and other vehicles. Master mechanics repair virtually any part on the vehicle or specialize in the transmission system. Test drive vehicles, and test components and systems, using equipment such as infrared engine analyzers, compression gauges, and computerized diagnostic devices. Examine vehicles to determine extent of damage or malfunctions. Repair, reline, replace, and adjust brakes. Follow checklists to ensure all important parts are examined, including belts, hoses, steering systems, spark plugs, brake and fuel systems, wheel bearings, and other potentially troublesome areas. Confer with customers to obtain descriptions of vehicle problems, and to discuss work to be performed and future repair requirements. Perform routine and scheduled maintenance services such as oil changes, lubrications, and tune-ups. Repair and service air conditioning, heating, engine-cooling, and electrical systems. Test and adjust repaired systems to meet manufacturers' performance specifications. Review work orders and discuss work with supervisors. Tear down, repair, and rebuild faulty assemblies such as power systems, steering systems, and linkages. Plan work procedures, using charts, technical manuals, and experience. Disassemble units and inspect parts for wear, using micrometers, calipers, and gauges. Repair or replace parts such as pistons, rods, gears, valves, and bearings. Rewire ignition systems, lights, and instrument panels. Repair manual and automatic transmissions. Install and repair accessories such as radios, heaters, mirrors, and windshield wipers. Maintain cleanliness of work area. Repair or replace shock absorbers. Replace and adjust headlights. Overhaul or replace carburetors, blowers, generators, distributors, starters, and pumps. Repair radiator leaks. Align vehicles' front ends. Rebuild parts such as crankshafts and cylinder blocks. Repair damaged automobile bodies.

Related Knowledge/Courses: Mechanical Devices; Engineering and Technology; Physics; Design; Chemistry; Computers and Electronics.

Personality Types: Realistic-Investigative.

Skills: Repairing; Equipment Maintenance; Installation; Troubleshooting; Equipment Selection; Operation and Control; Quality Control Analysis; Operation Monitoring.

Work Environment: Standing; using hands; bending or twisting the body; repetitive motions; noise; very hot or cold; bright or inadequate lighting; contaminants; cramped work space; hazardous conditions; hazardous equipment; minor burns, cuts, bites, or stings.

Job Specialization: Automotive Specialty Technicians

Repair only one system or component on a vehicle, such as brakes, suspension, or radiator. Examine vehicles, compile estimates of repair costs, and secure customers' approval to perform repairs. Repair, overhaul, and adjust automobile brake systems. Use electronic test equipment to locate and correct malfunctions in fuel, ignition, and emissions control systems. Repair and replace defective balljoint suspensions, brakeshoes, and wheelbearings. Inspect and test new vehicles for damage, then record findings so that necessary repairs can be made. Test electronic computer components in automobiles to ensure that they are working properly. Tune automobile engines to ensure proper and efficient functioning. Install and repair air conditioners, and service components such as compressors, condensers, and controls. Repair, replace, and adjust defective carburetor parts and gasoline filters. Remove and replace defective mufflers and tailpipes. Repair and replace automobile leaf springs. Rebuild, repair, and test automotive fuel injection units. Align and repair wheels, axles, frames, torsion bars, and steering mechanisms of automobiles, using special alignment equipment and wheel-balancing machines. Repair, install, and adjust hydraulic and electromagnetic automatic lift mechanisms used to raise and lower automobile windows, seats, and tops. Repair and rebuild clutch systems. Convert vehicle fuel systems from gasoline to butane gas operations, and repair and service operating butane fuel units.

Related Knowledge/Courses: Mechanical Devices; Physics; Engineering and Technology;

Customer and Personal Service; Sales and Marketing; Administration and Management.

Personality Types:
Realistic-Investigative-Conventional.

Skills: Repairing; Equipment Maintenance; Troubleshooting; Operation and Control; Equipment Selection; Installation; Quality Control Analysis; Operation Monitoring.

Work Environment: Standing; walking and running; kneeling, crouching, stooping, or crawling; using hands; bending or twisting the body; repetitive motions; noise; very hot or cold; bright or inadequate lighting; contaminants; cramped work space; hazardous conditions; hazardous equipment; minor burns, cuts, bites, or stings.

Bill and Account Collectors

- ❀ Average Annual Earnings (All): $31,920
- ❀ Average Annual Earnings (Recent Veterans): $29,470
- ❀ Earnings Growth Potential: Low (32.5%)
- ❀ Growth: 14.2%
- ❀ Annual Job Openings: 13,550
- ❀ Veteran Employment by Sector: For-Profit, 83.6%; Nonprofit, 0.0%; Government, 13.2%; Self-Employed, 3.2%.

Considerations for Job Outlook: Job prospects should be excellent for this occupation. Workers frequently leave the occupation, which leads to numerous job openings. Prospects should be best for applicants who have worked in a call center before because some companies prefer to hire collectors with this kind of experience. Unlike many other occupations, collections jobs usually remain stable during economic downturns. When the economy weakens, many consumers

and businesses fall behind on their financial obligations, increasing the amount of debt to be collected. However, the success rate of collectors decreases because fewer people can afford to pay their debts.

Locate and notify customers of delinquent accounts by mail, telephone, or personal visit to solicit payment. Receive payments, and post amounts paid to customer accounts. Locate and monitor overdue accounts, using computers and a variety of automated systems. Record information about financial status of customers and status of collection efforts. Confer with customers by telephone or in person to determine reasons for overdue payments and to review the terms of sales, service, or credit contracts. Advise customers of necessary actions and strategies for debt repayment. Persuade customers to pay amounts due on credit accounts, damage claims, or nonpayable checks or to return merchandise. Sort and file correspondence, and perform miscellaneous clerical duties such as answering correspondence and writing reports. Perform various administrative functions for assigned accounts, such as recording address changes and purging the records of deceased customers. Arrange for debt repayment, or establish repayment schedules based on customers' financial situations. Negotiate credit extensions when necessary. Trace delinquent customers to new addresses by inquiring at post offices, telephone companies, or credit bureaus or through the questioning of neighbors. Notify credit departments, order merchandise repossession or service disconnection, and turn over account records to attorneys when customers fail to respond to collection attempts.

Related Military Specializations: None. **Average Educational Level of Vets:** One or more years of college, no degree. **Usual Educational Requirement:** High school diploma or equivalent. **Relevant Educational Program:** Banking and Financial Support

Services. **Related Knowledge/Courses:** Clerical Practices; Economics and Accounting; Customer and Personal Service; Law and Government; Computers and Electronics. **Work Experience Needed:** None. **On-the-Job Training Needed:** Moderate-term on-the-job training. **Certification/Licensure:** None.

Personality Types: Conventional-Enterprising. **Key Career Cluster:** 06 Finance. **Key Career Pathway:** 6.3 Banking and Related Services. **Top Industries for Vets:** Business Support Services; Nondepository Credit and Related Activities; Banking and Related Activities; National Security and International Affairs; Electric Power Generation, Transmission and Distribution.

Skills: Persuasion; Negotiation; Speaking; Active Listening; Social Perceptiveness; Mathematics; Writing; Critical Thinking.

Work Environment: Indoors; sitting; using hands; repetitive motions; noise.

Billing and Posting Clerks

- ❋ Average Annual Earnings (All): $32,880
- ❋ Average Annual Earnings (Recent Veterans): $26,190
- ❋ Earnings Growth Potential: Low (31.0%)
- ❋ Growth: 19.7%
- ❋ Annual Job Openings: 18,760
- ❋ Veteran Employment by Sector: For-Profit, 78.2%; Nonprofit, 7.9%; Government, 12.3%; Self-Employed, 1.6%.

Considerations for Job Outlook: Job prospects for financial clerks should be favorable, because many workers are expected to leave this occupation. Employers will need to hire new workers to replace those leaving the occupation.

Compile, compute, and record billing, accounting, statistical, and other numerical data for billing purposes. For task data, see Job Specializations.

Related Military Specializations: None. **Average Educational Level of Vets:** One or more years of college, no degree. **Usual Educational Requirement:** High school diploma or equivalent. **Relevant Educational Program:** Accounting Technology/Technician and Bookkeeping. **Work Experience Needed:** None. **On-the-Job Training Needed:** Short-term on-the-job training. **Certification/Licensure:** None.

Key Career Cluster: 16 Transportation, Distribution, and Logistics. **Key Career Pathway:** 16.7 Sales and Service. **Top Industries for Vets:** Hospitals; Offices of Physicians; Broadcasting, Including Internet Publishing and Web Search Portals; Outpatient Care Centers; Accounting, Tax Preparation, Bookkeeping and Payroll Services.

Job Specialization: Billing, Cost, and Rate Clerks

Compile data, compute fees and charges, and prepare invoices for billing purposes. Duties include computing costs and calculating rates for goods, services, and shipment of goods; posting data; and keeping other relevant records. May involve use of computer or typewriter, calculator, and adding and bookkeeping machines. Verify accuracy of billing data, and revise any errors. Operate typing, adding, calculating, and billing machines. Prepare itemized statements, bills, or invoices, and record amounts due for items purchased or services rendered. Review documents such as purchase orders, sales tickets, charge slips, or hospital records to compute fees and charges due. Perform bookkeeping work, including posting data and keeping other records concerning costs of goods and services and the shipment of goods. Keep records of invoices and support documents. Resolve discrepancies in accounting records. Type billing documents, shipping labels, credit memoranda, and credit forms, using typewriters or computers. Contact customers to obtain or relay account information. Compute credit terms, discounts, shipment charges, and rates for goods and services to complete billing documents. Answer mail and telephone inquiries regarding rates, routing, and procedures. Track accumulated hours and dollar amounts charged to each client job to calculate client fees for professional services such as legal and accounting services. Review compiled data on operating costs and revenues to set rates. Compile reports of cost factors, such as labor, production, storage, and equipment. Consult sources such as rate books, manuals, and insurance company representatives to determine specific charges and information such as rules, regulations, and government tax and tariff information.

Related Knowledge/Courses: Clerical Practices; Economics and Accounting; Computers and Electronics.

Personality Types: Conventional-Enterprising.

Skills: Programming; Mathematics; Active Listening; Service Orientation.

Work Environment: Indoors; sitting.

Job Specialization: Statement Clerks

Prepare and distribute bank statements to customers, answer inquiries, and reconcile discrepancies in records and accounts. Encode and cancel checks, using bank machines. Take orders for imprinted checks. Compare previously prepared bank statements with canceled checks, and reconcile discrepancies. Verify signatures and required information on checks. Post stop-payment notices to prevent payment of protested checks. Maintain files of canceled checks and

customers' signatures. Match statements with batches of canceled checks by account numbers. Weigh envelopes containing statements to determine correct postage, and affix postage using stamps or metering equipment. Load machines with statements, canceled checks, and envelopes to prepare statements for distribution to customers, or stuff envelopes by hand. Retrieve checks returned to customers in error, adjusting customer accounts and answering inquiries about errors as necessary. Route statements for mailing or over-the-counter delivery to customers. Monitor equipment to ensure proper operation. Fix minor problems, such as equipment jams, and notify repair personnel of major equipment problems.

Related Knowledge/Courses: Economics and Accounting; Clerical Practices; Administration and Management.

Personality Types: Conventional-Enterprising-Social.

Skills: Programming.

Work Environment: Indoors; sitting; repetitive motions.

Biological Technicians

* Average Annual Earnings (All): $39,480
* Average Annual Earnings (Recent Veterans): $38,200
* Earnings Growth Potential: Medium (36.8%)
* Growth: 13.5%
* Annual Job Openings: 3,790
* Veteran Employment by Sector: For-Profit, 41.3%; Nonprofit, 9.1%; Government, 49.2%; Self-Employed, 0.4%.

Considerations for Job Outlook: Strong competition for jobs is expected. There have been large increases in the number of bachelor's degrees in biology and other life sciences awarded each year, and this trend is expected to continue. Applicants who have laboratory experience, either through coursework or previous work experience, should have the best opportunities.

Assist biological and medical scientists in laboratories. Keep detailed logs of all work-related activities. Monitor laboratory work to ensure compliance with set standards. Isolate, identify, and prepare specimens for examination. Use computers, computer-interfaced equipment, robotics, or high-technology industrial applications to perform work duties. Conduct research or assist in the conduct of research, including the collection of information and samples such as blood, water, soil, plants, and animals. Set up, adjust, calibrate, clean, maintain, and troubleshoot laboratory and field equipment. Provide technical support and services for scientists and engineers working in fields such as agriculture, environmental science, resource management, biology, and health sciences. Clean, maintain, and prepare supplies and work areas. Participate in the research, development, or manufacturing of medicinal and pharmaceutical preparations. Conduct standardized biological, microbiological, or biochemical tests and laboratory analyses to evaluate the quantity or quality of physical or chemical substances in food or other products. Analyze experimental data and interpret results to write reports and summaries of findings. Measure or weigh compounds and solutions for use in testing or animal feed. Monitor and observe experiments, recording production and test data for evaluation by research personnel. Examine animals and specimens to detect the presence of disease or other problems.

Related Military Specialization: Biological Sciences Assistant. **Average Educational Level of Vets:** One or more years of college, no degree. **Usual Educational Requirement:** Bachelor's degree. **Relevant Educational Program:** Biology Technician/Biotechnology Laboratory Technician Training. **Related Knowledge/Courses:** Biology; Chemistry; Computers and Electronics; Mathematics; Mechanical Devices; Engineering and Technology. **Work Experience Needed:** None. **On-the-Job Training Needed:** None. **Certification/Licensure:** None.

Personality Types: Realistic-Investigative-Conventional. **Key Career Cluster:** 15 Science, Technology, Engineering, and Mathematics. **Key Career Pathway:** 15.2 Science and Mathematics. **Top Industries for Vets:** Scientific Research and Development Services; National Security and International Affairs; Architectural, Engineering, and Related Services; Colleges and Universities, Including Junior Colleges; Administration of Environmental Quality and Housing Programs.

Skills: Science; Programming; Troubleshooting; Mathematics; Reading Comprehension; Quality Control Analysis; Operation and Control; Equipment Maintenance.

Work Environment: Indoors; sitting; using hands; repetitive motions; contaminants.

Bookkeeping, Accounting, and Auditing Clerks

❀ Average Annual Earnings (All): $34,740

❀ Average Annual Earnings (Recent Veterans): $31,430

❀ Earnings Growth Potential: Medium (38.3%)

❀ Growth: 13.6%

❀ Annual Job Openings: 46,780

❀ Veteran Employment by Sector: For-Profit, 58.7%; Nonprofit, 5.6%; Government, 35.1%; Self-Employed, 0.6%.

Considerations for Job Outlook: Because this is a large occupation, there will be a large number of job openings from workers leaving the occupation. This means that opportunities to enter the occupation should be plentiful.

Compute, classify, and record numerical data to keep financial records complete. Operate computers programmed with accounting software to record, store, and analyze information. Check figures, postings, and documents for correct entry, mathematical accuracy, and proper codes. Comply with federal, state, and company policies, procedures, and regulations. Debit, credit, and total accounts on computer spreadsheets and databases, using specialized accounting software. Classify, record, and summarize numerical and financial data to compile and keep financial records, using journals and ledgers or computers. Calculate, prepare, and issue bills, invoices, account statements, and other financial statements according to established procedures. Code documents according to company procedures. Compile statistical, financial, accounting, or auditing reports and tables pertaining to such matters as cash receipts, expenditures, accounts payable and receivable, and profits and losses. Operate 10-key calculators, typewriters, and copy machines to perform calculations and produce documents. Access computerized financial information to answer general questions as well as those related to specific accounts. Reconcile or note and report discrepancies found in records. Perform financial calculations such as amounts due, interest charges, balances, discounts, equity, and principal. Perform general office duties such as filing, answering telephones, and handling routine correspondence.

Related Military Specializations: Accounting Specialist; Aviation Storekeeper; Disbursing Afloat Automated Systems Specialist; Financial Management Resource Analyst; Financial Management Technician; Machine Accountant; NAF Audit Technician; Relational Supply Force Advanced Technical Specialist; Relational Supply Force Technical Specialist; Relational Supply Unit Advanced Technical Specialist; Relational Supply Unit Technical Specialist; Storekeeper; Supply and Accounting (SUADPS R/T) Advanced Technical Specialist; others. **Average Educational Level of Vets:** One or more years of college, no degree. **Usual Educational Requirement:** High school diploma or equivalent. **Relevant Educational Program:** Accounting Technology/Technician and Bookkeeping. **Related Knowledge/Courses:** Economics and Accounting; Clerical Practices; Mathematics; Computers and Electronics. **Work Experience Needed:** None. **On-the-Job Training Needed:** Moderate-term on-the-job training. **Certification/Licensure:** None.

Personality Types: Conventional-Enterprising. **Key Career Cluster:** 04 Business, Management, and Administration. **Key Career Pathway:** 4.2 Business Financial Management and Accounting. **Top Industries for Vets:** National Security and International Affairs; Accounting, Tax Preparation, Bookkeeping and Payroll Services;

B

Traveler Accommodation; Banking and Related Activities; Construction.

Skills: Management of Financial Resources; Mathematics; Active Listening; Reading Comprehension; Time Management; Writing; Speaking.

Work Environment: Indoors; sitting; using hands; repetitive motions.

Budget Analysts

- ❀ Average Annual Earnings (All): $69,090
- ❀ Average Annual Earnings (Recent Veterans): $65,480
- ❀ Earnings Growth Potential: Low (34.3%)
- ❀ Growth: 10.4%
- ❀ Annual Job Openings: 1,960
- ❀ Veteran Employment by Sector: For-Profit, 22.6%; Nonprofit, 0.0%; Government, 77.4%; Self-Employed, 0.0%.

Considerations for Job Outlook: The greater complexity of the job and its expanding job duties are expected to create a need for more budget analysts. Efficient use of public funds is increasingly expected.

Examine budget estimates for completeness, accuracy, and conformance with procedures and regulations. Direct the preparation of regular and special budget reports. Consult with managers to ensure that budget adjustments are made in accordance with program changes. Match appropriations for specific programs with appropriations for broader programs, including items for emergency funds. Provide advice and technical assistance with cost analysis, fiscal allocation, and budget preparation. Summarize budgets, and submit recommendations for the approval or disapproval of funds requests. Seek new ways to improve efficiency and increase profits. Review operating budgets to analyze trends affecting budget needs. Perform cost-benefit analyses to compare operating programs, review financial requests, or explore alternative financing methods. Interpret budget directives, and establish policies for carrying out directives. Compile and analyze accounting records and other data to determine the financial resources required to implement a program. Testify before examining and fund-granting authorities, clarifying and promoting the proposed budgets.

Related Military Specializations: Accounting Officer; Budget Officer; Designated Project Business Administrator; Financial Management Specialist; Planning, Programming, and Budgeting System Officer; Program/Budget. **Average Educational Level of Vets:** Bachelor's degree. **Usual Educational Requirement:** Bachelor's degree. **Relevant Educational Programs:** Accounting; Accounting and Finance; Finance, General; Public Finance. **Related Knowledge/Courses:** Economics and Accounting; Clerical Practices; Administration and Management; Mathematics; Personnel and Human Resources; Law and Government. **Work Experience Needed:** None. **On-the-Job Training Needed:** None. **Certification/Licensure:** None.

Personality Types: Conventional-Enterprising-Investigative. **Key Career Cluster:** 04 Business, Management, and Administration. **Key Career Pathway:** 4.4 Business Analysis. **Top Industries for Vets:** National Security and International Affairs; Public Finance Activities; Executive Offices and Legislative Bodies; Aerospace Products and Parts; Elementary and Secondary Schools.

Skills: Management of Financial Resources; Operations Analysis; Systems Analysis;

Mathematics; Management of Material Resources; Systems Evaluation; Judgment and Decision Making; Active Learning.

Work Environment: Indoors; sitting; repetitive motions.

Bus and Truck Mechanics and Diesel Engine Specialists

- ❈ Average Annual Earnings (All): $41,640
- ❈ Average Annual Earnings (Recent Veterans): $38,200
- ❈ Earnings Growth Potential: Medium (36.4%)
- ❈ Growth: 14.5%
- ❈ Annual Job Openings: 8,780
- ❈ Veteran Employment by Sector: For-Profit, 54.6%; Nonprofit, 0.5%; Government, 44.2%; Self-Employed, 0.8%.

Considerations for Job Outlook: Job opportunities should be good for those who have completed formal postsecondary education and have strong technical skills, as employers sometimes report difficulty finding qualified workers. Workers without formal training often require more supervision and on-the-job instruction than others— an expensive and time-consuming process for employers. Because of this, untrained candidates will face strong competition for jobs.

Diagnose, adjust, repair, or overhaul buses and trucks, or maintain and repair any type of diesel engines. Use hand tools such as screwdrivers, pliers, wrenches, pressure gauges, and precision instruments, as well as power tools such as pneumatic wrenches, lathes, welding equipment, and jacks and hoists. Inspect brake systems, steering mechanisms, wheel bearings, and other important parts to ensure that they are in proper operating condition. Adjust and reline brakes, align wheels, tighten bolts and screws, and reassemble equipment. Raise trucks, buses, and heavy parts or equipment using hydraulic jacks or hoists. Perform routine maintenance such as changing oil, checking batteries, and lubricating equipment and machinery. Test drive trucks and buses to diagnose malfunctions or to ensure that they are working properly. Examine and adjust protective guards, loose bolts, and specified safety devices. Attach test instruments to equipment, and read dials and gauges to diagnose malfunctions. Inspect, test, and listen to defective equipment to diagnose malfunctions, using test instruments such as handheld computers, motor analyzers, chassis charts, and pressure gauges. Inspect, repair, and maintain automotive and mechanical equipment and machinery such as pumps and compressors. Rewire ignition systems, lights, and instrument panels. Diagnose and repair vehicle heating and cooling systems. Recondition and replace parts, pistons, bearings, gears, and valves. Inspect and verify dimensions and clearances of parts to ensure conformance to factory specifications. Disassemble and overhaul internal combustion engines, pumps, generators, transmissions, clutches, and differential units. Specialize in repairing and maintaining parts of the engine, such as fuel injection systems. Repair and adjust seats, doors, and windows, and install and repair accessories. Rebuild gas or diesel engines. Align front ends and suspension systems. Operate valve-grinding machines to grind and reset valves.

Related Military Specializations: 16V146TI Diesel Engine/Waste Heat System Technician; Advanced Construction Mechanic; ALCO (251C), and General Motors EMD (645) Diesel Engine Technician; Assault Amphibious Vehicle (AAV) Repairer/Technician; Assault Breacher Vehicle/Joint Assault Bridge (JAB) Mechanic; Aviation Support Equipment Technician Basic;

Aviation Support Equipmentman; Battle Force Intermediate Maintenance Activity (BFIMA) Governor and Injector Repair Technician; others. **Average Educational Level of Vets:** High school diploma or equivalent. **Usual Educational Requirement:** High school diploma or equivalent. **Relevant Educational Programs:** Diesel Mechanics Technology/Technician; Medium/Heavy Vehicle and Truck Technology/Technician. **Related Knowledge/Courses:** Mechanical Devices; Transportation; Physics; Public Safety and Security; Engineering and Technology; Mathematics. **Work Experience Needed:** None. **On-the-Job Training Needed:** Long-term on-the-job training. **Certification/Licensure:** Voluntary certification by association.

Personality Types: Realistic-Conventional. **Key Career Cluster:** 16 Transportation, Distribution, and Logistics. **Key Career Pathway:** 16.4 Facility and Mobile Equipment Maintenance. **Top Industries for Vets:** National Security and International Affairs; Automotive Repair and Maintenance; Truck Transportation; Bus Service and Urban Transit; Elementary and Secondary Schools.

Skills: Repairing; Equipment Maintenance; Troubleshooting; Equipment Selection; Operation and Control; Quality Control Analysis; Operation Monitoring; Installation.

Work Environment: Outdoors; standing; walking and running; kneeling, crouching, stooping, or crawling; using hands; bending or twisting the body; repetitive motions; noise; very hot or cold; bright or inadequate lighting; contaminants; cramped work space; hazardous conditions; hazardous equipment; minor burns, cuts, bites, or stings.

Bus Drivers, Transit and Intercity

- ❋ Average Annual Earnings (All): $35,720
- ❋ Average Annual Earnings (Recent Veterans): $23,570
- ❋ Earnings Growth Potential: High (41.0%)
- ❋ Growth: 14.8%
- ❋ Annual Job Openings: 6,350
- ❋ Veteran Employment by Sector: For-Profit, 46.7%; Nonprofit, 4.0%; Government, 47.8%; Self-Employed, 1.4%.

Considerations for Job Outlook: Job opportunities for bus drivers should be favorable, especially for school bus drivers, as many drivers leave the occupation. Those willing to work part time or irregular shifts should have the best prospects. Prospects for motor coach drivers will depend on tourism, which fluctuates with the economy.

Drive bus or motor coach, including regular route operations, charters, and private carriage. Inspect vehicles, and check gas, oil, and water levels prior to departure. Park vehicles at loading areas so that passengers can board. Report delays or accidents. Advise passengers to be seated and orderly while on vehicles. Regulate heating, lighting, and ventilating systems for passenger comfort. Drive vehicles over specified routes or to specified destinations according to time schedules, complying with traffic regulations to ensure that passengers have a smooth and safe ride. Assist passengers, such as elderly or disabled individuals, on and off bus, ensure they are seated properly, help carry baggage, and answer questions about bus schedules or routes. Handle passenger emergencies or disruptions. Record information, such as cash receipts and ticket fares, and maintain log book. Collect tickets or cash fares from passengers. Maintain cleanliness of bus or motor coach.

Related Military Specialization: Vehicle Operations Journeyman. **Average Educational Level of Vets:** High school diploma or equivalent. **Usual Educational Requirement:** High school diploma or equivalent. **Relevant Educational Program:** Truck and Bus Driver Training/ Commercial Vehicle Operator and Instructor Training. **Related Knowledge/Courses:** Transportation; Public Safety and Security; Geography; Psychology; Telecommunications; Customer and Personal Service. **Work Experience Needed:** None. **On-the-Job Training Needed:** Moderate-term on-the-job training. **Certification/Licensure:** Licensure.

Personality Types: Realistic-Social. **Key Career Cluster:** 16 Transportation, Distribution, and Logistics. **Key Career Pathway:** 16.1 Transportation Operations. **Top Industries for Vets:** Bus Service and Urban Transit; Elementary and Secondary Schools; National Security and International Affairs; Travel Arrangements and Reservation Services; Scenic and Sightseeing Transportation.

Skills: Operation and Control; Operation Monitoring; Troubleshooting; Equipment Maintenance; Repairing.

Work Environment: Outdoors; sitting; using hands; repetitive motions; noise; very hot or cold; bright or inadequate lighting; contaminants; exposed to disease or infections.

Business Operations Specialists, All Other

- ❋ Average Annual Earnings (All): $64,030
- ❋ Average Annual Earnings (Recent Veterans): $56,750
- ❋ Earnings Growth Potential: High (46.5%)
- ❋ Growth: 11.6%
- ❋ Annual Job Openings: 32,720
- ❋ Veteran Employment by Sector: For-Profit, 38.1%; Nonprofit, 3.5%; Government, 57.2%; Self-Employed, 1.1%.

Considerations for Job Outlook: In federal government, a small increase is expected as positions with specialized titles in areas such as defense and energy increase.

All business operations specialists not listed separately. For task data, see Job Specializations.

Related Military Specializations: Civil Affairs Noncommissioned Officer; Civil Affairs Non-Commissioned Officer; Civil Affairs Specialist; Civil Affairs Specialist (RC); Civil Air Patrol (CAP)-USAF Reserve Assistance NCO; Defense Attaché; Disaster Preparedness Operations and Training Specialist; Emergency Management Apprentice; Emergency Management Craftsman; Emergency Management Helper; Emergency Management Journeyman; Emergency Management Superintendent; Expeditionary Force—Maritime Civil Affairs; others. **Average Educational Level of Vets:** Bachelor's degree. **Usual Educational Requirement:** High school diploma or equivalent. **Relevant Educational Program:** Business Administration and Management, General. **Work Experience Needed:** Less than 1 year. **On-the-Job Training Needed:** Long-term on-the-job training.

Certification/Licensure: Licensure for some specializations; voluntary certification by association.

Key Career Cluster: 04 Business, Management, and Administration. **Key Career Pathway:** 4.1 Management. **Top Industries for Vets:** National Security and International Affairs; Architectural, Engineering, and Related Services; Administration of Human Resource Programs; Management, Scientific and Technical Consulting Services; Construction.

Job Specialization: Business Continuity Planners

Develop, maintain, and implement business continuity and disaster recovery strategies and solutions. Perform risk analyses. Act as a coordinator for recovery efforts in emergency situations. Write reports to summarize testing activities, including descriptions of goals, planning, scheduling, execution, results, analysis, conclusions, and recommendations. Maintain and update organization information technology applications and network systems blueprints. Interpret government regulations and applicable codes to ensure compliance. Identify individual or transaction targets to direct intelligence collection. Establish, maintain, or test call trees to ensure appropriate communication during disaster. Design or implement products and services to mitigate risk, or facilitate use of technology-based tools and methods. Create business continuity and disaster recovery budgets. Create or administer training and awareness presentations or materials. Attend professional meetings, read literature, and participate in training or other educational offerings to keep abreast of new developments and technologies related to disaster recovery and business continuity. Test documented disaster recovery strategies and plans. Review existing disaster recovery, crisis management, or business continuity plans. Recommend or implement methods to monitor, evaluate, or enable resolution of safety, operations, or compliance interruptions. Prepare reports summarizing operational results, financial performance, or accomplishments of specified objectives, goals, or plans.

Related Knowledge/Courses: Public Safety and Security; Telecommunications; Administration and Management; Communications and Media; Geography; Economics and Accounting.

Personality Types: No data available.

Skills: Management of Financial Resources; Management of Material Resources; Complex Problem Solving; Systems Analysis; Systems Evaluation; Judgment and Decision Making; Operations Analysis; Critical Thinking.

Work Environment: Indoors; sitting.

Job Specialization: Customs Brokers

Prepare customs documentation and ensure that shipments meet all applicable laws to facilitate the import and export of goods. Determine and track duties and taxes payable and process payments on behalf of client. Sign documents under a power of attorney. Represent clients in meetings with customs officials and apply for duty refunds and tariff reclassifications. Coordinate transportation and storage of imported goods. Sign documents on behalf of clients, using powers of attorney. Provide advice on transportation options, types of carriers, or shipping routes. Post bonds for the products being imported, or assist clients in obtaining bonds. Insure cargo against loss, damage, or pilferage. Obtain line releases for frequent shippers of low-risk commodities, high-volume entries, or multiple-container loads. Contract with freight forwarders for destination services. Arrange for transportation, warehousing, or product distribution of imported or exported products. Suggest best methods of packaging or labeling products. Request or compile necessary import documentation, such as customs invoices, certificates of origin, and cargo-control documents. Stay abreast of changes in import or export laws or regulations by reading current literature, attending meetings or conferences, or conferring with colleagues. Quote duty and tax rates on goods to be imported, based on federal tariffs and excise taxes. Prepare papers for shippers to appeal duty charges. Pay, or arrange for payment of, taxes and duties on shipments. Monitor or trace the location of goods. Maintain relationships with customs brokers in other ports to expedite clearing of cargo. Inform importers and exporters of steps to reduce duties and taxes. Confer with officials in various agencies to facilitate clearance of goods through customs and quarantine. Classify goods according to tariff coding system.

Related Knowledge/Courses: Clerical Practices; Geography; Transportation; Sales and Marketing; Law and Government; Economics and Accounting.

Personality Types: Enterprising-Conventional.

Skills: Management of Financial Resources; Management of Material Resources; Negotiation; Programming; Mathematics; Management of Personnel Resources; Writing; Systems Analysis.

Work Environment: Indoors; sitting.

Job Specialization: Energy Auditors

Conduct energy audits of buildings, building systems, and process systems. May also conduct investment grade audits of buildings or systems. Identify and prioritize energy-saving measures. Prepare audit reports containing energy analysis results and recommendations for energy cost savings. Inspect or evaluate building envelopes, mechanical systems, electrical systems, or process systems to determine the energy consumption of each system. Collect and analyze field data related to energy usage. Perform tests such as blower-door tests to locate air leaks. Calculate potential for energy savings. Educate customers on energy efficiency, or answer questions on topics such as the costs of running household appliances and the selection of energy-efficient appliances. Recommend energy-efficient technologies or alternate energy sources. Prepare job specification sheets for home energy improvements such as attic insulation, window retrofits, and heating system upgrades. Quantify energy consumption to establish baselines for energy use and need. Identify opportunities to improve the operation, maintenance, or energy efficiency of building or process systems. Analyze technical feasibility of energy-saving measures using knowledge of engineering, energy production, energy use, construction, maintenance, system operation, or process systems. Analyze energy bills including utility rates or tariffs to gather historical energy-usage data.

Related Knowledge/Courses: Building and Construction; Physics; Sales and Marketing; Design; Clerical Practices; Mechanical Devices.

Personality Types: Conventional-Enterprising.

Skills: Operations Analysis; Science; Systems Evaluation; Systems Analysis; Mathematics; Management of Financial Resources; Operation and Control; Writing.

Work Environment: More often outdoors than indoors; standing; using hands; very hot or cold; bright or inadequate lighting; contaminants; cramped work space; high places.

Job Specialization: Online Merchants

Plan, direct, or coordinate retail activities of businesses operating online. May perform duties such as preparing business strategies, buying merchandise, managing inventory, implementing marketing activities, fulfilling

and shipping online orders, and balancing financial records. Participate in online forums and conferences to stay abreast of online retailing trends, techniques, and security threats. Upload digital media, such as photos, video, or scanned images to online storefront, auction sites, or other shopping websites. Order or purchase merchandise to maintain optimal inventory levels. Maintain inventory of shipping supplies, such as boxes, labels, tape, bubble wrap, loose packing materials, and tape guns. Integrate online retailing strategy with physical and catalogue retailing operations. Determine and set product prices. Disclose merchant information and terms and policies of transactions in online and offline materials. Deliver e-mail confirmation of completed transactions and shipment. Create, manage, and automate orders and invoices using order management and invoicing software. Create and maintain database of customer accounts. Create and distribute offline promotional material, such as brochures, pamphlets, business cards, stationary, and signage. Collaborate with search engine shopping specialists to place marketing content in desired online locations. Cancel orders based on customer requests or problems with inventory or delivery. Transfer digital media, such as music, video, and software, to customers via the Internet. Select and purchase technical web services, such as web hosting services, online merchant accounts, shopping cart software, payment gateway software, and spyware.

Related Knowledge/Courses: No data available.

Personality Types:
Enterprising-Conventional-Realistic.

Skills: No data available.

Work Environment: No data available.

Job Specialization: Security Management Specialists

Conduct security assessments for organizations, and design security systems and processes. May specialize in areas such as physical security, personnel security, and information security. May work in fields such as health care, banking, gaming, security engineering, or manufacturing. Prepare documentation for case reports or court proceedings. Review design drawings or technical documents for completeness, correctness, or appropriateness. Monitor tapes or digital recordings to identify the source of losses. Interview witnesses or suspects to identify persons responsible for security breaches, establish losses, pursue prosecutions, or obtain restitution. Budget and schedule security design work. Develop conceptual designs of security systems. Respond to emergency situations on an on-call basis. Train personnel in security procedures or use of security equipment. Prepare, maintain, or update security procedures, security system drawings, or related documentation. Monitor the work of contractors in the design, construction, and startup phases of security systems. Inspect security design features, installations, or programs to ensure compliance with applicable standards or regulations. Inspect fire, intruder detection, or other security systems. Engineer, install, maintain, or repair security systems, programmable logic controls, or other security-related electronic systems. Recommend improvements in security systems or procedures. Develop or review specifications for design or construction of security systems. Design security policies, programs, or practices to ensure adequate security relating to issues such as protection of assets, alarm response, and access card use.

Related Knowledge/Courses: No data available.

Personality Types:
Realistic-Investigative-Conventional.

Skills: No data available.

Work Environment: No data available.

Job Specialization: Sustainability Specialists

Address organizational sustainability issues, such as waste stream management, green building practices, and green procurement plans. Review and revise sustainability proposals or policies. Research or review regulatory, technical, or market issues related to sustainability. Identify or investigate violations of natural resources, waste management, recycling, or other environmental policies. Identify or create new sustainability indicators. Write grant applications, rebate applications, or project proposals to secure funding for sustainability projects. Provide technical or administrative support for sustainability programs or issues. Identify or procure needed resources to implement sustainability programs or projects. Create or maintain plans or other documents related to sustainability projects. Develop reports or presentations to communicate the effectiveness of sustainability initiatives. Create marketing or outreach media, such as brochures or websites, to communicate sustainability issues, procedures, or objectives. Collect information about waste stream management or green building practices to inform decision-makers. Assess or propose sustainability initiatives, considering factors such as cost effectiveness, technical feasibility, and acceptance. Monitor or track sustainability indicators, such as energy usage, natural resource usage, waste generation, and recycling. Develop sustainability project goals, objectives, initiatives, or strategies in collaboration with other sustainability professionals.

Related Knowledge/Courses: No data available.

Personality Types: No data available.

Skills: No data available.

Work Environment: No data available.

Captains, Mates, and Pilots of Water Vessels

* Average Annual Earnings (All): $63,920

* Average Annual Earnings (Recent Veterans): $43,650

* Earnings Growth Potential: Very high (51.8%)

* Growth: 20.4%

* Annual Job Openings: 2,070

* Veteran Employment by Sector: For-Profit, 37.7%; Nonprofit, 0.0%; Government, 60.2%; Self-Employed, 2.2%.

Considerations for Job Outlook: Job prospects should be favorable. Many workers leave water transportation occupations, especially sailors and marine oilers, because recently hired workers often decide they do not enjoy spending a lot of time away at sea. In addition, a number of officers and engineers are approaching retirement, creating job openings. The number of applicants for all types of jobs may be limited by high regulatory and security requirements.

Command or supervise operations of ships and water vessels, such as tugboats and ferryboats. For task data, see Job Specializations.

Related Military Specializations: Boatswain's Mate; Causeway Barge Ferry Coxswain; Causeway Barge Ferry Pilot; Causeway Lighterage Craftmaster; Chief of The Boat (All Submarines); Deep Submergence Vehicle Crewmember; Deep Submergence Vehicle Operator; Harbor/Docking Pilot; Landing Craft Utility Craftsmaster; LCAC Loadmaster; Minesweeping Boatswain's Mate; Navy Lighterage Deck Supervisor; Quartermaster; Tugmaster; Unmanned Undersea Vehicle (UUV) Operator; Watercraft Operator.

Average Educational Level of Vets: High school diploma or equivalent. **Usual Educational Requirement:** Bachelor's degree. **Relevant Educational Programs:** Commercial Fishing; Marine Science/Merchant Marine Officer. **Work Experience Needed:** None. **On-the-Job Training Needed:** None. **Certification/Licensure:** Licensure.

Key Career Cluster: 16 Transportation, Distribution, and Logistics. **Key Career Pathway:** 16.1 Transportation Operations. **Top Industries for Vets:** National Security and International Affairs; Water Transportation; Services Incidental to Transportation; Administration of Economic Programs and Space Research; Architectural, Engineering, and Related Services.

Job Specialization: Mates—Ship, Boat, and Barge

Supervise and coordinate activities of crew aboard ships, boats, barges, or dredges. Determine geographical positions of ships, using lorans, azimuths of celestial bodies, or computers, and use this information to determine the course and speed of a ship. Supervise crews in cleaning and maintaining decks, superstructures, and bridges. Supervise crew members in the repair or replacement of defective gear and equipment. Steer vessels, utilizing navigational devices such as compasses and sextons, and navigational aids such as lighthouses and buoys. Observe water from ships' mastheads in order to advise on navigational direction. Inspect equipment such as cargo-handling gear, lifesaving equipment, visual-signaling equipment, and fishing, towing, or dredging gear, in order to detect problems. Arrange for ships to be stocked, fueled, and repaired. Assume command of vessels in the event that ships' masters become incapacitated. Participate in activities related to maintenance

of vessel security. Stand watches on vessels during specified periods while vessels are under way. Observe loading and unloading of cargo and equipment to ensure that handling and storage are performed according to specifications.

Related Knowledge/Courses: Transportation; Geography; Public Safety and Security; Telecommunications; Personnel and Human Resources; Mechanical Devices.

Personality Types: Enterprising-Realistic-Conventional.

Skills: Repairing; Equipment Maintenance; Operation and Control; Troubleshooting; Operation Monitoring; Equipment Selection; Quality Control Analysis; Management of Personnel Resources.

Work Environment: More often outdoors than indoors; standing; balancing; using hands; noise; very hot or cold; bright or inadequate lighting; contaminants; cramped work space; whole-body vibration; high places; hazardous conditions; hazardous equipment; minor burns, cuts, bites, or stings.

Job Specialization: Pilots, Ship

Command ships to steer them into and out of harbors, estuaries, straits, and sounds and on rivers, lakes, and bays. Must be licensed by U.S. Coast Guard with limitations indicating class and tonnage of vessels for which licenses are valid and routes and waters that may be piloted. Maintain and repair boats and equipment. Give directions to crew members who are steering ships. Make nautical maps. Set ships' courses that avoid reefs, outlying shoals, and other hazards, utilizing navigational aids such as lighthouses and buoys. Report to appropriate authorities any violations of federal or state pilotage laws. Relieve crew members on tugs and launches. Provide assistance to vessels approaching or leaving seacoasts, navigating harbors, and docking and undocking. Provide assistance in maritime rescue operations. Prevent ships under their navigational control from engaging in unsafe operations. Operate amphibious craft during troop landings. Maintain ship logs. Learn to operate new technology systems and procedures, through the use of instruction, simulators, and models. Advise ships' masters on harbor rules and customs procedures. Steer ships into and out of berths, or signal tugboat captains to berth and unberth ships. Serve as a vessel's docking master upon arrival at a port and when at a berth. Operate ship-to-shore radios to exchange information needed for ship operations. Consult maps, charts, weather reports, and navigation equipment to determine and direct ship movements. Direct courses and speeds of ships, based on specialized knowledge of local winds, weather, water depths, tides, currents, and hazards. Oversee cargo storage on or below decks.

Related Knowledge/Courses: Transportation; Geography; Public Safety and Security; Telecommunications; Mechanical Devices; Law and Government.

Personality Types:
Realistic-Conventional-Investigative.

Skills: Operation and Control; Operation Monitoring; Troubleshooting; Equipment Maintenance; Management of Personnel Resources; Repairing; Quality Control Analysis; Complex Problem Solving.

Work Environment: More often outdoors than indoors; standing; using hands; noise; very hot or cold; bright or inadequate lighting; contaminants; whole-body vibration; hazardous conditions.

Job Specialization: Ship and Boat Captains

Command vessels in oceans, bays, lakes, rivers, and coastal waters. Assign watches and living quarters to crew members. Sort logs, form log booms, and salvage lost logs. Perform various marine duties such as checking for oil spills or other pollutants around ports and harbors, and patrolling beaches. Contact buyers to sell cargo such as fish. Tow and maneuver barges, or signal tugboats to tow barges to destinations. Signal passing vessels, using whistles, flashing lights, flags, and radios. Resolve questions or problems with customs officials. Read gauges to verify sufficient levels of hydraulic fluid, air pressure, and oxygen. Purchase supplies and equipment. Measure depths of water, using depth-measuring equipment. Maintain boats and equipment on board, such as engines, winches, navigational systems, fire extinguishers, and life preservers. Collect fares from customers, or signal ferryboat helpers to collect fares. Arrange for ships to be fueled, restocked with supplies, and/or repaired. Signal crew members or deckhands to rig tow lines, open or close gates and ramps, and pull guard chains across entries. Maintain records of daily activities, personnel reports, ship positions and movements, ports of call, weather and sea conditions, pollution control efforts, and/or cargo and passenger status. Inspect vessels to ensure efficient and safe operation of vessels and equipment, and conformance to regulations. Direct and coordinate crew members or workers performing activities such as loading and unloading cargo, steering vessels, operating engines, and operating, maintaining, and repairing ship equipment. Compute positions, set courses, and determine speeds, by using charts, area plotting sheets, compasses, sextants, and knowledge of local conditions. Calculate sightings of land, using electronic sounding devices, and following contour lines on charts. Monitor the loading and discharging of cargo or passengers. Interview and hire crew members.

Related Knowledge/Courses: Transportation; Public Safety and Security; Geography; Telecommunications; Mechanical Devices; Psychology.

Personality Types: Enterprising-Realistic.

Skills: Operation and Control; Repairing; Management of Material Resources; Management of Financial Resources; Equipment Maintenance; Troubleshooting; Operation Monitoring; Equipment Selection.

Work Environment: More often outdoors than indoors; standing; using hands; repetitive motions; noise; very hot or cold; bright or inadequate lighting; contaminants; whole-body vibration; hazardous equipment; minor burns, cuts, bites, or stings.

Cardiovascular Technologists and Technicians

- ❋ Average Annual Earnings (All): $51,020
- ❋ Average Annual Earnings (Recent Veterans): $43,650
- ❋ Earnings Growth Potential: High (46.2%)
- ❋ Growth: 29.3%
- ❋ Annual Job Openings: 2,210
- ❋ Veteran Employment by Sector: For-Profit, 48.2%; Nonprofit, 18.5%; Government, 32.5%; Self-Employed, 0.8%.

Considerations for Job Outlook: Job prospects should be best for those who have multiple professional credentials and are trained to do a wide range of procedures. Technologists or technicians

who are willing to move or to work irregular hours also should have better opportunities.

Conduct tests on pulmonary or cardiovascular systems of patients for diagnostic purposes. Monitor patients' blood pressure and heart rate using electrocardiogram (EKG) equipment during diagnostic and therapeutic procedures to notify the physician if something appears wrong. Monitor patients' comfort and safety during tests, alerting physicians to abnormalities or changes in patient responses. Explain testing procedures to patient to obtain cooperation and reduce anxiety. Prepare reports of diagnostic procedures for interpretation by physician. Observe gauges, recorder, and video screens of data analysis system during imaging of cardiovascular system. Conduct electrocardiogram (EKG), phonocardiogram, echocardiogram, stress testing, or other cardiovascular tests to record patients' cardiac activity, using specialized electronic test equipment, recording devices, and laboratory instruments. Prepare and position patients for testing. Obtain and record patient identification, medical history or test results. Attach electrodes to the patients' chests, arms, and legs, connect electrodes to leads from the electrocardiogram (EKG) machine, and operate the EKG machine to obtain a reading. Adjust equipment and controls according to physicians' orders or established protocol. Check, test, and maintain cardiology equipment, making minor repairs when necessary, to ensure proper operation. Supervise and train other cardiology technologists and students. Assist physicians in diagnosis and treatment of cardiac and peripheral vascular treatments, for example, assisting with balloon angioplasties to treat blood vessel blockages. Operate diagnostic imaging equipment to produce contrast enhanced radiographs of heart and cardiovascular system. Inject contrast medium into patients' blood vessels. Observe ultrasound display screen and listen to signals to record vascular information such as blood pressure, limb volume changes, oxygen saturation and cerebral circulation. Assess cardiac physiology and calculate valve areas from blood flow velocity measurements.

Related Military Specializations: Cardiopulmonary Laboratory Apprentice; Cardiopulmonary Laboratory Craftsman; Cardiopulmonary Laboratory Helper; Cardiopulmonary Laboratory Journeyman; Cardiopulmonary Laboratory Manager; Cardiopulmonary Laboratory Superintendent; Cardiovascular Technician. **Average Educational Level of Vets:** Associate degree. **Usual Educational Requirement:** Associate degree. **Relevant Educational Programs:** Cardiopulmonary Technology/Technologist; Cardiovascular Technology/Technologist; Electrocardiograph Technology/Technician; Perfusion Technology/Perfusionist. **Related Knowledge/Courses:** Medicine and Dentistry; Biology; Psychology; Customer and Personal Service; Sociology and Anthropology; Chemistry. **Work Experience Needed:** None. **On-the-Job Training Needed:** None. **Certification/ Licensure:** Voluntary certification by association.

Personality Types: Realistic-Investigative-Social. **Key Career Cluster:** 08 Health Science. **Key Career Pathway:** 8.2 Diagnostics Services. **Top Industries for Vets:** Hospitals; National Security and International Affairs; Other Health Care Services; Offices of Physicians; Outpatient Care Centers.

Skills: Science; Equipment Maintenance; Operation and Control; Repairing; Operation Monitoring; Service Orientation; Equipment Selection; Troubleshooting.

Work Environment: Indoors; standing; walking and running; using hands; repetitive motions; exposed to radiation; exposed to disease or infections.

Carpenters

- Average Annual Earnings (All): $40,010
- Average Annual Earnings (Recent Veterans): $29,360
- Earnings Growth Potential: Medium (37.8%)
- Growth: 19.6%
- Annual Job Openings: 40,830
- Veteran Employment by Sector: For-Profit, 71.8%; Nonprofit, 0.8%; Government, 8.2%; Self-Employed, 19.2%.

Considerations for Job Outlook: Overall job prospects for carpenters should improve over the coming decade as construction activity rebounds from the recent recession. The number of openings is expected to vary by geographic area. Because construction activity parallels the movement of people and businesses, areas of the country with the largest population increases will require the most carpenters. Employment of carpenters, like that of many other construction workers, is sensitive to fluctuations in the economy. On the one hand, workers in these trades may experience periods of unemployment when the overall level of construction falls. On the other hand, peak periods of building activity may produce shortages of carpenters. Experienced carpenters should have the best job opportunities.

Construct, erect, install, or repair structures and fixtures made of wood. For task data, see Job Specializations.

Related Military Specializations: Basic Engineer, Construction, and Equipment Marine; Builder; Builder—Heavy; Builder—Light; Builder Basic; Carpentry and Masonry Specialist; Carpentry and Masonry Specialist; Combat

Engineer; Structural Apprentice; Structural Helper; Structural Journeyman. **Average Educational Level of Vets:** High school diploma or equivalent. **Usual Educational Requirement:** High school diploma or equivalent. **Relevant Educational Program:** Carpentry/Carpenter. **Work Experience Needed:** None. **On-the-Job Training Needed:** Apprenticeship. **Certification/Licensure:** None.

Key Career Cluster: 02 Architecture and Construction. **Key Career Pathway:** 2.2 Construction. **Top Industries for Vets:** Construction; National Security and International Affairs; Furniture and Related Products; Ship and Boat Building; Prefabricated Wood Buildings and Mobile Homes.

Job Specialization: Construction Carpenters

Construct, erect, install, and repair structures and fixtures of wood, plywood, and wallboard, using carpenter's hand tools and power tools. Measure and mark cutting lines on materials, using ruler, pencil, chalk, and marking gauge. Follow established safety rules and regulations, and maintain a safe and clean environment. Verify trueness of structure using plumb bob and level. Shape or cut materials to specified measurements using hand tools, machines, or power saw. Study specifications in blueprints, sketches, or building plans to prepare project layout and determine dimensions and materials required. Assemble and fasten materials to make framework or props using hand tools and wood screws, nails, dowel pins, or glue. Build or repair cabinets, doors, frameworks, floors, and other wooden fixtures included in buildings using woodworking machines, carpenter's hand tools, and power tools. Erect scaffolding and ladders for assembling structures above ground level. Remove damaged or defective parts or sections of structures, and repair or replace using hand tools. Install structures and fixtures, such as windows, frames, floorings, and trim, or hardware, using carpenter's hand and power tools. Select and order lumber and other required materials. Maintain records, document actions, and present written progress reports. Finish surfaces of woodwork or wallboard in houses and buildings using paint, hand tools, and paneling. Prepare cost estimates for clients or employers. Arrange for subcontractors to deal with special areas such as heating and electrical wiring work.

Related Knowledge/Courses: Building and Construction; Design; Mechanical Devices; Engineering and Technology; Production and Processing; Mathematics.

Personality Types: Realistic-Conventional-Investigative.

Skills: Repairing; Equipment Selection; Installation; Quality Control Analysis; Equipment Maintenance; Operation and Control; Troubleshooting; Management of Material Resources.

Work Environment: Outdoors; standing; walking and running; kneeling, crouching, stooping, or crawling; using hands; bending or twisting the body; repetitive motions; noise; very hot or cold; bright or inadequate lighting; contaminants; cramped work space; high places; hazardous equipment; minor burns, cuts, bites, or stings.

Job Specialization: Rough Carpenters

Build rough wooden structures, such as concrete forms, scaffolds, tunnel, bridge, or sewer supports, billboard signs, and temporary frame shelters, according to sketches, blueprints, or oral instructions. Study blueprints and diagrams to determine dimensions of structure or form to be constructed. Measure materials or distances, using square, measuring tape, or rule to lay out work. Cut or saw boards, timbers, or plywood to required size, using handsaw, power saw, or woodworking machine. Assemble and fasten material together to construct wood or metal framework of structure, using bolts, nails, or screws. Anchor and brace forms and other structures in place, using nails, bolts, anchor rods, steel cables, planks, wedges, and timbers. Mark cutting lines on materials, using pencil and scriber. Erect forms, framework, scaffolds, hoists, roof supports, or chutes, using hand tools, plumb rule, and level. Install rough door and window frames, subflooring, fixtures, or temporary supports in structures undergoing construction or repair. Examine structural timbers and supports to detect decay and replace timbers as required, using hand tools, nuts, and bolts. Bore boltholes in timber, masonry, or concrete walls, using power drill. Fabricate parts, using woodworking and metalworking machines. Dig or direct digging of post holes and set poles to support structures. Build sleds from logs and timbers for use in hauling camp buildings and machinery through wooded areas. Build chutes for pouring concrete.

Related Knowledge/Courses: Building and Construction; Design; Mechanical Devices; Production and Processing; Public Safety and Security; Mathematics.

Personality Types:
Realistic-Conventional-Investigative.

Skills: Repairing; Equipment Maintenance; Troubleshooting; Operation and Control; Installation; Mathematics; Operation Monitoring; Coordination.

Work Environment: Outdoors; standing; walking and running; kneeling, crouching, stooping, or crawling; balancing; using hands; bending or twisting the body; repetitive motions; noise; very hot or cold; contaminants; cramped work space; high places; hazardous equipment; minor burns, cuts, bites, or stings.

Civil Engineering Technicians

- ❋ Average Annual Earnings (All): $46,900
- ❋ Average Annual Earnings (Recent Veterans): $48,460
- ❋ Earnings Growth Potential: Medium (38.3%)
- ❋ Growth: 12.0%
- ❋ Annual Job Openings: 2,460
- ❋ Veteran Employment by Sector: For-Profit, 60.8%; Nonprofit, 0.8%; Government, 37.8%; Self-Employed, 0.5%.

Considerations for Job Outlook: Civil engineering technicians learn to use design software that civil engineers typically do not. Thus, those who master it, keep their skills current, and stay abreast of the latest software will likely improve their chances for employment.

Apply theory and principles of civil engineering under the direction of engineering staff or physical scientists. Calculate dimensions, square footage, profile and component specifications, and material quantities using calculator or computer. Draft detailed dimensional drawings, and design layouts for projects and to ensure conformance to specifications. Analyze proposed site factors, and design maps, graphs, tracings, and diagrams to illustrate findings. Read and review project blueprints and structural specifications to determine dimensions of structure or system and material requirements. Prepare reports, and document project activities and data. Confer with supervisor to determine project details such as plan preparation, acceptance testing, and evaluation of field conditions. Inspect project site, and evaluate contractor work to detect design malfunctions and ensure conformance to design specifications and applicable codes. Plan and conduct field surveys to locate new sites, and analyze details of project sites. Develop plans and estimate costs for installation of systems, utilization of facilities, or construction of structures. Report maintenance problems occurring at project site to supervisor, and negotiate changes to resolve system conflicts. Conduct materials test and analysis using tools and equipment and applying engineering knowledge. Respond to public suggestions and complaints. Evaluate facility to determine suitability for occupancy and square footage availability.

Related Military Specializations: Advanced Engineering Aide; Civil Engineering Assistant; Engineer Assistant; Engineering Apprentice; Engineering Craftsman; Engineering Helper; Engineering Journeyman; Engineering Superintendent; Technical Engineer; Technical Engineering Specialist. **Average Educational Level of Vets:** One or more years of college, no degree. **Usual Educational Requirement:** Associate degree. **Relevant Educational Programs:** Building Construction Technology; Civil Engineering Technology/Technician; Construction Engineering Technology/Technician. **Related Knowledge/Courses:** Building and Construction; Engineering and Technology; Design; Geography; Transportation; Physics. **Work Experience Needed:** None. **On-the-Job Training Needed:** None. **Certification/Licensure:** Voluntary certification by association.

Personality Types: Realistic-Conventional-Investigative. **Key Career Cluster:** 02 Architecture and Construction. **Key Career Pathway:** 2.1 Design/Pre-construction. **Top Industries for Vets:** National Security and International Affairs; Architectural, Engineering, and Related Services; Electronic Components and Products, Not Elsewhere Classified; Wired Telecommunications Carriers; Broadcasting, Including Internet Publishing and Web Search Portals.

Skills: Operations Analysis; Operation Monitoring; Operation and Control; Mathematics; Science; Management of Financial Resources; Management of Material Resources; Active Listening.

Work Environment: More often indoors than outdoors; sitting; using hands; repetitive motions.

Claims Adjusters, Examiners, and Investigators

- ❋ Average Annual Earnings (All): $59,320
- ❋ Average Annual Earnings (Recent Veterans): $41,470
- ❋ Earnings Growth Potential: Medium (38.8%)
- ❋ Growth: 3.0%
- ❋ Annual Job Openings: 7,990
- ❋ Veteran Employment by Sector: For-Profit, 86.2%; Nonprofit, 1.7%; Government, 11.5%; Self-Employed, 0.6%.

Considerations for Job Outlook: Job opportunities for claims adjusters and examiners should be best in the health insurance industry as the number of health insurance customers expands. Additionally, prospects for claims adjusters in property and casualty insurance will likely be best in areas susceptible to natural disasters.

Review settled claims to determine that payments and settlements are made in accordance with company practices and procedures. For task data, see Job Specializations.

Related Military Specializations: None. **Average Educational Level of Vets:** Bachelor's degree. **Usual Educational Requirement:** High school diploma or equivalent. **Relevant**

Educational Programs: Health/Medical Claims Examiner Training; Insurance. **Work Experience Needed:** None. **On-the-Job Training Needed:** Long-term on-the-job training. **Certification/Licensure:** Licensure in some states for some specializations.

Key Career Cluster: 06 Finance. **Key Career Pathway:** 6.4 Insurance Services. **Top Industries for Vets:** Insurance Carriers and Related Activities; Banking and Related Activities.

Job Specialization: Claims Examiners, Property and Casualty Insurance

Review settled insurance claims to determine that payments and settlements have been made in accordance with company practices and procedures. Report overpayments, underpayments, and other irregularities. Confer with legal counsel on claims requiring litigation. Investigate, evaluate, and settle claims, applying technical knowledge and human relations skills to effect fair and prompt disposal of cases and to contribute to a reduced loss ratio. Pay and process claims within designated authority level. Adjust reserves or provide reserve recommendations to ensure that reserve activities are consistent with corporate policies. Enter claim payments, reserves, and new claims on computer system, inputting concise yet sufficient file documentation. Resolve complex severe exposure claims, using high-service-oriented file handling. Maintain claim files such as records of settled claims and an inventory of claims requiring detailed analysis. Verify and analyze data used in settling claims to ensure that claims are valid and that settlements are made according to company practices and procedures. Examine claims investigated by insurance adjusters, further investigating questionable claims to determine whether to authorize payments. Present cases, and participate in their discussion at claim committee meetings. Contact or interview claimants, doctors, medical specialists, or employers to get additional information. Confer with legal counsel on claims requiring litigation. Report overpayments, underpayments, and other irregularities. Communicate with reinsurance brokers to obtain information necessary for processing claims. Supervise claims adjusters to ensure that adjusters have followed proper methods.

Related Knowledge/Courses: Customer and Personal Service; Law and Government; Building and Construction; Administration and Management; English Language; Clerical Practices.

Personality Types: Conventional-Enterprising.

Skills: Negotiation; Persuasion; Service Orientation; Reading Comprehension; Writing; Critical Thinking; Management of Financial Resources; Mathematics.

Work Environment: Indoors; sitting; repetitive motions; noise.

Job Specialization: Insurance Adjusters, Examiners, and Investigators

Investigate, analyze, and determine the extent of insurance company's liability concerning personal, casualty, or property loss or damages and attempt to effect settlement with claimants. Correspond with or interview medical specialists, agents, witnesses, or claimants to compile information. Calculate benefit payments and approve payment of claims within a certain monetary limit. Interview or correspond with claimant and witnesses, consult police and hospital records, and inspect property damage to determine extent of liability. Investigate and assess damage to property. Examine claims forms and other records to determine insurance coverage. Analyze information gathered by investigation, and report findings and recommendations. Negotiate claim settlements, and recommend litigation when settlement cannot be negotiated.

C

Collect evidence to support contested claims in court. Prepare report of findings of investigation. Interview or correspond with agents and claimants to correct errors or omissions and to investigate questionable claims. Refer questionable claims to investigator or claims adjuster for investigation or settlement. Examine titles to property to determine validity, and act as company agent in transactions with property owners. Obtain credit information from banks and other credit services. Communicate with former associates to verify employment record and to obtain background information regarding persons or businesses applying for credit.

Related Knowledge/Courses: Customer and Personal Service; Clerical Practices; Building and Construction; English Language; Law and Government; Mathematics.

Personality Types: Conventional-Enterprising.

Skills: Management of Financial Resources; Negotiation; Mathematics; Critical Thinking; Active Listening; Speaking; Reading Comprehension; Writing.

Work Environment: Indoors; sitting; repetitive motions.

Clergy

- ❋ Average Annual Earnings (All): $44,140

- ❋ Average Annual Earnings (Recent Veterans): $39,290

- ❋ Earnings Growth Potential: High (46.6%)

- ❋ Growth: 17.5%

- ❋ Annual Job Openings: 7,990

- ❋ Veteran Employment by Sector: For-Profit, 0.3%; Nonprofit, 75.1%; Government, 24.5%; Self-Employed, 0.1%.

Considerations for Job Outlook: Faster than average employment growth is projected.

Conduct religious worship and perform other spiritual functions associated with beliefs and practices of religious faith or denomination. Pray and promote spirituality. Read from sacred texts such as the Bible, Torah, or Koran. Prepare and deliver sermons and other talks. Organize and lead regular religious services. Share information about religious issues by writing articles, giving speeches, or teaching. Instruct people who seek conversion to a particular faith. Visit people in homes, hospitals, and prisons to provide them with comfort and support. Counsel individuals and groups concerning their spiritual, emotional, and personal needs. Train leaders of church, community, and youth groups. Administer religious rites or ordinances. Study and interpret religious laws, doctrines, and/or traditions. Conduct special ceremonies such as weddings, funerals, and confirmations. Plan and lead religious education programs for their congregations. Respond to requests for assistance during emergencies or crises. Devise ways in which congregation membership can be expanded. Collaborate with committees and individuals to address financial and administrative issues pertaining to congregations. Prepare people for participation in religious ceremonies. Perform administrative duties such as overseeing building management, ordering supplies, contracting for services and repairs, and supervising the work of staff members and volunteers. Refer people to community support services, psychologists, and/or doctors as necessary. Participate in fundraising activities to support congregation activities and facilities. Organize and engage in interfaith, community, civic, educational, and recreational activities sponsored by or related to their religion.

Related Military Specializations: Chaplain; Chaplain Candidate Program Officer; Chaplain Selectee; Chaplain Specialist; Chaplain,

Buddhist; Chaplain, Jewish; Chaplain, Muslim; Chaplain, Orthodox; Chaplain, Protestant; Chaplain, Roman Catholic; Claimant Chaplain; Clinical Pastoral Educator; Command and Unit Chaplain; Force Chaplain; Group Chaplain; Strategic/Joint Chaplain; Supervisory Chaplain; Tactical Chaplain. **Average Educational Level of Vets:** Master's degree. **Usual Educational Requirement:** Bachelor's degree. **Relevant Educational Programs:** Clinical Pastoral Counseling/Patient Counseling; Divinity/Ministry (BD, MDiv.); Pastoral Studies/Counseling; Pre-Theology/Pre-Ministerial Studies; Rabbinical Studies (M.H.L./Rav); Theological and Ministerial Studies, Other; Theology/Theological Studies; Urban Ministry; Youth Ministry. **Related Knowledge/Courses:** Philosophy and Theology; Therapy and Counseling; Sociology and Anthropology; Psychology; Public Safety and Security; Customer and Personal Service. **Work Experience Needed:** None. **On-the-Job Training Needed:** Moderate-term on-the-job training. **Certification/Licensure:** None.

Personality Types: Social-Enterprising-Artistic. **Key Career Cluster:** 10 Human Services. **Key Career Pathway:** 10.3 Family and Community Services. **Top Industries for Vets:** Religious Organizations; National Security and International Affairs; Hospitals; Justice, Public Order, and Safety Activities; Business, Professional, Political and Similar Organizations.

Skills: Management of Financial Resources; Social Perceptiveness; Persuasion; Negotiation; Learning Strategies; Management of Material Resources; Service Orientation; Systems Evaluation.

Work Environment: Indoors; sitting.

Coaches and Scouts

- ❋ Average Annual Earnings (All): $28,470

- ❋ Average Annual Earnings (Recent Veterans): $23,570

- ❋ Earnings Growth Potential: Medium (39.9%)

- ❋ Growth: 29.4%

- ❋ Annual Job Openings: 13,300

- ❋ Veteran Employment by Sector: For-Profit, 59.8%; Nonprofit, 17.9%; Government, 19.6%; Self-Employed, 2.7%.

Considerations for Job Outlook: Those who have a degree or are state-certified to teach academic subjects should have the best prospects for getting coaching and instructor jobs at high schools. The need to replace the many high school coaches who change occupations or leave the labor force also will provide some jobs. Coaches in girls' and women's sports may have better job opportunities and face less competition for positions. Strong competition is expected for higher-paying jobs at the college level and will be even greater for jobs in professional sports. Competition should also be strong for paying jobs as scouts, particularly for professional teams, because there are few available jobs.

Instruct or coach groups or individuals in the fundamentals of sports. Plan, organize, and conduct practice sessions. Provide training direction, encouragement, and motivation to prepare athletes for games, competitive events, or tours. Identify and recruit potential athletes, arranging and offering incentives such as athletic scholarships. Plan strategies and choose team members for individual games or sports seasons. Plan and direct physical conditioning programs that will enable athletes to achieve maximum performance. Adjust coaching techniques based on the strengths and weaknesses of athletes. File scouting reports that detail player assessments, provide recommendations on athlete recruitment, and identify locations and individuals to be targeted for future recruitment efforts. Keep records of athlete, team, and opposing team performance. Instruct individuals or groups in sports rules, game strategies, and performance principles such as specific ways of moving the body, hands, and feet in order to achieve desired results. Analyze the strengths and weaknesses of opposing teams to develop game strategies. Evaluate athletes' skills and review performance records to determine their fitness and potential in a particular area of athletics. Keep abreast of changing rules, techniques, technologies, and philosophies relevant to their sport. Monitor athletes' use of equipment to ensure safe and proper use. Explain and enforce safety rules and regulations. Develop and arrange competition schedules and programs.

Related Military Specializations: None. **Average Educational Level of Vets:** High school diploma or equivalent. **Usual Educational Requirement:** High school diploma or equivalent. **Relevant Educational Programs:** Health and Physical Education, General; Physical Education Teaching and Coaching; Sport and Fitness Administration/Management. **Related Knowledge/Courses:** Education and Training; Therapy and Counseling; Sales and Marketing; Personnel and Human Resources; Psychology; English Language. **Work Experience Needed:** None. **On-the-Job Training Needed:** Long-term on-the-job training. **Certification/Licensure:** Licensure in some states for some specializations.

Personality Types: Social-Realistic-Enterprising. **Key Career Cluster:** 05 Education and Training. **Key Career Pathway:** 5.3 Teaching/Training. **Top Industries for Vets:** Other Amusement, Gambling, and Recreation Industries; Elementary and Secondary Schools; Independent Artists, Performing Arts, Spectator Sports and Related Industries; Other Schools and Instruction, and Educational Support Services; Colleges and Universities, Including Junior Colleges.

Skills: Management of Personnel Resources; Instructing; Systems Evaluation; Monitoring; Management of Material Resources; Negotiation; Learning Strategies; Persuasion.

Work Environment: Indoors; standing; noise; very hot or cold.

Commercial and Industrial Designers

- ❋ Average Annual Earnings (All): $60,760
- ❋ Average Annual Earnings (Recent Veterans): $41,470
- ❋ Earnings Growth Potential: High (43.2%)
- ❋ Growth: 10.5%
- ❋ Annual Job Openings: 1,690
- ❋ Veteran Employment by Sector: For-Profit, 77.9%; Nonprofit, 1.7%; Government, 9.5%; Self-Employed, 10.9%.

Considerations for Job Outlook: Prospects are best for job applicants with a strong background in computer-aided design (CAD) and computer-aided industrial design (CAID).

Develop and design manufactured products, such as cars, home appliances, and children's toys. Prepare sketches of ideas and detailed drawings, illustrations, artwork, or blueprints, using drafting instruments, paints and brushes, or computer-aided design equipment. Direct and coordinate the fabrication of models or samples and the drafting of working drawings and specification sheets from sketches. Modify and refine designs, using working models, to conform with customer specifications, production limitations, or changes in design trends. Coordinate the look and function of product lines. Confer with engineering, marketing, production, or sales departments, or with customers, to establish and evaluate design concepts for manufactured products. Present designs and reports to customers or design committees for approval, and discuss need for modification. Evaluate feasibility of design ideas based on factors such as appearance, safety, function, serviceability, budget, production costs/methods, and market characteristics. Read publications, attend showings, and study competing products and design styles and motifs to obtain perspective and generate design concepts. Research production specifications, costs, production materials, and manufacturing methods, and provide cost estimates and itemized production requirements. Design graphic material for use as ornamentation, illustration, or advertising on manufactured materials and packaging or containers.

Related Military Specializations: None. **Average Educational Level of Vets:** Bachelor's degree. **Usual Educational Requirement:** Bachelor's degree. **Relevant Educational Programs:** Commercial and Advertising Art; Design and Visual Communications, General; Energy Management and Systems Technology/Technician; Industrial and Product Design; Packaging Science. **Related Knowledge/Courses:** Design; Engineering and Technology; Mechanical Devices; Production and Processing; Physics; Fine Arts. **Work Experience Needed:** None. **On-the-Job Training Needed:** None. **Certification/Licensure:** None.

Personality Types: Artistic-Enterprising-Realistic. **Key Career Cluster:** 03 Arts, Audiovisual Technology, and Communications. **Key Career Pathway:** 3.3 Visual Arts. **Top Industries for Vets:** Architectural, Engineering, and Related Services; Specialized Design Services; Advertising and Related Services; National Security and International Affairs; Computer Systems Design and Related Services.

Skills: Technology Design; Operations Analysis; Systems Evaluation; Science; Mathematics; Active Learning; Systems Analysis; Quality Control Analysis.

Work Environment: Indoors; sitting; using hands; noise.

Commercial Pilots

- ❀ Average Annual Earnings (All): $70,000
- ❀ Average Annual Earnings (Recent Veterans): $87,310
- ❀ Earnings Growth Potential: High (48.2%)
- ❀ Growth: 21.2%
- ❀ Annual Job Openings: 1,930
- ❀ Veteran Employment by Sector: For-Profit, 59.5%; Nonprofit, 0.7%; Government, 39.2%; Self-Employed, 0.7%.

Considerations for Job Outlook: As older pilots retire and younger pilots advance, entry-level positions may open up. And the demand for flight instructors may increase as they are needed to train a greater number of student pilots. Job prospects should be best with regional airlines, on low-cost carriers, or in general aviation, because these segments are anticipated to grow faster than the major airlines. In addition, entry-level requirements are lower for regional and commercial jobs. However, pilots with less than 500 flight hours will probably need to accumulate hours as flight instructors or commercial pilots before qualifying for regional airline jobs.

Pilot and navigate the flight of fixed-wing aircraft on nonscheduled air carrier routes,

or helicopters. Check aircraft prior to flights to ensure that the engines, controls, instruments, and other systems are functioning properly. Start engines, operate controls, and pilot airplanes to transport passengers, mail, or freight while adhering to flight plans, regulations, and procedures. Contact control towers for takeoff clearances, arrival instructions, and other information, using radio equipment. Monitor engine operation, fuel consumption, and functioning of aircraft systems during flights. Consider airport altitudes, outside temperatures, plane weights, and wind speeds and directions to calculate the speed needed to become airborne. Order changes in fuel supplies, loads, routes, or schedules to ensure safety of flights. Obtain and review data such as load weights, fuel supplies, weather conditions, and flight schedules to determine flight plans and to see if changes might be necessary. Plan flights, following government and company regulations, using aeronautical charts and navigation instruments. Use instrumentation to pilot aircraft when visibility is poor. Check baggage or cargo to ensure that it has been loaded correctly. Request changes in altitudes or routes as circumstances dictate. Choose routes, altitudes, and speeds that will provide the fastest, safest, and smoothest flights. Coordinate flight activities with ground crews and air-traffic control, and inform crew members of flight and test procedures.

Related Military Specializations: Aviation Pilot; Light Plane Pilot. **Average Educational Level of Vets:** Bachelor's degree. **Usual Educational Requirement:** Postsecondary vocational training. **Relevant Educational Programs:** Airline/Commercial/Professional Pilot and Flight Crew Training; Flight Instructor Training. **Related Knowledge/Courses:** Transportation; Geography; Mechanical Devices; Physics; Telecommunications; Psychology. **Work Experience Needed:** None. **On-the-Job**

Training Needed: None. **Certification/Licensure:** Licensure.

Personality Types: Realistic-Investigative-Enterprising. **Key Career Cluster:** 16 Transportation, Distribution, and Logistics. **Key Career Pathway:** 16.1 Transportation Operations. **Top Industries for Vets:** Air Transportation; National Security and International Affairs; Couriers and Messengers; Justice, Public Order, and Safety Activities; Other Health Care Services.

Skills: Operation and Control; Operation Monitoring; Science; Instructing; Troubleshooting; Operations Analysis; Judgment and Decision Making; Complex Problem Solving.

Work Environment: Outdoors; sitting; using hands; noise; very hot or cold; contaminants; cramped work space.

Compensation, Benefits, and Job Analysis Specialists

- Average Annual Earnings (All): $57,960
- Average Annual Earnings (Recent Veterans): $56,750
- Earnings Growth Potential: Medium (36.5%)
- Growth: 5.0%
- Annual Job Openings: 2,400
- Veteran Employment by Sector: For-Profit, 38.1%; Nonprofit, 3.5%; Government, 57.2%; Self-Employed, 1.1%.

Considerations for Job Outlook: In most industries, a small decrease is expected as compensation and benefits work is outsourced overseas and to the employment services industry; however, this should cause a moderate increase in the employment services industry.

Conduct programs of compensation and benefits and job analysis for employer. Evaluate job positions, determining classification, exempt or nonexempt status, and salary. Ensure company compliance with federal and state laws, including reporting requirements. Advise managers and employees on state and federal employment regulations, collective agreements, benefit and compensation policies, personnel procedures, and classification programs. Plan, develop, evaluate, improve, and communicate methods and techniques for selecting, promoting, compensating, evaluating, and training workers. Provide advice on the resolution of classification and salary complaints. Prepare occupational classifications, job descriptions, and salary scales. Assist in preparing and maintaining personnel records and handbooks. Prepare reports, such as organization and flow charts, and career path reports, to summarize job analysis and evaluation and compensation analysis information. Administer employee insurance, pension and savings plans, working with insurance brokers and plan carriers. Negotiate collective agreements on behalf of employers or workers, and mediate labor disputes and grievances. Develop, implement, administer, and evaluate personnel and labor relations programs, including performance appraisal, affirmative action, and employment equity programs. Perform multifactor data and cost analyses that may be used in areas such as support of collective bargaining agreements. Research employee benefit and health and safety practices and recommend changes or modifications to existing policies. Analyze organizational, occupational, and industrial data to facilitate organizational functions and provide technical information to business, industry, and government. Advise staff of individuals' qualifications. Assess need for and develop job analysis instruments and materials.

Related Military Specializations: None. **Average Educational Level of Vets:** Bachelor's degree. **Usual Educational Requirement:** Bachelor's degree. **Relevant Educational Program:** Human Resources Management/Personnel Administration, General. **Related Knowledge/Courses:** Personnel and Human Resources; Economics and Accounting; Law and Government; Administration and Management; Mathematics; English Language. **Work Experience Needed:** None. **On-the-Job Training Needed:** None. **Certification/Licensure:** None.

Personality Types: Conventional-Enterprising. **Key Career Cluster:** 04 Business, Management, and Administration. **Key Career Pathway:** 4.3 Human Resources. **Top Industries for Vets:** National Security and International Affairs; Architectural, Engineering, and Related Services; Administration of Human Resource Programs; Management, Scientific and Technical Consulting Services; Construction.

Skills: Operations Analysis; Science; Systems Analysis; Mathematics; Programming; Systems Evaluation; Management of Financial Resources; Speaking.

Work Environment: Indoors; sitting.

Compliance Officers

- ✳ Average Annual Earnings (All): $60,740
- ✳ Average Annual Earnings (Recent Veterans): $54,240
- ✳ Earnings Growth Potential: High (42.5%)
- ✳ Growth: 15.0%
- ✳ Annual Job Openings: 5,860
- ✳ Veteran Employment by Sector: For-Profit, 10.2%; Nonprofit, 1.9%; Government, 87.9%; Self-Employed, 0.0%.

Considerations for Job Outlook: Much faster than average employment growth is projected.

Examine, evaluate, and investigate eligibility for or conformity with laws and regulations governing contract compliance of licenses and permits. For task data, see Job Specializations.

Related Military Specializations: Equal Opportunity Superintendent; Equal Opportunity Advisor; Equal Opportunity Advisor (EOA); Equal Opportunity Craftsman; Equal Opportunity Helper; Equal Opportunity Journeyman; Equal Opportunity Manager; Equal Opportunity Specialist. **Average Educational Level of Vets:** Bachelor's degree. **Usual Educational Requirement:** Bachelor's degree. **Relevant Educational Program:** Business Administration and Management, General. **Work Experience Needed:** None. **On-the-Job Training Needed:** Moderate-term on-the-job training. **Certification/Licensure:** Licensure for some specializations.

Key Career Cluster: 07 Government and Public Administration. **Key Career Pathway:** 7.6 Regulation. **Top Industries for Vets:** National Security and International Affairs; Administration of Economic Programs and Space Research; Executive Offices and Legislative Bodies; Justice, Public Order, and Safety Activities; Administration of Environmental Quality and Housing Programs.

Job Specialization: Coroners

Direct activities such as autopsies, pathological and toxicological analyses, and inquests relating to the investigation of deaths occurring within a legal jurisdiction to determine cause of death or to fix responsibility for accidental, violent, or unexplained deaths. Perform medico-legal examinations and autopsies, conducting preliminary examinations of the body in order to identify victims, to locate signs of trauma, and to identify factors that would indicate time of death. Inquire into the cause, manner, and circumstances of human deaths, and establish the identities of deceased persons. Direct activities of workers who conduct autopsies, perform pathological and toxicological analyses, and prepare documents for permanent records. Complete death certificates, including the assignment of a cause and manner of death. Observe and record the positions and conditions of bodies and of related evidence. Collect and document any pertinent medical history information. Observe, record, and preserve any objects or personal property related to deaths, including objects such as medication containers and suicide notes. Complete reports and forms required to finalize cases. Remove or supervise removal of bodies from death scenes, using the proper equipment and supplies, and arrange for transportation to morgues. Testify at inquests, hearings, and court trials. Interview persons present at death scenes to obtain information useful in determining the manner of death. Provide information concerning the circumstances of death to relatives of the deceased. Locate and document information regarding the next of kin, including their relationship to the deceased and the status of notification attempts.

Related Knowledge/Courses: Medicine and Dentistry; Biology; Psychology; Therapy and Counseling; Chemistry; Law and Government.

Personality Types: Investigative-Realistic-Conventional.

Skills: Science; Social Perceptiveness; Speaking; Critical Thinking; Management of Personnel Resources; Writing; Learning Strategies; Instructing.

Work Environment: More often indoors than outdoors; sitting; using hands; contaminants; exposed to disease or infections; hazardous equipment.

Job Specialization: Environmental Compliance Inspectors

Inspect and investigate sources of pollution to protect the public and environment and ensure conformance with federal, state, and local regulations and ordinances. Determine the nature of code violations and actions to be taken; issue written notices of violation; and participate in enforcement hearings as necessary. Examine permits, licenses, applications, and records to ensure compliance with licensing requirements. Prepare, organize, and maintain inspection records. Interview individuals to determine the nature of suspected violations and to obtain evidence of violations. Prepare written, oral, tabular, and graphic reports summarizing requirements and regulations, including enforcement and chain of custody documentation. Monitor follow-up actions in cases where violations were found, and review compliance-monitoring reports. Investigate complaints and suspected violations regarding illegal dumping, pollution, pesticides, product quality, or labeling laws. Inspect waste pretreatment, treatment, and disposal facilities and systems for conformance to federal, state, or local regulations. Inform individuals and groups of pollution control regulations and inspection findings, and explain how problems can be corrected. Determine sampling locations and methods, and collect water or wastewater samples for analysis, preserving samples with appropriate containers and preservation methods. Verify that hazardous chemicals are handled, stored, and disposed of in accordance with regulations. Research and keep informed of pertinent information and developments in areas such as EPA laws and regulations.

Related Knowledge/Courses: Biology; Chemistry; Law and Government; Geography; Physics; Engineering and Technology.

Personality Types: Conventional-Investigative-Realistic.

Skills: Quality Control Analysis; Science; Programming; Troubleshooting; Mathematics; Reading Comprehension; Writing; Active Learning.

Work Environment: More often indoors than outdoors; sitting; contaminants.

Job Specialization: Equal Opportunity Representatives and Officers

Monitor and evaluate compliance with equal opportunity laws, guidelines, and policies to ensure that employment practices and contracting arrangements give equal opportunity without regard to race, religion, color, national origin, sex, age, or disability. Investigate employment practices and alleged violations of laws to document and correct discriminatory factors. Interpret civil rights laws and equal opportunity regulations for individuals and employers. Study equal opportunity complaints to clarify issues. Meet with persons involved in equal opportunity complaints to verify case information and to arbitrate and settle disputes. Coordinate, monitor, and revise complaint procedures to ensure timely processing and review of complaints. Prepare reports of selection, survey, and other statistics and recommendations for corrective action. Conduct surveys and evaluate findings to determine whether systematic discrimination exists. Develop guidelines for nondiscriminatory employment practices, and monitor their implementation and impact. Review company contracts to determine actions required to meet governmental equal opportunity provisions. Counsel newly hired members of minority and disadvantaged groups, informing them about details of civil rights laws. Provide information, technical assistance, and training to supervisors, managers, and employees on topics such as employee supervision, hiring, grievance procedures, and staff development. Verify that all job descriptions are submitted for review and approval and that descriptions meet regulatory standards. Act as liaisons between minority placement agencies and employers or between job search committees and other equal opportunity administrators.

Related Knowledge/Courses: Law and Government; Personnel and Human Resources; Clerical Practices; English Language; Customer and Personal Service; Administration and Management.

Personality Types:
Social-Enterprising-Conventional.

Skills: Persuasion; Reading Comprehension; Active Listening; Active Learning; Programming; Negotiation; Writing; Speaking.

Work Environment: Indoors; sitting; repetitive motions.

Job Specialization: Government Property Inspectors and Investigators

Investigate or inspect government property to ensure compliance with contract agreements and government regulations. Prepare correspondence, reports of inspections or investigations, and recommendations for action. Inspect government-owned equipment and materials in the possession of private contractors to ensure compliance with contracts and regulations and to prevent misuse. Examine records, reports, and documents to establish facts and detect discrepancies. Inspect manufactured or processed products to ensure compliance with contract specifications and legal requirements. Locate and interview plaintiffs, witnesses, or representatives of business or government to gather facts relevant to inspections or alleged violations. Recommend legal or administrative action to protect government property. Submit samples of products to government laboratories for testing as required. Coordinate with and assist law enforcement agencies in matters of mutual

concern. Testify in court or at administrative proceedings concerning findings of investigations. Collect, identify, evaluate, and preserve case evidence. Monitor investigations of suspected offenders to ensure that they are conducted in accordance with constitutional requirements. Investigate applications for special licenses or permits, as well as alleged violations of licenses or permits.

Related Knowledge/Courses: Building and Construction; Engineering and Technology; Public Safety and Security; Mechanical Devices; Transportation; Computers and Electronics.

Personality Types:
Conventional-Enterprising-Realistic.

Skills: Quality Control Analysis; Programming; Persuasion; Operation and Control; Writing; Systems Evaluation; Speaking; Judgment and Decision Making.

Work Environment: More often outdoors than indoors; sitting; noise; very hot or cold; contaminants.

Job Specialization: Licensing Examiners and Inspectors

Examine, evaluate, and investigate eligibility for, conformity with, or liability under licenses or permits. Issue licenses to individuals meeting standards. Evaluate applications, records, and documents in order to gather information about eligibility or liability issues. Administer oral, written, road, or flight tests to license applicants. Score tests and observe equipment operation and control in order to rate ability of applicants. Advise licensees and other individuals or groups concerning licensing, permit, or passport regulations. Warn violators of infractions or penalties. Prepare reports of activities, evaluations, recommendations, and decisions. Prepare correspondence to inform concerned parties of licensing decisions and of appeals processes. Confer with and interview officials, technical or professional specialists, and applicants in order to obtain information or to clarify facts relevant to licensing decisions. Report law or regulation violations to appropriate boards and agencies. Visit establishments to verify that valid licenses and permits are displayed and that licensing standards are being upheld.

Related Knowledge/Courses: Clerical Practices; Customer and Personal Service; Law and Government; Foreign Language; Psychology; Public Safety and Security.

Personality Types: Conventional-Enterprising.

Skills: Quality Control Analysis; Judgment and Decision Making; Social Perceptiveness; Speaking; Operation Monitoring; Service Orientation; Systems Evaluation; Negotiation.

Work Environment: More often indoors than outdoors; sitting; using hands; repetitive motions; contaminants.

Job Specialization: Regulatory Affairs Specialists

Coordinate and document internal regulatory processes, such as internal audits, inspections, license renewals, or registrations. May compile and prepare materials for submission to regulatory agencies. Coordinate, prepare, or review regulatory submissions for domestic or international projects. Provide technical review of data or reports that will be incorporated into regulatory submissions to assure scientific rigor, accuracy, and clarity of presentation. Review product promotional materials, labeling, batch records, specification sheets, or test methods for compliance with applicable regulations and policies. Maintain current knowledge base of existing and emerging regulations, standards, or guidance documents. Interpret regulatory rules or rule changes and ensure that they are communicated through corporate policies and procedures. Advise project teams on subjects

such as premarket regulatory requirements, export and labeling requirements, and clinical study compliance issues. Determine the types of regulatory submissions or internal documentation that are required in situations such as proposed device changes and labeling changes. Prepare or maintain technical files as necessary to obtain and sustain product approval. Coordinate efforts associated with the preparation of regulatory documents or submissions. Prepare or direct the preparation of additional information or responses as requested by regulatory agencies. Analyze product complaints, and make recommendations regarding their reportability. Escort government inspectors during inspections, and provide post-inspection follow-up information as requested.

Related Knowledge/Courses: Law and Government; Biology; Medicine and Dentistry; Clerical Practices; English Language; Chemistry.

Personality Types: Conventional-Enterprising.

Skills: Systems Analysis; Systems Evaluation; Judgment and Decision Making; Persuasion; Writing; Speaking; Coordination; Reading Comprehension.

Work Environment: Indoors; sitting.

Computer Programmers

- ❋ Average Annual Earnings (All): $72,630
- ❋ Average Annual Earnings (Recent Veterans): $60,020
- ❋ Earnings Growth Potential: High (42.6%)
- ❋ Growth: 12.0%
- ❋ Annual Job Openings: 12,800
- ❋ Veteran Employment by Sector: For-Profit, 63.5%; Nonprofit, 1.5%; Government, 32.3%; Self-Employed, 2.7%.

Considerations for Job Outlook: Job prospects will be best for programmers who have a bachelor's degree or higher and knowledge of a variety of programming languages. Keeping up to date with the newest programming tools will also improve prospects. As employers increasingly contract with outside firms to do programming jobs, more opportunities are expected to arise for experienced programmers who have expertise in a specific area to work as consultants.

Create, modify, and test the code, forms, and script that allow computer applications to run. Correct errors by making appropriate changes and rechecking the program to ensure that the desired results are produced. Conduct trial runs of programs and software applications to be sure they will produce the desired information and that the instructions are correct. Compile and write documentation of program development and subsequent revisions, inserting comments in the coded instructions so others can understand the program. Write, update, and maintain computer programs or software packages to handle specific jobs such as tracking inventory, storing or retrieving data, or controlling other equipment. Consult with managerial, engineering, and technical personnel to clarify program intent, identify problems, and suggest changes. Perform or direct revision, repair, or expansion of existing programs to increase operating efficiency or adapt to new requirements. Write, analyze, review, and rewrite programs, using workflow chart and diagram, and applying knowledge of computer capabilities, subject matter, and symbolic logic. Write or contribute to instructions or manuals to guide end users. Investigate whether networks, workstations, the central processing unit of the system, or peripheral equipment are responding to a program's instructions. Prepare detailed workflow charts and diagrams that describe input, output, and logical operation, and convert them into a series of instructions coded in a computer language.

Perform systems analysis and programming tasks to maintain and control the use of computer systems software as a systems programmer. Consult with and assist computer operators or system analysts to define and resolve problems in running computer programs. Assign, coordinate, and review work and activities of programming personnel. Collaborate with computer manufacturers and other users to develop new programming methods. Train subordinates in programming and program coding.

Related Military Specializations: Communications—Computer Systems Programming Apprentice; Communications—Computer Systems Programming Craftsman; Communications—Computer Systems Programming Helper; Communications—Computer Systems Programming Journeyman; Computer Programmer (FORTRAN); Computer Systems Programming Apprentice; Computer Systems Programming Craftsman; Computer Systems Programming Helper; Computer Systems Programming Journeyman; Entry Level Programmer/Analyst; Programmer, ADA; Small Computer Systems Operator/Programmer. **Average Educational Level of Vets:** Bachelor's degree. **Usual Educational Requirement:** Bachelor's degree. **Relevant Educational Programs:** Computer Graphics; Computer Programming, Other; Computer Programming, Specific Applications; Computer Programming, Vendor/Product Certification; Computer Programming/Programmer, General; Computer Science; Computer Software Technology/Technician; Management Information Systems, General; Medical Office Computer Specialist/Assistant Training; Modeling, Virtual Environments and Simulation. **Related Knowledge/Courses:** Computers and Electronics; Mathematics; Design; Administration and Management; English Language; Communications and Media.

Work Experience Needed: None. **On-the-Job Training Needed:** None. **Certification/Licensure:** Voluntary certification by vendor or association.

Personality Types: Investigative-Conventional. **Key Career Cluster:** 11 Information Technology. **Key Career Pathway:** 11.4 Programming and Software Development. **Top Industries for Vets:** Computer Systems Design and Related Services; National Security and International Affairs; Executive Offices and Legislative Bodies; Insurance Carriers and Related Activities; Colleges and Universities, Including Junior Colleges.

Skills: Programming; Quality Control Analysis; Operations Analysis; Technology Design; Science; Systems Evaluation; Mathematics; Systems Analysis.

Work Environment: Indoors; sitting; using hands; repetitive motions.

Computer Systems Analysts

* Average Annual Earnings (All): $78,770

* Average Annual Earnings (Recent Veterans): $65,480

* Earnings Growth Potential: Medium (37.3%)

* Growth: 22.1%

* Annual Job Openings: 22,250

* Veteran Employment by Sector: For-Profit, 58.3%; Nonprofit, 2.7%; Government, 37.7%; Self-Employed, 1.3%.

Considerations for Job Outlook: Job applicants with a background in business may have better prospects because this occupation often requires knowledge of an organization's business needs.

An understanding of the specific field an analyst is working in is also helpful. For example, a hospital may desire an analyst with a background or coursework in health management.

Analyze science, engineering, business, and other data processing problems to implement and improve computer systems. Provide staff and users with assistance solving computer-related problems, such as malfunctions and program problems. Test, maintain, and monitor computer programs and systems, including coordinating the installation of computer programs and systems. Use object-oriented programming languages, as well as client and server applications development processes and multimedia and Internet technology. Confer with clients regarding the nature of the information processing or computation needs a computer program is to address. Coordinate and link the computer systems within an organization to increase compatibility and so information can be shared. Consult with management to ensure agreement on system principles. Expand or modify system to serve new purposes or improve work flow. Interview or survey workers, observe job performance or perform the job to determine what information is processed and how it is processed. Determine computer software or hardware needed to set up or alter system. Train staff and users to work with computer systems and programs. Analyze information processing or computation needs and plan and design computer systems, using techniques such as structured analysis, data modeling and information engineering. Assess the usefulness of predeveloped application packages and adapt them to a user environment. Define the goals of the system and devise flow charts and diagrams describing logical operational steps of programs. Develop, document, and revise system design procedures, test procedures, and quality standards. Review and analyze computer printouts and performance indicators to locate code problems, and correct errors by correcting codes. Recommend new equipment or software packages. Read manuals, periodicals, and technical reports to learn how to develop programs that meet staff and user requirements. Supervise computer programmers or other systems analysts or serve as project leaders for particular systems projects.

Related Military Specialization: Computer Systems Analyst. **Average Educational Level of Vets:** Bachelor's degree. **Usual Educational Requirement:** Bachelor's degree. **Relevant Educational Programs:** Computer and Information Sciences, General; Computer Systems Analysis/Analyst; Computer Systems Networking and Telecommunications; Information Technology. **Related Knowledge/Courses:** Computers and Electronics; Engineering and Technology; Mathematics; Telecommunications; Clerical Practices; English Language. **Work Experience Needed:** None. **On-the-Job Training Needed:** None. **Certification/Licensure:** None.

Personality Types: Investigative-Conventional-Realistic. **Key Career Cluster:** 11 Information Technology. **Key Career Pathway:** 11.4 Programming and Software Development. **Top Industries for Vets:** Computer Systems Design and Related Services; National Security and International Affairs; Architectural, Engineering, and Related Services; Management, Scientific and Technical Consulting Services; Scientific Research and Development Services.

Skills: Programming; Technology Design; Troubleshooting; Quality Control Analysis; Systems Evaluation; Operations Analysis; Systems Analysis; Mathematics.

Work Environment: Indoors; sitting; using hands; repetitive motions; noise.

Job Specialization: Informatics Nurse Specialists

Apply knowledge of nursing and informatics to assist in the design, development, and ongoing modification of computerized health-care systems. May educate staff and assist in problem solving to promote the implementation of the health-care system. Design, develop, select, test, implement, and evaluate new or modified informatics solutions, data structures, and decision-support mechanisms to support patients, health-care professionals, and their information management and human-computer and human-technology interactions within health-care contexts. Disseminate information about nursing informatics science and practice to the profession, other health-care professions, nursing students, and the public. Translate nursing practice information between nurses and systems engineers, analysts, or designers using object-oriented models or other techniques. Plan, install, repair, or troubleshoot telehealth-technology applications or systems in homes. Use informatics science to design or implement health information technology applications to resolve clinical or health-care administrative problems. Develop, implement, or evaluate health information technology applications, tools, processes, or structures to assist nurses with data management. Analyze and interpret patient, nursing, or information systems data to improve nursing services. Analyze computer and information technologies to determine applicability to nursing practice, education, administration, and research. Apply knowledge of computer science, information science, nursing, and informatics theory to nursing practice, education, administration, or research, in collaboration with other health informatics specialists.

Related Knowledge/Courses: Medicine and Dentistry; Sociology and Anthropology; Education and Training; Engineering and

Technology; Computers and Electronics; Clerical Practices.

Personality Types: Social-Investigative.

Skills: Programming; Technology Design; Science; Systems Evaluation; Operations Analysis; Systems Analysis; Equipment Selection; Active Learning.

Work Environment: Indoors; sitting; using hands; repetitive motions.

Construction and Building Inspectors

❈ Average Annual Earnings (All): $53,180

❈ Average Annual Earnings (Recent Veterans): $41,580

❈ Earnings Growth Potential: Medium (39.7%)

❈ Growth: 17.9%

❈ Annual Job Openings: 4,860

❈ Veteran Employment by Sector: For-Profit, 27.0%; Nonprofit, 2.0%; Government, 63.0%; Self-Employed, 8.0%.

Considerations for Job Outlook: Construction and building inspectors who are certified and can do a variety of inspections should have the best job opportunities. Inspectors with construction-related work experience or training in engineering, architecture, construction technology, or related fields will likely also have better job prospects. In addition, inspectors with thorough knowledge of construction practices and skills, such as reading and evaluating blueprints and plans, should have better job opportunities.

Inspect structures using engineering skills to determine structural soundness and compliance with specifications, building codes, and other regulations. Issue violation notices and stop-work orders, conferring with owners, violators, and authorities to explain regulations and recommend rectifications. Inspect bridges, dams, highways, buildings, wiring, plumbing, electrical circuits, sewers, heating systems, and foundations during and after construction for structural quality, general safety, and conformance to specifications and codes. Approve and sign plans that meet required specifications. Review and interpret plans, blueprints, site layouts, specifications, and construction methods to ensure compliance to legal requirements and safety regulations. Monitor installation of plumbing, wiring, equipment, and appliances to ensure that installation is performed properly and is in compliance with applicable regulations. Inspect and monitor construction sites to ensure adherence to safety standards, building codes, and specifications. Measure dimensions and verify level, alignment, and elevation of structures and fixtures to ensure compliance to building plans and codes. Maintain daily logs, and supplement inspection records with photographs. Use survey instruments, metering devices, tape measures, and test equipment such as concrete strength measurers to perform inspections. Train, direct, and supervise other construction inspectors. Issue permits for construction, relocation, demolition, and occupancy.

Related Military Specializations: Construction Inspector; Seabee Technical Security Specialist (STSS). **Average Educational Level of Vets:** One or more years of college, no degree. **Usual Educational Requirement:** High school diploma or equivalent. **Relevant Educational Program:** Building/Home/Construction Inspection/Inspector. **Related Knowledge/Courses:** Building and Construction; Engineering and Technology; Design; Physics; Public Safety and Security; Mechanical Devices. **Work Experience**

Needed: More than 5 years. **On-the-Job Training Needed:** Moderate-term on-the-job training. **Certification/Licensure:** Licensure in most states.

Personality Types: Realistic-Conventional-Investigative. **Key Career Cluster:** 02 Architecture and Construction. **Key Career Pathway:** 2.2 Construction. **Top Industries for Vets:** Construction; Real Estate; National Security and International Affairs; Architectural, Engineering, and Related Services; Administration of Economic Programs and Space Research.

Skills: Science; Quality Control Analysis; Operation and Control; Systems Evaluation; Mathematics; Systems Analysis; Operation Monitoring; Troubleshooting.

Work Environment: More often outdoors than indoors; standing; noise; very hot or cold; bright or inadequate lighting; contaminants; cramped work space; high places.

Construction Laborers

- ✳ Average Annual Earnings (All): $29,730
- ✳ Average Annual Earnings (Recent Veterans): $24,880
- ✳ Earnings Growth Potential: Medium (36.7%)
- ✳ Growth: 21.3%
- ✳ Annual Job Openings: 29,240
- ✳ Veteran Employment by Sector: For-Profit, 75.6%; Nonprofit, 0.9%; Government, 11.7%; Self-Employed, 11.8%.

Considerations for Job Outlook: Construction laborers with the most skills should have the best job opportunities. Opportunities also will vary by occupation; for example, carpenters' helpers should have the best job prospects, while painters', paperhangers', plasterers', and stucco masons' helpers will likely find fewer job openings. Prospective employees with military service often have better opportunities when applying for a job. Employment of construction laborers and helpers is especially sensitive to the fluctuations of the economy. On the one hand, workers in these trades may experience periods of unemployment when the overall level of construction falls. On the other hand, shortages of these workers may occur in some areas during peak periods of building activity.

Perform tasks involving physical labor at construction sites. Clean and prepare construction sites to eliminate possible hazards. Read and interpret plans, instructions, and specifications to determine work activities. Control traffic passing near, in, and around work zones. Signal equipment operators to facilitate alignment, movement, and adjustment of machinery, equipment, and materials. Dig ditches or trenches, backfill excavations, and compact and level earth to grade specifications, using picks, shovels, pneumatic tampers, and rakes. Measure, mark, and record openings and distances to lay out areas where construction work will be performed. Position, join, align, and seal structural components such as concrete wall sections and pipes. Load, unload, and identify building materials, machinery, and tools, and distribute them to the appropriate locations according to project plans and specifications. Erect and disassemble scaffolding, shoring, braces, traffic barricades, ramps, and other temporary structures. Build and position forms for pouring concrete, and dismantle forms after use, using saws, hammers, nails, or bolts. Lubricate, clean, and repair machinery, equipment, and tools. Operate jackhammers and drills to break up concrete or pavement. Smooth and finish freshly poured cement or concrete using floats, trowels, screeds, or powered cement-finishing tools. Operate, read, and maintain air-monitoring and other sampling devices in confined or hazardous environments.

Related Military Specializations: Builder Basic; Structural Helper. **Average Educational Level of Vets:** High school diploma or equivalent. **Usual Educational Requirement:** Less than high school diploma or equivalent. **Relevant Educational Program:** Construction Trades, Other. **Related Knowledge/Courses:** Building and Construction; Design; Mechanical Devices; Transportation; Public Safety and Security; Engineering and Technology. **Work Experience Needed:** None. **On-the-Job Training Needed:** Short-term on-the-job training. **Certification/ Licensure:** None.

Personality Types: Realistic-Conventional. **Key Career Cluster:** 02 Architecture and Construction. **Key Career Pathway:** 2.2 Construction. **Top Industries for Vets:** Construction; National Security and International Affairs; Electric Power Generation, Transmission and Distribution; Employment Services; Miscellaneous Manufacturing, Not Elsewhere Classified.

Skills: Operation and Control; Equipment Selection; Installation; Equipment Maintenance; Operation Monitoring; Troubleshooting; Repairing; Quality Control Analysis.

Work Environment: Outdoors; standing; using hands; bending or twisting the body; repetitive motions; noise; very hot or cold; bright or inadequate lighting; contaminants; whole-body vibration; hazardous equipment; minor burns, cuts, bites, or stings.

Construction Managers

* Average Annual Earnings (All): $84,240

* Average Annual Earnings (Recent Veterans): $52,380

* Earnings Growth Potential: Medium (39.9%)

* Growth: 16.6%

* Annual Job Openings: 12,040

* Veteran Employment by Sector: For-Profit, 64.1%; Nonprofit, 0.3%; Government, 8.6%; Self-Employed, 27.1%.

Considerations for Job Outlook: Job opportunities for qualified job seekers are expected to be good. Those with a bachelor's degree in construction science, construction management, or civil engineering, coupled with construction experience, will have the best job prospects. Employment growth will provide many new job openings. A substantial number of construction managers are expected to retire over the next decade, resulting in additional job opportunities. Employment of construction managers, like that of many other construction workers, is sensitive to fluctuations in the economy.

Plan, direct, or coordinate activities concerned with the construction and maintenance of structures, facilities, and systems. Schedule the project in logical steps, and budget time required to meet deadlines. Confer with supervisory personnel, owners, contractors, and design professionals to discuss and resolve matters such as work procedures, complaints, and construction problems. Prepare contracts, and negotiate revisions, changes, and additions to contractual agreements with architects, consultants, clients, suppliers, and subcontractors. Prepare and submit budget estimates and progress and cost-tracking reports. Interpret and explain plans and contract terms to administrative staff, workers, and clients, representing the owner or developer. Plan, organize, and direct activities concerned with the construction and maintenance of structures, facilities, and systems. Take actions to deal with the results of delays, bad weather, or emergencies at construction sites. Inspect and review projects to monitor compliance with building and safety codes and other regulations. Study job specifications to determine appropriate construction methods. Select, contract, and oversee workers who complete specific pieces of the project, such as painting or plumbing. Obtain all necessary permits and licenses. Direct and supervise workers. Develop and implement quality control programs. Investigate damage, accidents, or delays at construction sites to ensure that proper procedures are being carried out. Determine labor requirements, and dispatch workers to construction sites.

Related Military Specializations: Combat Engineer Officer; Commanding Officer, Naval Construction Forces; Company Officer, Naval Construction Forces; Executive Officer, Naval Construction Forces; Facilities Construction/ Facilities Services Officer; Facilities Engineering Officer; Facilities Planning and Programming Officer; Facilities/Contract Construction Management Engineer (FCCME); Officer in Charge, Naval Construction Battalion Unit; Operations Officer, Naval Construction Forces; Public Works Planning Officer; Staff Civil Engineer; Systems Development. **Average Educational Level of Vets:** Bachelor's degree. **Usual Educational Requirement:** Associate degree. **Relevant Educational Programs:** Business Administration and Management, General; Business/Commerce, General; Construction Engineering Technology/ Technician; Construction Management; Operations Management and Supervision. **Related Knowledge/Courses:** Building

and Construction; Design; Engineering and Technology; Mechanical Devices; Administration and Management; Personnel and Human Resources. **Work Experience Needed:** More than 5 years. **On-the-Job Training Needed:** None. **Certification/Licensure:** Licensure for some specializations; voluntary certification by association.

Personality Types: Enterprising-Realistic-Conventional. **Key Career Cluster:** 02 Architecture and Construction. **Key Career Pathway:** 2.2 Construction. **Top Industries for Vets:** Construction; National Security and International Affairs; Architectural, Engineering, and Related Services; Real Estate; Machinery, Equipment, and Supplies Merchant Wholesalers.

Skills: Management of Financial Resources; Management of Material Resources; Operations Analysis; Management of Personnel Resources; Negotiation; Mathematics; Persuasion; Systems Evaluation.

Work Environment: More often outdoors than indoors; sitting; noise; contaminants; hazardous equipment.

Credit Counselors

- ❋ Average Annual Earnings (All): $38,430
- ❋ Average Annual Earnings (Recent Veterans): $41,470
- ❋ Earnings Growth Potential: Low (29.8%)
- ❋ Growth: 20.3%
- ❋ Annual Job Openings: 1,520
- ❋ Veteran Employment by Sector: For-Profit, 88.0%; Nonprofit, 2.6%; Government, 1.5%; Self-Employed, 8.0%.

Considerations for Job Outlook: Efforts to recruit and retain employees, the growing importance of employee training, and new legal standards are expected to increase employment of these workers. College graduates and those with certification should have the best opportunities.

Advise and educate individuals or organizations on acquiring and managing debt. Assess clients' overall financial situation by reviewing income, assets, debts, expenses, credit reports, or other financial information. Calculate clients' available monthly income to meet debt obligations. Create debt management plans, spending plans, or budgets to assist clients to meet financial goals. Estimate time for debt repayment given amount of debt, interest rates, and available funds. Explain services or policies to clients, such as debt management program rules, the advantages and disadvantages of using services, or creditor concession policies. Interview clients by telephone or in person to gather financial information. Maintain or update records of client account activity, including financial transactions, counseling session notes, correspondence, document images, or client inquiries. Negotiate with creditors on behalf of clients to arrange for payment adjustments, interest rate reductions, time extensions, or to set up payment plans. Prepare written documents to establish contracts with or communicate financial recommendations to clients. Prioritize client debt repayment to avoid dire consequences, such as bankruptcy or foreclosure or to reduce overall costs, such as by paying high-interest or short-term loans first. Recommend educational materials or resources to clients on matters such as financial planning, budgeting, or credit. Recommend strategies for clients to meet their financial goals, such as borrowing money through loans or loan programs, declaring bankruptcy, making budget adjustments, or enrolling in debt management plans. Refer clients to social service or community resources for needs beyond those of credit or debt counseling. Review changes to financial, family, or employment

situations to determine whether changes to existing debt management plans, spending plans, or budgets are needed. Advise clients on housing matters, such as housing rental, homeownership, mortgage delinquency, or foreclosure prevention.

Related Military Specializations: None. **Average Educational Level of Vets:** Bachelor's degree. **Usual Educational Requirement:** Bachelor's degree. **Relevant Educational Programs:** Banking and Financial Support Services; Credit Management; Financial Planning and Services. **Work Experience Needed:** None. **On-the-Job Training Needed:** Moderate-term on-the-job training. **Certification/Licensure:** Licensure in some states for some specializations.

Key Career Cluster: 10 Human Services. **Key Career Pathway:** 10.5 Consumer Services. **Top Industries for Vets:** Nondepository Credit and Related Activities; Banking and Related Activities; Individual and Family Services; Insurance Carriers and Related Activities; Furniture and Related Products.

Job Specialization: Loan Counselors

Provide guidance to prospective loan applicants who have problems qualifying for traditional loans. Guidance may include determining the best type of loan and explaining loan requirements or restrictions. Check loan agreements to ensure that they are complete and accurate, according to policies. Refer loans to loan committees for approval. Approve loans within specified limits. Submit applications to credit analysts for verification and recommendation. Analyze applicants' financial status, credit, and property evaluations to determine feasibility of granting loans. Interview applicants and request specified information for loan applications. Establish payment priorities according to credit terms and interest rates to reduce clients' overall costs. Contact applicants or creditors to resolve questions about applications or to assist with completion of paperwork. Maintain current knowledge of credit regulations. Calculate amount of debt and funds available to plan methods of payoff and to estimate time for debt liquidation. Analyze potential loan markets to find opportunities to promote loans and financial services. Review billing for accuracy. Supervise loan personnel. Maintain and review account records, updating and recategorizing them according to status changes. Assist in selection of financial award candidates using electronic databases to certify loan eligibility. Confer with underwriters to resolve mortgage application problems. Inform individuals and groups about the financial assistance available to college or university students. Match students' needs and eligibility with available financial aid programs to provide informed recommendations. Contact creditors to explain clients' financial situations and to arrange for payment adjustments so that payments are feasible for clients and agreeable to creditors. Petition courts to transfer titles and deeds of collateral to banks. Contact borrowers with delinquent accounts to obtain payment in full or to negotiate repayment plans. Compare data on student aid applications with eligibility requirements of assistance programs.

Related Knowledge/Courses: Economics and Accounting; Law and Government; Clerical Practices; Customer and Personal Service; Fine Arts; Administration and Management.

Personality Types: Enterprising-Social-Conventional.

Skills: Service Orientation; Learning Strategies; Mathematics; Instructing; Persuasion; Judgment and Decision Making; Time Management; Social Perceptiveness.

Work Environment: More often indoors than outdoors; sitting; noise.

Customer Service Representatives

❋ Average Annual Earnings (All): $30,610

❋ Average Annual Earnings (Recent Veterans): $26,080

❋ Earnings Growth Potential: Medium (35.9%)

❋ Growth: 15.5%

❋ Annual Job Openings: 95,960

❋ Veteran Employment by Sector: For-Profit, 83.3%; Nonprofit, 1.2%; Government, 15.3%; Self-Employed, 0.2%.

Considerations for Job Outlook: Job prospects for customer service representatives are expected to be good. Many job openings will arise from the need to replace workers who leave the occupation. There will be greater competition for in-house customer service jobs—which often have higher pay and greater advancement potential—than for those jobs in the call center industry.

Interact with customers to provide information in response to inquiries about products and services and to handle and resolve complaints. Confer with customers by telephone or in person to provide information about products and services, to take orders or cancel accounts, or to obtain details of complaints. Keep records of customer interactions and transactions, recording details of inquiries, complaints, and comments, as well as actions taken. Resolve customers' service or billing complaints by performing activities such as exchanging merchandise, refunding money, and adjusting bills. Check to ensure that appropriate changes were made to resolve customers' problems. Contact customers to respond to inquiries or to notify them of claim-investigation results and any planned adjustments. Refer unresolved customer grievances to designated departments for further investigation. Determine charges for services requested, collect deposits or payments, or arrange for billing. Complete contract forms, prepare change of address records, and issue service-discontinuance orders, using computers. Obtain and examine all relevant information to assess validity of complaints and to determine possible causes, such as extreme weather conditions, that could increase utility bills. Solicit sale of new or additional services or products. Review insurance policy terms to determine whether a particular loss is covered by insurance. Review claims adjustments with dealers, examining parts claimed to be defective and approving or disapproving dealers' claims.

Related Military Specializations: None. **Average Educational Level of Vets:** One or more years of college, no degree. **Usual Educational Requirement:** High school diploma or equivalent. **Relevant Educational Programs:** Customer Service Support/Call Center/Teleservice Operation; Receptionist Training. **Related Knowledge/Courses:** Clerical Practices; Customer and Personal Service; English Language. **Work Experience Needed:** None. **On-the-Job Training Needed:** Short-term on-the-job training. **Certification/Licensure:** Licensure for some specializations.

Personality Types: Enterprising-Social-Conventional. **Key Career Cluster:** 14 Marketing, Sales, and Service. **Key Career Pathway:** 14.3 Buying and Merchandising. **Top Industries for Vets:** National Security and International Affairs; Business Support Services; Building Material and Supplies Dealers; Other Telecommunication Services; Wired Telecommunications Carriers.

Skills: Service Orientation; Persuasion; Negotiation; Active Listening; Speaking; Reading Comprehension.

Work Environment: Indoors; sitting; using hands; repetitive motions; noise.

Job Specialization: Patient Representatives

Assist patients in obtaining services, understanding policies, and making health-care decisions. Explain policies, procedures, or services to patients using medical or administrative knowledge. Coordinate communication between patients, family members, medical staff, administrative staff, or regulatory agencies. Investigate and direct patient inquiries or complaints to appropriate medical staff members, and follow up to ensure satisfactory resolution. Interview patients or their representatives to identify problems relating to care. Refer patients to appropriate health-care services or resources. Analyze patients' abilities to pay to determine charges on a sliding scale. Collect and report data on topics such as patient encounters and inter-institutional problems, making recommendations for change when appropriate. Develop and distribute newsletters, brochures, or other printed materials to share information with patients or medical staff. Teach patients to use home health-care equipment. Identify and share research, recommendations, or other information regarding legal liabilities, risk management, or quality of care. Read current literature, talk with colleagues, continue education, or participate in professional organizations or conferences to keep abreast of developments in the field. Maintain knowledge of community services and resources available to patients. Provide consultation or training to volunteers or staff on topics such as guest relations, patients' rights, and medical issues.

Related Knowledge/Courses: Therapy and Counseling; Psychology; Customer and Personal Service; Sociology and Anthropology; Philosophy and Theology; Medicine and Dentistry.

Personality Types: Social-Enterprising.

Skills: Service Orientation; Persuasion; Social Perceptiveness; Negotiation; Systems Evaluation; Instructing; Critical Thinking; Systems Analysis.

Work Environment: Indoors; sitting; noise; exposed to disease or infections.

Database Administrators

* Average Annual Earnings (All): $75,190

* Average Annual Earnings (Recent Veterans): $61,120

* Earnings Growth Potential: High (43.7%)

* Growth: 30.6%

* Annual Job Openings: 5,270

* Veteran Employment by Sector: For-Profit, 56.9%; Nonprofit, 3.2%; Government, 39.9%; Self-Employed, 0.0%.

Considerations for Job Outlook: Job prospects should be favorable. Database administrators are in high demand, and firms sometimes have difficulty finding qualified workers. Applicants who have experience with new technology should have the best prospects.

Administer, test, and implement computer databases, applying knowledge of database management systems. Develop standards and guidelines to guide the use and acquisition of software and to protect vulnerable information. Modify existing databases and database management systems or direct programmers and analysts to make changes. Test programs or databases, correct errors and make necessary modifications. Plan, coordinate, and implement security measures to safeguard information in computer files against accidental or unauthorized damage, modification, or disclosure. Approve, schedule, plan, and supervise the installation and testing of new products and improvements to computer systems such as the installation of new databases. Train users and answer questions. Establish and calculate optimum values for database parameters, using manuals and calculator. Specify users and user access levels for each segment of database. Develop data model describing data elements and how they are used, following procedures and using pen, template, or computer software. Develop methods for integrating different products so they work properly together such as customizing commercial databases to fit specific needs. Review project requests describing database user needs to estimate time and cost required to accomplish project. Review procedures in database management system manuals for making changes to database. Work as part of a project team to coordinate database development and determine project scope and limitations. Select and enter codes to monitor database performance and to create production database. Identify and evaluate industry trends in database systems to serve as a source of information and advice for upper management. Write and code logical and physical database descriptions and specify identifiers of database to management system or direct others in coding descriptions. Review workflow charts developed by programmer analyst to understand tasks computer will perform, such as updating records. Revise company definition of data as defined in data dictionary.

Related Military Specializations: Database Administrator; Mission Distribution System Operator; Naval Aviation Logistics Command Management Information System (NALCOMIS) Data Base Administrator/Analyst (DBA/A); Optimized NALCOMIS Database Administrator/Analysis IMA; OSIS Baseline Upgrade (OBU) System Manager; OSIS

Baseline Upgrade (OBU) User/Analyst. **Average Educational Level of Vets:** Bachelor's degree. **Usual Educational Requirement:** Bachelor's degree. **Relevant Educational Programs:** Computer and Information Sciences, General; Computer and Information Systems Security/ Information Assurance; Data Modeling/ Warehousing and Database Administration. **Related Knowledge/Courses:** Computers and Electronics; Telecommunications; Clerical Practices; Communications and Media; Engineering and Technology; Mathematics. **Work Experience Needed:** 1 to 5 years. **On-the-Job Training Needed:** None. **Certification/ Licensure:** Voluntary certification by vendors or association.

Personality Types: Conventional-Investigative. **Key Career Cluster:** 11 Information Technology. **Key Career Pathway:** 11.1 Network Systems. **Top Industries for Vets:** National Security and International Affairs; Computer Systems Design and Related Services; Architectural, Engineering, and Related Services; Insurance Carriers and Related Activities; Other Telecommunication Services.

Skills: Programming; Technology Design; Troubleshooting; Systems Evaluation; Operations Analysis; Management of Financial Resources; Systems Analysis; Mathematics.

Work Environment: Indoors; sitting; using hands; repetitive motions; noise.

Dental Assistants

- ✽ Average Annual Earnings (All): $34,140
- ✽ Average Annual Earnings (Recent Veterans): $27,280
- ✽ Earnings Growth Potential: Low (32.4%)
- ✽ Growth: 30.8%
- ✽ Annual Job Openings: 15,400
- ✽ Veteran Employment by Sector: For-Profit, 48.6%; Nonprofit, 2.5%; Government, 48.9%; Self-Employed, 0.0%.

Considerations for Job Outlook: Ongoing research linking oral health and general health will likely continue to increase the demand for preventive dental services. Dentists will continue to hire more dental assistants to complete routine tasks, allowing the dentist to see more patients in their practice and spend their time on more complex procedures. As dental practices grow, more dental assistants will be needed. As the large baby-boom population ages, and as people keep more of their original teeth than did previous generations, the need to maintain and treat teeth will continue to increase the need for dental assistants.

Assist dentist, set up equipment, prepare patient for treatment, and keep records. Prepare patient, sterilize and disinfect instruments, set up instrument trays, prepare materials, and assist dentist during dental procedures. Expose dental diagnostic X-rays. Record treatment information in patient records. Take and record medical and dental histories and vital signs of patients. Provide postoperative instructions prescribed by dentist. Assist dentist in management of medical and dental emergencies. Pour, trim, and polish study casts. Instruct patients in oral hygiene and plaque-control programs. Make preliminary impressions for study casts and occlusal registrations for mounting study casts. Clean and polish removable appliances. Clean teeth, using dental instruments. Apply protective coating of fluoride to teeth. Fabricate temporary restorations and custom impressions from preliminary impressions. Schedule appointments, prepare bills, and receive payment for dental services; complete insurance forms; and maintain records, manually or using computer.

Related Military Specializations: Advanced Dental Assistant; Dental Assistant; Dental Assistant Apprentice; Dental Assistant Craftsman; Dental Assistant Craftsman, Dental Hygienist; Dental Assistant Helper; Dental Assistant Journeyman; Dental Assistant Journeyman, Dental Hygienist; Dental Department Administrative Assistant; Dental Specialist; Dental Surgical Technologist; Dental Technician; others. **Average Educational Level of Vets:** One or more years of college, no degree. **Usual Educational Requirement:** Postsecondary vocational training. **Relevant Educational Program:** Dental Assisting/Assistant. **Related Knowledge/Courses:** Medicine and Dentistry; Customer and Personal Service; Psychology; Sales and Marketing. **Work Experience Needed:** None. **On-the-Job Training Needed:** None. **Certification/Licensure:** Licensure for some specializations; voluntary certification by association.

Personality Types: Conventional-Realistic-Social. **Key Career Cluster:** 08 Health Science. **Key Career Pathway:** 8.1 Therapeutic Services. **Top Industries for Vets:** Offices of Dentists; National Security and International Affairs; Colleges and Universities, Including Junior Colleges; Hospitals; Justice, Public Order, and Safety Activities.

Skills: Repairing; Equipment Maintenance; Operation Monitoring; Equipment Selection; Science; Service Orientation; Operation and Control; Quality Control Analysis.

Work Environment: Indoors; standing; walking and running; using hands; bending or twisting the body; repetitive motions; contaminants; exposed to radiation; exposed to disease or infections; hazardous conditions.

Detectives and Criminal Investigators

- ❋ Average Annual Earnings (All): $71,770
- ❋ Average Annual Earnings (Recent Veterans): $64,390
- ❋ Earnings Growth Potential: High (44.7%)
- ❋ Growth: 2.9%
- ❋ Annual Job Openings: 3,010
- ❋ Veteran Employment by Sector: For-Profit, 2.7%; Nonprofit, 0.6%; Government, 95.1%; Self-Employed, 1.6%.

Considerations for Job Outlook: Continued demand for public safety will lead to new openings for officers in local departments; however, both state and federal jobs may be more competitive. Because they typically offer low salaries, many local departments face high turnover rates, making opportunities more plentiful for qualified applicants. However, some smaller departments may have fewer opportunities as budgets limit the ability to hire additional officers. Jobs in state and federal agencies will remain more competitive as they often offer high pay and more opportunities for both promotions and interagency transfers. Bilingual applicants with a bachelor's degree and law enforcement or military experience, especially investigative experience, should have the best opportunities in federal agencies.

Conduct investigations related to suspected violations of federal, state, or local laws to prevent or solve crimes. For task data, see Job Specializations.

Related Military Specializations: CID Special Agent; Forensic Psycho-physiologist (Polygraph Examiner); GWOT IA/ILO Detainee Operations Interrogator; Investigator; Military Investigator; Military Police Investigator (MPI); Special Investigations Craftsman; Special Investigations Helper; Special Investigations Journeyman. **Average Educational Level of Vets:** Bachelor's degree. **Usual Educational Requirement:** High school diploma or equivalent. **Relevant Educational Programs:** Criminal Justice/Police Science; Criminalistics and Criminal Science; Cultural/Archaeological Resources Protection; Cyber/Computer Forensics and Counterterrorism; Financial Forensics and Fraud Investigation; Law Enforcement Intelligence Analysis; Law Enforcement Investigation and Interviewing; Law Enforcement Record-Keeping and Evidence Management; Maritime Law Enforcement; Natural Resources Law Enforcement and Protective Services; Suspension and Debarment Investigation. **Work Experience Needed:** 1 to 5 years. **On-the-Job Training Needed:** Moderate-term on-the-job training. **Certification/Licensure:** Licensure in some states.

Key Career Cluster: 07 Government and Public Administration. **Key Career Pathway:** 7.6 Regulation. **Top Industries for Vets:** Justice, Public Order, and Safety Activities; National Security and International Affairs; Investigation and Security Services; Administration of Human Resource Programs; Executive Offices and Legislative Bodies.

Job Specialization: Criminal Investigators and Special Agents

Investigate alleged or suspected criminal violations of federal, state, or local laws to determine if evidence is sufficient to recommend prosecution. Record evidence and documents, using equipment such as cameras and photocopy machines. Obtain and verify evidence by interviewing and observing suspects and witnesses or by analyzing records. Examine records to locate links in chains of evidence or information. Prepare reports that detail investigation findings. Determine scope, timing, and direction of investigations. Collaborate with other offices and agencies to exchange information and coordinate activities. Testify before grand juries concerning criminal activity investigations. Analyze evidence in laboratories or in the field. Investigate organized crime, public corruption, financial crime, copyright infringement, civil rights violations, bank robbery, extortion, kidnapping, and other violations of federal or state statutes. Identify case issues and evidence needed, based on analysis of charges, complaints, or allegations of law violations. Obtain and use search and arrest warrants. Serve subpoenas or other official papers. Collaborate with other authorities on activities such as surveillance, transcription, and research. Develop relationships with informants to obtain information related to cases. Search for and collect evidence such as fingerprints, using investigative equipment. Collect and record physical information about arrested suspects, including fingerprints, height and weight measurements, and photographs.

Related Knowledge/Courses: Public Safety and Security; Psychology; Law and Government; Customer and Personal Service; Sociology and Anthropology; Therapy and Counseling.

Personality Types: Enterprising-Investigative.

Skills: Negotiation; Science; Complex Problem Solving; Persuasion; Judgment and Decision Making; Speaking; Critical Thinking; Social Perceptiveness.

Work Environment: Indoors; sitting; noise; very hot or cold; contaminants; exposed to disease or infections.

Job Specialization: Immigration and Customs Inspectors

Investigate and inspect persons, common carriers, goods, and merchandise arriving in or departing from the United States or moving between states to detect violations of immigration and customs laws and regulations. Examine immigration applications, visas, and passports and interview persons to determine eligibility for admission, residence, and travel in the United States. Detain persons found to be in violation of customs or immigration laws, and arrange for legal action such as deportation. Locate and seize contraband or undeclared merchandise and vehicles, aircraft, or boats that contain such merchandise. Interpret and explain laws and regulations to travelers, prospective immigrants, shippers, and manufacturers. Inspect cargo, baggage, and personal articles entering or leaving U.S. for compliance with revenue laws and U.S. Customs Service regulations. Record and report job-related activities, findings, transactions, violations, discrepancies, and decisions. Institute civil and criminal prosecutions, and cooperate with other law enforcement agencies in the investigation and prosecution of those in violation of immigration or customs laws. Testify regarding decisions at immigration appeals or in federal court. Determine duty and taxes to be paid on goods. Collect samples of merchandise for examination, appraisal, or testing. Investigate applications for duty refunds, and petition

for remission or mitigation of penalties when warranted.

Related Knowledge/Courses: Public Safety and Security; Law and Government; Foreign Language; Geography; Customer and Personal Service; Philosophy and Theology.

Personality Types: Conventional-Enterprising-Realistic.

Skills: Active Listening; Persuasion; Negotiation; Operation and Control; Speaking; Social Perceptiveness; Time Management; Judgment and Decision Making.

Work Environment: More often outdoors than indoors; more often sitting than standing; using hands; repetitive motions; noise; very hot or cold; bright or inadequate lighting; contaminants; cramped work space; exposed to radiation; hazardous equipment.

Job Specialization: Intelligence Analysts

Gather, analyze, and evaluate information from a variety of sources, such as law enforcement databases, surveillance, intelligence networks, and geographic information systems. Use data to anticipate and prevent organized crime activities, such as terrorism. Predict future gang, organized crime, or terrorist activity, using analyses of intelligence data. Study activities relating to narcotics, money laundering, gangs, auto theft rings, terrorism, or other national security threats. Design, use, or maintain databases and software applications, such as geographic information systems (GIS) mapping and artificial intelligence tools. Establish criminal profiles to aid in connecting criminal organizations with their members. Evaluate records of communications, such as telephone calls, to plot activity and determine the size and location of criminal groups and members. Gather and evaluate information, using tools such as aerial photographs, radar equipment, or sensitive radio equipment. Gather intelligence information by field observation, confidential information sources, or public records. Gather, analyze, correlate, or evaluate information from a variety of resources, such as law enforcement databases. Link or chart suspects to criminal organizations or events to determine activities and interrelationships. Operate cameras, radios, or other surveillance equipment to intercept communications or document activities. Prepare comprehensive written reports, presentations, maps, or charts based on research, collection, and analysis of intelligence data. Prepare plans to intercept foreign communications transmissions. Study the assets of criminal suspects to determine the flow of money from or to targeted groups.

Related Knowledge/Courses: No data available.

Personality Types: No data available.

Skills: No data available.

Work Environment: No data available.

Job Specialization: Police Detectives

Conduct investigations to prevent crimes or solve criminal cases. Examine crime scenes to obtain clues and evidence, such as loose hairs, fibers, clothing, or weapons. Secure deceased body and obtain evidence from it, preventing bystanders from tampering with it prior to medical examiner's arrival. Obtain evidence from suspects. Provide testimony as a witness in court. Analyze completed police reports to determine what additional information and investigative work is needed. Prepare charges or responses to charges, or information for court cases, according to formalized procedures. Note, mark, and photograph location of objects found, such as footprints, tire tracks, bullets and bloodstains, and take measurements of the scene. Obtain facts or statements from complainants, witnesses, and accused persons and record interviews, using recording device. Obtain summary of incident from officer in charge at crime scene, taking care to avoid disturbing evidence. Examine records and governmental agency files to find identifying data about suspects. Prepare and serve search and arrest warrants. Block or rope off scene and check perimeter to ensure that entire scene is secured. Summon medical help for injured individuals and alert medical personnel to take statements from them. Provide information to lab personnel concerning the source of an item of evidence and tests to be performed. Monitor conditions of victims who are unconscious so that arrangements can be made to take statements if consciousness is regained. Secure persons at scene, keeping witnesses from conversing or leaving the scene before investigators arrive. Preserve, process, and analyze items of evidence obtained from crime scenes and suspects, placing them in proper containers and destroying evidence no longer needed. Record progress of investigation, maintain informational files on suspects, and submit reports to commanding officer or magistrate to authorize warrants.

Related Knowledge/Courses: Public Safety and Security; Law and Government; Psychology; Therapy and Counseling; Customer and Personal Service; Philosophy and Theology.

Personality Types: Enterprising-Investigative.

Skills: Science; Negotiation; Operation and Control; Social Perceptiveness; Operation Monitoring; Service Orientation; Active Learning; Critical Thinking.

Work Environment: More often outdoors than indoors; sitting; noise; very hot or cold; contaminants; exposed to disease or infections.

Job Specialization: Police Identification and Records Officers

Collect evidence at crime scene, classify and identify fingerprints, and photograph evidence for use in criminal and civil cases. Photograph crime or accident scenes for evidence records. Analyze and process evidence at crime scenes and in the laboratory, wearing protective equipment and using powders and chemicals. Look for trace evidence, such as fingerprints, hairs, fibers, or shoe impressions, using alternative light sources when necessary. Dust selected areas of crime scene, and lift latent fingerprints, adhering to proper preservation procedures. Testify in court, and present evidence. Package, store, and retrieve evidence. Serve as technical advisor and coordinate with other law enforcement workers to exchange information on crime-scene collection activities. Perform emergency work during off-hours. Submit evidence to supervisors. Process film and prints from crime or accident scenes. Identify, classify, and file fingerprints, using systems such as the Henry Classification system.

Related Knowledge/Courses: Public Safety and Security; Law and Government; Chemistry; Customer and Personal Service; Clerical Practices; Telecommunications.

Personality Types: Conventional-Realistic-Investigative.

Skills: Operation and Control; Speaking; Negotiation; Operation Monitoring; Critical Thinking; Active Listening; Persuasion; Technology Design.

Work Environment: Indoors; sitting; using hands; noise; contaminants; exposed to disease or infections; hazardous conditions.

Diagnostic Medical Sonographers

- ❋ Average Annual Earnings (All): $65,210
- ❋ Average Annual Earnings (Recent Veterans): $43,650
- ❋ Earnings Growth Potential: Low (31.1%)
- ❋ Growth: 43.5%
- ❋ Annual Job Openings: 3,170
- ❋ Veteran Employment by Sector: For-Profit, 48.2%; Nonprofit, 18.5%; Government, 32.5%; Self-Employed, 0.8%.

Considerations for Job Outlook: Sonographers who are certified in more than one specialty are expected to have better job opportunities.

Produce ultrasonic recordings of internal organs for use by physicians. Decide which images to include, looking for differences between healthy and pathological areas. Observe screen during scan to ensure that image produced is satisfactory for diagnostic purposes, making adjustments to equipment as required. Observe and care for patients throughout examinations to ensure their safety and comfort. Provide sonogram and oral or written summary of technical findings to physician for use in medical diagnosis. Operate ultrasound equipment to produce and record images of the motion, shape, and composition of blood, organs, tissues, and bodily masses such as fluid accumulations. Select appropriate equipment settings and adjust patient positions to obtain the best sites and angles. Determine whether scope of exam should be extended, based on findings. Process and code film from procedures and complete appropriate documentation. Obtain and record accurate patient history, including prior test results and information from physical examinations. Record and store suitable images, using camera unit connected to the ultrasound equipment. Prepare patients for exam by explaining procedure, transferring them to ultrasound table, scrubbing skin and applying gel, and positioning them properly. Coordinate work with physicians and other health-care team members, including providing assistance during invasive procedures. Maintain records that include patient information, sonographs and interpretations, files of correspondence, publications and regulations, or quality assurance records such as pathology, biopsy, or postoperative reports. Perform legal and ethical duties including preparing safety and accident reports, obtaining written consent from patient to perform invasive procedures, and reporting symptoms of abuse and neglect. Supervise and train students and other medical sonographers. Maintain stock and supplies, preparing supplies for special examinations and ordering supplies when necessary.

Related Military Specializations: Advanced X-Ray Technician; Diagnostic Imaging Apprentice, Ultrasound; Diagnostic Imaging Craftsman; Diagnostic Imaging Craftsman, Ultrasound; Diagnostic Imaging Helper, Ultrasound; Diagnostic Imaging Journeyman; Diagnostic Imaging Journeyman, Ultrasound. **Average Educational Level of Vets:** Associate degree. **Usual Educational Requirement:** Associate degree. **Relevant Educational Program:** Diagnostic Medical Sonography/ Sonographer and Ultrasound Technician Training. **Related Knowledge/Courses:** Medicine and Dentistry; Physics; Biology; Customer and Personal Service; Psychology; Clerical Practices. **Work Experience Needed:** None. **On-the-Job Training Needed:** None. **Certification/Licensure:** Voluntary certification by association.

Personality Types: Investigative-Social-Realistic. **Key Career Cluster:** 08 Health Science. **Key**

Career Pathway: 8.2 Diagnostics Services. **Top Industries for Vets:** Hospitals; National Security and International Affairs; Other Health Care Services; Offices of Physicians; Outpatient Care Centers.

Skills: Science; Equipment Maintenance; Equipment Selection; Repairing; Operation and Control; Troubleshooting; Operation Monitoring; Quality Control Analysis.

Work Environment: Indoors; more often sitting than standing; using hands; bending or twisting the body; repetitive motions; contaminants; exposed to disease or infections.

Electrical Power-Line Installers and Repairers

* Average Annual Earnings (All): $60,190
* Average Annual Earnings (Recent Veterans): $51,290
* Earnings Growth Potential: High (42.5%)
* Growth: 13.2%
* Annual Job Openings: 5,270
* Veteran Employment by Sector: For-Profit, 81.5%; Nonprofit, 3.6%; Government, 14.9%; Self-Employed, 0.0%.

Considerations for Job Outlook: Good job opportunities are expected overall. Highly skilled workers with apprenticeship training or a 2-year associate degree in telecommunications, electronics, or electricity should have the best job opportunities. Employment opportunities should be particularly good for electrical power-line installers and repairers, as many workers in this field are expected to retire. Because of layoffs in the 1990s, more of the electrical power industry is near retirement age than in most industries. This is of special concern for electrical line workers who must be in good physical shape and cannot necessarily put off retirement.

Install or repair cables or wires used in electrical power or distribution systems. Adhere to safety practices and procedures, such as checking equipment regularly and erecting barriers around work areas. Open switches or attach grounding devices to remove electrical hazards from disturbed or fallen lines or to facilitate repairs. Climb poles or use truck-mounted buckets to access equipment. Place insulating or fireproofing materials over conductors and joints. Install, maintain, and repair electrical distribution and transmission systems, including conduits; cables; wires; and related equipment such as transformers, circuit breakers, and switches. Identify defective sectionalizing devices, circuit breakers, fuses, voltage regulators, transformers, switches, relays, or wiring, using wiring diagrams and electrical-testing instruments. Drive vehicles equipped with tools and materials to job sites. Coordinate work-assignment preparation and completion with other workers. String wire conductors and cables between poles, towers, trenches, pylons, and buildings, setting lines in place and using winches to adjust tension. Inspect and test power lines and auxiliary equipment to locate and identify problems, using reading and testing instruments. Test conductors according to electrical diagrams and specifications to identify corresponding conductors and to prevent incorrect connections. Replace damaged poles with new poles, and straighten the poles. Install watt-hour meters, and connect service drops between power lines and consumers' facilities.

Related Military Specializations: Cable and Antenna Systems Apprentice; Cable and Antenna Systems Craftsman; Cable and Antenna Systems Helper; Cable and Antenna Systems Journeyman; Cable Splicing Technician; Communications Antenna Systems Journeyman; Communications Cable and Antenna Systems, Journeyman; Construction Electrician; Powerline Distribution Specialist (RC); SSN Radio Frequency (RF)Equipment Operator; Transmission and Distribution Specialist (RC). **Average Educational Level of Vets:** High school diploma or equivalent. **Usual Educational Requirement:** High school diploma or equivalent. **Relevant Educational Programs:** Electrical and Power Transmission Installation/Installer, General; Electrical and Power Transmission Installers, Other; Lineworker. **Related Knowledge/Courses:** Building and Construction; Mechanical Devices; Customer and Personal Service; Engineering and Technology; Transportation; Design. **Work Experience Needed:** None. **On-the-Job Training Needed:** Long-term on-the-job training. **Certification/Licensure:** Voluntary certification by association.

Personality Types: Realistic-Investigative-Conventional. **Key Career Cluster:** 02 Architecture and Construction. **Key Career Pathway:** 2.2 Construction. **Top Industries for Vets:** Electric Power Generation, Transmission and Distribution; Construction; Electric and Gas, and Other Combinations; National Security and International Affairs; Wired Telecommunications Carriers.

Skills: Repairing; Troubleshooting; Equipment Maintenance; Operation and Control; Quality Control Analysis; Operation Monitoring; Installation; Equipment Selection.

Work Environment: Outdoors; standing; walking and running; using hands; bending or twisting the body; repetitive motions; noise; very hot or cold; bright or inadequate lighting; contaminants; cramped work space; high places; hazardous conditions; hazardous equipment; minor burns, cuts, bites, or stings.

Electricians

- ❋ Average Annual Earnings (All): $49,320
- ❋ Average Annual Earnings (Recent Veterans): $37,540
- ❋ Earnings Growth Potential: Medium (38.4%)
- ❋ Growth: 23.2%
- ❋ Annual Job Openings: 28,920
- ❋ Veteran Employment by Sector: For-Profit, 71.6%; Nonprofit, 1.2%; Government, 24.6%; Self-Employed, 2.7%.

Considerations for Job Outlook: Employment of electricians fluctuates with the overall economy. On the one hand, there is great demand for electricians during peak periods of building and manufacturing. On the other hand, workers may experience periods of unemployment when the overall level of construction falls. Inside electricians in factories tend to have the most stable employment.

Install, maintain, and repair electrical wiring, equipment, and fixtures. Maintain current electrician's license or identification card to meet governmental regulations. Connect wires to circuit breakers, transformers, or other components. Repair or replace wiring, equipment, and fixtures, using hand tools and power tools. Assemble, install, test, and maintain electrical or electronic wiring, equipment, appliances, apparatus, and fixtures, using hand tools and power tools. Test electrical systems and continuity of circuits in electrical wiring, equipment, and fixtures, using testing devices such as ohmmeters, voltmeters, and oscilloscopes, to ensure compatibility and safety of system. Use a variety of tools and equipment such as power construction equipment, measuring devices, power tools, and testing equipment, including oscilloscopes, ammeters, and test lamps. Plan layout and installation of electrical wiring, equipment, and fixtures based on job specifications and local codes. Inspect electrical systems, equipment, and components to identify hazards, defects, and the need for adjustment or repair and to ensure compliance with codes. Direct and train workers to install, maintain, or repair electrical wiring, equipment, and fixtures. Diagnose malfunctioning systems, apparatus, and components, using test equipment and hand tools, to locate the cause of a breakdown and correct the problem. Prepare sketches or follow blueprints to determine the location of wiring and equipment and to ensure conformance to building and safety codes.

Related Military Specializations: Advanced Construction Electrician; Construction Electrician; DD-963/LHD-1 Electrical Component Maintenance Technician; Electrical Systems Apprentice; Electrical Systems Craftsman; Electrical Systems Helper; Electrical Systems Journeyman; Electrician; Electrolytic Oxygen Generator (Model 6L16) Electrical Technician; FFG-7 Class Auxiliaries Electrical System Technician; Interior Electrician; Planning Series—Oxygen Generating Plant Electrical/Electronic Maintenance Technician; others. **Average Educational Level of Vets:** High school diploma or equivalent. **Usual Educational Requirement:** High school diploma or equivalent. **Relevant Educational Program:** Electrician. **Related Knowledge/ Courses:** Building and Construction; Mechanical Devices; Design; Physics; Telecommunications; Engineering and Technology. **Work Experience Needed:** None. **On-the-Job Training Needed:** Apprenticeship. **Certification/Licensure:** Licensure.

Personality Types: Realistic-Investigative-Conventional. **Key Career Cluster:** 02 Architecture and Construction. **Key Career**

Pathway: 2.2 Construction. **Top Industries for Vets:** Construction; National Security and International Affairs; Ship and Boat Building; Electric Power Generation, Transmission and Distribution; Iron and Steel Mills and Steel Products.

Skills: Installation; Repairing; Equipment Maintenance; Troubleshooting; Equipment Selection; Quality Control Analysis; Operation and Control; Management of Financial Resources.

Work Environment: More often outdoors than indoors; standing; climbing; walking and running; using hands; bending or twisting the body; repetitive motions; noise; very hot or cold; bright or inadequate lighting; contaminants; cramped work space; high places; hazardous conditions; hazardous equipment; minor burns, cuts, bites, or stings.

Emergency Medical Technicians and Paramedics

- ✸ Average Annual Earnings (All): $30,710

- ✸ Average Annual Earnings (Recent Veterans): $36,670

- ✸ Earnings Growth Potential: Medium (35.3%)

- ✸ Growth: 33.3%

- ✸ Annual Job Openings: 12,080

- ✸ Veteran Employment by Sector: For-Profit, 44.0%; Nonprofit, 11.8%; Government, 44.2%; Self-Employed, 0.0%.

Considerations for Job Outlook: Emergencies such as car crashes, natural disasters, and violence will continue to create demand for EMTs and paramedics. There will also continue to be demand for part-time, volunteer EMTs and paramedics in rural areas and smaller metropolitan areas. Growth in the middle-aged and elderly population will lead to an increase in the number of age-related health emergencies, such as heart attacks or strokes.

Assess injuries, administer emergency medical care, and extricate trapped individuals. Transport injured or sick persons to medical facilities. Administer first-aid treatment and life-support care to sick or injured persons in prehospital setting. Operate equipment such as electrocardiograms (EKGs), external defibrillators, and bag-valve mask resuscitators in advanced life-support environments. Assess nature and extent of illness or injury to establish and prioritize medical procedures. Maintain vehicles and medical and communication equipment, and replenish first-aid equipment and supplies. Observe, record, and report to physician the patient's condition or injury, the treatment provided, and reactions to drugs and treatment. Perform emergency diagnostic and treatment procedures, such as stomach suction, airway management or heart monitoring, during ambulance ride. Administer drugs, orally or by injection, and perform intravenous procedures under a physician's direction. Comfort and reassure patients. Communicate with dispatchers and treatment center personnel to provide information about situation, to arrange reception of victims, and to receive instructions for further treatment. Immobilize patient for placement on stretcher and ambulance transport, using backboard or other spinal immobilization device. Coordinate work with other emergency medical team members and police and fire department personnel. Decontaminate ambulance interior following treatment of patient with infectious disease and report case to proper authorities. Drive mobile intensive care unit to specified location, following instructions from emergency medical dispatcher. Coordinate with treatment center personnel to obtain patients' vital statistics and medical history, to determine the circumstances of the emergency, and to administer emergency treatment.

Related Military Specializations: Aerospace Medical Service Apprentice; Aerospace Medical Service Apprentice, Allergy/immunology; Aerospace Medical Service Apprentice, Neurology; Aerospace Medical Service Craftsman; Aerospace Medical Service Craftsman, Independent Duty Medical Technician; Aerospace Medical Service Helper; Aerospace Medical Service Helper, Allergy/immunology; Aerospace Medical Service Helper, Neurology; Aerospace Medical Service Journeyman; Aerospace Medical Service Journeyman, Allergy/immunology; others.
Average Educational Level of Vets: One or more years of college, no degree. **Usual Educational Requirement:** Postsecondary vocational training. **Relevant Educational Program:** Emergency Medical Technology/Technician (EMT Paramedic). **Related Knowledge/Courses:** Medicine and Dentistry; Customer and Personal Service; Therapy and Counseling; Psychology; Transportation; Education and Training. **Work Experience Needed:** None. **On-the-Job Training Needed:** None. **Certification/Licensure:** Licensure.

Personality Types: Social-Investigative-Realistic. **Key Career Cluster:** 12 Law, Public Safety, Corrections, and Security. **Key Career Pathway:** 12.2 Emergency and Fire Management Services. **Top Industries for Vets:** Other Health Care Services; Hospitals; National Security and International Affairs; Justice, Public Order, and Safety Activities; Offices of Other Health Practitioners.

Skills: Science; Operation and Control; Service Orientation; Coordination; Operation Monitoring; Active Learning; Troubleshooting; Equipment Selection.

Work Environment: More often outdoors than indoors; standing; using hands; bending or twisting the body; repetitive motions; noise; very hot or cold; bright or inadequate lighting; contaminants; cramped work space; exposed to disease or infections; hazardous conditions; hazardous equipment; minor burns, cuts, bites, or stings.

Environmental Engineering Technicians

* Average Annual Earnings (All): $44,850
* Average Annual Earnings (Recent Veterans): $48,460
* Earnings Growth Potential: Medium (36.8%)
* Growth: 24.3%
* Annual Job Openings: 820
* Veteran Employment by Sector: For-Profit, 60.8%; Nonprofit, 0.8%; Government, 37.8%; Self-Employed, 0.5%.

Considerations for Job Outlook: Employment in this occupation is typically tied to projects created by environmental engineers. State and local governments are expected to focus efforts and resources on efficient water use and wastewater treatment, which will support the demand for environmental engineering technicians.

Apply theory and principles of environmental engineering to modify, test, and operate equipment and devices used in the prevention, control, and remediation of environmental problems. Receive, set up, test, and decontaminate equipment. Maintain project logbook records and computer program files. Perform environmental quality work in field and office settings. Conduct pollution surveys, collecting and analyzing samples such as air and groundwater. Review technical documents to ensure completeness and conformance to requirements. Perform laboratory work such as logging numerical and visual observations, preparing and packaging samples, recording test results, and performing photo documentation. Review work plans to schedule activities. Obtain product information, identify vendors and suppliers, and order materials and equipment to maintain inventory. Arrange for the disposal of lead, asbestos, and other hazardous materials. Inspect facilities to monitor compliance with regulations governing substances such as asbestos, lead, and wastewater. Provide technical engineering support in the planning of projects such as wastewater treatment plants to ensure compliance with environmental regulations and policies. Improve chemical processes to reduce toxic emissions. Oversee support staff. Assist in the cleanup of hazardous material spills. Produce environmental assessment reports, tabulating data and preparing charts, graphs, and sketches. Maintain process parameters, and evaluate process anomalies. Work with customers to assess the environmental impact of proposed construction and to develop pollution prevention programs.

Related Military Specializations: None. **Average Educational Level of Vets:** One or more years of college, no degree. **Usual Educational Requirement:** Associate degree. **Relevant Educational Programs:** Environmental Engineering Technology/Environmental Technology; Hazardous Materials Information Systems Technology/Technician. **Related Knowledge/Courses:** Biology; Building and Construction; Physics; Chemistry; Engineering and Technology; Design. **Work Experience Needed:** None. **On-the-Job Training Needed:** None. **Certification/Licensure:** None.

Personality Types: Realistic-Investigative-Conventional. **Key Career Cluster:** 01

Agriculture, Food, and Natural Resources. **Key Career Pathway:** 1.6 Environmental Service Systems. **Top Industries for Vets:** National Security and International Affairs; Architectural, Engineering, and Related Services; Electronic Components and Products, Not Elsewhere Classified; Wired Telecommunications Carriers; Broadcasting, Including Internet Publishing and Web Search Portals.

Skills: Science; Mathematics; Equipment Maintenance; Quality Control Analysis; Management of Material Resources; Equipment Selection; Troubleshooting; Repairing.

Work Environment: Indoors.

Environmental Science and Protection Technicians, Including Health

- Average Annual Earnings (All): $42,270
- Average Annual Earnings (Recent Veterans): $36,670
- Earnings Growth Potential: Medium (36.8%)
- Growth: 23.6%
- Annual Job Openings: 1,950
- Veteran Employment by Sector: For-Profit, 42.6%; Nonprofit, 10.3%; Government, 46.6%; Self-Employed, 0.5%.

Considerations for Job Outlook: Environmental science and protection technicians should have good opportunities for employment. In addition to openings due to growth, many job openings are expected to be created by those who retire or leave the occupation for other reasons. Job candidates with an associate degree or experience should have the best opportunities. Job opportunities available in state and local governments will vary from year to year with the budgets of state and local environmental protection agencies.

Perform laboratory and field tests to monitor the environment and investigate sources of pollution under the direction of an environmental scientist, engineer, or other specialist. Collect samples of gases, soils, water, industrial wastewater, and asbestos products to conduct tests on pollutant levels and identify sources of pollution. Record test data, and prepare reports, summaries, and charts that interpret test results. Develop and implement programs for monitoring of environmental pollution and radiation. Discuss test results and analyses with customers. Set up equipment or stations to monitor and collect pollutants from sites such as smokestacks, manufacturing plants, or mechanical equipment. Maintain files, such as hazardous waste databases, chemical usage data, personnel exposure information, and diagrams showing equipment locations. Develop testing procedures or direct activities of workers in laboratory. Prepare samples or photomicrographs for testing and analysis. Calibrate microscopes, and test instruments. Examine and analyze material for presence and concentration of contaminants such as asbestos, using variety of microscopes. Calculate amount of pollutant in samples or compute air pollution or gas flow in industrial processes, using chemical and mathematical formulas. Make recommendations to control or eliminate unsafe conditions at workplaces or public facilities. Weigh, analyze, and measure collected sample particles such as lead, coal dust, or rock to determine concentration of pollutants.

Related Military Specializations: None. **Average Educational Level of Vets:** One or more years of college, no degree. **Usual Educational Requirement:** Associate degree. **Relevant Educational Programs:** Physical Science Technologies/Technicians, Other; Science Technologies/Technicians, Other. **Related Knowledge/Courses:** Biology; Chemistry; Geography; Physics; Computers and Electronics; Building and Construction. **Work Experience Needed:** None. **On-the-Job Training Needed:** Moderate-term on-the-job training. **Certification/Licensure:** Licensure for some specializations.

Personality Types: Investigative-Realistic-Conventional. **Key Career Cluster:** 01 Agriculture, Food, and Natural Resources. **Key Career Pathway:** 1.6 Environmental Service Systems. **Top Industries for Vets:** Scientific Research and Development Services; National Security and International Affairs; Architectural, Engineering, and Related Services; Colleges and Universities, Including Junior Colleges; Management, Scientific and Technical Consulting Services.

Skills: Science; Equipment Maintenance; Troubleshooting; Operation and Control; Operations Analysis; Repairing; Equipment Selection; Mathematics.

Work Environment: More often outdoors than indoors; standing; using hands; noise; very hot or cold; bright or inadequate lighting; contaminants; hazardous conditions; hazardous equipment; minor burns, cuts, bites, or stings.

Executive Secretaries and Executive Administrative Assistants

- ❋ Average Annual Earnings (All): $45,580
- ❋ Average Annual Earnings (Recent Veterans): $32,410
- ❋ Earnings Growth Potential: Low (33.5%)
- ❋ Growth: 12.6%
- ❋ Annual Job Openings: 32,180
- ❋ Veteran Employment by Sector: For-Profit, 40.8%; Nonprofit, 9.3%; Government, 49.0%; Self-Employed, 0.9%.

Considerations for Job Outlook: In addition to jobs coming from employment growth, numerous job openings will arise from the need to replace secretaries and administrative assistants who transfer to other occupations or retire. Job opportunities should be best for applicants with extensive knowledge of computer software applications. Applicants with a bachelor's degree are expected to be in great demand and will act as managerial assistants who perform more complex tasks.

Provide high-level administrative support by conducting research, preparing statistical reports, handling information requests, and performing clerical functions. Manage and maintain executives' schedules. Prepare invoices, reports, memos, letters, financial statements, and other documents, using word processing, spreadsheet, database, or presentation software. Open, sort, and distribute incoming correspondence, including faxes and e-mail. Read and analyze incoming memos, submissions, and reports to determine their significance and plan their distribution. File and retrieve corporate documents, records, and reports. Greet visitors, and determine whether they should be given access to specific individuals. Prepare responses to correspondence containing routine inquiries. Perform general office duties such as ordering supplies, maintaining records-management systems, and performing basic bookkeeping work. Prepare agendas and make arrangements for committee, board, and other meetings. Make travel arrangements for executives. Conduct research, compile data, and prepare papers for consideration and presentation by executives, committees, and boards of directors. Compile, transcribe, and distribute minutes of meetings. Attend meetings to record minutes. Coordinate and direct office services, such as records and budget preparation, personnel, and housekeeping, to aid executives. Meet with individuals, special-interest groups, and others on behalf of executives, committees, and boards of directors. Set up and oversee administrative policies and procedures for offices or organizations. Supervise and train other clerical staff.

Related Military Specializations: Executive Administrative Assistant; Flag Officer Writer; Marine Aide. **Average Educational Level of Vets:** One or more years of college, no degree. **Usual Educational Requirement:** High school diploma or equivalent. **Relevant Educational Programs:** Administrative Assistant and Secretarial Science, General; Executive Assistant/Executive Secretary Training. **Related Knowledge/Courses:** Clerical Practices; Personnel and Human Resources. **Work Experience Needed:** 1 to 5 years. **On-the-Job Training Needed:** None. **Certification/Licensure:** Voluntary certification by association.

Personality Types: Conventional-Enterprising. **Key Career Cluster:** 04 Business, Management, and Administration. **Key Career Pathway:** 4.6 Administrative and Information Support. **Top Industries for Vets:** National Security and International Affairs; Hospitals; Legal Services; Colleges and Universities, Including Junior

Colleges; Justice, Public Order, and Safety Activities.

Skills: Service Orientation; Programming; Active Listening; Writing; Speaking; Time Management; Reading Comprehension; Monitoring.

Work Environment: Indoors; sitting; repetitive motions; noise.

Firefighters

- ❈ Average Annual Earnings (All): $45,420
- ❈ Average Annual Earnings (Recent Veterans): $49,110
- ❈ Earnings Growth Potential: High (50.5%)
- ❈ Growth: 8.6%
- ❈ Annual Job Openings: 11,230
- ❈ Veteran Employment by Sector: For-Profit, 0.3%; Nonprofit, 0.0%; Government, 99.7%; Self-Employed, 0.0%.

Considerations for Job Outlook: Prospective firefighters will face tough competition for positions. Many people are attracted to the job's challenge, opportunity for public service, relatively low formal educational requirements, and pensions that are usually guaranteed after 25 years of service. As a result, a department often receives hundreds or thousands of applicants for a single position. Physically fit applicants with high test scores, some postsecondary firefighter education, and paramedic training have the best prospects.

Control and extinguish fires or respond to emergency situations where life, property, or the environment is at risk. For task data, see Job Specializations.

Related Military Specializations: Aircraft Rescue and Firefighting Specialist; Aviation

Boatswain's Mate (Aircraft Handling); Damage Control Basic; Damage Controlman; Fire Protection Apprentice; Fire Protection Helper; Fire Protection Journeyman; Firefighter; Shipboard Aircraft Rescue, Firefighting and Salvage Specialists; Shore Base Airport and Aircraft Firefighter. **Average Educational Level of Vets:** One or more years of college, no degree. **Usual Educational Requirement:** Postsecondary vocational training. **Relevant Educational Programs:** Fire Prevention and Safety Technology/Technician; Fire Protection, Other; Fire Science/Firefighting; Natural Resources Law Enforcement and Protective Services; Wildland/Forest Firefighting and Investigation. **Work Experience Needed:** None. **On-the-Job Training Needed:** Long-term on-the-job training. **Certification/Licensure:** Licensure in some states; certification by association; municipal examination.

Key Career Cluster: 12 Law, Public Safety, Corrections, and Security. **Key Career Pathway:** 12.2 Emergency and Fire Management Services. **Top Industries for Vets:** Justice, Public Order, and Safety Activities; National Security and International Affairs; Executive Offices and Legislative Bodies; Services Incidental to Transportation; Administration of Economic Programs and Space Research.

Job Specialization: Forest Firefighters

Control and suppress fires in forests or vacant public land. Maintain contact with fire dispatchers at all times to notify them of the need for additional firefighters and supplies or to detail any difficulties encountered. Rescue fire victims, and administer emergency medical aid. Collaborate with other firefighters as a member of a firefighting crew. Patrol burned areas after fires to locate and eliminate hot spots that may restart fires. Extinguish flames and embers to suppress fires using shovels or engine- or hand-driven water or chemical pumps. Fell trees, cut and clear brush, and dig trenches to create firelines using axes, chain saws, or shovels. Maintain knowledge of current firefighting practices by participating in drills and by attending seminars, conventions, and conferences. Operate pumps connected to high-pressure hoses. Participate in physical training to maintain high levels of physical fitness. Establish water supplies, connect hoses, and direct water onto fires. Maintain fire equipment and firehouse living quarters. Inform and educate the public about fire prevention. Take action to contain any hazardous chemicals that could catch fire, leak, or spill. Organize fire caches, positioning equipment for the most effective response. Transport personnel and cargo to and from fire areas. Participate in fire-prevention and inspection programs. Perform forest-maintenance and improvement tasks such as cutting brush, planting trees, building trails, and marking timber.

Related Knowledge/Courses: Geography; Building and Construction; Telecommunications; Mechanical Devices; Public Safety and Security; Customer and Personal Service.

Personality Types: Realistic-Social.

Skills: Repairing; Equipment Maintenance; Equipment Selection; Operation and Control; Troubleshooting; Quality Control Analysis; Operation Monitoring; Coordination.

Work Environment: Outdoors; standing; walking and running; using hands; bending or twisting the body; repetitive motions; noise; very hot or cold; bright or inadequate lighting; contaminants; hazardous conditions; hazardous equipment; minor burns, cuts, bites, or stings.

Job Specialization: Municipal Firefighters

Control and extinguish municipal fires, protect life and property, and conduct rescue efforts. Administer first aid and cardiopulmonary resuscitation to injured persons. Rescue victims from burning buildings and accident sites. Search burning buildings to locate fire victims. Drive and operate firefighting vehicles and equipment. Move toward the source of a fire, using knowledge of types of fires, construction design, building materials, and physical layout of properties. Dress with equipment such as fire-resistant clothing and breathing apparatus. Position and climb ladders to gain access to upper levels of buildings or to rescue individuals from burning structures. Take action to contain hazardous chemicals that might catch fire, leak, or spill. Assess fires and situations, and report conditions to superiors to receive instructions using two-way radios. Respond to fire alarms and other calls for assistance such as automobile and industrial accidents. Operate pumps connected to high-pressure hoses. Select and attach hose nozzles, depending on fire type, and direct streams of water or chemicals onto fires. Create openings in buildings for ventilation or entrance, using axes, chisels, crowbars, electric saws, or core cutters. Inspect fire sites after flames have been extinguished to ensure that there is no further danger. Lay hose lines, and connect them to water supplies. Protect property from water and smoke using waterproof salvage covers, smoke ejectors, and deodorants. Participate in physical training activities to maintain a high level of physical fitness.

Related Knowledge/Courses: Building and Construction; Public Safety and Security; Mechanical Devices; Customer and Personal Service; Physics; Geography.

Personality Types: Realistic-Social-Enterprising.

Skills: Equipment Maintenance; Repairing; Troubleshooting; Operation and Control;

Equipment Selection; Science; Operation Monitoring; Quality Control Analysis.

Work Environment: More often outdoors than indoors; standing; using hands; noise; very hot or cold; bright or inadequate lighting; contaminants; cramped work space; exposed to disease or infections; hazardous conditions; hazardous equipment; minor burns, cuts, bites, or stings.

First-Line Supervisors of Fire Fighting and Prevention Workers

- ❋ Average Annual Earnings (All): $69,510
- ❋ Average Annual Earnings (Recent Veterans): $54,570
- ❋ Earnings Growth Potential: High (41.7%)
- ❋ Growth: 8.2%
- ❋ Annual Job Openings: 3,310
- ❋ Veteran Employment by Sector: For-Profit, 0.7%; Nonprofit, 0.0%; Government, 99.3%; Self-Employed, 0.0%.

Considerations for Job Outlook: Most job growth will stem from the conversion of volunteer firefighting positions into paid positions. Job seekers are expected to face keen competition. Those who have completed some firefighter education at a community college and have EMT or paramedic certification should have the best prospects.

Directly supervise and coordinate activities of workers engaged in fire fighting and fire prevention and control. For task data, see Job Specializations.

Related Military Specializations: Fire Protection Craftsman; Fire Protection Manager;

Fire Protection Superintendent. **Average Educational Level of Vets:** One or more years of college, no degree. **Usual Educational Requirement:** Postsecondary vocational training. **Relevant Educational Programs:** Fire Protection, Other; Fire Services Administration; Natural Resources Law Enforcement and Protective Services. **Work Experience Needed:** 1 to 5 years. **On-the-Job Training Needed:** None. **Certification/Licensure:** Licensure in some states; certification by association; municipal examination.

Key Career Cluster: 12 Law, Public Safety, Corrections, and Security. **Key Career Pathway:** 12.2 Emergency and Fire Management Services. **Top Industries for Vets:** Justice, Public Order, and Safety Activities; National Security and International Affairs; Forestry Except Logging; Coal Mining.

Job Specialization: Forest Fire Fighting and Prevention Supervisors

Supervise firefighters who control and suppress fires in forests or vacant public land. Communicate fire details to superiors, subordinates, and interagency dispatch centers, using two-way radios. Serve as working leader of an engine, hand, helicopter, or prescribed fire crew of three or more firefighters. Maintain fire suppression equipment in good condition, checking equipment periodically to ensure that it is ready for use. Evaluate size, location, and condition of forest fires in order to request and dispatch crews and position equipment so fires can be contained safely and effectively. Operate wildland fire engines and hoselays. Direct and supervise prescribed burn projects, and prepare post-burn reports analyzing burn conditions and results. Monitor prescribed burns to ensure that they are conducted safely and effectively. Identify staff training and development needs to ensure that appropriate training can be arranged. Maintain knowledge of forest fire laws and fire prevention techniques and tactics. Recommend equipment modifications or new equipment purchases. Perform administrative duties such as compiling and maintaining records, completing forms, preparing reports, and composing correspondence. Recruit and hire forest firefighting personnel. Train workers in such skills as parachute jumping, fire suppression, aerial observation, and radio communication, both in the classroom and on the job. Review and evaluate employee performance.

Related Knowledge/Courses: Public Safety and Security; Building and Construction; Mechanical Devices; Customer and Personal Service; Personnel and Human Resources; Transportation.

Personality Types:
Enterprising-Realistic-Conventional.

Skills: Operations Analysis; Equipment Maintenance; Operation and Control; Management of Personnel Resources; Coordination; Operation Monitoring; Monitoring; Equipment Selection.

Work Environment: Outdoors; standing; walking and running; using hands; noise; very hot or cold; bright or inadequate lighting; contaminants; cramped work space; hazardous equipment; minor burns, cuts, bites, or stings.

Job Specialization: Municipal Fire Fighting and Prevention Supervisors

Supervise firefighters who control and extinguish municipal fires, protect life and property, and conduct rescue efforts. Assign firefighters to jobs at strategic locations to facilitate rescue of persons and maximize application of extinguishing agents. Provide emergency medical services as required, and perform light to heavy rescue functions at emergencies. Assess nature and extent of fire, condition of building, danger to adjacent buildings, and water supply status to determine crew or company requirements. Instruct and drill fire department personnel in assigned duties, including firefighting, medical care, hazardous materials response, fire prevention, and related subjects. Inspect and test new and existing fire protection systems, fire detection systems, and fire safety equipment to ensure that they are operating properly. Compile and maintain records on personnel, accidents, equipment, and supplies. Perform maintenance and minor repairs on firefighting equipment, including vehicles, and write and submit proposals to modify, replace, and repair equipment. Prepare activity reports listing fire call locations, actions taken, fire types and probable causes, damage estimates, and situation dispositions. Evaluate the performance of assigned firefighting personnel. Direct the training of firefighters, assigning of instructors to training classes, and providing of supervisors with reports on training progress and status. Maintain required maps and records. Present and interpret fire prevention and fire code information to citizens' groups, organizations, contractors, engineers, and developers. Recommend personnel actions related to disciplinary procedures, performance, leaves of absence, and grievances. Direct firefighters in station maintenance duties, and participate in these duties. Attend in-service training classes to remain current in knowledge of codes, laws, ordinances, and regulations. Evaluate fire station procedures to ensure efficiency and enforcement of departmental regulations. Coordinate the distribution of fire prevention promotional materials.

Related Knowledge/Courses: Building and Construction; Public Safety and Security; Medicine and Dentistry; Mechanical Devices; Chemistry; Personnel and Human Resources.

Personality Types: Enterprising-Realistic-Social.

Skills: Operation and Control; Science; Equipment Selection; Repairing; Equipment Maintenance; Quality Control Analysis; Management of Personnel Resources; Systems Analysis.

Work Environment: More often outdoors than indoors; standing; using hands; noise; very hot or cold; bright or inadequate lighting; contaminants; cramped work space; exposed to disease or infections; high places; hazardous conditions; hazardous equipment; minor burns, cuts, bites, or stings.

First-Line Supervisors of Helpers, Laborers, and Material Movers, Hand

- ❈ Average Annual Earnings (All): $44,580
- ❈ Average Annual Earnings (Recent Veterans): $43,650
- ❈ Earnings Growth Potential: Medium (37.3%)
- ❈ Growth: 27.2%
- ❈ Annual Job Openings: 8,000
- ❈ Veteran Employment by Sector: For-Profit, 71.7%; Nonprofit, 3.7%; Government, 21.8%; Self-Employed, 2.8%.

Considerations for Job Outlook: Slower than average employment growth is projected.

Directly supervise and coordinate the activities of helpers, laborers, or material movers. Plan work schedules and assign duties to maintain adequate staffing levels, to ensure that activities are performed effectively, and to respond to fluctuating workloads. Collaborate with workers and managers to solve work-related problems. Review work throughout the work process and at completion, in order to ensure that it has been performed properly. Transmit and explain work orders to laborers. Check specifications of materials loaded or unloaded against information contained in work orders. Examine freight to determine loading sequences. Inform designated employees or departments of items loaded, and problems encountered. Evaluate employee performance, and prepare performance appraisals. Perform the same work duties as those whom they supervise, and/or perform more difficult or skilled tasks or assist in their performance. Prepare and maintain work records and reports that include information such as employee time and wages, daily receipts, and inspection results. Conduct staff meetings to relay general information or to address specific topics such as safety. Counsel employees in work-related activities, personal growth, and career development. Inspect equipment for wear and for conformance to specifications. Resolve personnel problems, complaints, and formal grievances when possible, or refer them to higher-level supervisors for resolution. Recommend or initiate personnel actions such as promotions, transfers, and disciplinary measures. Assess training needs of staff; then arrange for or provide appropriate instruction. Schedule times of shipment and modes of transportation for materials. Quote prices to customers. Estimate material, time, and staffing requirements for a given project, based on work orders, job specifications, and experience. Provide assistance in balancing books, tracking, monitoring, and projecting a unit's budget needs, and in developing unit policies and procedures.

Related Military Specializations: None. **Average Educational Level of Vets:** One or more years of college, no degree. **Usual Educational Requirement:** High school diploma or equivalent. **Relevant Educational Program:** No related CIP programs; this job is learned through work experience in a related occupation. **Related**

Knowledge/Courses: Production and Processing; Transportation; Personnel and Human Resources; Administration and Management; Public Safety and Security; Psychology. **Work Experience Needed:** 1 to 5 years. **On-the-Job Training Needed:** None. **Certification/Licensure:** None.

Personality Types: Enterprising-Realistic-Conventional. **Key Career Cluster:** 16 Transportation, Distribution, and Logistics. **Key Career Pathway:** 16.3 Warehousing and Distribution Center Operations. **Top Industries for Vets:** National Security and International Affairs; Couriers and Messengers; Services Incidental to Transportation; Truck Transportation; Rail Transportation.

Skills: Management of Material Resources; Management of Financial Resources; Management of Personnel Resources; Negotiation; Persuasion; Operations Analysis; Time Management; Systems Evaluation.

Work Environment: Indoors; standing; walking and running; noise; very hot or cold; contaminants.

Job Specialization: Recycling Coordinators

Supervise curbside and drop-off recycling programs for municipal governments or private firms. Oversee recycling pick-up or drop-off programs to ensure compliance with community ordinances. Supervise recycling technicians, community service workers, or other recycling operations employees or volunteers. Assign truck drivers or recycling technicians to routes. Coordinate recycling collection schedules to optimize service and efficiency. Coordinate shipments of recycling materials with shipping brokers or processing companies. Create or manage recycling operations budgets. Design community solid and hazardous waste management programs. Develop community or corporate recycling plans and goals to minimize waste and conform to resource constraints. Implement grant-funded projects, monitoring and reporting progress in accordance with sponsoring agency requirements. Investigate violations of solid waste or recycling ordinances. Make presentations to educate the public on how to recycle or on the environmental advantages of recycling. Negotiate contracts with waste management or other firms. Operate fork lifts, skid loaders, or trucks to move or store recyclable materials. Operate recycling processing equipment, such as sorters, balers, crushers, and granulators to sort and process materials. Oversee campaigns to promote recycling or waste reduction programs in communities or private companies. Prepare grant applications to fund recycling programs or program enhancements. Schedule movement of recycling materials into and out of storage areas. Identify or investigate new opportunities for materials to be collected and recycled. Inspect physical condition of recycling or hazardous waste facility for compliance with safety, quality, and service standards. Maintain logs of recycling materials received or shipped to processing companies. Prepare bills of lading, statements of shipping records, or customer receipts related to recycling or hazardous material services.

Related Knowledge/Courses: No data available.

Personality Types: No data available.

Skills: No data available.

Work Environment: No data available.

First-Line Supervisors of Landscaping, Lawn Service, and Groundskeeping Workers

- ❀ Average Annual Earnings (All): $42,050
- ❀ Average Annual Earnings (Recent Veterans): $21,830
- ❀ Earnings Growth Potential: Medium (36.4%)
- ❀ Growth: 15.1%
- ❀ Annual Job Openings: 6,010
- ❀ Veteran Employment by Sector: For-Profit, 55.7%; Nonprofit, 2.7%; Government, 4.4%; Self-Employed, 37.3%.

Considerations for Job Outlook: Demand for lawn care and landscaping services is expected to grow, resulting in employment growth for these workers. Job prospects are expected to be good. Opportunities for year-round work should be best in regions with temperate climates.

Directly supervise and coordinate activities of workers engaged in landscaping or groundskeeping activities. Establish and enforce operating procedures and work standards that will ensure adequate performance and personnel safety. Inspect completed work to ensure conformance to specifications, standards, and contract requirements. Direct activities of workers who perform duties such as landscaping, cultivating lawns, or pruning trees and shrubs. Schedule work for crews depending on work priorities, crew and equipment availability, and weather conditions. Plant and maintain vegetation through activities such as mulching, fertilizing, watering, mowing, and pruning. Monitor project activities to ensure that instructions are followed, deadlines are met, and schedules are maintained. Train workers in tasks such as transplanting and pruning trees and shrubs, finishing cement, using equipment, and caring for turf. Inventory supplies of tools, equipment, and materials to ensure that sufficient supplies are available and items are in usable condition. Provide workers with assistance in performing duties as necessary to meet deadlines. Confer with other supervisors to coordinate work activities with those of other departments or units. Perform personnel-related activities such as hiring workers, evaluating staff performance, and taking disciplinary actions when performance problems occur. Direct or perform mixing and application of fertilizers, insecticides, herbicides, and fungicides. Review contracts or work assignments to determine service, machine, and workforce requirements for jobs. Maintain required records such as personnel information and project records. Prepare and maintain required records such as work activity and personnel reports. Order the performance of corrective work when problems occur, and recommend procedural changes to avoid such problems. Identify diseases and pests affecting landscaping, and order appropriate treatments. Investigate work-related complaints in order to verify problems, and to determine responses.

Related Military Specializations: None. **Average Educational Level of Vets:** High school diploma or equivalent. **Usual Educational Requirement:** High school diploma or equivalent. **Relevant Educational Programs:** Applied Horticulture/Horticulture Operations, General; Golf Course Operation and Grounds Management; Greenhouse Operations and Management; Landscaping and Groundskeeping; Ornamental Horticulture; Plant Nursery Operations and Management; Turf and Turfgrass Management. **Related Knowledge/Courses:** Mechanical Devices; Building and Construction; Design; Biology; Chemistry; Education and Training. **Work Experience Needed:** 1 to 5 years. **On-the-Job Training Needed:** None. **Certification/Licensure:** None.

Personality Types: Enterprising-Realistic-Conventional. **Key Career Cluster:** 01 Agriculture, Food, and Natural Resources. **Key Career Pathway:** 1.2 Plant Systems. **Top Industries for Vets:** Landscaping Services; Other Amusement, Gambling, and Recreation Industries; National Security and International Affairs; Museums, Art Galleries, Historical Sites, and Similar Institutions; Architectural, Engineering, and Related Services.

Skills: Operation and Control; Repairing; Equipment Maintenance; Operation Monitoring; Management of Financial Resources; Management of Material Resources; Troubleshooting; Quality Control Analysis.

Work Environment: More often outdoors than indoors; standing; walking and running; using hands; noise; very hot or cold; bright or inadequate lighting; contaminants; hazardous equipment; minor burns, cuts, bites, or stings.

First-Line Supervisors of Mechanics, Installers, and Repairers

- ❋ Average Annual Earnings (All): $59,850
- ❋ Average Annual Earnings (Recent Veterans): $52,380
- ❋ Earnings Growth Potential: Medium (39.6%)
- ❋ Growth: 11.9%
- ❋ Annual Job Openings: 16,490
- ❋ Veteran Employment by Sector: For-Profit, 40.8%; Nonprofit, 1.9%; Government, 57.1%; Self-Employed, 0.3%.

Considerations for Job Outlook: Slower than average employment growth is projected.

Directly supervise and coordinate the activities of mechanics, installers, and repairers. Determine schedules, sequences, and assignments for work activities, based on work priority, quantity of equipment, and skill of personnel. Monitor employees' work levels, and review work performance. Monitor tool and part inventories and the condition and maintenance of shops to ensure adequate working conditions. Recommend or initiate personnel actions such as hires, promotions, transfers, discharges, and disciplinary measures. Investigate accidents and injuries, and prepare reports of findings. Compile operational and personnel records such as time and production records, inventory data, repair and maintenance statistics, and test results. Develop, implement, and evaluate maintenance policies and procedures. Counsel employees about work-related issues, and assist employees to correct job-skill deficiencies. Examine objects, systems, or facilities, and analyze information to determine needed installations, services, or repairs. Conduct or arrange for worker training in safety, repair, and maintenance techniques, operational procedures, or equipment use. Inspect and monitor work areas, examine tools and equipment, and provide employee safety training to prevent, detect, and correct unsafe conditions or violations of procedures and safety rules. Inspect, test, and measure completed work, using devices such as hand tools and gauges to verify conformance to standards and repair requirements. Requisition materials and supplies such as tools, equipment, and replacement parts.

Related Military Specializations: A-10, F-15, and U-2 Avionics Systems Craftsman; Advanced Aircraft Electrical/Instrument/Flight Control Systems Technician, IMA; Advanced Aircraft Electronic Countermeasures Technician, IMA; Advanced Consolidated Automatic Support

System (CASS) Technician IMA; AEGIS Ballistic Missile Defense Weapon System Supervisor; AEGIS Combat System (BL4) Maintenance Supervisor; AEGIS Weapon System MK 7 Technician; AEGIS Weapon System MK-7 (TK-II) Supervisor; others. **Average Educational Level of Vets:** One or more years of college, no degree. **Usual Educational Requirement:** High school diploma or equivalent. **Relevant Educational Programs:** Electrical and Power Transmission Installation/Installer, General; High Performance and Custom Engine Technician/Mechanic Training; Lineworker; Operations Management and Supervision; Recreation Vehicle (RV) Service Technician Training; Vehicle Maintenance and Repair Technologies, General. **Related Knowledge/Courses:** Mechanical Devices; Personnel and Human Resources; Production and Processing; Building and Construction; Engineering and Technology; Economics and Accounting. **Work Experience Needed:** 1 to 5 years. **On-the-Job Training Needed:** None. **Certification/Licensure:** None.

Personality Types: Enterprising-Conventional-Realistic. **Key Career Cluster:** 13 Manufacturing. **Key Career Pathway:** 13.3 Maintenance, Installation and Repair. **Top Industries for Vets:** National Security and International Affairs; Automobile Dealers; Wired Telecommunications Carriers; Air Transportation; Real Estate.

Skills: Repairing; Management of Financial Resources; Equipment Maintenance; Troubleshooting; Management of Material Resources; Equipment Selection; Quality Control Analysis; Operation and Control.

Work Environment: More often indoors than outdoors; standing; noise; contaminants; hazardous conditions.

First-Line Supervisors of Non-Retail Sales Workers

- ✹ Average Annual Earnings (All): $70,520
- ✹ Average Annual Earnings (Recent Veterans): $43,650
- ✹ Earnings Growth Potential: High (47.4%)
- ✹ Growth: 4.0%
- ✹ Annual Job Openings: 12,350
- ✹ Veteran Employment by Sector: For-Profit, 81.7%; Nonprofit, 2.4%; Government, 5.0%; Self-Employed, 10.9%.

Considerations for Job Outlook: In the Postal Service, a very large decrease is expected because sales staff will be cut as post offices attempt to cut costs.

Directly supervise and coordinate activities of sales workers other than retail sales workers. Listen to and resolve customer complaints regarding services, products, or personnel. Monitor sales staff performance to ensure that goals are met. Hire, train, and evaluate personnel. Confer with company officials to develop methods and procedures to increase sales, expand markets, and promote business. Direct and supervise employees engaged in sales, inventory-taking, reconciling cash receipts, or performing specific services such as pumping gasoline for customers. Provide staff members with assistance in performing difficult or complicated duties. Plan and prepare work schedules, and assign employees to specific duties. Attend company meetings to exchange product information and coordinate work activities with other departments. Prepare sales and inventory reports for management and budget departments. Formulate pricing policies on merchandise according to profitability requirements. Examine merchandise to ensure correct pricing and display, and ensure that it functions as advertised. Analyze details of sales territories to assess their growth potential and to set quotas. Visit retailers and sales representatives to promote products and gather information. Keep records pertaining to purchases, sales, and requisitions. Coordinate sales promotion activities, and prepare merchandise displays and advertising copy. Prepare rental or lease agreements, specifying charges and payment procedures for use of machinery, tools, or other items.

Related Military Specializations: None. **Average Educational Level of Vets:** One or more years of college, no degree. **Usual Educational Requirement:** High school diploma or equivalent. **Relevant Educational Programs:** General Merchandising, Sales, and Related Marketing Operations, Other; Selling Skills and Sales Operations; Special Products Marketing Operations. **Related Knowledge/Courses:** Sales and Marketing; Economics and Accounting; Personnel and Human Resources; Administration and Management; Mathematics; Clerical Practices. **Work Experience Needed:** More than 5 years. **On-the-Job Training Needed:** None. **Certification/Licensure:** None.

Personality Types: Enterprising-Conventional-Social. **Key Career Cluster:** 14 Marketing, Sales, and Service. **Key Career Pathway:** 14.2 Professional Sales and Marketing. **Top Industries for Vets:** Insurance Carriers and Related Activities; Automotive Repair and Maintenance; Groceries and Related Products Merchant Wholesalers; Machinery, Equipment, and Supplies Merchant Wholesalers; Video Tape and Disc Rental.

Skills: Management of Financial Resources; Management of Material Resources; Systems Evaluation; Instructing; Negotiation;

Management of Personnel Resources; Persuasion; Monitoring.

Work Environment: Indoors; noise.

First-Line Supervisors of Office and Administrative Support Workers

- ❋ Average Annual Earnings (All): $48,810
- ❋ Average Annual Earnings (Recent Veterans): $48,350
- ❋ Earnings Growth Potential: Medium (37.9%)
- ❋ Growth: 14.3%
- ❋ Annual Job Openings: 58,440
- ❋ Veteran Employment by Sector: For-Profit, 37.0%; Nonprofit, 2.4%; Government, 60.2%; Self-Employed, 0.5%.

Considerations for Job Outlook: Employment growth is expected to be tempered by technological advances that increase the productivity of—and thus decrease the need for—these workers and the workers they supervise. Keen competition is expected.

Directly supervise and coordinate the activities of clerical and administrative support workers. Resolve customer complaints, and answer customers' questions regarding policies and procedures. Supervise the work of office, administrative, or customer service employees to ensure adherence to quality standards, deadlines, and proper procedures, correcting errors or problems. Provide employees with guidance in handling difficult or complex problems and in resolving escalated complaints or disputes. Implement corporate and departmental policies, procedures, and service standards in conjunction with management. Discuss job performance problems with employees to identify causes and issues and to work on resolving problems. Train and instruct employees in job duties and company policies, or arrange for training to be provided. Evaluate employees' job performance and conformance to regulations, and recommend appropriate personnel action. Recruit, interview, and select employees. Review records and reports pertaining to activities such as production, payroll, and shipping to verify details, monitor work activities, and evaluate performance. Interpret and communicate work procedures and company policies to staff. Prepare and issue work schedules, deadlines, and duty assignments of office or administrative staff. Maintain records pertaining to inventory, personnel, orders, supplies, and machine maintenance. Compute figures such as balances, totals, and commissions.

Related Military Specializations:
Communications—Computer Systems Manager; Communications—Computer Systems Operations Craftsman; Communications—Computer Systems Superintendent; Data Processing Chief; Defense Message System (DMS) Chief; Finance Senior Sergeant; Financial Management and Comptroller Manager; Financial Management and Comptroller Superintendent; Force Support Manager; Health Services Management Manager; Health Services Management Superintendent; Information Center Supervisor; Information Systems Chief; others. **Average Educational Level of Vets:** One or more years of college, no degree. **Usual Educational Requirement:** High school diploma or equivalent. **Relevant Educational Programs:** Agricultural Business Technology; Customer Service Management; E-Commerce/Electronic Commerce; Medical Office Management/Administration; Medical/Health Management and Clinical Assistant/Specialist Training; Office Management and Supervision. **Related**

Knowledge/Courses: Clerical Practices; Economics and Accounting; Administration and Management; Personnel and Human Resources; Customer and Personal Service; Education and Training. **Work Experience Needed:** 1 to 5 years. **On-the-Job Training Needed:** None. **Certification/Licensure:** None.

Personality Types: Enterprising-Conventional-Social. **Key Career Cluster:** 04 Business, Management, and Administration. **Key Career Pathway:** 4.6 Administrative and Information Support. **Top Industries for Vets:** National Security and International Affairs; Postal Service; Architectural, Engineering, and Related Services; Justice, Public Order, and Safety Activities; Investigation and Security Services.

Skills: Management of Financial Resources; Management of Material Resources; Negotiation; Monitoring; Management of Personnel Resources; Learning Strategies; Persuasion; Time Management.

Work Environment: Indoors; sitting; noise.

First-Line Supervisors of Police and Detectives

* Average Annual Earnings (All): $77,890
* Average Annual Earnings (Recent Veterans): $54,570
* Earnings Growth Potential: High (40.0%)
* Growth: 2.1%
* Annual Job Openings: 3,870
* Veteran Employment by Sector: For-Profit, 0.0%; Nonprofit, 0.0%; Government, 100.0%; Self-Employed, 0.0%.

Considerations for Job Outlook: Population growth is the main source of demand for police services. Overall, opportunities in local police departments should be favorable for qualified applicants.

Directly supervise and coordinate activities of members of police force. Supervise and coordinate the investigation of criminal cases, offering guidance and expertise to investigators, and ensuring that procedures are conducted in accordance with laws and regulations. Maintain logs, prepare reports, and direct the preparation, handling, and maintenance of departmental records. Explain police operations to subordinates to assist them in performing their job duties. Cooperate with court personnel and officials from other law enforcement agencies, and testify in court as necessary. Review contents of written orders to ensure adherence to legal requirements. Investigate and resolve personnel problems within organization and charges of misconduct against staff. Direct collection, preparation, and handling of evidence and personal property of prisoners. Inform personnel of changes in regulations and policies, implications of new or amended laws, and new techniques of police work. Train staff in proper police work procedures. Monitor and evaluate the job performance of subordinates, and authorize promotions and transfers. Prepare work schedules, and assign duties to subordinates. Conduct raids, and order detention of witnesses and suspects for questioning. Discipline staff members for violation of departmental rules and regulations. Develop, implement, and revise departmental policies and procedures. Inspect facilities, supplies, vehicles, and equipment to ensure conformance to standards. Requisition and issue equipment and supplies.

Related Military Specializations: Correctional Custody Supervisor; Criminal Investigator CID Agent; Security Forces Manager; Security Forces Superintendent; Special Investigations Manager;

Special Investigations Superintendent. **Average Educational Level of Vets:** Bachelor's degree. **Usual Educational Requirement:** High school diploma or equivalent. **Relevant Educational Programs:** Corrections; Criminal Justice/Law Enforcement Administration; Criminal Justice/Safety Studies; Crisis/Emergency/Disaster Management; Critical Incident Response/Special Police Operations; Critical Infrastructure Protection; Cultural/Archaeological Resources Protection; Homeland Security; Law Enforcement Record-Keeping and Evidence Management; Maritime Law Enforcement; Natural Resources Law Enforcement and Protective Services; Protective Services Operations; Terrorism and Counterterrorism Operations. **Related Knowledge/Courses:** Public Safety and Security; Law and Government; Psychology; Sociology and Anthropology; Therapy and Counseling; Personnel and Human Resources. **Work Experience Needed:** 1 to 5 years. **On-the-Job Training Needed:** Moderate-term on-the-job training. **Certification/Licensure:** Licensure in some states.

Personality Types: Enterprising-Social-Conventional. **Key Career Cluster:** 12 Law, Public Safety, Corrections, and Security. **Key Career Pathway:** 12.4 Law Enforcement Services. **Top Industries for Vets:** Justice, Public Order, and Safety Activities; National Security and International Affairs.

Skills: Management of Financial Resources; Management of Personnel Resources; Persuasion; Management of Material Resources; Monitoring; Learning Strategies; Time Management; Instructing.

Work Environment: More often indoors than outdoors; sitting; noise; very hot or cold; bright or inadequate lighting; contaminants; hazardous equipment.

First-Line Supervisors of Production and Operating Workers

⊛ Average Annual Earnings (All): $53,670

⊛ Average Annual Earnings (Recent Veterans): $48,460

⊛ Earnings Growth Potential: Medium (39.6%)

⊛ Growth: 1.9%

⊛ Annual Job Openings: 8,790

⊛ Veteran Employment by Sector: For-Profit, 83.9%; Nonprofit, 0.4%; Government, 13.9%; Self-Employed, 1.8%.

Considerations for Job Outlook: Little change in employment is projected.

Directly supervise and coordinate the activities of production and operating workers. Enforce safety and sanitation regulations. Direct and coordinate the activities of employees engaged in the production or processing of goods, such as inspectors, machine setters, and fabricators. Read and analyze charts, work orders, production schedules, and other records and reports to determine production requirements and to evaluate current production estimates and outputs. Confer with other supervisors to coordinate operations and activities within or between departments. Plan and establish work schedules, assignments, and production sequences to meet production goals. Inspect materials, products, or equipment to detect defects or malfunctions. Observe work and monitor gauges, dials, and other indicators to ensure that operators conform to production or processing standards. Confer with management or subordinates to resolve worker problems, complaints, or grievances. Interpret specifications, blueprints, job orders, and company policies and procedures for workers. Maintain operations data, such as time, production, and cost records, and prepare management reports of production results. Recommend or implement measures to motivate employees and to improve production methods, equipment performance, product quality, or efficiency. Determine standards, budgets, production goals, and rates, based on company policies, equipment and labor availability, and workloads. Requisition materials, supplies, equipment parts, or repair services. Set up and adjust machines and equipment. Conduct employee training in equipment operations or work and safety procedures, or assign employee training to experienced workers. Keep records of employees' attendance and hours worked. Recommend or execute personnel actions, such as hirings, evaluations, and promotions. Calculate labor and equipment requirements and production specifications, using standard formulas. Plan and develop new products and production processes.

Related Military Specializations: Facility Systems Superintendent; Fuels Manager; Fuels Superintendent; Infrastructure Systems Superintendent; Instrumentation and Telemetry Systems Manager; Nuclear Qualified Engineering Department Master Chief (EDMC); Nuclear Qualified Reactor Department Master Chief (RDMC); Precision Measurement Equipment Laboratory Manager; Precision Measurement Equipment Laboratory Superintendent; Shipboard Engineering Plant Program Manager; others. **Average Educational Level of Vets:** One or more years of college, no degree. **Usual Educational Requirement:** Postsecondary vocational training. **Relevant Educational Program:** Operations Management and Supervision. **Related Knowledge/Courses:** Mechanical Devices; Production and Processing; Engineering and Technology; Design; Personnel and Human Resources; Administration and Management.

Work Experience Needed: 1 to 5 years. **On-the-Job Training Needed:** None. **Certification/Licensure:** None.

Personality Types: Enterprising-Realistic-Conventional. **Key Career Cluster:** 13 Manufacturing. **Key Career Pathway:** 13.1 Production. **Top Industries for Vets:** Motor Vehicles and Motor Vehicle Equipment; National Security and International Affairs; Aircraft and Parts; Structural Metals, and Boiler, Tank, and Shipping Containers; Plastics Products.

Skills: Management of Financial Resources; Repairing; Management of Personnel Resources; Equipment Maintenance; Management of Material Resources; Operations Analysis; Equipment Selection; Quality Control Analysis.

Work Environment: Standing; walking and running; noise; very hot or cold; contaminants; hazardous equipment; minor burns, cuts, bites, or stings.

First-Line Supervisors of Retail Sales Workers

- ❋ Average Annual Earnings (All): $36,480
- ❋ Average Annual Earnings (Recent Veterans): $33,500
- ❋ Earnings Growth Potential: Medium (36.1%)
- ❋ Growth: 8.4%
- ❋ Annual Job Openings: 51,370
- ❋ Veteran Employment by Sector: For-Profit, 88.3%; Nonprofit, 1.6%; Government, 1.9%; Self-Employed, 8.2%.

Considerations for Job Outlook: Limited job growth is expected as retailers increase the responsibilities of existing sales worker supervisors and as the retail industry grows slowly overall. Competition is expected. Job seekers with college degrees and retail experience should have the best prospects.

Directly supervise and coordinate activities of retail sales workers in an establishment or department. Provide customer service by greeting and assisting customers and responding to customer inquiries and complaints. Direct and supervise employees engaged in sales, inventory-taking, reconciling cash receipts, or performing services for customers. Monitor sales activities to ensure that customers receive satisfactory service and quality goods. Inventory stock and reorder when inventory drops to a specified level. Instruct staff on how to handle difficult and complicated sales. Hire, train, and evaluate personnel in sales or marketing establishments, promoting or firing workers when appropriate. Assign employees to specific duties. Enforce safety, health, and security rules. Examine merchandise to ensure that it is correctly priced and displayed and that it functions as advertised. Plan budgets and authorize payments and merchandise returns. Perform work activities of subordinates, such as cleaning and organizing shelves and displays and selling merchandise.

Related Military Specializations: Automated Afloat Sales and Service Manager; Resale Management Specialist; Services Craftsman; Services Superintendent; Ship's Store Afloat Resale Operations Management (ROM) II Manager. **Average Educational Level of Vets:** One or more years of college, no degree. **Usual Educational Requirement:** High school diploma or equivalent. **Relevant Educational Programs:** Consumer Merchandising/Retailing

Management; E-Commerce/Electronic Commerce; Floriculture/Floristry Operations and Management; General Merchandising, Sales, and Related Marketing Operations, Other; Retail Management; Retailing and Retail Operations; Selling Skills and Sales Operations; Special Products Marketing Operations. **Related Knowledge/Courses:** Sales and Marketing; Customer and Personal Service; Personnel and Human Resources; Administration and Management; Economics and Accounting; Education and Training. **Work Experience Needed:** 1 to 5 years. **On-the-Job Training Needed:** None. **Certification/Licensure:** None.

Personality Types: Enterprising-Conventional-Social. **Key Career Cluster:** 01 Agriculture, Food, and Natural Resources. **Key Career Pathway:** 1.3 Animal Systems. **Top Industries for Vets:** Department and Discount Stores; Grocery Stores; Building Material and Supplies Dealers; Auto Parts, Accessories, and Tire Stores; Automobile Dealers.

Skills: Management of Financial Resources; Management of Material Resources; Negotiation; Management of Personnel Resources; Persuasion; Systems Evaluation; Learning Strategies; Instructing.

Work Environment: Indoors; standing; walking and running; using hands; repetitive motions; noise.

First-Line Supervisors of Transportation and Material-Moving Machine and Vehicle Operators

❋ Average Annual Earnings (All): $52,950

❋ Average Annual Earnings (Recent Veterans): $43,650

❋ Earnings Growth Potential: High (40.1%)

❋ Growth: 14.3%

❋ Annual Job Openings: 6,930

❋ Veteran Employment by Sector: For-Profit, 71.7%; Nonprofit, 3.7%; Government, 21.8%; Self-Employed, 2.8%.

Considerations for Job Outlook: About average increase in employment is projected.

Directly supervise and coordinate activities of transportation and material-moving machine and vehicle operators and helpers. Enforce safety rules and regulations. Plan work assignments and equipment allocations in order to meet transportation, operations, or production goals. Confer with customers, supervisors, contractors, and other personnel to exchange information and to resolve problems. Direct workers in transportation or related services, such as pumping, moving, storing, and loading/unloading of materials or people. Resolve worker problems, or collaborate with employees to assist in problem resolution. Review orders, production schedules, blueprints, and shipping/receiving notices to determine work sequences and material shipping dates, types, volumes, and destinations. Monitor field work to ensure that it is being performed properly and that materials are being used as they should be. Recommend and implement measures to improve worker motivation, equipment performance, work methods, and customer services. Maintain or verify records of time, materials, expenditures, and crew activities. Interpret transportation and tariff regulations, shipping orders, safety regulations, and company policies and procedures for workers. Explain and demonstrate work tasks to new workers, or assign workers to more experienced workers for further training. Prepare, compile, and submit reports on work activities, operations, production, and work-related accidents. Recommend or implement personnel actions such as employee selection, evaluation, and rewards or disciplinary actions. Requisition needed personnel, supplies, equipment, parts, or repair services. Plan and establish transportation routes. Inspect or test materials, stock, vehicles, equipment, and facilities to ensure that they are safe, free of defects, and meet specifications. Compute and estimate cash, payroll, transportation, personnel, and storage requirements. Dispatch personnel and vehicles in response to telephone or radio reports of emergencies. Perform or schedule repairs and preventive maintenance of vehicles and other equipment.

Related Military Specializations: Motor Transport Operations Chief; Railway Senior Sergeant (RC); Transportation Senior Sergeant; Vehicle Operations Craftsman; Vehicle Operations Manager; Vehicle Operations Superintendent. **Average Educational Level of Vets:** One or more years of college, no degree. **Usual Educational Requirement:** High school diploma or equivalent. **Relevant Educational Program:** Railroad and Railway Transportation. **Related Knowledge/Courses:** Transportation; Production and Processing; Personnel and Human Resources; Customer and Personal Service; Public Safety and Security; Administration and Management. **Work Experience Needed:** 1 to 5 years. **On-the-Job Training Needed:** None. **Certification/Licensure:** None.

Personality Types: Enterprising-Conventional-Realistic. **Key Career Cluster:** 16 Transportation, Distribution, and Logistics. **Key Career Pathway:** 16.3 Warehousing and Distribution Center Operations. **Top Industries for Vets:** National Security and International Affairs; Couriers and Messengers; Services Incidental to Transportation; Truck Transportation; Rail Transportation.

Skills: Management of Material Resources; Management of Financial Resources; Management of Personnel Resources; Systems Evaluation; Systems Analysis; Operations Analysis; Time Management; Negotiation.

Work Environment: Indoors; sitting; noise; contaminants.

Fitness Trainers and Aerobics Instructors

- ❋ Average Annual Earnings (All): $31,030
- ❋ Average Annual Earnings (Recent Veterans): $20,950
- ❋ Earnings Growth Potential: High (44.1%)
- ❋ Growth: 24.0%
- ❋ Annual Job Openings: 10,060
- ❋ Veteran Employment by Sector: For-Profit, 55.5%; Nonprofit, 8.5%; Government, 23.9%; Self-Employed, 12.1%.

Considerations for Job Outlook: Job prospects should be best for workers with professional certification or increased levels of formal education in health or fitness.

Instruct or coach groups or individuals in exercise activities. Explain and enforce safety rules and regulations governing sports, recreational activities, and the use of exercise equipment. Offer alternatives during classes to accommodate different levels of fitness. Plan routines, choose appropriate music, and choose different movements for each set of muscles, depending on participants' capabilities and limitations. Observe participants, and inform them of corrective measures necessary for skill improvement. Teach proper breathing techniques used during physical exertion. Teach and demonstrate use of gymnastic and training equipment such as trampolines and weights. Instruct participants in maintaining exertion levels to maximize benefits from exercise routines. Maintain fitness equipment. Conduct therapeutic, recreational, or athletic activities. Monitor participants' progress, and adapt programs as needed. Evaluate individuals' abilities, needs, and physical conditions, and develop suitable training programs to meet any special requirements. Plan physical education programs to promote development of participants' physical attributes and social skills. Provide students with information and resources regarding nutrition, weight control, and lifestyle issues. Administer emergency first aid, wrap injuries, treat minor chronic disabilities, or refer injured persons to physicians. Advise clients about proper clothing and shoes.

Related Military Specializations: Drill Instructor; Martial Arts Instructor; Water Safety/Survival Instructor; Weapons and Tactics Instructor. **Average Educational Level of Vets:** One or more years of college, no degree. **Usual Educational Requirement:** High school diploma or equivalent. **Relevant Educational Programs:** Health and Physical Education, General; Physical Education Teaching and Coaching; Physical Fitness Technician Training; Sport and Fitness Administration/Management; Yoga Teacher Training/Yoga Therapy. **Related Knowledge/ Courses:** Education and Training; Therapy and Counseling; Psychology; Customer and Personal Service; Medicine and Dentistry; Biology.

Work Experience Needed: None. **On-the-Job Training Needed:** Short-term on-the-job training. **Certification/Licensure:** Voluntary certification by association.

Personality Types: Social-Realistic-Enterprising. **Key Career Cluster:** 10 Human Services. **Key Career Pathway:** 10.4 Personal Care Services. **Top Industries for Vets:** Other Amusement, Gambling, and Recreation Industries; National Security and International Affairs; Recreational Vehicle Parks and Camps, and Rooming and Boarding Houses; Colleges and Universities, Including Junior Colleges; Museums, Art Galleries, Historical Sites, and Similar Institutions.

Skills: Learning Strategies; Service Orientation; Operations Analysis; Instructing; Social Perceptiveness; Technology Design; Systems Evaluation; Persuasion.

Work Environment: Indoors; standing; walking and running; bending or twisting the body; repetitive motions.

Forensic Science Technicians

- ❋ Average Annual Earnings (All): $52,180
- ❋ Average Annual Earnings (Recent Veterans): $36,670
- ❋ Earnings Growth Potential: Medium (37.2%)
- ❋ Growth: 18.6%
- ❋ Annual Job Openings: 790
- ❋ Veteran Employment by Sector: For-Profit, 42.6%; Nonprofit, 10.3%; Government, 46.6%; Self-Employed, 0.5%.

Considerations for Job Outlook: Competition for jobs should be stiff because of the substantial interest in forensic science and crime scene investigation spurred by its portrayal in popular media. Applicants with experience or a bachelor's degree in forensic science or a related field should have the best opportunities. Year to year, the number of job openings available will vary based on federal, state, and local law enforcement budgets.

Collect, identify, classify, and analyze physical evidence related to criminal investigations. Collect evidence from crime scenes, storing it in conditions that preserve its integrity. Keep records and prepare reports detailing findings, investigative methods, and laboratory techniques. Use chemicals and other substances to examine latent fingerprint evidence and compare developed prints to those of known persons in databases. Testify in court about investigative and analytical methods and findings. Visit morgues, examine scenes of crimes, or contact other sources to obtain evidence or information to be used in investigations. Take photographs of evidence. Collect impressions of dust from surfaces to obtain and identify fingerprints. Reconstruct crime scenes to determine relationships among pieces of evidence. Operate and maintain laboratory equipment and apparatus. Train new technicians and other personnel on forensic science techniques. Examine and analyze blood stain patterns at crime scenes. Prepare solutions, reagents, and sample formulations needed for laboratory work. Confer with ballistics, fingerprinting, handwriting, documents, electronics, medical, chemical, or metallurgical experts concerning evidence and its interpretation. Interpret laboratory findings and test results to identify and classify substances, materials, and other evidence collected at crime scenes. Examine physical evidence such as hair, fiber, wood, or soil residues to obtain information about its source and composition. Examine firearms to determine mechanical condition and legal status, performing restoration work on damaged firearms to obtain information such as serial numbers. Analyze gunshot residue and bullet paths to determine how shootings occurred. Compare objects such as tools with impression marks to determine whether a specific object is responsible for a specific mark. Determine types of bullets used in shooting and if fired from a specific weapon. Identify and quantify drugs and poisons found in biological fluids and tissues, in foods, and at crime scenes.

Related Military Specializations: None.
Average Educational Level of Vets: One or more years of college, no degree. **Usual Educational Requirement:** Bachelor's degree. **Relevant Educational Programs:** Forensic Chemistry; Forensic Science and Technology. **Related Knowledge/Courses:** Chemistry; Biology; Clerical Practices; Design; Law and Government; Customer and Personal Service. **Work Experience Needed:** None. **On-the-Job Training Needed:** Moderate-term on-the-job training. **Certification/Licensure:** Licensure in some states for Polygraph Operators.

Personality Types: Investigative-Realistic-Conventional. **Key Career Cluster:** 12 Law, Public Safety, Corrections, and Security. **Key Career Pathway:** 12.4 Law Enforcement Services. **Top Industries for Vets:** Scientific Research and Development Services; National Security and International Affairs; Architectural, Engineering, and Related Services; Colleges and Universities, Including Junior Colleges; Management, Scientific and Technical Consulting Services.

Skills: Science; Instructing; Speaking; Writing; Critical Thinking; Reading Comprehension; Mathematics; Operation and Control.

Work Environment: More often indoors than outdoors; sitting; using hands; contaminants; hazardous conditions.

General and Operations Managers

* Average Annual Earnings (All): $95,150
* Average Annual Earnings (Recent Veterans): $65,480
* Earnings Growth Potential: High (50.0%)
* Growth: 4.6%
* Annual Job Openings: 41,010
* Veteran Employment by Sector: For-Profit, 68.5%; Nonprofit, 1.7%; Government, 28.4%; Self-Employed, 1.4%.

Considerations for Job Outlook: Educational requirements vary by industry, but candidates who can demonstrate strong leadership abilities and experience getting positive results will have better job opportunities.

Plan, direct, or coordinate the operations of public or private sector organizations. Oversee activities directly related to making products or providing services. Direct and coordinate activities of businesses or departments concerned with the production, pricing, sales, or distribution of products. Review financial statements, sales and activity reports, and other performance data to measure productivity and goal achievement and to determine areas needing cost reduction and program improvement. Manage staff, preparing work schedules and assigning specific duties. Direct and coordinate organization's financial and budget activities to fund operations, maximize investments, and increase efficiency. Establish and implement departmental policies, goals, objectives, and procedures, conferring with board members, organization officials, and staff members as necessary. Determine staffing requirements, and interview, hire, and train new employees, or oversee those personnel processes. Plan and direct activities such as sales promotions, coordinating with other department heads as required. Determine goods and services to be sold, and set prices and credit terms based on forecasts of customer demand. Monitor businesses and agencies to ensure that they efficiently and effectively provide needed services while staying within budgetary limits. Locate, select, and procure merchandise for resale, representing management in purchase negotiations. Perform sales floor work such as greeting and assisting customers, stocking shelves, and taking inventory.

Related Military Specializations: None. **Average Educational Level of Vets:** Bachelor's degree. **Usual Educational Requirement:** Associate degree. **Relevant Educational Programs:** Business Administration and Management, General; Business/Commerce, General; Entrepreneurship/Entrepreneurial Studies; Finance, General; International Business/Trade/Commerce; Management Science; Parks, Recreation and Leisure Facilities Management, Other; Public Administration; Retail Management. **Related Knowledge/ Courses:** Economics and Accounting; Personnel and Human Resources; Administration and Management; Sales and Marketing; Building and Construction; Clerical Practices. **Work Experience Needed:** 1 to 5 years. **On-the-Job Training Needed:** None. **Certification/ Licensure:** Licensure for some specializations.

Personality Types: Enterprising-Conventional-Social. **Key Career Cluster:** 04 Business, Management, and Administration. **Key Career Pathway:** 4.1 Management. **Top Industries for Vets:** National Security and International Affairs; Restaurants and Other Food Services; Truck Transportation; Architectural, Engineering, and Related Services; Construction.

Skills: Management of Material Resources; Management of Financial Resources; Operations Analysis; Management of Personnel Resources; Negotiation; Systems Analysis; Coordination; Systems Evaluation.

Work Environment: Indoors; more often sitting than standing; noise.

Geological and Petroleum Technicians

* Average Annual Earnings (All): $49,690

* Average Annual Earnings (Recent Veterans): $37,110

* Earnings Growth Potential: High (42.4%)

* Growth: 14.7%

* Annual Job Openings: 700

* Veteran Employment by Sector: For-Profit, 42.7%; Nonprofit, 10.0%; Government, 46.8%; Self-Employed, 0.5%.

Considerations for Job Outlook: High prices and growing demand for natural resources—especially oil and natural gas—are expected to increase demand for geological exploration and extraction in the future. Historically, when oil and natural gas prices are low, companies limit exploration and hire fewer technicians. When prices are high, however, companies explore and extract more. If oil prices remain high over the long run, the demand for geological and petroleum technicians will remain high as well.

Assist scientists or engineers in the use of electronic, sonic, or nuclear measuring instruments in both laboratory and production activities to obtain data indicating potential resources. For task data, see Job Specializations.

Related Military Specializations: Oil Analysis Operator/Evaluator; Petroleum Laboratory Specialist. **Average Educational Level of Vets:** One or more years of college, no degree. **Usual Educational Requirement:** Associate degree. **Relevant Educational Programs:** Mining and Petroleum Technologies/Technicians, Other; Petroleum Technology/Technician. **Work Experience Needed:** None. **On-the-Job Training Needed:** Moderate-term on-the-job training. **Certification/Licensure:** None.

Key Career Cluster: 01 Agriculture, Food, and Natural Resources. **Key Career Pathway:** 1.5 Natural Resources Systems. **Top Industries for Vets:** Scientific Research and Development Services; National Security and International Affairs; Architectural, Engineering, and Related Services; Colleges and Universities, Including Junior Colleges; Management, Scientific and Technical Consulting Services.

Job Specialization: Geological Sample Test Technicians

Test and analyze geological samples, crude oil, or petroleum products to detect presence of petroleum, gas, or mineral deposits indicating potential for exploration and production or to determine physical and chemical properties to ensure that products meet quality standards. Test and analyze samples in order to determine their content and characteristics, using laboratory apparatus and testing equipment. Collect and prepare solid and fluid samples for analysis. Assemble, operate, and maintain field and laboratory testing, measuring, and mechanical equipment, working as part of a crew when required. Compile and record testing and operational data for review and further analysis. Adjust and repair testing, electrical, and mechanical equipment and devices. Supervise well exploration and drilling activities, and well completions. Inspect engines for wear and defective parts, using equipment and measuring devices. Prepare notes, sketches, geological maps, and cross sections. Participate in geological, geophysical, geochemical, hydrographic, or oceanographic surveys, prospecting field trips, exploratory drilling, well logging or underground mine survey programs. Plot information from aerial photographs, well logs, section descriptions, and other databases. Assess the environmental impacts of development projects on subsurface materials. Collaborate with hydrogeologists in order to evaluate groundwater and well circulation. Prepare, transcribe, and/or analyze seismic, gravimetric, well log, or other geophysical and survey data. Participate in the evaluation of possible mining locations.

Related Knowledge/Courses: Chemistry; Geography; Mechanical Devices; Physics; Mathematics; Clerical Practices.

Personality Types:
Realistic-Investigative-Conventional.

Skills: Repairing; Science; Equipment Selection; Equipment Maintenance; Troubleshooting; Mathematics; Operation and Control; Quality Control Analysis.

Work Environment: Indoors; more often sitting than standing; using hands; noise; contaminants; hazardous equipment.

Job Specialization: Geophysical Data Technicians

Measure, record, and evaluate geological data by using sonic, electronic, electrical, seismic, or gravity-measuring instruments to prospect for oil or gas. May collect and evaluate core samples and cuttings. Prepare notes, sketches, geological maps and cross-sections. Read and study reports in order to compile information and data for geological and geophysical prospecting.

Interview individuals, and research public databases in order to obtain information. Assemble, maintain, and distribute information for library or record systems. Operate and adjust equipment and apparatus used to obtain geological data. Plan and direct activities of workers who operate equipment to collect data. Set up or direct setup of instruments used to collect geological data. Record readings in order to compile data used in prospecting for oil or gas. Supervise oil, water, and gas well drilling activities. Collect samples and cuttings, using equipment and hand tools. Develop and print photographic recordings of information, using equipment. Measure geological characteristics used in prospecting for oil or gas, using measuring instruments. Evaluate and interpret core samples and cuttings, and other geological data used in prospecting for oil or gas. Diagnose and repair malfunctioning instruments and equipment, using manufacturers' manuals and hand tools. Prepare and attach packing instructions to shipping containers. Develop and design packing materials and handling procedures for shipping of objects.

Related Knowledge/Courses: Geography; Engineering and Technology; Physics; Computers and Electronics; Mathematics; Chemistry.

Personality Types:
Conventional-Realistic-Investigative.

Skills: Science; Operation and Control; Operation Monitoring; Reading Comprehension; Operations Analysis; Writing; Technology Design; Troubleshooting.

Work Environment: Indoors; sitting.

Graphic Designers

- ✺ Average Annual Earnings (All): $44,010
- ✺ Average Annual Earnings (Recent Veterans): $41,470
- ✺ Earnings Growth Potential: High (40.4%)
- ✺ Growth: 13.4%
- ✺ Annual Job Openings: 12,380
- ✺ Veteran Employment by Sector: For-Profit, 77.9%; Nonprofit, 1.7%; Government, 9.5%; Self-Employed, 10.9%.

Considerations for Job Outlook: Graphic designers are expected to face competition for available positions. Many talented individuals are attracted to careers as graphic designers. Prospects will be best for job applicants with website design and other interactive media experience.

Design or create graphics to meet specific commercial or promotional needs, such as packaging, displays, or logos. Create designs, concepts, and sample layouts based on knowledge of layout principles and esthetic design concepts. Determine size and arrangement of illustrative material and copy; and select style and size of type. Confer with clients to discuss and determine layout designs. Develop graphics and layouts for product illustrations, company logos, and Internet websites. Review final layouts, and suggest improvements as needed. Prepare illustrations or rough sketches of material, discussing them with clients or supervisors and making necessary changes. Use computer software to generate new images. Key information into computer equipment to create layouts for client or supervisor. Maintain archive of images, photos, or previous work products. Prepare notes and instructions for workers who assemble and prepare final layouts for printing. Draw and print charts, graphs, illustrations, and other artwork, using computer. Study illustrations and photographs to plan presentations of materials, products, or services. Research new software or design concepts. Mark up, paste, and assemble final layouts to prepare layouts for printer. Produce still and animated graphics for on-air and taped portions of television news broadcasts, using electronic video equipment. Photograph layouts, using cameras, to make layout prints for supervisors or clients. Develop negatives and prints to produce layout photographs, using negative and print developing equipment and tools.

Related Military Specializations: Combat Illustrator; Graphic Illustrator; Illustrator Draftsman; Illustrator Draftsman Tracking NEC. **Average Educational Level of Vets:** Bachelor's degree. **Usual Educational Requirement:** Bachelor's degree. **Relevant Educational Programs:** Agricultural Communication/Journalism; Commercial and Advertising Art; Computer Graphics; Design and Visual Communications, General; Digital Arts; Graphic Design; Industrial and Product Design; Web Page, Digital/Multimedia, and Information Resources Design. **Related Knowledge/Courses:** Fine Arts; Design; Communications and Media; Sales and Marketing; Sociology and Anthropology; Computers and Electronics. **Work Experience Needed:** None. **On-the-Job Training Needed:** None. **Certification/Licensure:** None.

Personality Types: Artistic-Realistic-Enterprising. **Key Career Cluster:** 03 Arts, Audiovisual Technology, and Communications. **Key Career Pathway:** 3.1 Audio and Video Technologies. **Top Industries for Vets:** Architectural, Engineering, and Related Services; Specialized Design Services; Advertising and Related Services; National Security and International Affairs; Computer Systems Design and Related Services.

Skills: Operations Analysis; Technology Design; Negotiation; Management of Financial Resources; Time Management; Complex Problem Solving; Reading Comprehension; Writing.

Work Environment: Indoors; sitting; using hands; repetitive motions.

Health Educators

* Average Annual Earnings (All): $47,940
* Average Annual Earnings (Recent Veterans): $37,110
* Earnings Growth Potential: High (44.0%)
* Growth: 36.5%
* Annual Job Openings: 3,690
* Veteran Employment by Sector: For-Profit, 5.0%; Nonprofit, 18.3%; Government, 76.7%; Self-Employed, 0.0%.

Considerations for Job Outlook: Growth will be driven by efforts to reduce health-care costs by teaching people about healthy habits and behaviors. As health-care costs continue to rise, insurance companies, employers, and governments are trying to find ways to curb costs. One way is to employ health educators, who teach people how to live healthy lives and avoid costly diseases.

Provide and manage health education programs that help individuals, families, and their communities maximize and maintain healthy lifestyles. Document activities, recording information such as the numbers of applications completed, presentations conducted, and persons assisted. Develop and present health education and promotion programs such as training workshops, conferences, and school or community presentations. Develop and maintain cooperative working relationships with agencies and organizations interested in public health care. Prepare and distribute health education materials, including reports, bulletins, and visual aids such as films, videotapes, photographs, and posters. Develop operational plans and policies necessary to achieve health education objectives and services. Collaborate with health specialists and civic groups to determine community health needs and the availability of services, and to develop goals for meeting needs. Maintain databases, mailing lists, telephone networks, and other information to facilitate the functioning of health education programs. Supervise professional and technical staff in implementing health programs, objectives, and goals. Design and conduct evaluations and diagnostic studies to assess the quality and performance of health education programs. Provide program information to the public by preparing and presenting press releases, conducting media campaigns, and/or maintaining program-related websites. Develop, prepare, and coordinate grant applications and grant-related activities to obtain funding for health education programs and related work. Provide guidance to agencies and organizations in the assessment of health education needs, and in the development and delivery of health education programs. Develop and maintain health education libraries to provide resources for staff and community agencies. Develop, conduct, or coordinate health needs assessments and other public health surveys.

Related Military Specializations: None. **Average Educational Level of Vets:** Bachelor's degree. **Usual Educational Requirement:** Bachelor's degree. **Relevant Educational Programs:** Behavioral Aspects of Health; Community Health Services/Liaison/Counseling; Dental Public Health and Education (Cert., MS/MPH, PhD/DPH); Health and Wellness, General; Health Communication; International Public Health/International Health; Maternal and Child Health; Public Health Education and Promotion; Public Health, General. **Related Knowledge/Courses:** Sociology and Anthropology; Customer and Personal Service; Education and Training; Personnel and Human Resources; Therapy and Counseling; Psychology. **Work Experience Needed:** None. **On-the-Job Training Needed:** None. **Certification/Licensure:** None.

Personality Types: Social-Enterprising. **Key Career Cluster:** 08 Health Science. **Key Career Pathway:** 8.3 Health Informatics. **Top Industries for Vets:** Justice, Public Order, and Safety Activities; Administration of Human Resource Programs; National Security and International Affairs; Civic, Social, Advocacy Organizations, and Grantmaking and Giving Services; Individual and Family Services.

Skills: Operations Analysis; Science; Writing; Learning Strategies; Speaking; Persuasion; Social Perceptiveness; Service Orientation.

Work Environment: Indoors; sitting; using hands; exposed to disease or infections.

Health Technologists and Technicians, All Other

- ❋ Average Annual Earnings (All): $38,080
- ❋ Average Annual Earnings (Recent Veterans): $32,740
- ❋ Earnings Growth Potential: Low (32.9%)
- ❋ Growth: 23.2%
- ❋ Annual Job Openings: 4,040
- ❋ Veteran Employment by Sector: For-Profit, 47.4%; Nonprofit, 8.0%; Government, 42.5%; Self-Employed, 2.1%.

Considerations for Job Outlook: Rapid employment growth is projected.

All health technologists and technicians not listed separately. For task data, see Job Specializations.

Related Military Specializations: Aerospace and Operational Physiology Apprentice; Aerospace and Operational Physiology Craftsman; Aerospace and Operational Physiology Helper; Aerospace and Operational Physiology Journeyman; Aerospace and Operational Physiology Manager; Aerospace and Operational Physiology Superintendent; Electroneurodiagnostic Technologist; Eye Specialist. **Average Educational Level of Vets:** One or more years of college, no degree. **Usual Educational Requirement:** Postsecondary vocational training. **Relevant Educational Programs:** Electroneurodiagnostic/Electroencephalographic Technology/Technologist; Gene/Genetic Therapy; Polysomnography; Radiologist Assistant Training; Renal/Dialysis Technologist/Technician Training. **Work Experience Needed:** None. **On-the-Job Training Needed:** Short-term on-the-job training. **Certification/Licensure:** Licensure for some specializations.

Key Career Cluster: 08 Health Science. **Key Career Pathway:** 8.2 Diagnostics Services. **Top Industries for Vets:** Hospitals; National Security and International Affairs; Medical Equipment and Supplies; Outpatient Care Centers; Other Health Care Services.

Job Specialization: Neurodiagnostic Technologists

Conduct electroneurodiagnostic (END) tests such as electroencephalograms, evoked potentials, polysomnograms, or electronystagmograms. May perform nerve conduction studies. Attach electrodes to patients using adhesives.

Summarize technical data to assist physicians to diagnose brain, sleep, or nervous system disorders. Conduct tests or studies such as electroencephalography (EEG), polysomnography (PSG), nerve conduction studies (NCS), electromyography (EMG), and intraoperative monitoring (IOM). Calibrate, troubleshoot, or repair equipment, and correct malfunctions as needed. Conduct tests to determine cerebral death, the absence of brain activity, or the probability of recovery from a coma. Measure visual, auditory, or somatosensory evoked potentials (EPs) to determine responses to stimuli. Indicate artifacts or interferences derived from sources outside of the brain, such as poor electrode contact or patient movement, on electroneurodiagnostic recordings. Measure patients' body parts, and mark locations where electrodes are to be placed. Monitor patients during tests or surgeries, using electroencephalographs (EEG), evoked potential (EP) instruments, or video recording equipment. Set up, program, or record montages or electrical combinations when testing peripheral nerve, spinal cord, subcortical, or cortical responses. Adjust equipment to optimize viewing of the nervous system. Collect patients' medical information needed to customize tests. Submit reports to physicians summarizing test results. Assist in training technicians, medical students, residents, or other staff members.

Related Knowledge/Courses: Medicine and Dentistry; Biology; Psychology; Computers and Electronics; Customer and Personal Service; Clerical Practices.

Personality Types: Realistic-Investigative.

Skills: Repairing; Troubleshooting; Equipment Maintenance; Operation and Control; Quality Control Analysis; Operation Monitoring; Science; Learning Strategies.

Work Environment: Indoors; sitting; using hands; contaminants; exposed to disease or infections.

Job Specialization: Ophthalmic Medical Technologists

Assist ophthalmologists by performing ophthalmic clinical functions and ophthalmic photography. Provide instruction and supervision to other ophthalmic personnel. Assist with minor surgical procedures, applying aseptic techniques and preparing instruments. May perform eye exams, administer eye medications, and instruct patients in care and use of corrective lenses. Administer topical ophthalmic or oral medications. Assess abnormalities of color vision, such as amblyopia. Assess refractive condition of eyes, using retinoscope. Assist physicians in performing ophthalmic procedures, including surgery. Calculate corrections for refractive errors. Collect ophthalmic measurements or other diagnostic information, using ultrasound equipment, such as A-scan ultrasound biometry or B-scan ultrasonography equipment. Conduct binocular disparity tests to assess depth perception. Conduct ocular motility tests to measure function of eye muscles. Conduct tests, such as the Amsler Grid test, to measure central visual field used in the early diagnosis of macular degeneration, glaucoma, or diseases of the eye. Conduct tonometry or tonography tests to measure intraocular pressure. Conduct visual field tests to measure field of vision. Create three-dimensional images of the eye, using computed tomography (CT). Measure and record lens power, using lensometers. Measure corneal curvature with keratometers or ophthalmometers to aid in the diagnosis of conditions, such as astigmatism. Measure corneal thickness, using pachymeter or contact ultrasound methods. Measure the thickness of the retinal nerve, using scanning laser polarimetry techniques to aid in diagnosis of glaucoma. Measure visual acuity, including near, distance, pinhole, or dynamic visual acuity, using appropriate tests. Perform advanced ophthalmic procedures, including electrophysiological, electrophysical, or microbial procedures. Perform fluorescein angiography of the eye. Perform slit lamp biomicroscopy procedures to diagnose disorders of the eye, such as retinitis, presbyopia, cataracts, or retinal detachment. Photograph patients' eye areas, using clinical photography techniques, to document retinal or corneal defects. Supervise or instruct ophthalmic staff. Take anatomical or functional ocular measurements of the eye or surrounding tissue, such as axial length measurements.

Related Knowledge/Courses: No data available.

Personality Types: No data available.

Skills: No data available.

Work Environment: No data available.

Job Specialization: Radiologic Technicians

Maintain and use equipment and supplies necessary to demonstrate portions of the human body on X-ray film or fluoroscopic screen for diagnostic purposes. Use beam-restrictive devices and patient-shielding techniques to minimize radiation exposure to patient and staff. Position X-ray equipment and adjust controls to set exposure factors, such as time and distance. Position patient on examining table, and set up and adjust equipment to obtain optimum view of specific body area as requested by physician. Determine patients' X-ray needs by reading requests or instructions from physicians. Make exposures necessary for the requested procedures, rejecting and repeating work that does not meet established standards. Process exposed radiographs using film processors or computer-generated methods. Explain procedures to patients to reduce anxieties and obtain cooperation. Perform procedures such as linear tomography, mammography, sonograms, joint and cyst aspirations, routine contrast studies, routine fluoroscopy,

and examinations of the head, trunk, and extremities under supervision of physician. Prepare and set up X-ray room for patient. Provide assistance to physicians or other technologists in the performance of more complex procedures. Provide students and other technologists with suggestions of additional views, alternate positioning, or improved techniques to ensure the images produced are of the highest quality. Coordinate work of other technicians or technologists when procedures require more than one person.

Related Knowledge/Courses: Physics; Medicine and Dentistry; Psychology; Biology; Chemistry; Customer and Personal Service.

Personality Types: Realistic-Conventional-Social.

Skills: Operation and Control; Science; Operation Monitoring; Service Orientation; Troubleshooting; Technology Design; Coordination; Quality Control Analysis.

Work Environment: Indoors; standing; walking and running; using hands; bending or twisting the body; repetitive motions; contaminants; exposed to radiation; exposed to disease or infections.

Job Specialization: Surgical Assistants

Assist surgeons during surgery by performing duties such as tissue retraction, insertion of tubes and intravenous lines, or closure of surgical wounds. Perform preoperative and postoperative duties to facilitate patient care. Adjust and maintain operating room temperature, humidity, or lighting, according to surgeon's specifications. Apply sutures, staples, clips, or other materials to close skin, fascia, or subcutaneous wound layers. Assess skin integrity or other body conditions upon completion of the procedure to determine if damage has occurred from body positioning. Assist in the insertion, positioning, or suturing of closed-wound drainage systems. Assist members of surgical team with gowning or gloving. Clamp, ligate, or cauterize blood vessels to control bleeding during surgical entry using hemostatic clamps, suture ligatures, or electrocautery equipment. Coordinate or participate in the positioning of patients using body-stabilizing equipment or protective padding to provide appropriate exposure for the procedure or to protect against nerve damage or circulation impairment. Coordinate with anesthesia personnel to maintain patient temperature. Discuss with surgeon the nature of the surgical procedure, including operative consent, methods of operative exposure, diagnostic or laboratory data, or patient-advanced directives or other needs. Incise tissue layers in lower extremities to harvest veins. Maintain an unobstructed operative field using surgical retractors, sponges, or suctioning and irrigating equipment. Monitor and maintain aseptic technique throughout procedures. Monitor patient's intra-operative status, including patient position, vital signs, or volume or color of blood.

Related Knowledge/Courses: No data available.

Personality Types: No data available.

Skills: No data available.

Work Environment: No data available.

Heating, Air Conditioning, and Refrigeration Mechanics and Installers

- ❀ Average Annual Earnings (All): $43,380
- ❀ Average Annual Earnings (Recent Veterans): $34,050
- ❀ Earnings Growth Potential: Medium (38.2%)
- ❀ Growth: 33.7%
- ❀ Annual Job Openings: 13,760
- ❀ Veteran Employment by Sector: For-Profit, 74.9%; Nonprofit, 4.4%; Government, 19.4%; Self-Employed, 1.2%.

Considerations for Job Outlook: Job opportunities for HVACR technicians are expected to be excellent, particularly for those who have completed training at an accredited technical school or through a formal apprenticeship. Candidates familiar with computers and electronics will have the best job opportunities as employers continue to have trouble finding qualified technicians to work on complex new systems. Technicians who specialize in installation work may experience periods of unemployment when the level of new construction activity declines. Maintenance and repair work, however, usually remains relatively stable. Businesses and homeowners depend on their climate-control or refrigeration systems and must keep them in good working order, regardless of economic conditions.

Install or repair heating, central air conditioning, or refrigeration systems, including oil burners, hot-air furnaces, and heating stoves. For task data, see Job Specializations.

Related Military Specializations: Aircraft Maintenance Support Equipment Electrician/Refrigeration Mechanic; Heating, Ventilation, Air Conditioning, and Refrigeration Apprentice; Heating, Ventilation, Air Conditioning, and Refrigeration Craftsman; Heating, Ventilation, Air Conditioning, and Refrigeration Helper; Heating, Ventilation, Air Conditioning, and Refrigeration Journeyman; NAMTS Air Conditioning and Refrigeration; Refrigeration and Air Conditioning Technician; Shore-Based Refrigeration and Air Conditioning Technician; others. **Average Educational Level of Vets:** High school diploma or equivalent. **Usual Educational Requirement:** Postsecondary vocational training. **Relevant Educational Programs:** Heating, Air Conditioning, Ventilation, and Refrigeration Maintenance Technology/Technician (HAC, HACR, HVAC, HVACR); Heating, Ventilation, Air Conditioning, and Refrigeration Engineering Technology/Technician. **Work Experience Needed:** None. **On-the-Job Training Needed:** Long-term on-the-job training. **Certification/Licensure:** Licensure.

Key Career Cluster: 02 Architecture and Construction. **Key Career Pathway:** 2.3 Maintenance/operations. **Top Industries for Vets:** Construction; National Security and International Affairs; Commercial and Industrial Machinery and Equipment Repair and Maintenance; Hospitals; Colleges and Universities, Including Junior Colleges.

Job Specialization: Heating and Air Conditioning Mechanics and Installers

Install, service, and repair heating and air conditioning systems in residences and commercial establishments. Obtain and maintain required certifications. Comply with all applicable standards, policies, and procedures, including safety procedures and the maintenance of a clean work area. Repair or replace defective equipment, components, or wiring. Test electrical circuits and components for continuity, using electrical test equipment. Reassemble and test equipment following repairs. Inspect and test system to verify system compliance with plans and specifications and to detect and locate malfunctions. Discuss heating-cooling system malfunctions with users to isolate problems or to verify that malfunctions have been corrected. Test pipe or tubing joints and connections for leaks, using pressure gauge or soap-and-water solution. Record and report all faults, deficiencies, and other unusual occurrences, as well as the time and materials expended on work orders. Adjust system controls to setting recommended by manufacturer to balance system, using hand tools. Recommend, develop, and perform preventive and general-maintenance procedures such as cleaning, power-washing, and vacuuming equipment; oiling parts; and changing filters. Lay out and connect electrical wiring between controls and equipment according to wiring diagram, using electrician's hand tools. Install auxiliary components to heating-cooling equipment, such as expansion and discharge valves, air ducts, pipes, blowers, dampers, flues, and stokers, following blueprints.

Related Knowledge/Courses: Mechanical Devices; Building and Construction; Physics; Chemistry; Design; Engineering and Technology.

Personality Types: Realistic-Conventional-Investigative.

Skills: Installation; Repairing; Equipment Maintenance; Troubleshooting; Equipment Selection; Operation and Control; Quality Control Analysis; Mathematics.

Work Environment: More often outdoors than indoors; standing; walking and running; kneeling, crouching, stooping, or crawling; using hands; bending or twisting the body; noise; very hot or cold; bright or inadequate lighting;

contaminants; cramped work space; high places; hazardous conditions; hazardous equipment; minor burns, cuts, bites, or stings.

Job Specialization: Refrigeration Mechanics and Installers

Install and repair industrial and commercial refrigerating systems. Braze or solder parts to repair defective joints and leaks. Observe and test system operation, using gauges and instruments. Test lines, components, and connections for leaks. Dismantle malfunctioning systems, and test components using electrical, mechanical, and pneumatic testing equipment. Adjust or replace worn or defective mechanisms and parts, and reassemble repaired systems. Read blueprints to determine location, size, capacity, and type of components needed to build refrigeration system. Supervise and instruct assistants. Perform mechanical overhauls and refrigerant reclaiming. Install wiring to connect components to an electric power source. Cut, bend, thread, and connect pipe to functional components and water, power, or refrigeration system. Adjust valves according to specifications, and charge system with proper type of refrigerant by pumping the specified gas or fluid into the system. Estimate, order, pick up, deliver, and install materials and supplies needed to maintain equipment in good working condition. Install expansion and control valves using acetylene torches and wrenches. Mount compressor, condenser, and other components in specified locations on frames using hand tools and acetylene welding equipment. Keep records of repairs and replacements made and causes of malfunctions. Schedule work with customers, and initiate work orders, house requisitions, and orders from stock.

Related Knowledge/Courses: Mechanical Devices; Physics; Building and Construction; Engineering and Technology; Design; Chemistry.

Personality Types: Realistic-Conventional-Enterprising.

Skills: Installation; Repairing; Equipment Maintenance; Troubleshooting; Equipment Selection; Operation and Control; Quality Control Analysis; Management of Material Resources.

Work Environment: More often outdoors than indoors; standing; walking and running; kneeling, crouching, stooping, or crawling; using hands; bending or twisting the body; repetitive motions; noise; very hot or cold; bright or inadequate lighting; contaminants; cramped work space; high places; hazardous conditions; hazardous equipment; minor burns, cuts, bites, or stings.

Heavy and Tractor-Trailer Truck Drivers

- ✱ Average Annual Earnings (All): $37,930
- ✱ Average Annual Earnings (Recent Veterans): $32,740
- ✱ Earnings Growth Potential: Low (34.4%)
- ✱ Growth: 20.6%
- ✱ Annual Job Openings: 64,940
- ✱ Veteran Employment by Sector: For-Profit, 83.4%; Nonprofit, 1.3%; Government, 9.3%; Self-Employed, 6.0%.

Considerations for Job Outlook: Job prospects for heavy and tractor-trailer truck drivers are expected to be favorable. Due to the somewhat difficult lifestyle and time spent away from home, many companies have trouble finding qualified long-haul drivers. Those who have the necessary experience and other qualifications should be able to find jobs.

Drive a tractor-trailer combination or a truck with a capacity of at least 26,000 pounds gross vehicle weight (GVW). Follow appropriate safety procedures when transporting dangerous goods. Check vehicles before driving them to ensure that mechanical, safety, and emergency equipment is in good working order. Maintain logs of working hours and of vehicle service and repair status, following applicable state and federal regulations. Obtain receipts or signatures when loads are delivered, and collect payment for services when required. Check all load-related documentation to ensure that it is complete and accurate. Maneuver trucks into loading or unloading positions, following signals from loading crew as needed; check that vehicle position is correct and any special loading equipment is properly positioned. Drive trucks with capacities greater than three tons, including tractor-trailer combinations, to transport and deliver products, livestock, or other materials. Secure cargo for transport, using ropes, blocks, chains, binders, or covers. Read bills of lading to determine assignment details. Report vehicle defects, accidents, traffic violations, or damage to the vehicles. Read and interpret maps to determine vehicle routes. Couple and uncouple trailers by changing trailer jack positions, connecting or disconnecting air and electrical lines, and manipulating fifth-wheel locks. Collect delivery instructions from appropriate sources, verifying instructions and routes. Drive trucks to weigh stations before and after loading and along routes to document weights and to comply with state regulations.

Related Military Specializations: Logistics Vehicle System Operator; Motor Transport Operator; Motor Vehicle Operator; Semitrailer Refueler Operator; Vehicle Operations Apprentice; Vehicle Operations Helper; Vehicle Operations Journeyman. **Average Educational Level of Vets:** High school diploma or equivalent. **Usual Educational Requirement:** High school diploma or equivalent. **Relevant Educational Program:** Truck and Bus Driver Training/Commercial Vehicle Operator and Instructor Training. **Related Knowledge/Courses:** Transportation; Food Production; Mechanical Devices; Building and Construction; Design; Personnel and Human Resources. **Work Experience Needed:** 1 to 5 years. **On-the-Job Training Needed:** Short-term on-the-job training. **Certification/Licensure:** Licensure.

Personality Types: Realistic-Conventional. **Key Career Cluster:** 16 Transportation, Distribution, and Logistics. **Key Career Pathway:** 16.1 Transportation Operations. **Top Industries for Vets:** Truck Transportation; National Security and International Affairs; Restaurants and Other Food Services; Construction; Groceries and Related Products Merchant Wholesalers.

Skills: Repairing; Operation and Control; Equipment Maintenance; Troubleshooting; Operation Monitoring; Equipment Selection; Quality Control Analysis; Installation.

Work Environment: Outdoors; sitting; using hands; repetitive motions; noise; very hot or cold; bright or inadequate lighting; contaminants; cramped work space; hazardous equipment.

Human Resources Assistants, Except Payroll and Timekeeping

❋ Average Annual Earnings (All): $37,250

❋ Average Annual Earnings (Recent Veterans): $34,920

❋ Earnings Growth Potential: Low (33.1%)

❋ Growth: 11.2%

❋ Annual Job Openings: 6,160

❋ Veteran Employment by Sector: For-Profit, 22.8%; Nonprofit, 4.8%; Government, 72.4%; Self-Employed, 0.0%.

Considerations for Job Outlook: Employment growth will vary by specialty. Projected employment change is most rapid for interviewers and correspondence clerks.

Compile and keep personnel records. Process, verify, and maintain personnel related documentation, including staffing, recruitment, training, grievances, performance evaluations, classifications, and employee leaves of absence. Explain company personnel policies, benefits, and procedures to employees or job applicants. Record data for each employee, including such information as addresses, weekly earnings, absences, amount of sales or production, supervisory reports on performance, and dates of and reasons for terminations. Gather personnel records from other departments or employees. Examine employee files to answer inquiries and provide information for personnel actions. Answer questions regarding examinations, eligibility, salaries, benefits, and other pertinent information. Compile and prepare reports and documents pertaining to personnel activities. Request information from law enforcement officials, previous employers, and other references to determine applicants' employment acceptability. Process and review employment applications to evaluate qualifications or eligibility of applicants. Arrange for advertising or posting of job vacancies, and notify eligible workers of position availability. Provide assistance in administering employee benefit programs and worker's compensation plans. Select applicants meeting specified job requirements and refer them to hiring personnel. Inform job applicants of their acceptance or rejection of employment. Interview job applicants to obtain and verify information used to screen and evaluate them. Search employee files to obtain information for authorized persons and organizations, such as credit bureaus and finance companies. Administer and score applicant and employee aptitude, personality, and interest assessment instruments. Prepare badges, passes, and identification cards, and perform other security-related duties. Arrange for in-house and external training activities.

Related Military Specializations: Human Resources Information Systems Management Specialist; Human Resources Specialist; Manpower Information Systems (MIS) Analyst; Personnel Actions Specialist; Personnel Administration Specialist; Personnel Apprentice; Personnel Clerk; Personnel Craftsman; Personnel Helper; Personnel Information Systems Management Specialist; Personnel Journeyman; Personnel Management Specialist; Personnel Records Specialist; Personnel Services Specialist; Personnel Specialist; others. **Average Educational Level of Vets:** One or more years of college, no degree. **Usual Educational Requirement:** High school diploma or equivalent. **Relevant Educational Program:** General Office Occupations and Clerical Services. **Related Knowledge/Courses:** Clerical Practices; Personnel and Human Resources; Customer and Personal Service; Economics and Accounting; Computers and Electronics; Law and

H

Government. **Work Experience Needed:** None. **On-the-Job Training Needed:** Short-term on-the-job training. **Certification/Licensure:** None.

Personality Types: Conventional-Enterprising-Social. **Key Career Cluster:** 04 Business, Management, and Administration. **Key Career Pathway:** 4.3 Human Resources. **Top Industries for Vets:** National Security and International Affairs; Administration of Human Resource Programs; Construction; Hospitals; Sawmills and Wood Preservation.

Skills: Active Listening; Reading Comprehension; Service Orientation; Writing; Speaking; Social Perceptiveness; Management of Personnel Resources.

Work Environment: Indoors; sitting; repetitive motions.

Industrial Machinery Mechanics

* Average Annual Earnings (All): $46,270

* Average Annual Earnings (Recent Veterans): $43,650

* Earnings Growth Potential: Low (33.5%)

* Growth: 21.6%

* Annual Job Openings: 11,710

* Veteran Employment by Sector: For-Profit, 81.0%; Nonprofit, 1.3%; Government, 16.9%; Self-Employed, 0.8%.

Considerations for Job Outlook: Applicants with a broad range of skills in machine repair should have good job prospects overall. The need to replace the many older workers who are expected to retire, as well as those who leave the occupation for other reasons, should result in numerous job openings. Some employers have reported difficulty in recruiting young workers with the necessary skills. Mechanics are not as affected by changes in production levels as are other manufacturing workers because mechanics often are kept during production downtime to complete overhauls to major equipment and to keep expensive machinery in working order.

Repair, install, adjust, or maintain industrial production and processing machinery or refinery and pipeline distribution systems. Disassemble machinery and equipment to remove parts and make repairs. Repair and replace broken or malfunctioning components of machinery and equipment. Repair and maintain the operating condition of industrial production and processing machinery and equipment. Examine parts for defects such as breakage and excessive wear. Reassemble equipment after completion of inspections, testing, or repairs. Observe and test the operation of machinery and equipment to diagnose malfunctions, using voltmeters and other testing devices. Operate newly repaired machinery and equipment to verify the adequacy of repairs. Clean, lubricate, and adjust parts, equipment, and machinery. Analyze test results, machine error messages, and information obtained from operators to diagnose equipment problems. Record repairs and maintenance performed. Study blueprints and manufacturers' manuals to determine correct installation and operation of machinery. Record parts and materials used, ordering or requisitioning new parts and materials as necessary. Cut and weld metal to repair broken metal parts, fabricate new parts, and assemble new equipment. Demonstrate equipment functions and features to machine operators. Enter codes and instructions to program computer-controlled machinery.

Related Military Specializations: Afloat Mobile Electric Power Plant Technician; Aviation Fuels Maintenance Technician; Battle

Force Intermediate Maintenance Activity (BFIMA) Boiler ACC Technician; Causeway Section Powered/Side Loadable Warping Tug (CSP/SLWT) Engineer; CG Smart Ship Engineering Control System Equipment (ECSE) Operator and Maintenance Technician; Crash Equipment Technician (SEA); Diesel Engine Inspector; Electronic Automatic Boiler Controls Maintenance Technician; High and Low Pressure Cryogenic Technician; others. **Average Educational Level of Vets:** High school diploma or equivalent. **Usual Educational Requirement:** High school diploma or equivalent. **Relevant Educational Program:** Industrial Mechanics and Maintenance Technology. **Related Knowledge/ Courses:** Mechanical Devices; Engineering and Technology; Building and Construction; Design; Chemistry; Physics. **Work Experience Needed:** None. **On-the-Job Training Needed:** Long-term on-the-job training. **Certification/Licensure:** None.

Personality Types: Realistic-Investigative-Conventional. **Key Career Cluster:** 13 Manufacturing. **Key Career Pathway:** 13.3 Maintenance, Installation and Repair. **Top Industries for Vets:** National Security and International Affairs; Motor Vehicles and Motor Vehicle Equipment; Commercial and Industrial Machinery and Equipment Repair and Maintenance; Machinery, Equipment, and Supplies Merchant Wholesalers; Industrial and Miscellaneous Chemicals.

Skills: Repairing; Equipment Maintenance; Troubleshooting; Installation; Operation Monitoring; Equipment Selection; Operation and Control; Quality Control Analysis.

Work Environment: Standing; walking and running; kneeling, crouching, stooping, or crawling; using hands; bending or twisting the body; repetitive motions; noise; very hot or cold; contaminants; cramped work space; high places;

hazardous conditions; hazardous equipment; minor burns, cuts, bites, or stings.

Industrial Truck and Tractor Operators

- ❋ Average Annual Earnings (All): $30,010
- ❋ Average Annual Earnings (Recent Veterans): $26,190
- ❋ Earnings Growth Potential: Low (32.3%)
- ❋ Growth: 11.8%
- ❋ Annual Job Openings: 20,950
- ❋ Veteran Employment by Sector: For-Profit, 93.2%; Nonprofit, 0.1%; Government, 6.4%; Self-Employed, 0.2%.

Considerations for Job Outlook: Job prospects should be favorable. A high number of job openings should be created by the need to replace workers who leave this occupation. As automation increases, the technology used by this occupation will become more complex.

Operate industrial trucks or tractors equipped to move materials around a warehouse, storage yard, factory, construction site, or similar location. Move controls to drive gasoline- or electric-powered trucks, cars, or tractors and transport materials between loading, processing, and storage areas. Move levers and controls that operate lifting devices, such as forklifts, lift beams and swivel-hooks, hoists, and elevating platforms, to load, unload, transport, and stack material. Position lifting devices under, over, or around loaded pallets, skids, and boxes, and secure material or products for transport to designated areas. Manually load or unload materials onto or off pallets, skids, platforms, cars, or lifting devices. Perform routine maintenance on vehicles and auxiliary equipment, such as cleaning, lubricating, recharging batteries, fueling, or replacing liquefied-gas tank. Weigh materials or products, and record weight and other production data on tags or labels. Operate or tend automatic stacking, loading, packaging, or cutting machines. Signal workers to discharge, dump, or level materials. Hook tow trucks to trailer hitches and fasten attachments, such as graders, plows, rollers, and winch cables to tractors, using hitchpins. Turn valves and open chutes to dump, spray, or release materials from dump cars or storage bins into hoppers.

Related Military Specialization: Vehicle Recovery Operator. **Average Educational Level of Vets:** High school diploma or equivalent. **Usual Educational Requirement:** Less than high school diploma or equivalent. **Relevant Educational Program:** Ground Transportation, Other. **Related Knowledge/Courses:** Production and Processing. **Work Experience Needed:** Less than 1 year. **On-the-Job Training Needed:** Short-term on-the-job training. **Certification/ Licensure:** None.

Personality Types: Realistic-Conventional. **Key Career Cluster:** 16 Transportation, Distribution, and Logistics. **Key Career Pathway:** 16.1 Transportation Operations. **Top Industries for Vets:** Warehousing and Storage; Truck Transportation; Construction; Motor Vehicles and Motor Vehicle Equipment; Building Material and Supplies Dealers.

Skills: Equipment Maintenance; Operation and Control; Operation Monitoring; Troubleshooting; Repairing.

Work Environment: Indoors; sitting; using hands; bending or twisting the body; repetitive motions; noise; very hot or cold; contaminants; hazardous equipment.

Insurance Sales Agents

- Average Annual Earnings (All): $47,450
- Average Annual Earnings (Recent Veterans): $32,740
- Earnings Growth Potential: High (45.4%)
- Growth: 21.9%
- Annual Job Openings: 18,440
- Veteran Employment by Sector: For-Profit, 72.3%; Nonprofit, 1.7%; Government, 2.2%; Self-Employed, 23.7%.

Considerations for Job Outlook: College graduates who have sales ability, excellent customer-service skills, and expertise in a range of insurance and financial services products should enjoy the best prospects. Multilingual agents should have an advantage, because they can serve a wider customer base. Additionally, insurance language is often technical, so agents who have a firm understanding of the relevant technical and legal terms should also be desirable to employers.

Sell life, property, casualty, health, automotive, or other types of insurance. Call on policyholders to deliver and explain policy, to analyze insurance program and suggest additions or changes, or to change beneficiaries. Calculate premiums, and establish payment method. Customize insurance programs to suit individual customers, often covering a variety of risks. Sell various types of insurance policies to businesses and individuals on behalf of insurance companies, including automobile, fire, life, property, medical, and dental insurance or specialized policies such as marine, farm/crop, and medical malpractice. Interview prospective clients to obtain data about their financial resources and needs and the physical condition of the person or property to be insured and to discuss any existing coverage. Seek out new clients and develop clientele by networking to find new customers and generate lists of prospective clients. Explain features, advantages, and disadvantages of various policies to promote sale of insurance plans. Contact underwriter, and submit forms to obtain binder coverage. Ensure that policy requirements are fulfilled, including any necessary medical examinations and the completion of appropriate forms. Confer with clients to obtain and provide information when claims are made on a policy. Perform administrative tasks, such as maintaining records and handling policy renewals. Select company that offers type of coverage requested by client to underwrite policy.

Related Military Specializations: None. **Average Educational Level of Vets:** Bachelor's degree. **Usual Educational Requirement:** High school diploma or equivalent. **Relevant Educational Program:** Insurance. **Related Knowledge/Courses:** Sales and Marketing; Economics and Accounting; Customer and Personal Service; Clerical Practices; Law and Government; Computers and Electronics. **Work Experience Needed:** None. **On-the-Job Training Needed:** Moderate-term on-the-job training. **Certification/Licensure:** Licensure; voluntary certification by association.

Personality Types: Enterprising-Conventional-Social. **Key Career Cluster:** 06 Finance. **Key Career Pathway:** 6.4 Insurance Services. **Top Industries for Vets:** Insurance Carriers and Related Activities; Securities, Commodities, Funds, Trusts, and Other Financial Investments; Nondepository Credit and Related Activities.

Skills: Negotiation; Persuasion; Service Orientation; Active Listening; Speaking; Systems Analysis; Active Learning; Systems Evaluation.

Work Environment: Indoors; sitting.

Interior Designers

* Average Annual Earnings (All): $47,620
* Average Annual Earnings (Recent Veterans): $41,470
* Earnings Growth Potential: High (46.0%)
* Growth: 19.3%
* Annual Job Openings: 2,840
* Veteran Employment by Sector: For-Profit, 77.9%; Nonprofit, 1.7%; Government, 9.5%; Self-Employed, 10.9%.

Considerations for Job Outlook: Job prospects should be better in higher income areas, because wealthier clients are more likely to engage in remodeling or renovating their homes. Interior designers who specialize, such as those who design kitchens, may benefit by becoming an expert in their particular area. By specializing in a unique area of design, interior designers can use their knowledge of products to better fulfill customer requests.

Plan, design, and furnish interiors of residential, commercial, or industrial buildings. Estimate material requirements and costs, and present design to client for approval. Confer with client to determine factors affecting planning interior environments, such as budget, architectural preferences, and purpose and function. Advise client on interior design factors such as space planning, layout, utilization of furnishings or equipment, and color coordination. Select or design and purchase furnishings, artwork, and accessories. Formulate environmental plan to be practical, aesthetic, and conducive to intended purposes such as raising productivity or selling merchandise. Subcontract fabrication, installation, and arrangement of carpeting, fixtures, accessories, draperies, paint and wall coverings, artwork, furniture, and related items. Render design ideas in form of paste-ups or drawings. Plan and design interior environments for boats, planes, buses, trains, and other enclosed spaces.

Related Military Specializations: None. **Average Educational Level of Vets:** Bachelor's degree. **Usual Educational Requirement:** Bachelor's degree. **Relevant Educational Programs:** Facilities Planning and Management; Interior Architecture; Interior Design; Textile Science. **Related Knowledge/Courses:** Design; Fine Arts; Building and Construction; Sales and Marketing; History and Archeology; Psychology. **Work Experience Needed:** None. **On-the-Job Training Needed:** None. **Certification/ Licensure:** Licensure in many states; voluntary certification for some specializations.

Personality Types: Artistic-Enterprising. **Key Career Cluster:** 02 Architecture and Construction. **Key Career Pathway:** 2.1 Design/Pre-construction. **Top Industries for Vets:** Architectural, Engineering, and Related Services; Specialized Design Services; Advertising and Related Services; National Security and International Affairs; Computer Systems Design and Related Services.

Skills: Management of Financial Resources; Operations Analysis; Management of Material Resources; Negotiation; Persuasion; Service Orientation; Coordination; Mathematics.

Work Environment: Indoors; sitting.

Laborers and Freight, Stock, and Material Movers, Hand

- ❋ Average Annual Earnings (All): $23,750
- ❋ Average Annual Earnings (Recent Veterans): $24,990
- ❋ Earnings Growth Potential: Low (27.6%)
- ❋ Growth: 15.4%
- ❋ Annual Job Openings: 98,020
- ❋ Veteran Employment by Sector: For-Profit, 81.6%; Nonprofit, 1.1%; Government, 16.4%; Self-Employed, 0.9%.

Considerations for Job Outlook: Job prospects for hand laborers and material movers should be favorable. Despite slower growth in this occupation, the need to replace workers who leave the occupation should create a large number of job openings. As automation increases, the technology used by workers in this occupation will become more complex. Employers will likely prefer workers who are comfortable using technology such as tablet computers and handheld scanners.

Manually move freight, stock, or other materials or perform other general labor. Attach identifying tags to containers, or mark them with identifying information. Read work orders or receive oral instructions to determine work assignments and material and equipment needs. Record numbers of units handled and moved, using daily production sheets or work tickets. Move freight, stock, and other materials to and from storage and production areas, loading docks, delivery vehicles, ships, and containers, by hand or using trucks, tractors, and other equipment. Sort cargo before loading and unloading. Assemble product containers and crates, using hand tools and pre-cut lumber. Load and unload ship cargo, using winches and other hoisting devices. Connect hoses and operate equipment to move liquid materials into and out of storage tanks on vessels. Pack containers and repack damaged containers. Carry needed tools and supplies from storage or trucks, and return them after use. Install protective devices, such as bracing, padding, or strapping, to prevent shifting or damage to items being transported. Maintain equipment storage areas to ensure that inventory is protected. Attach slings, hooks, and other devices to lift cargo and guide loads. Carry out general yard duties such as performing shunting on railway lines. Adjust controls to guide, position, and move equipment such as cranes, booms, and cameras. Guide loads being lifted in order to prevent swinging. Adjust or replace equipment parts such as rollers, belts, plugs, and caps, using hand tools. Stack cargo in locations such as transit sheds or in holds of ships as directed, using pallets or cargo boards. Connect electrical equipment to power sources so that it can be tested before use. Set up the equipment needed to produce special lighting and sound effects during performances. Bundle and band material such as fodder and tobacco leaves, using banding machines. Rig and dismantle props and equipment such as frames, scaffolding, platforms, or backdrops, using hand tools.

Related Military Specializations: None. **Average Educational Level of Vets:** High school diploma or equivalent. **Usual Educational Requirement:** Less than high school diploma or equivalent. **Relevant Educational Program:** No related CIP programs; this job is learned through informal short-term on-the-job training. **Related Knowledge/Courses:** Transportation; Public Safety and Security; Production and Processing. **Work Experience Needed:** None. **On-the-Job Training Needed:** Short-term on-the-job training. **Certification/Licensure:** None.

Personality Types: Realistic. **Key Career Cluster:** 16 Transportation, Distribution, and Logistics. **Key Career Pathway:** 16.3 Warehousing and Distribution Center Operations. **Top Industries for Vets:** National Security and International Affairs; Couriers and Messengers; Department and Discount Stores; Warehousing and Storage; Truck Transportation.

Skills: Repairing; Equipment Maintenance; Troubleshooting; Operation and Control; Equipment Selection; Quality Control Analysis; Operation Monitoring; Installation.

Work Environment: Outdoors; standing; walking and running; using hands; bending or twisting the body; repetitive motions; noise; very hot or cold; contaminants; cramped work space; hazardous equipment.

Landscaping and Groundskeeping Workers

- ✱ Average Annual Earnings (All): $23,410
- ✱ Average Annual Earnings (Recent Veterans): $20,080
- ✱ Earnings Growth Potential: Low (26.8%)
- ✱ Growth: 20.9%
- ✱ Annual Job Openings: 44,440
- ✱ Veteran Employment by Sector: For-Profit, 59.3%; Nonprofit, 3.2%; Government, 25.5%; Self-Employed, 11.9%.

Considerations for Job Outlook: Job prospects are expected to be favorable. Those with experience should have the best job opportunities. Most job openings will come from the need to replace many workers who leave or retire from this very large occupation.

Landscape or maintain grounds of property using hand or power tools or equipment.

Operate powered equipment such as mowers, tractors, twin-axle vehicles, snow blowers, chain saws, electric clippers, sod cutters, and pruning saws. Mow and edge lawns, using power mowers and edgers. Care for established lawns by mulching, aerating, weeding, grubbing and removing thatch, and trimming and edging around flower beds, walks, and walls. Shovel snow from walks, driveways, and parking lots, and spread salt in those areas. Use hand tools such as shovels, rakes, pruning saws, saws, hedge and brush trimmers, and axes. Prune and trim trees, shrubs, and hedges, using shears, pruners, or chain saws. Maintain and repair tools, equipment, and structures such as buildings, greenhouses, fences, and benches, using hand and power tools. Gather and remove litter. Mix and spray or spread fertilizers, herbicides, or insecticides onto grass, shrubs, and trees, using hand or automatic sprayers or spreaders. Provide proper upkeep of sidewalks, driveways, parking lots, fountains, planters, burial sites, and other grounds features. Water lawns, trees, and plants, using portable sprinkler systems, hoses, or watering cans. Trim and pick flowers, and clean flower beds. Rake, mulch, and compost leaves. Plant seeds, bulbs, foliage, flowering plants, grass, ground covers, trees, and shrubs, and apply mulch for protection, using gardening tools. Follow planned landscaping designs to determine where to lay sod, sow grass, or plant flowers and foliage. Decorate gardens with stones and plants. Maintain irrigation systems, including winterizing the systems and starting them up in spring. Care for natural turf fields, making sure the underlying soil has the required composition to allow proper drainage and to support the grasses used on the fields. Use irrigation methods to adjust the amount of water consumption and to prevent waste. Haul or spread topsoil, and spread straw over seeded soil to hold soil in place. Advise customers on plant selection and care.

Related Military Specializations: None. **Average Educational Level of Vets:** High school diploma or equivalent. **Usual Educational Requirement:** Less than high school diploma or equivalent. **Relevant Educational Program:** No related CIP programs; this job is learned through short-term on-the-job training. **Related Knowledge/Courses:** Mechanical Devices. **Work Experience Needed:** None. **On-the-Job Training Needed:** Short-term on-the-job training. **Certification/Licensure:** Licensure for some specializations; voluntary certification by association.

Personality Types: Realistic-Conventional. **Key Career Cluster:** 02 Architecture and Construction. **Key Career Pathway:** 2.3 Maintenance/operations. **Top Industries for Vets:** Landscaping Services; Museums, Art Galleries, Historical Sites, and Similar Institutions; Other Amusement, Gambling, and Recreation Industries; Elementary and Secondary Schools; National Security and International Affairs.

Skills: Operation and Control; Repairing; Equipment Maintenance; Troubleshooting; Operation Monitoring; Equipment Selection; Quality Control Analysis.

Work Environment: Outdoors; standing; walking and running; using hands; bending or twisting the body; repetitive motions; noise; very hot or cold; bright or inadequate lighting; contaminants; hazardous equipment; minor burns, cuts, bites, or stings.

Licensed Practical and Licensed Vocational Nurses

* Average Annual Earnings (All): $41,150
* Average Annual Earnings (Recent Veterans): $33,830
* Earnings Growth Potential: Low (25.5%)
* Growth: 22.4%
* Annual Job Openings: 36,920
* Veteran Employment by Sector: For-Profit, 50.4%; Nonprofit, 11.2%; Government, 36.5%; Self-Employed, 1.9%.

Considerations for Job Outlook: A large number of licensed practical and licensed vocational nurses are expected to retire over the coming decade. Job prospects should, therefore, be excellent for licensed and experienced LPNs and LVNs.

Care for ill, injured, or convalescing patients or persons with disabilities in hospitals, nursing homes, clinics, private homes, group homes, and similar institutions. Administer prescribed medications or start intravenous fluids, recording times and amounts on patients' charts. Observe patients, charting and reporting changes in patients' conditions, such as adverse reactions to medication or treatment, and taking any necessary actions. Provide basic patient care and treatments such as taking temperatures or blood pressures, dressing wounds, treating bedsores, giving enemas or douches, rubbing with alcohol, massaging, or performing catheterizations. Sterilize equipment and supplies, using germicides, sterilizer, or autoclave. Answer patients' calls, and determine how to assist them. Work as part of a health-care team to assess patient needs, plan and modify care, and implement interventions. Measure and record patients' vital signs, such as height, weight, temperature, blood pressure, pulse, and respiration. Collect samples such as blood, urine, and sputum from patients, and perform routine laboratory tests on samples. Prepare patients for examinations, tests, or treatments, and explain procedures. Assemble and use equipment such as catheters, tracheotomy tubes, and oxygen suppliers. Evaluate nursing intervention outcomes, conferring with other health-care team members as necessary. Record food and fluid intake and output. Help patients with bathing, dressing, maintaining personal hygiene, moving in bed, or standing and walking. Apply compresses, ice bags, and hot water bottles. Inventory and requisition supplies and instruments.

Related Military Specialization: Practical Nurse. **Average Educational Level of Vets:** One or more years of college, no degree. **Usual Educational Requirement:** Postsecondary vocational training. **Relevant Educational Programs:** Licensed Practical/Vocational Nurse Training; Practical Nursing, Vocational Nursing, and Nursing Assistant Training. **Related Knowledge/ Courses:** Psychology; Medicine and Dentistry; Therapy and Counseling; Biology; Philosophy and Theology; Customer and Personal Service. **Work Experience Needed:** None. **On-the-Job Training Needed:** None. **Certification/ Licensure:** Licensure.

Personality Types: Social-Realistic. **Key Career Cluster:** 08 Health Science. **Key Career Pathway:** 8.1 Therapeutic Services. **Top Industries for Vets:** Hospitals; Nursing Care Facilities; National Security and International Affairs; Outpatient Care Centers; Other Health Care Services.

Skills: Science; Social Perceptiveness; Service Orientation; Operation and Control; Persuasion; Negotiation; Speaking; Operations Analysis.

Work Environment: Indoors; standing; walking and running; using hands; repetitive motions; noise; contaminants; cramped work space; exposed to disease or infections.

Life, Physical, and Social Science Technicians, All Other

- ✵ Average Annual Earnings (All): $43,120
- ✵ Average Annual Earnings (Recent Veterans): $36,670
- ✵ Earnings Growth Potential: High (42.3%)
- ✵ Growth: 11.8%
- ✵ Annual Job Openings: 3,350
- ✵ Veteran Employment by Sector: For-Profit, 42.6%; Nonprofit, 10.3%; Government, 46.6%; Self-Employed, 0.5%.

Considerations for Job Outlook: Slower than average employment growth is projected.

All life, physical, and social science technicians not listed separately. For task data, see Job Specializations.

Related Military Specializations: Aerographer's Mate; Field Artillery Meteorological Crewmember; Marine Science Technician; Meteorology and Oceanography (METOC) Observer; Physical Sciences Assistant; Research, Analysis and Lessons Learned; Special Operations Weather Apprentice; Special Operations Weather Helper; Special Operations Weather Journeyman; Technical Applications Specialist; Weather Apprentice; Weather Apprentice, Advanced Battlefield Airman; Weather Apprentice, Battlefield Airman; Weather Apprentice, Forecaster; others. **Average Educational Level of Vets:** One or more years of college, no degree. **Usual Educational Requirement:** Associate degree. **Relevant Educational Programs:** Chemical Process Technology; Physical Science Technologies/Technicians, Other; Science Technologies/Technicians, General; Science Technologies/Technicians, Other. **Work Experience Needed:** None. **On-the-Job Training Needed:** Moderate-term on-the-job training. **Certification/Licensure:** None.

Key Career Cluster: 15 Science, Technology, Engineering, and Mathematics. **Key Career Pathway:** 15.2 Science and Mathematics. **Top Industries for Vets:** Scientific Research and Development Services; National Security and International Affairs; Architectural, Engineering, and Related Services; Colleges and Universities, Including Junior Colleges; Management, Scientific and Technical Consulting Services.

Job Specialization: Precision Agriculture Technicians

Apply geospatial technologies, including geographic information systems (GIS) and Global Positioning System (GPS), to agricultural production and management activities, such as pest scouting, site-specific pesticide application, yield mapping, and variable-rate irrigation. May use computers to develop and analyze maps and remote sensing images to compare physical topography with data on soils, fertilizer, pests, or weather. Collect information about soil and field attributes, yield data, or field boundaries, using field data recorders and basic geographic information systems (GIS). Create, layer, and analyze maps showing precision agricultural data such as crop yields, soil characteristics, input applications, terrain, drainage patterns, and field management history. Document and maintain records of precision agriculture information. Compile and analyze geospatial data to determine agricultural implications of factors such as soil quality, terrain, field productivity, fertilizers, and weather conditions. Divide agricultural fields into georeferenced zones based on soil characteristics and production potentials. Develop soil-sampling grids or identify sampling sites, using geospatial technology, for soil testing on characteristics such as nitrogen, phosphorus, and potassium content; pH; and micronutrients. Compare crop-yield maps with maps of soil-test data, chemical-application patterns, or other information to develop site-specific crop-management plans. Apply knowledge of government regulations when making agricultural recommendations. Recommend best crop varieties and seeding rates for specific field areas, based on analysis of geospatial data. Draw and read maps such as soil, contour, and plat maps. Process and analyze data from harvester monitors to develop yield maps.

Related Knowledge/Courses: Food Production; Geography; Biology; Chemistry; Sales and Marketing; Mechanical Devices.

Personality Types: Realistic-Investigative-Conventional.

Skills: Equipment Maintenance; Repairing; Science; Troubleshooting; Equipment Selection; Operations Analysis; Quality Control Analysis; Operation and Control.

Work Environment: Outdoors; very hot or cold.

Job Specialization: Quality Control Analysts

Conduct tests to determine quality of raw materials, bulk intermediate, and finished products. May conduct stability sample tests. Train other analysts to perform laboratory procedures and assays. Perform visual inspections of finished products. Serve as a technical liaison between quality control and other departments, vendors, or contractors. Participate in internal assessments and audits as required. Identify

and troubleshoot equipment problems. Evaluate new technologies and methods to make recommendations regarding their use. Ensure that lab cleanliness and safety standards are maintained. Develop and qualify new testing methods. Coordinate testing with contract laboratories and vendors. Write technical reports or documentation such as deviation reports, testing protocols, and trend analyses. Write or revise standard quality control operating procedures. Supply quality control data necessary for regulatory submissions. Receive and inspect raw materials. Review data from contract laboratories to ensure accuracy and regulatory compliance. Prepare or review required method transfer documentation, including technical transfer protocols or reports. Perform validations or transfers of analytical methods in accordance with applicable policies or guidelines. Participate in out-of-specification and failure investigations, and recommend corrective actions. Monitor testing procedures to ensure that all tests are performed according to established item specifications, standard test methods, or protocols. Investigate or report questionable test results.

Related Knowledge/Courses: No data available.

Personality Types: Conventional-Investigative-Realistic.

Skills: No data available.

Work Environment: No data available.

Job Specialization: Remote Sensing Technicians

Apply remote sensing technologies to assist scientists in areas such as natural resources, urban planning, and homeland security. May prepare flight plans and sensor configurations for flight trips. Participate in the planning and development of mapping projects. Maintain records of survey data. Document methods used, and write technical reports containing information collected. Develop specialized computer software routines to customize and integrate image analysis. Collect verification data on the ground using equipment such as global positioning receivers, digital cameras, and notebook computers. Verify integrity and accuracy of data contained in remote sensing image analysis systems. Prepare documentation and presentations including charts, photos, or graphs. Operate airborne remote sensing equipment such as survey cameras, sensors, and scanners. Monitor raw data quality during collection, and make equipment corrections as necessary. Merge scanned images or build photo mosaics of large areas using image processing software. Integrate remotely sensed data with other geospatial data. Evaluate remote sensing project requirements to determine the types of equipment or computer software necessary to meet project requirements such as specific image types and output resolutions. Develop and maintain geospatial information databases. Correct raw data for errors due to factors such as skew and atmospheric variation. Calibrate data collection equipment. Consult with remote sensing scientists, surveyors, cartographers, or engineers to determine project needs.

Related Knowledge/Courses: No data available.

Personality Types:
Realistic-Investigative-Conventional.

Skills: No data available.

Work Environment: No data available.

Light Truck or Delivery Services Drivers

- ❋ Average Annual Earnings (All): $29,080
- ❋ Average Annual Earnings (Recent Veterans): $32,740
- ❋ Earnings Growth Potential: Medium (38.0%)
- ❋ Growth: 14.7%
- ❋ Annual Job Openings: 29,590
- ❋ Veteran Employment by Sector: For-Profit, 83.4%; Nonprofit, 1.3%; Government, 9.3%; Self-Employed, 6.0%.

Considerations for Job Outlook: Delivery truck driver and driver/sales worker jobs are expected to be competitive. Because these drivers do not have to spend long periods away from home, these local jobs are more desirable than long-haul trucking jobs. Those with experience, or who work for the company in another occupation, should have the best job prospects.

Drive a light vehicle, such as a truck or van, with a capacity of less than 26,000 pounds gross vehicle weight (GVW), primarily to deliver or pick up merchandise or to deliver packages. Obey traffic laws, and follow established traffic and transportation procedures. Inspect and maintain vehicle supplies and equipment, such as gas, oil, water, tires, lights, and brakes in order to ensure that vehicles are in proper working condition. Report any mechanical problems encountered with vehicles. Present bills and receipts, and collect payments for goods delivered or loaded. Load and unload trucks, vans, or automobiles. Verify the contents of inventory loads against shipping papers. Turn in receipts and money received from deliveries.

Maintain records such as vehicle logs, records of cargo, or billing statements in accordance with regulations. Read maps, and follow written and verbal geographic directions. Report delays, accidents, or other traffic and transportation situations to bases or other vehicles, using telephones or mobile two-way radios. Sell and keep records of sales for products from truck inventory. Drive vehicles with capacities under three tons in order to transport materials to and from specified destinations such as railroad stations, plants, residences and offices, or within industrial yards. Drive trucks equipped with public address systems through city streets in order to broadcast announcements for advertising or publicity purposes. Use and maintain the tools and equipment found on commercial vehicles, such as weighing and measuring devices. Perform emergency repairs such as changing tires or installing light bulbs, fuses, tire chains, and spark plugs.

Related Military Specializations: Motor Transport Operator; Motor Vehicle Operator. **Average Educational Level of Vets:** High school diploma or equivalent. **Usual Educational Requirement:** High school diploma or equivalent. **Relevant Educational Program:** Truck and Bus Driver Training/Commercial Vehicle Operator and Instructor Training. **Related Knowledge/Courses:** Transportation. **Work Experience Needed:** None. **On-the-Job Training Needed:** Short-term on-the-job training. **Certification/Licensure:** Licensure in some states.

Personality Types: Realistic-Conventional. **Key Career Cluster:** 16 Transportation, Distribution, and Logistics. **Key Career Pathway:** 16.1 Transportation Operations. **Top Industries for Vets:** Truck Transportation; National Security and International Affairs; Restaurants and Other Food Services; Construction; Groceries and Related Products Merchant Wholesalers.

Skills: Repairing; Equipment Maintenance; Operation and Control; Equipment Selection; Quality Control Analysis; Troubleshooting; Operation Monitoring; Installation.

Work Environment: More often outdoors than indoors; using hands; bending or twisting the body; repetitive motions; noise; very hot or cold; bright or inadequate lighting; contaminants; cramped work space; whole-body vibration; minor burns, cuts, bites, or stings.

Loan Officers

- ❈ Average Annual Earnings (All): $58,030
- ❈ Average Annual Earnings (Recent Veterans): $41,470
- ❈ Earnings Growth Potential: High (44.7%)
- ❈ Growth: 14.2%
- ❈ Annual Job Openings: 11,520
- ❈ Veteran Employment by Sector: For-Profit, 88.0%; Nonprofit, 2.6%; Government, 1.5%; Self-Employed, 8.0%.

Considerations for Job Outlook: Prospects for loan officers should improve over the coming decade as lending activity rebounds from the recent recession. Job opportunities should be good for those with a college degree and lending, banking, or sales experience. In addition, some firms require loan officers to find their own clients, so candidates with established contacts and a referral network should have the best job opportunities.

Evaluate, authorize, or recommend approval of commercial, real estate, or credit loans. Meet with applicants to obtain information for loan applications and to answer questions about the process. Approve loans within specified limits, and refer loan applications outside those limits to management for approval. Analyze applicants' financial status, credit, and property evaluations to determine feasibility of granting loans. Explain to customers the different types of loans and credit options that are available, as well as the terms of those services. Obtain and compile copies of loan applicants' credit histories, corporate financial statements, and other financial information. Review and update credit and loan files. Review loan agreements to ensure that they are complete and accurate according to policy. Compute payment schedules. Stay abreast of new types of loans and other financial services and products to better meet customers' needs. Submit applications to credit analysts for verification and recommendation. Handle customer complaints, and take appropriate action to resolve them. Work with clients to identify their financial goals and to find ways of reaching those goals. Confer with underwriters to aid in resolving mortgage application problems. Negotiate payment arrangements with customers who have delinquent loans. Market bank products to individuals and firms, promoting bank services that may meet customers' needs. Supervise loan personnel. Set credit policies, credit lines, procedures, and standards in conjunction with senior managers.

Related Military Specializations: None. **Average Educational Level of Vets:** Bachelor's degree. **Usual Educational Requirement:** High school diploma or equivalent. **Relevant Educational Programs:** Credit Management; Finance, General. **Related Knowledge/Courses:** Sales and Marketing; Economics and Accounting; Customer and Personal Service; Law and Government; Clerical Practices; Mathematics. **Work Experience Needed:** None. **On-the-Job Training Needed:** Moderate-term on-the-job training. **Certification/Licensure:** Voluntary certification by association.

Personality Types: Conventional-Enterprising-Social. **Key Career Cluster:** 06 Finance.

Key Career Pathway: 6.3 Banking and Related Services. **Top Industries for Vets:** Nondepository Credit and Related Activities; Banking and Related Activities; Individual and Family Services; Insurance Carriers and Related Activities; Furniture and Related Products.

Skills: Service Orientation; Mathematics; Judgment and Decision Making; Speaking; Negotiation; Active Listening; Critical Thinking; Reading Comprehension.

Work Environment: More often indoors than outdoors; sitting.

Logisticians

* Average Annual Earnings (All): $71,910
* Average Annual Earnings (Recent Veterans): $57,840
* Earnings Growth Potential: Medium (37.7%)
* Growth: 25.5%
* Annual Job Openings: 4,870
* Veteran Employment by Sector: For-Profit, 36.3%; Nonprofit, 1.0%; Government, 61.8%; Self-Employed, 0.8%.

Considerations for Job Outlook: Job prospects should be good for those with a bachelor's degree in supply chain management, industrial engineering, business, or a related field. Prospects should be best for those with a college degree and work experience related to logistics, particularly previous experience using logistical software or doing logistical work for the military.

Analyze and coordinate the logistical functions of a firm or organization. Maintain and develop positive business relationships with a customer's key personnel involved in or directly relevant to a logistics activity. Develop an understanding of customers' needs, and take actions to ensure that such needs are met. Direct availability and allocation of materials, supplies, and finished products. Collaborate with other departments as necessary to meet customer requirements, to take advantage of sales opportunities, or, in the case of shortages, to minimize negative impacts on a business. Protect and control proprietary materials. Review logistics performance with customers against targets, benchmarks, and service agreements. Develop and implement technical project-management tools such as plans, schedules, and responsibility and compliance matrices. Direct team activities, establishing task priorities, scheduling and tracking work assignments, providing guidance, and ensuring the availability of resources. Report project plans, progress, and results. Direct and support the compilation and analysis of technical source data necessary for product development. Explain proposed solutions to customers, management, or other interested parties through written proposals and oral presentations. Provide project-management services, including the provision and analysis of technical data. Develop proposals that include documentation for estimates.

Related Military Specializations: Acquisition Logistics Specialist; Basic Distribution Management Marine; Distribution Management Specialist; Expeditionary Force Logistic Support—Deployed; Expeditionary Force Logistic Support—Not Deployed; Logistics Plans Apprentice; Logistics Plans Craftsman; Logistics Plans Helper; Logistics Plans Journeyman; Senior Noncommissioned Logistician; Vehicle Management and Analysis Apprentice; Vehicle Management and Analysis Helper; Vehicle Management and Analysis Journeyman; others. **Average Educational Level of Vets:** Bachelor's degree. **Usual Educational Requirement:** Bachelor's degree. **Relevant**

Educational Program: Operations Management and Supervision. **Related Knowledge/Courses:** Telecommunications; Geography; Computers and Electronics; Economics and Accounting; Administration and Management; Public Safety and Security. **Work Experience Needed:** 1 to 5 years. **On-the-Job Training Needed:** None. **Certification/Licensure:** Licensure for some specializations; voluntary certification by association.

Personality Types: Enterprising-Conventional. **Key Career Cluster:** 16 Transportation, Distribution, and Logistics Cluster. **Key Career Pathway:** 16.2 Logistics, Planning, and Management Services. **Top Industries for Vets:** National Security and International Affairs; Architectural, Engineering, and Related Services; Management, Scientific and Technical Consulting Services; Computer Systems Design and Related Services; Services Incidental to Transportation.

Skills: Operations Analysis; Management of Personnel Resources; Programming; Coordination; Monitoring; Systems Evaluation; Persuasion; Systems Analysis.

Work Environment: Indoors; sitting.

Job Specialization: Logistics Analysts

Analyze product delivery or supply chain processes to identify or recommend changes. May manage route activity including invoicing, electronic bills, and shipment tracing. Identify opportunities for inventory reductions. Monitor industry standards, trends, or practices to identify developments in logistics planning or execution. Enter logistics-related data into databases. Develop and maintain payment systems to ensure accuracy of vendor payments. Determine packaging requirements. Develop and maintain freight-rate databases for use by supply-chain departments to determine the most economical modes of transportation. Contact potential vendors to determine material availability. Contact carriers for rates or schedules. Communicate with and monitor service providers, such as ocean carriers, air freight forwarders, global consolidators, customs brokers, and trucking companies. Track product flow from origin to final delivery. Write or revise standard operating procedures for logistics processes. Review procedures such as distribution and inventory management to ensure maximum efficiency and minimum cost. Recommend improvements to existing or planned logistics processes. Provide ongoing analyses in areas such as transportation costs, parts procurement, back orders, and delivery processes. Prepare reports on logistics performance measures. Manage systems to ensure that pricing structures adequately reflect logistics costing. Monitor inventory transactions at warehouse facilities to assess receiving, storage, shipping, or inventory integrity. Maintain databases of logistics information. Maintain logistics records in accordance with corporate policies.

Related Knowledge/Courses: Transportation; Geography; Computers and Electronics; Production and Processing; Mathematics; Engineering and Technology.

Personality Types: Conventional-Enterprising-Investigative.

Skills: Mathematics; Systems Analysis; Systems Evaluation; Management of Financial Resources; Programming; Technology Design; Management of Material Resources; Active Learning.

Work Environment: Indoors; sitting.

Job Specialization: Logistics Engineers

Design and analyze operational solutions for projects such as transportation optimization, network modeling, process and methods analysis, cost containment, capacity enhancement, routing and shipment optimization, and information management. Propose logistics solutions for customers. Prepare production strategies and conceptual designs for production facilities. Interview key staff or tour facilities to identify efficiency-improvement, cost-reduction, or service-delivery opportunities. Direct the work of logistics analysts. Design plant distribution centers. Develop specifications for equipment, tools, facility layouts, or material-handling systems. Review contractual commitments, customer specifications, or related information to determine logistics and support requirements. Prepare or validate documentation on automated logistics or maintenance-data reporting and management-information systems. Identify cost-reduction and process-improvement opportunities. Identify or develop business rules and standard operating procedures to streamline operating processes. Develop metrics, internal analysis tools, or key performance indicators for business units within logistics. Develop and maintain cost estimates, forecasts, or cost models. Determine feasibility of designing new facilities or modifying existing facilities, based on such factors as cost, available space, schedule, technical requirements, and ergonomics. Determine logistics support requirements, such as facility details, staffing needs, and safety or maintenance plans. Conduct logistics studies and analyses, such as time studies, zero-base analyses, rate analyses, network analyses, flow-path analyses, and supply chain analyses.

Related Knowledge/Courses: Engineering and Technology; Design; Transportation; Telecommunications; Mechanical Devices; Production and Processing.

Personality Types: Investigative-Conventional-Realistic.

Skills: Equipment Selection; Programming; Systems Evaluation; Operations Analysis; Systems Analysis; Management of Material Resources;

Mathematics; Management of Financial Resources.

Work Environment: Indoors; sitting.

Machinists

* Average Annual Earnings (All): $39,220

* Average Annual Earnings (Recent Veterans): $31,100

* Earnings Growth Potential: Medium (37.8%)

* Growth: 8.5%

* Annual Job Openings: 9,950

* Veteran Employment by Sector: For-Profit, 75.9%; Nonprofit, 1.7%; Government, 21.3%; Self-Employed, 1.1%.

Considerations for Job Outlook: Job opportunities for machinists and tool and die makers should be excellent as employers continue to value the wide-ranging skills of these workers. Also, many young people with the educational and personal qualifications needed to become machinists or tool and die makers prefer to attend college or may not wish to enter production occupations. In fact, employers in certain parts of the country report difficulty attracting skilled workers and apprenticeship candidates with the abilities necessary to fill job openings. Therefore, the number of workers learning to be machinists or tool and die makers is expected to be smaller than the number of job openings arising each year from the need to replace experienced machinists who retire or leave the occupation for other reasons.

Set up and operate a variety of machine tools to produce precision parts and instruments. Calculate dimensions and tolerances using knowledge of mathematics and instruments such as micrometers and vernier calipers. Machine parts to specifications using machine tools such as lathes, milling machines, shapers, or grinders. Measure, examine, and test completed units to detect defects and ensure conformance to specifications, using precision instruments such as micrometers. Set up, adjust, and operate all of the basic machine tools and many specialized or advanced variation tools to perform precision machining operations. Align and secure holding fixtures, cutting tools, attachments, accessories, and materials onto machines. Monitor the feed and speed of machines during the machining process. Study sample parts, blueprints, drawings, and engineering information to determine methods and sequences of operations needed to fabricate products, and determine product dimensions and tolerances. Select the appropriate tools, machines, and materials to be used in preparation of machinery work. Lay out, measure, and mark metal stock to display placement of cuts. Observe and listen to operating machines or equipment to diagnose machine malfunctions and to determine need for adjustments or repairs. Check work pieces to ensure that they are properly lubricated and cooled. Maintain industrial machines, applying knowledge of mechanics, shop mathematics, metal properties, layout, and machining procedures. Position and fasten work pieces. Operate equipment to verify operational efficiency. Install repaired parts into equipment, or install new equipment. Clean and lubricate machines, tools, and equipment to remove grease, rust, stains, and foreign matter. Advise clients about the materials being used for finished products. Set controls to regulate machining, or enter commands to retrieve, input, or edit computerized machine control media. Program computers and electronic instruments such as numerically controlled machine tools.

Related Military Specializations: Advanced Machinery Repairman; Aircraft Metals

Technology Apprentice; Aircraft Metals Technology Craftsman; Aircraft Metals Technology Helper; Aircraft Metals Technology Journeyman; Allied Trades Specialist; Machinery Repairman; Machinist; NAMTS Inside Machinist; NAMTS Outside Machinist; NAMTS Sheetmetal Worker. **Average Educational Level of Vets:** High school diploma or equivalent. **Usual Educational Requirement:** High school diploma or equivalent. **Relevant Educational Programs:** Machine Shop Technology/Assistant; Machine Tool Technology/ Machinist. **Related Knowledge/Courses:** Mechanical Devices; Design; Engineering and Technology; Production and Processing; Mathematics. **Work Experience Needed:** None. **On-the-Job Training Needed:** Long-term on-the-job training. **Certification/Licensure:** Voluntary certification by association.

Personality Types: Realistic-Conventional-Investigative. **Key Career Cluster:** 13 Manufacturing. **Key Career Pathway:** 13.1 Production. **Top Industries for Vets:** Machine Shops; Turned Products; Screws, Nuts and Bolts; National Security and International Affairs; Machinery, Not Elsewhere Classified; Construction, and Mining and Oil and Gas Field Machinery; Motor Vehicles and Motor Vehicle Equipment.

Skills: Equipment Maintenance; Installation; Repairing; Equipment Selection; Quality Control Analysis; Technology Design; Troubleshooting; Operation and Control.

Work Environment: Standing; walking and running; using hands; repetitive motions; noise; contaminants; hazardous equipment; minor burns, cuts, bites, or stings.

Maintenance and Repair Workers, General

- Average Annual Earnings (All): $35,030
- Average Annual Earnings (Recent Veterans): $37,870
- Earnings Growth Potential: High (40.6%)
- Growth: 11.0%
- Annual Job Openings: 37,910
- Veteran Employment by Sector: For-Profit, 49.1%; Nonprofit, 2.0%; Government, 47.6%; Self-Employed, 1.3%.

Considerations for Job Outlook: There should be many job openings for general maintenance and repair workers, due to growth and the need to replace workers who leave the occupation. Many job openings are expected as experienced workers retire. Those with experience in repair- or maintenance-related fields should continue to have the best job prospects.

Perform work involving the skills of two or more maintenance or craft occupations to keep machines, mechanical equipment, or the structure of an establishment in repair. Repair or replace defective equipment parts, using hand tools and power tools, and reassemble equipment. Perform routine preventive maintenance to ensure that machines continue to run smoothly, building systems operate efficiently, or the physical condition of buildings does not deteriorate. Inspect drives, motors, and belts, check fluid levels, replace filters, or perform other maintenance actions, following checklists. Use tools ranging from common hand and power tools, such as hammers, hoists, saws, drills, and wrenches, to precision measuring instruments and electrical and electronic testing devices. Assemble, install, or repair wiring, electrical or electronic components, pipe systems, plumbing, machinery, or equipment. Diagnose mechanical problems and determine how to correct them, checking blueprints, repair manuals, or parts catalogs, as necessary. Inspect, operate, or test machinery or equipment to diagnose machine malfunctions. Record type and cost of maintenance or repair work. Clean or lubricate shafts, bearings, gears, or other parts of machinery. Dismantle devices to access and remove defective parts, using hoists, cranes, hand tools, and power tools. Plan and lay out repair work, using diagrams, drawings, blueprints, maintenance manuals, or schematic diagrams. Order parts, supplies, and equipment from catalogs and suppliers, or obtain them from storerooms. Adjust functional parts of devices or control instruments, using hand tools, levels, plumb bobs, or straightedges. Paint or repair roofs, windows, doors, floors, woodwork, plaster, drywall, or other parts of building structures. Operate cutting torches or welding equipment to cut or join metal parts. Maintain and repair specialized equipment and machinery found in cafeterias, laundries, hospitals, stores, offices, or factories. Provide grounds keeping services, such as landscaping and snow removal. Perform general cleaning of buildings or properties.

Related Military Specializations: Aircraft Armament Systems Apprentice, A10; Aircraft Armament Systems Apprentice, All Other; Aircraft Armament Systems Apprentice, B-1; Aircraft Armament Systems Apprentice, B-52; Aircraft Armament Systems Apprentice, F/A-22; Aircraft Armament Systems Apprentice, F-4; Aircraft Armament Systems Apprentice, F-15; Aircraft Armament Systems Apprentice, F-16; Aircraft Armament Systems Apprentice, F-35; Aircraft Armament Systems Apprentice, F-111; Aircraft Armament Systems Craftsman; others. **Average Educational Level of Vets:** High

school diploma or equivalent. **Usual Educational Requirement:** High school diploma or equivalent. **Relevant Educational Program:** Building/Property Maintenance. **Related Knowledge/Courses:** Building and Construction; Mechanical Devices; Design; Public Safety and Security; Physics; Engineering and Technology. **Work Experience Needed:** None. **On-the-Job Training Needed:** Moderate-term on-the-job training. **Certification/Licensure:** Voluntary certification for some specializations.

Personality Types: Realistic-Conventional-Investigative. **Key Career Cluster:** 02 Architecture and Construction. **Key Career Pathway:** 2.2 Construction. **Top Industries for Vets:** National Security and International Affairs; Architectural, Engineering, and Related Services; Real Estate; Machinery, Equipment, and Supplies Merchant Wholesalers; Machinery, Not Elsewhere Classified.

Skills: Repairing; Equipment Maintenance; Installation; Equipment Selection; Troubleshooting; Operation and Control; Quality Control Analysis; Operation Monitoring.

Work Environment: Outdoors; standing; walking and running; kneeling, crouching, stooping, or crawling; using hands; bending or twisting the body; noise; very hot or cold; contaminants; cramped work space; hazardous equipment; minor burns, cuts, bites, or stings.

Managers, All Other

- ❋ Average Annual Earnings (All): $99,540

- ❋ Average Annual Earnings (Recent Veterans): $69,850

- ❋ Earnings Growth Potential: High (48.4%)

- ❋ Growth: 7.9%

- ❋ Annual Job Openings: 24,940

- ❋ Veteran Employment by Sector: For-Profit, 44.6%; Nonprofit, 2.4%; Government, 47.3%; Self-Employed, 5.6%.

Considerations for Job Outlook: Slower than average employment growth is projected.

All managers not listed separately. For task data, see Job Specializations.

Related Military Specializations: Aircraft Maintenance Officer; Aviation Ordnance Officer; Avionics Officer; Basic Operational Communications Officer; Circuit Control Officer; Communication Officer; Custodian of CMS Material; Director of Communications; Electronics Maintenance Officer (Ground); Electronics Maintenance Officer Aviation Command and Control (C2); Executive Officer; Generalist Remotely Piloted Aircraft Pilot; Health Services Materiel Officer; Health Services Plans, Operations, Intelligence, Security and Training; Information Systems Officer; Information Warfare Officer; others. **Average Educational Level of Vets:** Bachelor's degree. **Usual Educational Requirement:** High school diploma or equivalent. **Relevant Educational Programs:** American Government and Politics (United States); American History (United States); Anthropology; Anthropology, Other; Applied Behavior Analysis; Applied Economics; Applied Psychology; Archeology; Archives/Archival Administration; Arts, Entertainment, and Media Management, Other; Arts, Entertainment, and Media Management, General; Asian History; Business Administration and Management, General; Business/Commerce, General; Canadian Government and Politics; Canadian History; Clinical Child Psychology; Clinical Psychology; Clinical Research Coordinator; Clinical, Counseling and Applied Psychology, Other; Cognitive Psychology and Psycholinguistics; Community Psychology; Comparative Psychology; Counseling Psychology; Criminal Justice/Law Enforcement Administration; Criminology; Crisis/Emergency/Disaster Management; Critical Infrastructure Protection; Cultural Anthropology; Demography and Population Studies; Development Economics and International Development; others. **Work Experience Needed:** 1 to 5 years. **On-the-Job Training Needed:** None. **Certification/Licensure:** Licensure for some specializations.

Key Career Cluster: 04 Business, Management, and Administration. **Key Career Pathway:** 4.1 Management. **Top Industries for Vets:** National Security and International Affairs; Architectural, Engineering, and Related Services; Computer Systems Design and Related Services; Executive Offices and Legislative Bodies; Construction.

Job Specialization: Brownfield Redevelopment Specialists and Site Managers

Participate in planning and directing cleanup and redevelopment of contaminated properties for reuse. Does not include properties sufficiently contaminated to qualify as Superfund sites. Review or evaluate environmental-remediation project proposals. Review or evaluate designs for contaminant treatment or disposal facilities. Provide training on hazardous-material or waste-cleanup procedures and technologies.

Provide expert witness testimony on issues such as soil, air, or water contamination and associated cleanup measures. Prepare reports or presentations to communicate brownfield redevelopment needs, status, or progress. Negotiate contracts for services or materials needed for environmental remediation. Prepare and submit permit applications for demolition, cleanup, remediation, or construction projects. Maintain records of decisions, actions, and progress related to environmental-redevelopment projects. Inspect sites to assess environmental damage or monitor cleanup progress. Plan or implement brownfield redevelopment projects to ensure safety, quality, and compliance with applicable standards or requirements. Identify environmental-contamination sources. Estimate costs for environmental cleanup and remediation of land-redevelopment projects. Develop or implement plans for revegetation of brownfield sites. Design or implement plans for surface- or ground-water remediation. Design or implement plans for structural demolition and debris removal. Design or implement measures to improve the water, air, and soil quality of military test sites, abandoned mine land, or other contaminated sites. Design or conduct environmental-restoration studies.

Related Knowledge/Courses: No data available.

Personality Types: No data available.

Skills: No data available.

Work Environment: No data available.

Job Specialization: Compliance Managers

Plan, direct, or coordinate activities of an organization to ensure compliance with ethical or regulatory standards. Verify that software technology is in place to adequately provide oversight and monitoring in all required areas. Serve as a confidential point of contact for employees to communicate with management, seek clarification on issues or dilemmas, or report irregularities.

Maintain documentation of compliance activities such as complaints received and investigation outcomes. Consult with corporate attorneys as necessary to address difficult legal-compliance issues. Discuss emerging compliance issues with management or employees. Collaborate with human resources departments to ensure the implementation of consistent disciplinary action strategies in cases of compliance standard violations. Advise internal management or business partners on the implementation and operation of compliance programs. Review communications such as securities sales advertising to ensure there are no violations of standards or regulations. Provide employee training on compliance-related topics, policies, or procedures. Report violations of compliance or regulatory standards to duly authorized enforcement agencies as appropriate or required. Provide assistance to internal and external auditors in compliance reviews. Prepare management reports regarding compliance operations and progress. Oversee internal reporting systems such as corporate compliance hotlines, and inform employees about these systems. Monitor compliance systems to ensure their effectiveness.

Related Knowledge/Courses: No data available.

Personality Types:
Conventional-Enterprising-Realistic.

Skills: No data available.

Work Environment: No data available.

Job Specialization: Investment Fund Managers

Plan, direct, or coordinate investment strategy or operations for a large pool of liquid assets supplied by institutional investors or individual investors. Prepare for and respond to regulatory inquiries. Verify regulatory compliance of transaction reporting. Hire and evaluate staff. Direct activities of accounting or operations departments. Develop, implement, or monitor security valuation policies. Attend investment briefings or consult financial media to stay abreast of relevant investment markets. Review offering documents or marketing materials to ensure regulatory compliance. Perform or evaluate research, such as detailed company and industry analyses, to inform financial forecasting, decision making, or valuation. Present investment information, such as product risks, fees, and fund performance statistics. Monitor financial or operational performance of individual investments to ensure that portfolios meet risk goals. Monitor regulatory or tax law changes to ensure fund compliance or to capitalize on development opportunities. Meet with investors to determine investment goals or to discuss investment strategies. Identify group and individual target investors for a specific fund. Develop, or direct development of, offering documents or marketing materials. Evaluate the potential of new product developments or market opportunities according to factors such as business plans, technologies, and market potential. Develop and implement fund investment policies and strategies. Select and direct the execution of trades. Analyze acquisitions to ensure conformance with strategic goals or regulatory requirements.

Related Knowledge/Courses: No data available.

Personality Types: Enterprising-Conventional.

Skills: No data available.

Work Environment: No data available.

Job Specialization: Loss Prevention Managers

Plan and direct policies, procedures, or systems to prevent the loss of assets. Determine risk exposure or potential liability, and develop risk control measures. Review loss-prevention exception reports and cash discrepancies to ensure adherence to guidelines. Perform cash audits and deposit investigations to fully account for store cash. Provide recommendations and solutions in crisis situations such as workplace violence, protests, and demonstrations. Monitor and review paperwork procedures and systems to prevent error-related shortages. Maintain databases such as bad check logs, reports on multiple offenders, and alarm activation lists. Investigate or interview individuals suspected of shoplifting or internal theft. Direct installation of covert surveillance equipment, such as security cameras. Advise retail establishments on development of loss-investigation procedures. Visit stores to ensure compliance with company policies and procedures. Verify correct use and maintenance of physical security systems, such as closed-circuit television, merchandise tags, and burglar alarms. Train loss-prevention staff, retail managers, or store employees on loss control and prevention measures. Supervise surveillance, detection, or criminal processing related to theft and criminal cases. Recommend improvements in loss-prevention programs, staffing, scheduling, or training. Perform or direct inventory investigations in response to shrink results outside of acceptable ranges. Hire or supervise loss-prevention staff. Maintain documentation of all loss-prevention activity.

Related Knowledge/Courses: No data available.

Personality Types: Enterprising-Conventional.

Skills: No data available.

Work Environment: No data available.

Job Specialization: Regulatory Affairs Managers

Plan, direct, or coordinate production activities of an organization to ensure compliance with regulations and standard operating procedures. Direct the preparation and submission of regulatory agency applications, reports, or correspondence. Review all regulatory agency submission materials to ensure timeliness, accuracy, comprehensiveness, and compliance with regulatory standards. Provide regulatory guidance to departments or development project teams regarding design, development, evaluation, or marketing of products. Formulate or implement regulatory affairs policies and procedures to ensure that regulatory compliance is maintained or enhanced. Manage activities such as audits, regulatory agency inspections, and product recalls. Communicate regulatory information to multiple departments, and ensure that information is interpreted correctly. Develop regulatory strategies and implementation plans for the preparation and submission of new products. Provide responses to regulatory agencies regarding product information or issues. Maintain current knowledge of relevant regulations including proposed and final rules. Investigate product complaints, and prepare documentation and submissions to appropriate regulatory agencies as necessary. Review materials such as marketing literature and user manuals to ensure that regulatory agency requirements are met. Implement or monitor complaint processing systems to ensure effective and timely resolution of all complaint investigations. Represent organizations before domestic or international regulatory agencies on major policy matters or decisions regarding company products.

Related Knowledge/Courses: Biology; Medicine and Dentistry; Law and Government; Chemistry; Clerical Practices; Personnel and Human Resources.

Personality Types: Enterprising-Conventional.

Skills: Operations Analysis; Management of Personnel Resources; Systems Evaluation; Systems Analysis; Negotiation; Coordination; Science; Writing.

Work Environment: Indoors; sitting.

Job Specialization: Security Managers

Direct an organization's security functions, including physical security and safety of employees, facilities, and assets. Write or review security-related documents, such as incident reports, proposals, and tactical or strategic initiatives. Train subordinate security professionals or other organization members in security rules and procedures. Plan security for special and high-risk events. Review financial reports to ensure efficiency and quality of security operations. Develop budgets for security operations. Order security-related supplies and equipment as needed. Coordinate security operations or activities with public law enforcement, fire, and other agencies. Attend meetings, professional seminars, or conferences to keep abreast of changes in executive legislative directives or new technologies impacting security operations. Assist in emergency management and contingency planning. Arrange for or perform executive protection activities. Respond to medical emergencies, bomb threats, fire alarms, or intrusion alarms, following emergency response procedures. Recommend security procedures for security call centers, operations centers, domains, asset classification systems, system acquisition, system development, system maintenance, access control, program models, or reporting tools. Prepare reports or make presentations on internal investigations, losses, or violations of regulations, policies, and procedures. Identify, investigate, or resolve security breaches.

Related Knowledge/Courses: No data available.

Personality Types: No data available.

Skills: No data available.

Work Environment: No data available.

Job Specialization: Supply Chain Managers

Direct, or coordinate production, purchasing, warehousing, distribution, or financial forecasting services and activities to limit costs and improve accuracy, customer service and safety. Examine existing procedures and opportunities for streamlining activities to meet product distribution needs. Direct the movement, storage, and processing of inventory. Select transportation routes to maximize economy by combining shipments and consolidating warehousing and distribution. Diagram supply chain models to help facilitate discussions with customers. Develop material costs forecasts or standard cost lists. Assess appropriate material handling equipment needs and staffing levels to load, unload, move, or store materials. Appraise vendor manufacturing ability through on-site visits and measurements. Negotiate prices and terms with suppliers, vendors, or freight forwarders. Monitor supplier performance to assess ability to meet quality and delivery requirements. Monitor forecasts and quotas to identify changes or to determine their effect on supply chain activities. Meet with suppliers to discuss performance metrics, to provide performance feedback, or to discuss production forecasts or changes. Implement new or improved supply chain processes. Collaborate with other departments, such as procurement, engineering, and quality assurance, to identify or qualify new suppliers. Document physical supply chain processes, such as workflows, cycle times, position responsibilities, and system flows. Develop and implement procedures or systems to evaluate and select suppliers. Design and implement plant warehousing strategies for production materials or finished products. Confer with supply chain planners to forecast demand or create supply plans that ensure availability of materials and products.

Related Knowledge/Courses: Production and Processing; Transportation; Economics and Accounting; Administration and Management; Geography; Sales and Marketing.

Personality Types: Enterprising-Conventional.

Skills: Management of Material Resources; Management of Financial Resources; Systems Evaluation; Negotiation; Monitoring; Management of Personnel Resources; Systems Analysis; Complex Problem Solving.

Work Environment: Indoors; sitting.

Job Specialization: Wind Energy Operations Managers

Manage wind field operations, including personnel, maintenance activities, financial activities, and planning. Train, or coordinate the training of, employees in operations, safety, environmental issues, or technical issues. Track and maintain records for wind operations, such as site performance, downtime events, parts usage, and substation events. Provide technical support to wind field customers, employees, or subcontractors. Manage warranty repair or replacement services. Order parts, tools, or equipment needed to maintain, restore, or improve wind field operations. Maintain operations records, such as work orders, site inspection forms, or other documentation. Negotiate or review and approve wind farm contracts. Recruit or select wind operations employees, contractors, or subcontractors. Monitor and maintain records of daily facility operations. Estimate costs associated with operations, including repairs and preventive maintenance. Establish goals, objectives, or priorities for wind field operations. Develop relationships and communicate with customers, site managers, developers, land owners, authorities, utility representatives, or residents. Develop processes and procedures for wind operations, including

M

transitioning from construction to commercial operations. Prepare wind field operational budgets. Supervise employees or subcontractors to ensure quality of work or adherence to safety regulations or policies. Oversee the maintenance of wind field equipment or structures, such as towers, transformers, electrical collector systems, roadways, and other site assets.

Related Knowledge/Courses: No data available.

Personality Types: No data available.

Skills: No data available.

Work Environment: No data available.

Job Specialization: Wind Energy Project Managers

Lead or manage the development and evaluation of potential wind energy business opportunities, including environmental studies, permitting, and proposals. May also manage construction of projects. Supervise the work of subcontractors or consultants to ensure quality and conformance to specifications or budgets. Prepare requests for proposals (RFPs) for wind project construction or equipment acquisition. Manage site assessments or environmental studies for wind fields. Lead or support negotiations involving tax agreements or abatements, power purchase agreements, land use, or interconnection agreements. Update schedules, estimates, forecasts, or budgets for wind projects. Review or evaluate proposals or bids to make recommendations regarding awarding of contracts. Provide verbal or written project status reports to project teams, management, subcontractors, customers, or owners. Review civil design, engineering, or construction technical documentation to ensure compliance with applicable government or industrial codes, standards, requirements, or regulations. Provide technical support for the design, construction, or commissioning of wind

farm projects. Prepare wind project documentation, including diagrams or layouts. Manage wind project costs to stay within budget limits. Develop scope of work for wind project functions, such as design, site assessment, environmental studies, surveying, and field support services. Coordinate or direct development, energy assessment, engineering, or construction activities to ensure that wind project needs and objectives are met.

Related Knowledge/Courses: No data available.

Personality Types: No data available.

Skills: No data available.

Work Environment: No data available.

Mechanical Drafters

- ❋ Average Annual Earnings (All): $49,200
- ❋ Average Annual Earnings (Recent Veterans): $34,920
- ❋ Earnings Growth Potential: Low (34.4%)
- ❋ Growth: 11.1%
- ❋ Annual Job Openings: 2,050
- ❋ Veteran Employment by Sector: For-Profit, 80.4%; Nonprofit, 5.0%; Government, 5.4%; Self-Employed, 9.2%.

Considerations for Job Outlook: New software, such as PDM and BIM, will require drafters to work in collaboration with other professionals on projects, whether constructing a new building or manufacturing a new product. This new software, however, requires that someone build and maintain large databases. Workers with knowledge of drafting and of the software will be needed to oversee these databases. Many drafting jobs are in construction and manufacturing, so they are subject to the ups and downs of those industries.

Demand for particular drafting specialties varies across the country because jobs depend on the needs of local industries.

Prepare detailed working diagrams of machinery and mechanical devices, including dimensions, fastening methods, and other engineering information. Develop detailed design drawings and specifications for mechanical equipment, dies, tools, and controls, using computer-assisted drafting (CAD) equipment. Lay out and draw schematic, orthographic, or angle views to depict functional relationships of components, assemblies, systems, and machines. Coordinate with and consult other workers to design, lay out, or detail components and systems and to resolve design or other problems. Check dimensions of materials to be used and assign numbers to the materials. Review and analyze specifications, sketches, drawings, ideas, and related data to assess factors affecting component designs and the procedures and instructions to be followed. Modify and revise designs to correct operating deficiencies or to reduce production problems. Compute mathematical formulas to develop and design detailed specifications for components or machinery using computer-assisted equipment. Position instructions and comments onto drawings. Lay out, draw, and reproduce illustrations for reference manuals and technical publications to describe operation and maintenance of mechanical systems. Design scale or full-size blueprints of specialty items such as furniture and automobile body or chassis components. Confer with customer representatives to review schematics and answer questions pertaining to installation of systems. Supervise and train other drafters, technologists, and technicians. Draw freehand sketches of designs, trace finished drawings onto designated paper for the reproduction of blueprints, and reproduce working drawings on copy machines. Shade or color drawings to clarify and emphasize details and dimensions or eliminate background using ink, crayon, airbrush, and overlays.

Related Military Specializations: None. **Average Educational Level of Vets:** Associate degree. **Usual Educational Requirement:** Associate degree. **Relevant Educational Programs:** CAD/CADD Drafting and/or Design Technology/Technician; Drafting and Design Technology/Technician, General; Mechanical Drafting and Mechanical Drafting CAD/CADD. **Related Knowledge/Courses:** Design; Engineering and Technology; Mechanical Devices; Physics; Mathematics; Production and Processing. **Work Experience Needed:** None. **On-the-Job Training Needed:** None. **Certification/Licensure:** Voluntary certification by association.

Personality Types: Realistic-Conventional-Investigative. **Key Career Cluster:** 02 Architecture and Construction. **Key Career Pathway:** 2.1 Design/Pre-construction. **Top Industries for Vets:** Architectural, Engineering, and Related Services; Computer Systems Design and Related Services; Construction; Motor Vehicles and Motor Vehicle Equipment; Not Specified Industries.

Skills: Programming; Technology Design; Mathematics; Operations Analysis; Quality Control Analysis; Active Learning; Systems Evaluation; Systems Analysis.

Work Environment: Indoors; sitting; using hands; repetitive motions.

Medical and Clinical Laboratory Technicians

- ❊ Average Annual Earnings (All): $36,950

- ❊ Average Annual Earnings (Recent Veterans): $34,920

- ❊ Earnings Growth Potential: Low (33.5%)

- ❊ Growth: 14.7%

- ❊ Annual Job Openings: 5,510

- ❊ Veteran Employment by Sector: For-Profit, 29.1%; Nonprofit, 12.3%; Government, 58.2%; Self-Employed, 0.4%.

Considerations for Job Outlook: An increase in the aging population will lead to a greater need to diagnose medical conditions, such as cancer or type 2 diabetes, through laboratory procedures. Medical laboratory technologists and technicians will be needed to use and maintain the equipment needed for diagnosis and treatment.

Perform routine medical laboratory tests for the diagnosis, treatment, and prevention of disease. May work under the supervision of a medical technologist. Conduct chemical analyses of bodily fluids, such as blood and urine, using microscope or automatic analyzer to detect abnormalities or diseases, and enter findings into computer. Set up, adjust, maintain, and clean medical laboratory equipment. Analyze the results of tests and experiments to ensure conformity to specifications, using special mechanical and electrical devices. Analyze and record test data to issue reports that use charts, graphs, and narratives. Conduct blood tests for transfusion purposes, and perform blood counts. Perform medical research to further control and cure disease. Obtain specimens, cultivating, isolating, and identifying microorganisms for analysis. Examine cells stained with dye to locate abnormalities. Collect blood or tissue samples from patients, observing principles of asepsis to obtain blood sample. Consult with a pathologist to determine a final diagnosis when abnormal cells are found. Inoculate fertilized eggs, broths, or other bacteriological media with organisms. Cut, stain, and mount tissue samples for examination by pathologists. Supervise and instruct other technicians and laboratory assistants. Prepare standard volumetric solutions and reagents to be combined with samples, following standardized formulas or experimental procedures. Prepare vaccines and serums by standard laboratory methods, testing for virus inactivity and sterility.

Related Military Specializations: Cytotechnologist; Cytotechnology Apprentice; Cytotechnology Craftsman; Cytotechnology Helper; Cytotechnology Journeyman; Histopathology Apprentice; Histopathology Craftsman; Histopathology Helper; Histopathology Journeyman; Histopathology Technician; Medical Laboratory Apprentice; Medical Laboratory Craftsman; Medical Laboratory Helper; Medical Laboratory Journeyman; Medical Laboratory Manager; Medical Laboratory Specialist; Medical Laboratory Superintendent; others. **Average Educational Level of Vets:** One or more years of college, no degree. **Usual Educational Requirement:** Associate degree. **Relevant Educational Programs:** Blood Bank Technology Specialist Training; Clinical/Medical Laboratory Assistant Training; Clinical/Medical Laboratory Science and Allied Professions, Other; Clinical/Medical Laboratory Technician; Hematology Technology/Technician; Histologic Technician Training. **Related Knowledge/Courses:** Chemistry; Medicine and Dentistry; Biology; Mechanical Devices; Computers and Electronics; Production and Processing. **Work Experience Needed:** None. **On-the-Job Training Needed:**

None. **Certification/Licensure:** Voluntary certification by association.

Personality Types: Realistic-Investigative-Conventional. **Key Career Cluster:** 08 Health Science. **Key Career Pathway:** 8.2 Diagnostics Services. **Top Industries for Vets:** Hospitals; National Security and International Affairs; Other Health Care Services; Offices of Physicians; Scientific Research and Development Services.

Skills: Science; Equipment Maintenance; Equipment Selection; Troubleshooting; Repairing; Operation and Control; Quality Control Analysis; Operation Monitoring.

Work Environment: Indoors; standing; walking and running; using hands; repetitive motions; noise; contaminants; exposed to disease or infections; hazardous conditions.

Medical and Clinical Laboratory Technologists

- ❋ Average Annual Earnings (All): $57,010
- ❋ Average Annual Earnings (Recent Veterans): $34,920
- ❋ Earnings Growth Potential: Low (30.6%)
- ❋ Growth: 11.3%
- ❋ Annual Job Openings: 5,210
- ❋ Veteran Employment by Sector: For-Profit, 29.1%; Nonprofit, 12.3%; Government, 58.2%; Self-Employed, 0.4%.

Considerations for Job Outlook: An increase in the aging population will lead to a greater need to diagnose medical conditions, such as cancer or type 2 diabetes, through laboratory procedures. Medical laboratory technologists and technicians

will be needed to use and maintain the equipment needed for diagnosis and treatment.

Perform complex medical laboratory tests for diagnosis, treatment, and prevention of disease. May train or supervise staff. Analyze laboratory findings to check the accuracy of the results. Conduct chemical analysis of body fluids, including blood, urine, and spinal fluid, to determine presence of normal and abnormal components. Operate, calibrate and maintain equipment used in quantitative and qualitative analysis, such as spectrophotometers, calorimeters, flame photometers, and computer-controlled analyzers. Enter data from analysis of medical tests and clinical results into computer for storage. Analyze samples of biological material for chemical content or reaction. Establish and monitor programs to ensure the accuracy of laboratory results. Set up, clean, and maintain laboratory equipment. Provide technical information about test results to physicians, family members and researchers. Supervise, train, and direct lab assistants, medical and clinical laboratory technicians and technologists, and other medical laboratory workers engaged in laboratory testing. Develop, standardize, evaluate, and modify procedures, techniques and tests used in the analysis of specimens and in medical laboratory experiments. Cultivate, isolate, and assist in identifying microbial organisms, and perform various tests on these microorganisms. Study blood samples to determine the number of cells and their morphology, as well as the blood group, type, and compatibility for transfusion purposes, using microscopic technique. Obtain, cut, stain, and mount biological material on slides for microscopic study and diagnosis, following standard laboratory procedures. Select and prepare specimen and media for cell culture, using aseptic technique and knowledge of medium components and cell requirements. Conduct medical research under direction of microbiologist or biochemist. Harvest cell cultures at optimum time based on knowledge of cell cycle differences and culture conditions.

Related Military Specializations: Cytotechnologist; Cytotechnology Apprentice; Cytotechnology Craftsman; Cytotechnology Helper; Cytotechnology Journeyman; Histopathology Apprentice; Histopathology Craftsman; Histopathology Helper; Histopathology Journeyman; Histopathology Technician; Medical Laboratory Apprentice; Medical Laboratory Craftsman; Medical Laboratory Helper; Medical Laboratory Journeyman; Medical Laboratory Manager; Medical Laboratory Specialist; Medical Laboratory Superintendent; others. **Average Educational Level of Vets:** One or more years of college, no degree. **Usual Educational Requirement:** Bachelor's degree. **Relevant Educational Programs:** Clinical Laboratory Science/Medical Technology/Technologist Training; Clinical/Medical Laboratory Science and Allied Professions, Other; Cytogenetics/Genetics/Clinical Genetics Technology/Technologist; Cytotechnology/Cytotechnologist; Histologic Technology/Histotechnologist Training. **Related Knowledge/Courses:** Biology; Chemistry; Medicine and Dentistry; Mechanical Devices; Clerical Practices; Mathematics. **Work Experience Needed:** None. **On-the-Job Training Needed:** None. **Certification/Licensure:** Licensure.

Personality Types: Investigative-Realistic-Conventional. **Key Career Cluster:** 08 Health Science. **Key Career Pathway:** 8.2 Diagnostics Services. **Top Industries for Vets:** Hospitals; National Security and International Affairs; Other Health Care Services; Offices of Physicians; Scientific Research and Development Services.

Skills: Science; Equipment Selection; Equipment Maintenance; Quality Control Analysis; Programming; Troubleshooting; Operation Monitoring; Operation and Control.

Work Environment: Indoors; standing; using hands; repetitive motions; noise; contaminants; exposed to disease or infections; hazardous conditions.

Job Specialization: Cytogenetic Technologists

Analyze chromosomes found in biological specimens such as amniotic fluids, bone marrow, and blood to aid in the study, diagnosis, or treatment of genetic diseases. Develop and implement training programs for trainees, medical students, resident physicians, or post-doctoral fellows. Stain slides to make chromosomes visible for microscopy. Summarize test results and report to appropriate authorities. Select or prepare specimens and media for cell cultures using aseptic techniques, knowledge of medium components, or cell nutritional requirements. Select banding methods to permit identification of chromosome pairs. Identify appropriate methods of specimen collection, preservation, or transport. Prepare slides of cell cultures following standard procedures. Select appropriate methods of preparation and storage of media to maintain potential of hydrogen (pH), sterility, or ability to support growth. Harvest cell cultures using substances such as mitotic arrestants, cell releasing agents, and cell fixatives. Create chromosome images using computer imaging systems. Determine optimal time sequences and methods for manual or robotic cell harvests. Examine chromosomes found in biological specimens to detect abnormalities. Recognize and report abnormalities in the color, size, shape, composition, or pattern of cells. Communicate test results or technical information to patients, physicians, family members, or researchers. Prepare biological specimens such as amniotic fluids, bone marrow, tumors, chorionic villi, and blood for chromosome examinations.

Related Knowledge/Courses: Biology; Chemistry; Medicine and Dentistry; Education and Training.

Personality Types:
Investigative-Realistic-Conventional.

Skills: Science; Reading Comprehension; Writing; Active Learning; Speaking; Mathematics; Instructing; Active Listening.

Work Environment: Indoors; sitting; using hands; repetitive motions; contaminants; exposed to disease or infections; hazardous conditions.

Job Specialization: Cytotechnologists

Stain, mount, and study cells to detect evidence of cancer, hormonal abnormalities, and other pathological conditions following established standards and practices. Examine cell samples to detect abnormalities in the color, shape, or size of cellular components and patterns. Examine specimens using microscopes to evaluate specimen quality. Prepare and analyze samples, such as Papanicolaou (PAP) smear body fluids and fine needle aspirations (FNAs), to detect abnormal conditions. Provide patient clinical data or microscopic findings to assist pathologists in the preparation of pathology reports. Assist pathologists or other physicians to collect cell samples such as by FNA biopsies. Examine specimens to detect abnormal hormone conditions. Document specimens by verifying patients' and specimens' information. Maintain effective laboratory operations by adhering to standards of specimen collection, preparation, or laboratory safety. Perform karyotyping or organizing of chromosomes according to standardized ideograms. Prepare cell samples by applying special staining techniques, such as chromosomal staining, to differentiate cells or cell components.

Submit slides with abnormal cell structures to pathologists for further examination. Adjust, maintain, or repair laboratory equipment such as microscopes. Assign tasks or coordinate task assignments to ensure adequate performance of laboratory activities. Attend continuing education programs that address laboratory issues.

Related Knowledge/Courses: Biology; Medicine and Dentistry; Chemistry; Clerical Practices.

Personality Types: Investigative-Realistic.

Skills: Science; Reading Comprehension; Mathematics; Writing; Operation Monitoring; Judgment and Decision Making; Learning Strategies; Instructing.

Work Environment: Indoors; sitting; using hands; repetitive motions; contaminants; exposed to disease or infections; hazardous conditions.

Job Specialization: Histotechnologists and Histologic Technicians

Prepare histologic slides from tissue sections for microscopic examination and diagnosis by pathologists. May assist in research studies. Cut sections of body tissues for microscopic examination using microtomes. Embed tissue specimens into paraffin wax blocks, or infiltrate tissue specimens with wax. Freeze tissue specimens. Mount tissue specimens on glass slides. Stain tissue specimens with dyes or other chemicals to make cell details visible under microscopes. Examine slides under microscopes to ensure tissue preparation meets laboratory requirements. Identify tissue structures or cell components to be used in the diagnosis, prevention, or treatment of diseases. Operate computerized laboratory equipment to dehydrate, decalcify, or microincinerate tissue samples. Perform electron microscopy or mass spectrometry to analyze specimens. Perform procedures associated with histochemistry to prepare specimens

M

for immunofluorescence or microscopy. Maintain laboratory equipment such as microscopes, mass spectrometers, microtomes, immunostainers, tissue processors, embedding centers, and water baths. Prepare or use prepared tissue specimens for teaching, research, or diagnostic purposes. Supervise histology laboratory activities. Teach students or other staff.

Related Knowledge/Courses: Biology; Chemistry; Medicine and Dentistry; Production and Processing; Mechanical Devices; Education and Training.

Personality Types:
Realistic-Investigative-Conventional.

Skills: Science; Equipment Maintenance; Equipment Selection; Repairing; Operation and Control; Troubleshooting; Mathematics; Quality Control Analysis.

Work Environment: Indoors; sitting; using hands; repetitive motions; contaminants; exposed to disease or infections; hazardous conditions.

Medical Assistants

- ❋ Average Annual Earnings (All): $29,100
- ❋ Average Annual Earnings (Recent Veterans): $26,190
- ❋ Earnings Growth Potential: Low (28.2%)
- ❋ Growth: 30.9%
- ❋ Annual Job Openings: 24,380
- ❋ Veteran Employment by Sector: For-Profit, 59.8%; Nonprofit, 13.1%; Government, 26.7%; Self-Employed, 0.3%.

Considerations for Job Outlook: The growth of the aging baby-boom population will continue to spur demand for preventive medical services, which are often provided by physicians. As their practices expand, physicians will hire more assistants to perform routine administrative and clinical duties, allowing the physicians to see more patients. Assistants will likely continue to be used in place of more expensive workers, such as nurses, to reduce costs. In addition, an increasing number of group practices, clinics, and other health-care facilities need support workers, particularly medical assistants, to do both administrative and clinical duties.

Perform administrative and certain clinical duties under the direction of a physician. Record patients' medical history, vital statistics, and information such as test results in medical records. Prepare treatment rooms for patient examinations, keeping the rooms neat and clean. Interview patients to obtain medical information, and measure their vital signs, weights, and heights. Authorize drug refills, and provide prescription information to pharmacies. Clean and sterilize instruments, and dispose of contaminated supplies. Prepare and administer medications as directed by a physician. Show patients to examination rooms, and prepare them for the physician. Explain treatment procedures, medications, diets, and physicians' instructions to patients. Help physicians examine and treat patients, handing them instruments and materials or performing such tasks as giving injections or removing sutures. Collect blood, tissue, or other laboratory specimens, log the specimens, and prepare them for testing. Perform routine laboratory tests and sample analyses. Contact medical facilities or departments to schedule patients for tests or admission. Operate X-ray, electrocardiogram (EKG), and other equipment to administer routine diagnostic tests. Change dressings on wounds. Set up medical laboratory equipment. Perform general office duties such as answering telephones, taking dictation, or completing insurance forms. Greet and log in patients arriving at office or clinic. Schedule appointments for patients. Inventory and order medical, lab, or office supplies and equipment.

Related Military Specializations: Aeromedical Craftsman; Aeromedical Manager; Aeromedical Superintendent; Aerospace Medical Technician; Aerospace Physiology Technician; Dermatology Technician; Health Services Technician; Hemodialysis Technician; Hospital Corpsman; Hospitalman; Ocular Technician; Optometry Apprentice, Ophthalmology; Optometry Craftsman, Ophthalmology; Optometry Helper, Ophthalmology; Optometry Journeyman, Ophthalmology; Otolaryngology Technician; Urology Technician. **Average Educational Level of Vets:** One or more years of college, no degree. **Usual Educational Requirement:** High school diploma or equivalent. **Relevant Educational Programs:** Anesthesiologist Assistant Training; Chiropractic Assistant/Technician Training; Medical Administrative/Executive Assistant and Medical Secretary Training; Medical Insurance Coding Specialist/Coder Training; Medical Office Assistant/Specialist Training; Medical Reception/Receptionist; Medical/Clinical Assistant Training. **Related Knowledge/Courses:** Medicine and Dentistry; Clerical Practices; Psychology; Therapy and Counseling; Customer and Personal Service; Public Safety and Security. **Work Experience Needed:** None. **On-the-Job Training Needed:** Moderate-term on-the-job training. **Certification/Licensure:** Voluntary certification by association.

Personality Types: Social-Conventional-Realistic. **Key Career Cluster:** 08 Health Science. **Key Career Pathway:** 8.1 Therapeutic Services. **Top Industries for Vets:** Hospitals; Offices of Physicians; National Security and International Affairs; Other Health Care Services; Outpatient Care Centers.

Skills: Service Orientation; Active Listening; Science; Speaking; Social Perceptiveness; Negotiation; Operation Monitoring; Monitoring.

Work Environment: Indoors; standing; walking and running; using hands; repetitive motions; exposed to disease or infections.

Medical Equipment Repairers

- ✳ Average Annual Earnings (All): $44,870
- ✳ Average Annual Earnings (Recent Veterans): $44,750
- ✳ Earnings Growth Potential: High (41.5%)
- ✳ Growth: 31.5%
- ✳ Annual Job Openings: 2,230
- ✳ Veteran Employment by Sector: For-Profit, 65.9%; Nonprofit, 7.0%; Government, 27.1%; Self-Employed, 0.0%.

Considerations for Job Outlook: A combination of rapid employment growth and the need to replace workers leaving the occupation will likely result in excellent job opportunities from 2010 to 2020. Candidates who have an associate degree in biomedical equipment technology or engineering should have the best job prospects. Job opportunities should be even better for those who are willing to relocate, because often there are relatively few qualified applicants in rural areas.

Test, adjust, or repair biomedical or electromedical equipment. Inspect and test malfunctioning medical and related equipment following manufacturers' specifications, using test and analysis instruments. Examine medical equipment and facility's structural environment, and check for proper use of equipment to protect patients and staff from electrical or mechanical hazards and to ensure compliance with safety regulations.

M

Disassemble malfunctioning equipment, and remove, repair, and replace defective parts such as motors, clutches, or transformers. Keep records of maintenance, repair, and required updates of equipment. Perform preventive maintenance or service such as cleaning, lubricating, and adjusting equipment. Test and calibrate components and equipment, following manufacturers' manuals and troubleshooting techniques and using hand tools, power tools, and measuring devices. Explain and demonstrate correct operation and preventive maintenance of medical equipment to personnel. Study technical manuals and attend training sessions provided by equipment manufacturers to maintain current knowledge. Plan and carry out work assignments, using blueprints, schematic drawings, technical manuals, wiring diagrams, and liquid and air flow sheets, following prescribed regulations, directives, and other instructions as required. Solder loose connections, using soldering iron. Test, evaluate, and classify excess or in-use medical equipment, and determine serviceability, condition, and disposition in accordance with regulations.

Related Military Specializations: Advanced Biomedical Equipment Technician; Basic Biomedical Equipment System Technician; Biomedical Equipment Apprentice; Biomedical Equipment Craftsman; Biomedical Equipment Helper; Biomedical Equipment Journeyman; Biomedical Equipment Specialist; Biomedical Equipment Superintendent; Bio-Medical Equipment Technician; Dental Equipment Repair Technician; Hemodialysis Technician; Medical Equipment Repairer. **Average Educational Level of Vets:** One or more years of college, no degree. **Usual Educational Requirement:** Associate degree. **Relevant Educational Program:** Biomedical Technology/Technician. **Related Knowledge/Courses:** Mechanical Devices; Engineering and Technology; Physics; Telecommunications; Computers and Electronics;

Chemistry. **Work Experience Needed:** None. **On-the-Job Training Needed:** Moderate-term on-the-job training. **Certification/Licensure:** Voluntary certification by association.

Personality Types: Realistic-Investigative-Conventional. **Key Career Cluster:** 13 Manufacturing. **Key Career Pathway:** 13.3 Maintenance, Installation and Repair. **Top Industries for Vets:** Hospitals; National Security and International Affairs; Construction; Electronic and Precision Equipment Repair and Maintenance; Navigational, Measuring, Electromedical, and Control Instruments.

Skills: Equipment Maintenance; Repairing; Troubleshooting; Equipment Selection; Quality Control Analysis; Operation and Control; Installation; Operation Monitoring.

Work Environment: Indoors; standing; using hands; noise; bright or inadequate lighting; contaminants; cramped work space; exposed to disease or infections; hazardous conditions; hazardous equipment; minor burns, cuts, bites, or stings.

Medical Secretaries

- ❋ Average Annual Earnings (All): $31,060
- ❋ Average Annual Earnings (Recent Veterans): $32,410
- ❋ Earnings Growth Potential: Low (31.1%)
- ❋ Growth: 41.3%
- ❋ Annual Job Openings: 27,840
- ❋ Veteran Employment by Sector: For-Profit, 40.8%; Nonprofit, 9.3%; Government, 49.0%; Self-Employed, 0.9%.

Considerations for Job Outlook: In addition to jobs coming from employment growth, numerous job openings will arise from the need to replace secretaries and administrative assistants who transfer to other occupations or retire. Job opportunities should be best for applicants with extensive knowledge of computer software applications. Applicants with a bachelor's degree are expected to be in great demand and will act as managerial assistants who perform more complex tasks.

Perform secretarial duties using specific knowledge of medical terminology and hospital, clinic, or laboratory procedures. Answer telephones, and direct calls to appropriate staff. Schedule and confirm patient diagnostic appointments, surgeries, and medical consultations. Greet visitors, ascertain purpose of visit, and direct them to appropriate staff. Operate office equipment, such as voice mail messaging systems, and use word processing, spreadsheet, and other software applications to prepare reports, invoices, financial statements, letters, case histories, and medical records. Complete insurance and other claim forms. Interview patients to complete documents, case histories, and forms such as intake and insurance forms. Receive and route messages and documents such as laboratory results to appropriate staff. Compile and record medical charts, reports, and correspondence, using typewriter or personal computer. Transmit correspondence and medical records by mail, e-mail, or fax. Maintain medical records, technical library documents, and correspondence files. Perform various clerical and administrative functions, such as ordering and maintaining an inventory of supplies. Perform bookkeeping duties, such as credits and collections, preparing and sending financial statements and bills, and keeping financial records. Transcribe recorded messages and practitioners' diagnoses and recommendations into patients' medical records. Arrange hospital admissions for patients.

Related Military Specializations: None. **Average Educational Level of Vets:** One or more years of college, no degree. **Usual Educational Requirement:** High school diploma or equivalent. **Relevant Educational Programs:** Medical Administrative/Executive Assistant and Medical Secretary Training; Medical Insurance Specialist/Medical Biller Training; Medical Office Assistant/Specialist Training. **Related Knowledge/Courses:** Clerical Practices; Medicine and Dentistry; Customer and Personal Service; Computers and Electronics; Economics and Accounting. **Work Experience Needed:** None. **On-the-Job Training Needed:** Moderate-term on-the-job training. **Certification/Licensure:** Voluntary certification by association.

Personality Types: Conventional-Social. **Key Career Cluster:** 04 Business, Management, and Administration. **Key Career Pathway:** 4.6 Administrative and Information Support. **Top Industries for Vets:** National Security and International Affairs; Hospitals; Legal Services; Colleges and Universities, Including Junior Colleges; Justice, Public Order, and Safety Activities.

Skills: Service Orientation; Active Listening; Speaking.

Work Environment: Indoors; sitting; repetitive motions; exposed to disease or infections.

Meeting, Convention, and Event Planners

* Average Annual Earnings (All): $46,020

* Average Annual Earnings (Recent Veterans): $54,570

* Earnings Growth Potential: High (40.4%)

* Growth: 43.7%

* Annual Job Openings: 4,500

* Veteran Employment by Sector: For-Profit, 38.3%; Nonprofit, 3.9%; Government, 56.8%; Self-Employed, 1.0%.

Considerations for Job Outlook: In addition to rapid employment growth, many job openings are expected to arise from the need to replace workers who leave the occupation. However, job seekers can expect strong competition because the occupation usually attracts more applicants than job openings. Job opportunities should be best for people with a bachelor's degree in hospitality management. A Certified Meeting Planner (CMP) credential is also viewed favorably by potential employers. Those who have experience with virtual meeting software and social media outlets also should have an advantage in the job search. Event planners can expect strong competition for jobs. Those with related work experience should have the best job opportunities.

Coordinate activities of staff, convention personnel, or clients to make arrangements for group meetings, events, or conventions. Consult with customers to determine objectives and requirements for events such as meetings, conferences, and conventions. Monitor event activities to ensure compliance with applicable regulations and laws, satisfaction of participants, and resolution of any problems that arise. Confer with staff at a chosen event site to coordinate details. Review event bills for accuracy, and approve payment. Plan and develop programs, agendas, budgets, and services according to customer requirements. Coordinate services for events, such as accommodation and transportation for participants, facilities, catering, signage, displays, special needs requirements, printing and event security. Arrange the availability of audio-visual equipment, transportation, displays, and other event needs. Inspect event facilities to ensure that they conform to customer requirements. Maintain records of event aspects, including financial details. Conduct post-event evaluations to determine how future events could be improved. Negotiate contracts with such service providers and suppliers as hotels, convention centers, and speakers. Meet with sponsors and organizing committees to plan scope and format of events, to establish and monitor budgets, or to review administrative procedures and event progress. Direct administrative details such as financial operations, dissemination of promotional materials, and responses to inquiries. Evaluate and select providers of services according to customer requirements. Read trade publications, attend seminars, and consult with other meeting professionals to keep abreast of meeting management standards and trends. Organize registration of event participants. Design and implement efforts to publicize events and promote sponsorships. Hire, train, and supervise volunteers and support staff required for events. Obtain permits from fire and health departments to erect displays and exhibits and serve food at events.

Related Military Specializations: None. **Average Educational Level of Vets:** Bachelor's degree. **Usual Educational Requirement:** Bachelor's degree. **Relevant Educational Programs:** Facilities Planning and Management; Meeting and Event Planning. **Related Knowledge/Courses:** Sales and Marketing;

Clerical Practices; Customer and Personal Service; English Language; Economics and Accounting; Administration and Management. **Work Experience Needed:** Less than 1 year. **On-the-Job Training Needed:** None. **Certification/ Licensure:** Voluntary certification by association.

Personality Types: Enterprising-Conventional-Social. **Key Career Cluster:** 14 Marketing, Sales, and Service. **Key Career Pathway:** 14.2 Professional Sales and Marketing. **Top Industries for Vets:** National Security and International Affairs; Architectural, Engineering, and Related Services; Administration of Human Resource Programs; Construction; Management, Scientific and Technical Consulting Services.

Skills: Operations Analysis; Management of Financial Resources; Management of Material Resources; Negotiation; Systems Evaluation; Service Orientation; Time Management; Persuasion.

Work Environment: Indoors; sitting; noise.

Mobile Heavy Equipment Mechanics, Except Engines

* Average Annual Earnings (All): $45,600
* Average Annual Earnings (Recent Veterans): $40,380
* Earnings Growth Potential: Low (33.3%)
* Growth: 16.2%
* Annual Job Openings: 5,250
* Veteran Employment by Sector: For-Profit, 68.6%; Nonprofit, 1.8%; Government, 28.3%; Self-Employed, 1.3%.

Considerations for Job Outlook: Most job opportunities will come from the need to replace workers who retire or leave the occupation. Those with certificates from vocational schools or 2-year degrees from community colleges should have very good job opportunities as employers strongly prefer these candidates. Those without formal training will have difficulty finding jobs. The majority of job openings are expected to be in sectors that sell, rent, or lease heavy vehicles and mobile equipment, where a large proportion of service technicians are employed. The construction and mining industries, which use large numbers of heavy equipment, are sensitive to fluctuations in the economy. As a result, job opportunities for service technicians in these sectors will vary with overall economic conditions. Job opportunities for farm equipment mechanics are seasonal and are generally best during warmer months.

Diagnose, adjust, repair, or overhaul mobile mechanical, hydraulic, and pneumatic equipment. Test mechanical products and equipment after repair or assembly to ensure proper performance and compliance with manufacturers' specifications. Repair and replace damaged or worn parts. Diagnose faults or malfunctions to determine required repairs, using engine diagnostic equipment such as computerized test equipment and calibration devices. Operate and inspect machines or heavy equipment to diagnose defects. Dismantle and reassemble heavy equipment, using hoists and hand tools. Clean, lubricate, and perform other routine maintenance work on equipment and vehicles. Examine parts for damage or excessive wear, using micrometers and gauges. Read and understand operating manuals, blueprints, and technical drawings. Schedule maintenance for industrial machines and equipment, and keep equipment service records. Overhaul and test machines or equipment to ensure operating efficiency. Assemble gear systems, and align frames and gears. Fit bearings to adjust, repair, or overhaul mobile mechanical, hydraulic, and pneumatic equipment. Weld or solder broken parts and structural members, using electric or gas welders and soldering tools. Clean parts by spraying them with grease solvent or immersing them in tanks of solvent. Adjust, maintain, and repair or replace subassemblies, such as transmissions and crawler heads, using hand tools, jacks, and cranes. Adjust and maintain industrial machinery, using control and regulating devices. Fabricate needed parts or items from sheet metal.

Related Military Specializations: Afloat Support Equipment Technician; Airbrake Repairer (RC); Aircraft Maintenance Ground Support Equipment (GSE) Mechanic-Trainee; Aircraft Maintenance Support Equipment Hydraulic/Pneumatic/Structures Mechanic; Artillery Mechanic; BRADLEY Fighting Vehicle System Maintainer; BRADLEY Fighting Vehicle System Mechanic; Construction Equipment Repairer; Construction Mechanic; Construction Mechanic—Construction; Heavy Wheel Vehicle Mechanic; LCAC Deck Engineer; other. **Average Educational Level of Vets:** High school diploma or equivalent. **Usual Educational Requirement:** High school diploma or equivalent. **Relevant Educational Programs:** Agricultural Mechanics and Equipment/Machine Technology; Heavy Equipment Maintenance Technology/Technician. **Related Knowledge/Courses:** Mechanical Devices; Physics; Building and Construction; Engineering and Technology; Design; Transportation. **Work Experience Needed:** None. **On-the-Job Training Needed:** Long-term on-the-job training. **Certification/Licensure:** Voluntary certification by manufacturer.

Personality Types: Realistic-Conventional. **Key Career Cluster:** 16 Transportation, Distribution, and Logistics. **Key Career Pathway:** 16.4 Facility and Mobile Equipment Maintenance. **Top Industries for Vets:** Construction; National Security and International Affairs; Machinery,

Equipment, and Supplies Merchant Wholesalers; Rail Transportation; Machinery, Not Elsewhere Classified.

Skills: Repairing; Equipment Maintenance; Troubleshooting; Installation; Equipment Selection; Quality Control Analysis; Operation and Control; Operation Monitoring.

Work Environment: Outdoors; standing; walking and running; kneeling, crouching, stooping, or crawling; using hands; bending or twisting the body; repetitive motions; noise; very hot or cold; bright or inadequate lighting; contaminants; cramped work space; whole-body vibration; high places; hazardous conditions; hazardous equipment; minor burns, cuts, bites, or stings.

Music Directors and Composers

- ✽ Average Annual Earnings (All): $47,410
- ✽ Average Annual Earnings (Recent Veterans): $2,950
- ✽ Earnings Growth Potential: Very high (53.2%)
- ✽ Growth: 10.2%
- ✽ Annual Job Openings: 3,220
- ✽ Veteran Employment by Sector: For-Profit, 5.5%; Nonprofit, 5.7%; Government, 42.7%; Self-Employed, 46.1%.

Considerations for Job Outlook: Despite expected growth, strong competition for jobs is anticipated because of the large number of people who are interested in entering this field. In particular, there will be considerable competition for full-time positions. Those with exceptional musical talent and abilities should have the best opportunities. Many music directors and composers experience periods of unemployment or work in another occupation and attend auditions or write music outside of working hours.

Conduct, direct, plan, and lead instrumental or vocal performances by musical groups, such as orchestras, bands, choirs, and glee clubs. For task data, see Job Specializations.

Related Military Specializations: Army Bands; Arranger; Band; Band Master; Band Officer; Bandmaster; Bands Senior Sergeant; Ceremonial Conductor-Drum Major; Director/Assistant Director, "The President's Own" U.S. Marine Band; Drum Major; Enlisted Band Leader; Enlisted Conductor; Music Director; Musician Basic; Premier Band Manager; Premier Band Superintendent; Regional Band Apprentice, Music Arranger; Regional Band Craftsman, Music Arranger; Regional Band Helper; others. **Average Educational Level of Vets:** One or more years of college, no degree. **Usual Educational Requirement:** Bachelor's degree. **Relevant Educational Programs:** Conducting; Music Management; Music Performance, General; Music Technology; Music Theory and Composition; Music, Other; Musical Theatre; Musicology and Ethnomusicology; Religious/Sacred Music; Voice and Opera. **Work Experience Needed:** 1 to 5 years. **On-the-Job Training Needed:** None. **Certification/Licensure:** None.

Key Career Cluster: 03 Arts, Audiovisual Technology, and Communications. **Key Career Pathway:** 3.4 Performing Arts. **Top Industries for Vets:** Independent Artists, Performing Arts, Spectator Sports and Related Industries; National Security and International Affairs; Religious Organizations; Drinking Places, Alcoholic Beverages; Water Transportation.

Job Specialization: Music Composers and Arrangers

Write and transcribe musical scores. Copy parts from scores for individual performers. Transpose music from one voice or instrument to another to accommodate particular musicians. Use computers and synthesizers to compose, orchestrate, and arrange music. Write changes directly into compositions, or use computer software to make changes. Confer with producers and directors to define the nature and placement of film or television music. Guide musicians during rehearsals, performances, or recording sessions. Study original pieces of music to become familiar with them prior to making any changes. Study films or scripts to determine how musical scores can be used to create desired effects or moods. Write music for commercial mediums, including advertising jingles or film soundtracks. Accept commissions to create music for special occasions. Arrange music composed by others, changing the music to achieve desired effects. Write musical scores for orchestras, bands, choral groups, or individual instrumentalists or vocalists, using knowledge of music theory and of instrumental and vocal capabilities. Score compositions so that they are consistent with instrumental and vocal capabilities such as ranges and keys, using knowledge of music theory. Apply elements of music theory to create musical and tonal structures, including harmonies and melodies. Collaborate with other colleagues such as copyists to complete final scores.

Related Knowledge/Courses: Fine Arts; Communications and Media; Computers and Electronics; Sales and Marketing; Production and Processing; Design.

Personality Types: Artistic-Enterprising.

Skills: Operations Analysis; Writing; Coordination; Active Listening; Complex Problem Solving; Speaking.

Work Environment: Indoors; sitting; using hands; repetitive motions.

Job Specialization: Music Directors

Direct and conduct instrumental or vocal performances by musical groups such as orchestras or choirs. Study scores to learn the music in detail, and to develop interpretations. Consider such factors as ensemble size and abilities, availability of scores, and the need for musical variety in order to select music to be performed. Use gestures to shape the music being played, communicating desired tempo, phrasing, tone, color, pitch, volume, and other performance aspects. Engage services of composers to write scores. Plan and implement fundraising and promotional activities. Coordinate and organize tours, or hire touring companies to arrange concert dates, venues, accommodations, and transportation for longer tours. Confer with clergy to select music for church services. Transcribe musical compositions and melodic lines to adapt them to a particular group, or to create a particular musical style. Audition and select performers for musical presentations. Meet with composers to discuss interpretations of their works. Conduct guest soloists in addition to ensemble members. Collaborate with music librarians to ensure availability of scores. Assign and review staff work in such areas as scoring, arranging, copying music, and vocal coaching. Position members within groups to obtain balance among instrumental or vocal sections. Plan and schedule rehearsals and performances, and arrange details such as locations, accompanists, and instrumentalists. Meet with soloists and concertmasters to discuss and prepare for performances.

Related Knowledge/Courses: Fine Arts; Philosophy and Theology; Education and Training; History and Archeology; Communications and Media; Personnel and Human Resources.

Personality Types: Artistic-Enterprising-Social.

Skills: Instructing; Management of Personnel Resources; Systems Evaluation; Monitoring; Systems Analysis; Learning Strategies; Persuasion; Management of Financial Resources.

Work Environment: Sitting; standing.

Network and Computer Systems Administrators

* Average Annual Earnings (All): $70,970

* Average Annual Earnings (Recent Veterans): $64,390

* Earnings Growth Potential: Medium (38.8%)

* Growth: 27.8%

* Annual Job Openings: 15,530

* Veteran Employment by Sector: For-Profit, 59.2%; Nonprofit, 2.9%; Government, 37.5%; Self-Employed, 0.5%.

Considerations for Job Outlook: Job opportunities should be favorable for this occupation. Prospects should be best for applicants who have a bachelor's degree in computer science and who are up to date on the latest technology.

Install, configure, and support an organization's local area network (LAN), wide area network (WAN), and Internet systems or a segment of a network system. Perform data backups and disaster recovery operations. Maintain and administer computer networks and related computing environments including computer hardware, systems software, applications software, and all configurations. Plan, coordinate, and implement network security measures to protect data, software, and hardware. Operate master consoles to monitor the performance of computer systems and networks, and to coordinate computer network access and use. Perform routine network startup and shutdown procedures, and maintain control records. Design, configure, and test computer hardware, networking software and operating system software. Recommend changes to improve systems and network configurations, and determine hardware or software requirements related to such changes. Confer with network users about how to solve existing system problems. Monitor network performance to determine whether adjustments need to be made, and to determine where changes will need to be made in the future. Train people in computer system use. Load computer tapes and disks, and install software and printer paper or forms. Gather data pertaining to customer needs, and use the information to identify, predict, interpret, and evaluate system and network requirements. Analyze equipment performance records to determine the need for repair or replacement. Maintain logs related to network functions, as well as maintenance and repair records. Maintain an inventory of parts for emergency repairs. Coordinate with vendors and with company personnel to facilitate purchases. Diagnose, troubleshoot, and resolve hardware, software, or other network and system problems, and replace defective components when necessary. Configure, monitor, and maintain e-mail applications or virus protection software. Research new technologies by attending seminars, reading trade articles, or taking classes, and implement or recommend the implementation of new technologies.

Related Military Specializations: AN/UYK-65 System Supervisor (SNAP I); Aviation Logistics Tactical Information Systems (ALTIS) Specialist; Cryptologic Network Configuration Manager; Cyber Systems Operations Apprentice; Cyber Systems Operations Craftsman; Cyber

Systems Operations Helper; Cyber Systems Operations Journeyman; Data Chief; Data Network Technician; Defense Message System Administrator; GCCS-M System Administrator; Global Command and Control System-Maritime 4.X (GCCS-M 4.X) System Administrator; others. **Average Educational Level of Vets:** One or more years of college, no degree. **Usual Educational Requirement:** Bachelor's degree. **Relevant Educational Programs:** Computer and Information Sciences, General; Computer and Information Systems Security/Information Assurance; Network and System Administration/Administrator. **Related Knowledge/Courses:** Telecommunications; Computers and Electronics; Clerical Practices; Administration and Management; Engineering and Technology. **Work Experience Needed:** None. **On-the-Job Training Needed:** None. **Certification/Licensure:** Voluntary certification by vendor or association.

Personality Types: Investigative-Realistic-Conventional. **Key Career Cluster:** 11 Information Technology. **Key Career Pathway:** 11.1 Network Systems. **Top Industries for Vets:** Computer Systems Design and Related Services; National Security and International Affairs; Architectural, Engineering, and Related Services; Executive Offices and Legislative Bodies; Hospitals.

Skills: Programming; Equipment Maintenance; Troubleshooting; Equipment Selection; Technology Design; Repairing; Installation; Quality Control Analysis.

Work Environment: Indoors; sitting; using hands; repetitive motions; noise.

Nuclear Medicine Technologists

* Average Annual Earnings (All): $69,450

* Average Annual Earnings (Recent Veterans): $43,650

* Earnings Growth Potential: Low (28.5%)

* Growth: 18.9%

* Annual Job Openings: 750

* Veteran Employment by Sector: For-Profit, 48.2%; Nonprofit, 18.5%; Government, 32.5%; Self-Employed, 0.8%.

Considerations for Job Outlook: Nuclear medicine technologists can improve their job prospects by getting a specialty certification. A technologist can earn a certification in positron emission tomography (PET), nuclear cardiology (NCT), magnetic resonance imaging (MRI), or computed tomography (CT). The Nuclear Medicine Technology Certification Board (NMTCB) offers NCT and PET certification exams. The American Registry of Radiologic Technologists (ARRT) offers the CT and MRI certification exams.

Prepare, administer, and measure radioactive isotopes in therapeutic, diagnostic, and tracer studies using a variety of radioisotope equipment. Calculate, measure, and record radiation dosage or radiopharmaceuticals received, used, and disposed, using computer and following physician's prescription. Detect and map radiopharmaceuticals in patients' bodies, using a camera to produce photographic or computer images. Administer radiopharmaceuticals or radiation to patients to detect or treat diseases, using radioisotope equipment, under direction of physician. Explain test procedures and safety precautions to patients and provide them with assistance during test procedures. Produce a computer-generated or film image for interpretation by a physician. Process cardiac function studies, using computer. Dispose of radioactive materials and store radiopharmaceuticals, following radiation safety procedures. Record and process results of procedures. Prepare stock radiopharmaceuticals, adhering to safety standards that minimize radiation exposure to workers and patients. Maintain and calibrate radioisotope and laboratory equipment. Gather information on patients' illnesses and medical history to guide the choice of diagnostic procedures for therapy. Measure glandular activity, blood volume, red cell survival, and radioactivity of patient, using scanners, Geiger counters, scintillometers, and other laboratory equipment. Train and supervise student or subordinate nuclear medicine technologists. Position radiation fields, radiation beams, and patient to allow for most effective treatment of patient's disease, using computer. Add radioactive substances to biological specimens, such as blood, urine, and feces, to determine therapeutic drug or hormone levels. Develop treatment procedures for nuclear medicine treatment programs.

Related Military Specializations: Diagnostic Imaging Journeyman; Nuclear Medicine Technologist. **Average Educational Level of Vets:** Associate degree. **Usual Educational Requirement:** Associate degree. **Relevant Educational Program:** Nuclear Medical Technology/Technologist. **Related Knowledge/Courses:** Medicine and Dentistry; Biology; Chemistry; Physics; Customer and Personal Service; Therapy and Counseling. **Work Experience Needed:** None. **On-the-Job Training Needed:** None. **Certification/Licensure:** Voluntary certification by association.

Personality Types: Investigative-Realistic-Social. **Key Career Cluster:** 08 Health Science. **Key Career Pathway:** 8.2 Diagnostics Services. **Top Industries for Vets:** Hospitals; National Security and International Affairs; Other Health Care Services; Offices of Physicians; Outpatient Care Centers.

Skills: Science; Equipment Maintenance; Quality Control Analysis; Operation Monitoring; Repairing; Operation and Control; Troubleshooting; Service Orientation.

Work Environment: Indoors; standing; walking and running; using hands; contaminants; exposed to radiation; exposed to disease or infections; hazardous conditions.

Nuclear Technicians

- ✳ Average Annual Earnings (All): $68,030
- ✳ Average Annual Earnings (Recent Veterans): $36,670
- ✳ Earnings Growth Potential: Medium (39.8%)
- ✳ Growth: 13.5%
- ✳ Annual Job Openings: 330
- ✳ Veteran Employment by Sector: For-Profit, 42.6%; Nonprofit, 10.3%; Government, 46.6%; Self-Employed, 0.5%.

Considerations for Job Outlook: Nuclear technicians should have good job opportunities over the next decade. In the nuclear power industry, many openings should arise from technicians who retire or leave the occupation for other reasons.

Assist nuclear physicists, nuclear engineers, or other scientists in laboratory or production activities. For task data, see Job Specializations.

Related Military Specializations: Submarine Nuclear Propulsion Plant Operator; Surface Ship Nuclear Propulsion Plant Operator; Nuclear Propulsion Plant Operator Trainee. **Average**

Educational Level of Vets: One or more years of college, no degree. **Usual Educational Requirement:** Associate degree. **Relevant Educational Programs:** Industrial Radiologic Technology/Technician; Nuclear and Industrial Radiologic Technologies/Technicians, Other; Nuclear Engineering Technology/Technician; Nuclear/Nuclear Power Technology/Technician; Radiation Protection/Health Physics Technician Training. **Work Experience Needed:** None. **On-the-Job Training Needed:** Moderate-term on-the-job training. **Certification/Licensure:** Security clearance in some positions.

Key Career Cluster: 15 Science, Technology, Engineering, and Mathematics. **Key Career Pathway:** 15.2 Science and Mathematics. **Top Industries for Vets:** Scientific Research and Development Services; National Security and International Affairs; Architectural, Engineering, and Related Services; Colleges and Universities, Including Junior Colleges; Management, Scientific and Technical Consulting Services.

Job Specialization: Nuclear Equipment Operation Technicians

Operate equipment used for the release, control, and utilization of nuclear energy to assist scientists in laboratory and production activities. Follow policies and procedures for radiation workers to ensure personnel safety.

Related Knowledge/Courses: Physics; Chemistry; Mechanical Devices; Public Safety and Security; Engineering and Technology; Mathematics.

Personality Types: Realistic-Conventional-Investigative.

Skills: Repairing; Equipment Maintenance; Operation and Control; Troubleshooting; Operation Monitoring; Quality Control Analysis; Mathematics; Science.

Work Environment: More often indoors than outdoors; standing; walking and running; using hands; noise; very hot or cold; bright or inadequate lighting; contaminants; cramped work space; exposed to radiation; high places; hazardous conditions; hazardous equipment.

Job Specialization: Nuclear Monitoring Technicians

Collect and test samples to monitor results of nuclear experiments and contamination of humans, facilities, and environment. Calculate safe radiation exposure times for personnel using plant contamination readings and prescribed safe levels of radiation. Provide initial response to abnormal events and to alarms from radiation monitoring equipment. Monitor personnel to determine the amounts and intensities of radiation exposure. Inform supervisors when individual exposures or area radiation levels approach maximum permissible limits. Instruct personnel in radiation safety procedures and demonstrate use of protective clothing and equipment. Determine intensities and types of radiation in work areas, equipment, and materials, using radiation detectors and other instruments. Collect samples of air, water, gases, and solids to determine radioactivity levels of contamination. Set up equipment that automatically detects area radiation deviations and test detection equipment to ensure its accuracy.

Related Knowledge/Courses: Physics; Chemistry; Biology; Mathematics; Engineering and Technology; Public Safety and Security.

Personality Types: Realistic-Conventional-Investigative.

Skills: Operation Monitoring; Troubleshooting; Science; Quality Control Analysis; Operation and Control; Monitoring; Systems Analysis; Mathematics.

Work Environment: More often indoors than outdoors; sitting; using hands; noise; very hot or cold; bright or inadequate lighting; contaminants; exposed to radiation; high places; hazardous conditions; hazardous equipment.

Occupational Health and Safety Specialists

- ❋ Average Annual Earnings (All): $66,270
- ❋ Average Annual Earnings (Recent Veterans): $51,290
- ❋ Earnings Growth Potential: High (40.0%)
- ❋ Growth: 8.5%
- ❋ Annual Job Openings: 2,570
- ❋ Veteran Employment by Sector: For-Profit, 29.3%; Nonprofit, 2.3%; Government, 67.2%; Self-Employed, 1.1%.

Considerations for Job Outlook: New environmental regulations and laws will require specialists to create and enforce procedures in the workplace. The increased adoption of nuclear power as a source of energy may be a major factor for job growth for specialists in that field. These specialists will be needed to create and carry out programs to maintain the safety of both the workers and the environment. Insurance and workers' compensation costs have become a concern for many employers and insurance companies, especially with an aging population remaining in the workforce longer.

Review, evaluate, and analyze work environments and design programs and procedures to control, eliminate, and prevent disease or injury. Order suspension of activities that pose threats to workers' health and safety. Recommend measures to help protect workers from potentially hazardous work methods, processes, or materials. Investigate accidents to identify causes and to determine how such accidents might be prevented in the future. Investigate the adequacy of ventilation, exhaust equipment, lighting, and other conditions that could affect employee health, comfort, or performance. Develop and maintain hygiene programs such as noise surveys, continuous atmosphere monitoring, ventilation surveys, and asbestos management plans. Inspect and evaluate workplace environments, equipment, and practices in order to ensure compliance with safety standards and government regulations. Collaborate with engineers and physicians to institute control and remedial measures for hazardous and potentially hazardous conditions or equipment. Conduct safety training and education programs and demonstrate the use of safety equipment.

Related Military Specializations: Bioenvironmental Engineering Apprentice; Bioenvironmental Engineering Craftsman; Bioenvironmental Engineering Helper; Bioenvironmental Engineering Journeyman; Bioenvironmental Engineering Manager; Bioenvironmental Engineering Superintendent; Electroneurodiagnostic Technologist; Field Medical Service Technician; Ground Safety Specialist; Hazardous Materiel Control Management Technician; Preventive Medicine Specialist; Preventive Medicine Technician; Public Health Manager; others. **Average Educational Level of Vets:** Bachelor's degree. **Usual Educational Requirement:** Bachelor's degree. **Relevant Educational Programs:** Environmental Health; Industrial Safety Technology/Technician; Occupational Health and Industrial Hygiene; Occupational Safety and Health Technology/Technician. **Related Knowledge/Courses:** Chemistry; Biology; Physics; Engineering and Technology; Public Safety and Security; Building and Construction.

Work Experience Needed: None. **On-the-Job Training Needed:** Moderate-term on-the-job training. **Certification/Licensure:** Licensure for some specializations; voluntary certification by association.

Personality Types: Investigative-Conventional. **Key Career Cluster:** 01 Agriculture, Food, and Natural Resources. **Key Career Pathway:** 1.6 Environmental Service Systems. **Top Industries for Vets:** National Security and International Affairs; Construction; Hospitals; Administration of Human Resource Programs; Administration of Environmental Quality and Housing Programs.

Skills: Science; Operations Analysis; Quality Control Analysis; Operation Monitoring; Persuasion; Troubleshooting; Systems Evaluation; Programming.

Work Environment: More often indoors than outdoors; sitting; noise; contaminants.

Office Clerks, General

- ✺ Average Annual Earnings (All): $27,190
- ✺ Average Annual Earnings (Recent Veterans): $30,560
- ✺ Earnings Growth Potential: Low (34.8%)
- ✺ Growth: 16.6%
- ✺ Annual Job Openings: 101,150
- ✺ Veteran Employment by Sector: For-Profit, 28.5%; Nonprofit, 5.7%; Government, 65.5%; Self-Employed, 0.4%.

Considerations for Job Outlook: Job prospects are expected to be good in this large occupation. Workers will be needed to fill new jobs and replace those who leave the occupation. General office clerks who can learn new skills and adapt to changing technologies will have the best prospects.

Perform duties too varied and diverse to be classified in any specific office clerical occupation, requiring knowledge of office systems and procedures. Collect, count, and disburse money; do basic bookkeeping; and complete banking transactions. Communicate with customers, employees, and other individuals to answer questions, disseminate or explain information, take orders, and address complaints. Answer telephones, direct calls, and take messages. Compile, copy, sort, and file records of office activities, business transactions, and other activities. Complete and mail bills, contracts, policies, invoices, or checks. Operate office machines such as photocopiers and scanners, facsimile machines, voice mail systems, and personal computers. Compute, record, and proofread data and other information, such as records or reports. Maintain and update filing, inventory, mailing, and database systems, either manually or using a computer. Open, sort, and route incoming mail; answer correspondence; and prepare outgoing mail. Review files, records, and other documents to obtain information to respond to requests. Deliver messages, and run errands. Inventory and order materials, supplies, and services. Complete work schedules, manage calendars, and arrange appointments. Process and prepare documents such as business or government forms and expense reports. Monitor and direct the work of lower-level clerks. Type, format, proofread, and edit correspondence and other documents from notes or dictating machines, using computers or typewriters. Count, weigh, measure, or organize materials.

Related Military Specializations:
Administrative Clerk; Administrative Specialist; Cryptologic Technician (Administrative); Cryptologic Technician Administrative NEC; Education Assistant; Personnel Clerk; Personnel Journeyman; Personnel Specialist; Religious Program Specialist; Special Technical Operations (Enlisted); Special Technical Operations Marine; Yeoman. **Average Educational Level of Vets:** One or more years of college, no degree. **Usual Educational Requirement:** High school diploma or equivalent. **Relevant Educational Program:** General Office Occupations and Clerical Services. **Related Knowledge/Courses:** Clerical Practices; Customer and Personal Service; Computers and Electronics. **Work Experience Needed:** None. **On-the-Job Training Needed:** Short-term on-the-job training. **Certification/Licensure:** None.

Personality Types: Conventional-Enterprising-Realistic. **Key Career Cluster:** 14 Marketing, Sales, and Service. **Key Career Pathway:** 14.3 Buying and Merchandising. **Top Industries for Vets:** National Security and International Affairs; Colleges and Universities, Including Junior Colleges; Hospitals; Administration of Human Resource Programs; Executive Offices and Legislative Bodies.

Skills: Management of Material Resources; Service Orientation; Active Listening; Management of Financial Resources; Reading Comprehension; Speaking.

Work Environment: Indoors; sitting; repetitive motions.

Operating Engineers and Other Construction Equipment Operators

❋ Average Annual Earnings (All): $41,510

❋ Average Annual Earnings (Recent Veterans): $32,740

❋ Earnings Growth Potential: Medium (35.6%)

❋ Growth: 23.5%

❋ Annual Job Openings: 16,280

❋ Veteran Employment by Sector: For-Profit, 57.0%; Nonprofit, 1.3%; Government, 37.8%; Self-Employed, 3.9%.

Considerations for Job Outlook: Workers with the ability to operate multiple types of equipment should have the best job opportunities. As with many other construction workers, employment of construction equipment operators is sensitive to fluctuations of the economy. Workers may experience periods of unemployment when the overall level of construction falls. However, shortages of workers may occur in some areas during peak periods of building activity. Employment opportunities should be best in metropolitan areas, where most large commercial and multifamily buildings are constructed, and in states that are undertaking large transportation-related projects. In addition, the need to replace workers who leave the occupation should result in some job opportunities.

Operate one or several types of power construction equipment. Learn and follow safety regulations. Take actions to avoid potential hazards and obstructions such as utility lines, other equipment, other workers, and falling objects. Adjust handwheels and depress pedals to control attachments

such as blades, buckets, scrapers, and swing booms. Start engines; move throttles, switches, and levers; and depress pedals to operate machines such as bulldozers, trench excavators, road graders, and backhoes. Locate underground services, such as pipes and wires, prior to beginning work. Monitor operations to ensure that health and safety standards are met. Align machines, cutterheads, or depth gauge makers with reference stakes and guidelines, or ground or position equipment by following hand signals of other workers. Load and move dirt, rocks, equipment, and materials, using trucks, crawler tractors, power cranes, shovels, graders, and related equipment. Drive and maneuver equipment outfitted with blades in successive passes over working areas to remove topsoil, vegetation, and rocks and to distribute and level earth or terrain. Coordinate machine actions with other activities, positioning or moving loads in response to hand or audio signals from crew members. Operate tractors and bulldozers to perform such tasks as clearing land, mixing sludge, trimming backfills, and building roadways and parking lots. Repair and maintain equipment, making emergency adjustments or assisting with major repairs as necessary.

Related Military Specializations: Assault Breacher Vehicle (ABV)/Joint Assault Bridge (JAB) Operator; Construction Equipment Operator; Elevated Causeway System (Modular) Specialist; Engineer Equipment Operator; Engineer Tracked Vehicle Crewman; Equipment Operator; General Construction Equipment Operator; Heavy Construction Equipment Operator. **Average Educational Level of Vets:** High school diploma or equivalent. **Usual Educational Requirement:** High school diploma or equivalent. **Relevant Educational Programs:** Construction/Heavy Equipment/Earthmoving Equipment Operation; Mobile Crane Operation/Operator. **Related Knowledge/Courses:** Building and Construction; Mechanical Devices;

Engineering and Technology; Design; Production and Processing; Public Safety and Security. **Work Experience Needed:** None. **On-the-Job Training Needed:** Moderate-term on-the-job training. **Certification/Licensure:** Licensure for some specializations.

Personality Types: Realistic-Conventional-Investigative. **Key Career Cluster:** 02 Architecture and Construction. **Key Career Pathway:** 2.2 Construction. **Top Industries for Vets:** Construction; National Security and International Affairs; Executive Offices and Legislative Bodies; Support Activities For Mining; Electric Power Generation, Transmission and Distribution.

Skills: Operation and Control; Repairing; Equipment Maintenance; Troubleshooting; Operation Monitoring; Quality Control Analysis; Equipment Selection; Installation.

Work Environment: Outdoors; sitting; using hands; repetitive motions; noise; very hot or cold; bright or inadequate lighting; contaminants; whole-body vibration; hazardous equipment; minor burns, cuts, bites, or stings.

Painters, Construction and Maintenance

* Average Annual Earnings (All): $35,430

* Average Annual Earnings (Recent Veterans): $20,950

* Earnings Growth Potential: Low (34.6%)

* Growth: 18.5%

* Annual Job Openings: 15,730

* Veteran Employment by Sector: For-Profit, 57.1%; Nonprofit, 1.1%; Government, 11.6%; Self-Employed, 30.1%.

Considerations for Job Outlook: Overall job prospects should be good because of the need to replace workers who leave the occupation. There are no formal training requirements for entry into these jobs, so many people with limited skills work as painters for a relatively short time and then move on to other types of work with higher pay or better working conditions. Job opportunities for industrial painters should be excellent as the positions available should be greater than the pool of qualified individuals to fill them. Although industrial structures that require painting are located throughout the nation, the best employment opportunities should be in the Gulf Coast region, where strong demand and the largest concentration of workers exist. New painters and those with little experience should expect some periods of unemployment. In addition, many construction painting projects last only a short time. Employment of painters, like that of many other construction workers, is also sensitive to fluctuations in the economy.

Paint walls, equipment, buildings, bridges, and other structural surfaces, using brushes, rollers, and spray guns. Cover surfaces with dropcloths or masking tape and paper to protect surfaces during painting. Fill cracks, holes, and joints with caulk, putty, plaster, or other fillers, using caulking guns or putty knives. Apply primers or sealers to prepare new surfaces, such as bare wood or metal, for finish coats. Apply paint, stain, varnish, enamel, and other finishes to equipment, buildings, bridges, and/or other structures, using brushes, spray guns, or rollers. Calculate amounts of required materials and estimate costs, based on surface measurements and/or work orders. Read work orders or receive instructions from supervisors or homeowners in order to determine work requirements. Erect scaffolding and swing gates, or set up ladders, to work above ground level. Remove fixtures such as pictures, door knobs, lamps, and electric switch covers prior to painting. Wash and treat surfaces with oil, turpentine, mildew remover, or other preparations, and sand rough spots to ensure that finishes will adhere properly. Mix and match colors of paint, stain, or varnish with oil and thinning and drying additives in order to obtain desired colors and consistencies. Remove old finishes by stripping, sanding, wire brushing, burning, or using water and/or abrasive blasting. Select and purchase tools and finishes for surfaces to be covered, considering durability, ease of handling, methods of application, and customers' wishes. Smooth surfaces, using sandpaper, scrapers, brushes, steel wool, and/or sanding machines. Polish final coats to specified finishes. Use special finishing techniques such as sponging, ragging, layering, or faux finishing. Waterproof buildings, using waterproofers and caulking. Cut stencils, and brush and spray lettering and decorations on surfaces. Spray or brush hot plastics or pitch onto surfaces. Bake finishes on painted and enameled articles, using baking ovens.

Related Military Specializations: None. **Average Educational Level of Vets:** High school diploma or equivalent. **Usual Educational Requirement:** Less than high school diploma or equivalent. **Relevant Educational Program:** Painting/Painter and Wall Coverer Training. **Related Knowledge/Courses:** Building and Construction; Transportation; Design; Customer and Personal Service; Production and Processing; Administration and Management. **Work Experience Needed:** None. **On-the-Job Training Needed:** Moderate-term on-the-job training. **Certification/Licensure:** None.

Personality Types: Realistic-Conventional. **Key Career Cluster:** 02 Architecture and Construction. **Key Career Pathway:** 2.2 Construction. **Top Industries for Vets:** Construction; Real Estate; National Security and International Affairs; Services Incidental to Transportation; Other General Government and Support.

Skills: Operation and Control.

Work Environment: More often outdoors than indoors; standing; climbing; kneeling, crouching, stooping, or crawling; balancing; using hands; bending or twisting the body; repetitive motions; noise; contaminants; cramped work space; high places; hazardous conditions; minor burns, cuts, bites, or stings.

Paralegals and Legal Assistants

- ⊛ Average Annual Earnings (All): $46,730
- ⊛ Average Annual Earnings (Recent Veterans): $38,200
- ⊛ Earnings Growth Potential: Medium (37.1%)
- ⊛ Growth: 18.3%
- ⊛ Annual Job Openings: 8,340
- ⊛ Veteran Employment by Sector: For-Profit, 43.2%; Nonprofit, 0.5%; Government, 56.3%; Self-Employed, 0.0%.

Considerations for Job Outlook: This occupation attracts many applicants, and competition for jobs will be strong. Experienced, formally trained paralegals should have the best job prospects. In addition, many firms will prefer paralegals with experience and specialization in high-demand practice areas.

Assist lawyers by investigating facts, preparing legal documents, or researching legal precedent. Conduct research to support a legal proceeding, to formulate a defense, or to initiate legal action. Prepare legal documents, including briefs, pleadings, appeals, wills, contracts, and real estate closing statements. Prepare affidavits or other documents, maintain document file, and file pleadings with court clerk. Gather and analyze research data, such as statutes; decisions; and legal articles, codes, and documents. Investigate facts and law of cases to determine causes of action and to prepare cases. Call upon witnesses to testify at hearing. Direct and coordinate law office activity, including delivery of subpoenas. Arbitrate disputes between parties, and assist in real estate closing process. Keep and monitor legal volumes to ensure that law library is up to date. Appraise and inventory real and personal property for estate planning.

Related Military Specializations: Basic Legal Services Marine; Legal Services Specialist; Legal Specialist; Paralegal Apprentice; Paralegal Craftsman; Paralegal Helper; Paralegal Journeyman; Paralegal Manager; Paralegal Specialist; Paralegal Superintendent. **Average Educational Level of Vets:** Bachelor's degree. **Usual Educational Requirement:** Associate degree. **Relevant Educational Program:** Legal Assistant/Paralegal Training. **Related Knowledge/Courses:** Clerical Practices; Law and Government; English Language; Computers and Electronics; Communications and Media. **Work Experience Needed:** None. **On-the-Job Training Needed:** None. **Certification/Licensure:** Voluntary certification by association.

Personality Types: Conventional-Investigative-Enterprising. **Key Career Cluster:** 12 Law, Public Safety, Corrections, and Security. **Key Career Pathway:** 12.5 Legal Services. **Top Industries for Vets:** Legal Services; National Security and International Affairs; Justice, Public Order, and Safety Activities; Executive Offices and Legislative Bodies; Insurance Carriers and Related Activities.

Skills: Writing; Active Listening; Speaking; Service Orientation.

Work Environment: Indoors; sitting; repetitive motions.

Paving, Surfacing, and Tamping Equipment Operators

- ✳ Average Annual Earnings (All): $35,270
- ✳ Average Annual Earnings (Recent Veterans): $32,740
- ✳ Earnings Growth Potential: Low (32.7%)
- ✳ Growth: 22.1%
- ✳ Annual Job Openings: 2,200
- ✳ Veteran Employment by Sector: For-Profit, 57.3%; Nonprofit, 1.3%; Government, 36.9%; Self-Employed, 4.5%.

Considerations for Job Outlook: Workers with the ability to operate multiple types of equipment should have the best job opportunities. As with many other construction workers, employment of construction equipment operators is sensitive to fluctuations of the economy. Workers may experience periods of unemployment when the overall level of construction falls. However, shortages of workers may occur in some areas during peak periods of building activity. Employment opportunities should be best in metropolitan areas, where most large commercial and multifamily buildings are constructed, and in states that are undertaking large transportation-related projects. In addition, the need to replace workers who leave the occupation should result in some job opportunities.

Operate equipment used for applying concrete, asphalt, or other materials or for tamping gravel, dirt, or other materials. Start machine, engage clutch, and push and move levers to guide machine along forms or guidelines and to control the operation of machine attachments. Inspect, clean, maintain, and repair equipment, using mechanics' hand tools, or report malfunctions to supervisors. Operate machines to spread, smooth, level, or steel-reinforce stone, concrete, or asphalt on road beds. Coordinate truck dumping. Set up and tear down equipment. Operate tamping machines or manually roll surfaces to compact earth fills, foundation forms, and finished road materials, according to grade specifications. Shovel blacktop. Drive machines onto truck trailers, and drive trucks to transport machines and material to and from job sites. Observe distribution of paving material to adjust machine settings or material flow, and indicate low spots for workers to add material. Light burners or start heating units of machines, and regulate screed temperatures and asphalt flow rates. Fill tanks, hoppers, or machines with paving materials. Control traffic. Operate oil distributors, loaders, chip spreaders, dump trucks, and snow plows. Control paving machines to push dump trucks and to maintain a constant flow of asphalt or other material into hoppers or screeds. Set up forms and lay out guidelines for curbs, according to written specifications, using string, spray paint, and concrete/water mixes. Drive and operate curbing machines to extrude concrete or asphalt curbing. Cut or break up pavement and drive guardrail posts, using machines equipped with interchangeable hammers. Install dies, cutters, and extensions to screeds onto machines, using hand tools. Operate machines that clean or cut expansion joints in concrete or asphalt and that rout out cracks in pavement. Place strips of material such as cork, asphalt, or steel into joints, or place rolls of expansion-joint material on machines that automatically insert material.

Related Military Specializations: Advanced Equipment Operator; Concrete and Asphalt Equipment Operator; Pavements and Construction Equipment Apprentice; Pavements and Construction Equipment Helper; Pavements and Construction Equipment Journeyman. **Average Educational Level of Vets:** High school diploma or equivalent. **Usual Educational Requirement:** High school diploma or equivalent. **Relevant Educational Program:** Construction/Heavy Equipment/Earthmoving Equipment Operation. **Related Knowledge/ Courses:** Building and Construction; Transportation; Mechanical Devices; Engineering and Technology; Public Safety and Security; Production and Processing. **Work Experience Needed:** None. **On-the-Job Training Needed:** Moderate-term on-the-job training. **Certification/Licensure:** None.

Personality Types: Realistic-Conventional. **Key Career Cluster:** 02 Architecture and Construction. **Key Career Pathway:** 2.2 Construction. **Top Industries for Vets:** Construction; National Security and International Affairs; Executive Offices and Legislative Bodies; Support Activities For Mining; Electric Power Generation, Transmission and Distribution.

Skills: Repairing; Equipment Maintenance; Operation and Control; Equipment Selection; Troubleshooting; Operation Monitoring; Quality Control Analysis; Coordination.

Work Environment: Indoors; standing; using hands; bending or twisting the body; repetitive motions; noise; very hot or cold; bright or inadequate lighting; contaminants; whole-body vibration; hazardous equipment; minor burns, cuts, bites, or stings.

Payroll and Timekeeping Clerks

⊛ Average Annual Earnings (All): $37,160

⊛ Average Annual Earnings (Recent Veterans): $38,200

⊛ Earnings Growth Potential: Medium (35.3%)

⊛ Growth: 14.6%

⊛ Annual Job Openings: 6,570

⊛ Veteran Employment by Sector: For-Profit, 44.4%; Nonprofit, 0.8%; Government, 54.6%; Self-Employed, 0.2%.

Considerations for Job Outlook: Job prospects for financial clerks should be favorable, because many workers are expected to leave this occupation. Employers will need to hire new workers to replace those leaving the occupation.

Compile and record employee time and payroll data. Review time sheets, work charts, wage computation, and other information to detect and reconcile payroll discrepancies. Process paperwork for new employees and enter employee information into the payroll system. Verify attendance, hours worked, and pay adjustments, and post information onto designated records. Compute wages and deductions, and enter data into computers. Record employee information, such as exemptions, transfers, and resignations, to maintain and update payroll records. Process and issue employee paychecks and statements of earnings and deductions. Keep track of leave time, such as vacation, personal, and sick leave, for employees. Compile employee time, production, and payroll data from time sheets and other records. Distribute and collect timecards each pay period. Issue and record adjustments to pay related to previous errors or retroactive increases. Provide information to employees and managers on payroll matters, tax issues, benefit plans, and collective agreement provisions. Keep informed about changes in tax and deduction laws that apply to the payroll process. Compile statistical reports, statements, and summaries related to pay and benefits accounts, and submit them to appropriate departments. Conduct verifications of employment. Complete time sheets showing employees' arrival and departure times. Prepare and balance period-end reports, and reconcile issued payrolls to bank statements. Complete, verify, and process forms and documentation for administration of benefits such as pension plans, and unemployment and medical insurance. Post relevant work hours to client files to bill clients properly. Coordinate special programs, such as United Way campaigns, that involve payroll deductions.

Related Military Specializations: Basic Financial Management Marine; Disbursing Afloat Automated Systems Specialist; Disbursing Clerk; Disbursing Clerk Tracking NEC; Finance Specialist; Finance Technician; Financial Management and Comptroller Apprentice; Financial Management and Comptroller Craftsman; Financial Management and Comptroller Helper; Financial Management and Comptroller Journeyman. **Average Educational Level of Vets:** One or more years of college, no degree. **Usual Educational Requirement:** High school diploma or equivalent. **Relevant Educational Program:** Accounting Technology/Technician and Bookkeeping. **Related Knowledge/Courses:** Clerical Practices; Economics and Accounting; Personnel and Human Resources; Computers and Electronics. **Work Experience Needed:** None. **On-the-Job Training Needed:** Moderate-term on-the-job training. **Certification/Licensure:** Voluntary certification by association.

Personality Types: Conventional-Enterprising. **Key Career Cluster:** 04 Business, Management,

P

and Administration. **Key Career Pathway:** 4.2 Business Financial Management and Accounting. **Top Industries for Vets:** National Security and International Affairs; Accounting, Tax Preparation, Bookkeeping and Payroll Services; Computer Systems Design and Related Services; Employment Services; Advertising and Related Services.

Skills: Mathematics; Reading Comprehension; Writing; Management of Personnel Resources.

Work Environment: Indoors; sitting.

Personal Financial Advisors

- ❋ Average Annual Earnings (All): $66,580
- ❋ Average Annual Earnings (Recent Veterans): $52,380
- ❋ Earnings Growth Potential: High (50.7%)
- ❋ Growth: 32.1%
- ❋ Annual Job Openings: 9,020
- ❋ Veteran Employment by Sector: For-Profit, 69.6%; Nonprofit, 1.7%; Government, 10.5%; Self-Employed, 18.2%.

Considerations for Job Outlook: Personal financial advisors are expected to face competition as the combination of relatively high wages and few formal educational requirements attracts many applicants for each opening.

Advise clients on financial plans using knowledge of tax and investment strategies, securities, insurance, pension plans, and real estate. Prepare and interpret for clients information such as investment performance reports, financial document summaries, and income projections. Recommend strategies clients can use to achieve their financial goals and objectives, including specific recommendations in such areas as cash

management, insurance coverage, and investment planning. Build and maintain client bases, keeping current client plans up to date and recruiting new clients on an ongoing basis. Devise debt liquidation plans that include payoff priorities and timelines. Implement financial-planning recommendations, or refer clients to someone who can assist them with plan implementation. Interview clients to determine their current incomes, expenses, insurance coverages, tax statuses, financial objectives, risk tolerances, and other information needed to develop financial plans. Monitor financial market trends to ensure that plans are effective, and to identify any necessary updates. Explain and document for clients the types of services that are to be provided, and the responsibilities to be taken by personal financial advisors. Explain to individuals and groups the details of financial assistance available to college and university students, such as loans, grants, and scholarships. Guide clients in the gathering of information such as bank account records, income tax returns, life and disability insurance records, pension plan information, and wills.

Related Military Specializations: None. **Average Educational Level of Vets:** Bachelor's degree. **Usual Educational Requirement:** Bachelor's degree. **Relevant Educational Programs:** Finance, General; Financial Planning and Services. **Related Knowledge/Courses:** Economics and Accounting; Sales and Marketing; Law and Government; Customer and Personal Service; Mathematics; Computers and Electronics. **Work Experience Needed:** None. **On-the-Job Training Needed:** None. **Certification/Licensure:** None.

Personality Types: Enterprising-Conventional-Social. **Key Career Cluster:** 06 Finance. **Key Career Pathway:** 6.1 Financial and Investment Planning. **Top Industries for Vets:** Securities, Commodities, Funds, Trusts, and Other Financial Investments; National Security and International Affairs; Insurance Carriers and Related Activities; Nondepository Credit and Related Activities; Banking and Related Activities.

Skills: Operations Analysis; Management of Financial Resources; Mathematics; Persuasion; Service Orientation; Speaking; Writing; Reading Comprehension.

Work Environment: Indoors; sitting.

Pest Control Workers

- ❈ Average Annual Earnings (All): $30,220
- ❈ Average Annual Earnings (Recent Veterans): $29,140
- ❈ Earnings Growth Potential: Low (34.0%)
- ❈ Growth: 26.1%
- ❈ Annual Job Openings: 4,850
- ❈ Veteran Employment by Sector: For-Profit, 94.7%; Nonprofit, 2.3%; Government, 1.8%; Self-Employed, 1.2%.

Considerations for Job Outlook: Job opportunities are expected to be very good. The limited number of people seeking work in pest control, expected job growth, and the need to replace workers who leave this occupation should result in many job openings.

Apply or release chemical solutions or toxic gases and set traps to kill or remove pests and vermin that infest buildings and surrounding areas. Record work activities performed. Inspect premises to identify infestation source and extent of damage to property, wall and roof porosity, and access to infested locations. Spray or dust chemical solutions, powders, or gases into rooms, onto clothing, furnishings, or wood, and over marshlands, ditches, and catch-basins. Clean work site after completion of job. Direct and/or assist other workers in treatment and extermination processes to eliminate and control rodents, insects, and weeds. Drive truck equipped with power spraying equipment. Measure area dimensions requiring treatment, using rule, calculate fumigant requirements, and estimate cost for service. Post warning signs and lock building doors to secure area to be fumigated. Cut or bore openings in building or surrounding concrete, access infested areas, insert nozzle, and inject pesticide to impregnate ground. Study preliminary reports and diagrams of infested area and determine treatment type required to eliminate and prevent recurrence of infestation. Dig up and burn, or spray weeds with herbicides. Set mechanical traps and place poisonous paste or bait in sewers, burrows, and ditches. Clean and remove blockages from infested areas to facilitate spraying procedure and provide drainage, using broom, mop, shovel, and rake. Position and fasten edges of tarpaulins over building and tape vents to ensure air-tight environment and check for leaks.

Related Military Specializations: Pest Management Apprentice; Pest Management Craftsman; Pest Management Helper; Pest Management Journeyman. **Average Educational Level of Vets:** High school diploma or equivalent. **Usual Educational Requirement:** High school diploma or equivalent. **Relevant Educational Program:** Agricultural/Farm Supplies Retailing and Wholesaling. **Related Knowledge/ Courses:** Sales and Marketing; Chemistry; Biology; Building and Construction; Customer and Personal Service; Law and Government. **Work Experience Needed:** None. **On-the-Job Training Needed:** Moderate-term on-the-job training. **Certification/Licensure:** Licensure.

Personality Types: Realistic-Conventional. **Key Career Cluster:** 01 Agriculture, Food, and Natural Resources. **Key Career Pathway:** 1.6 Environmental Service Systems. **Top Industries**

for Vets: Services to Buildings and Dwellings, Except Construction Cleaning; Management, Scientific and Technical Consulting Services; Real Estate; Construction; Traveler Accommodation.

Skills: Equipment Selection; Repairing; Equipment Maintenance; Operation and Control; Troubleshooting; Mathematics; Persuasion; Systems Analysis.

Work Environment: More often outdoors than indoors; standing; walking and running; using hands; repetitive motions; very hot or cold; contaminants; cramped work space; hazardous conditions; minor burns, cuts, bites, or stings.

Pharmacy Technicians

- ✸ Average Annual Earnings (All): $28,940
- ✸ Average Annual Earnings (Recent Veterans): $30,560
- ✸ Earnings Growth Potential: Low (29.8%)
- ✸ Growth: 32.4%
- ✸ Annual Job Openings: 16,630
- ✸ Veteran Employment by Sector: For-Profit, 54.5%; Nonprofit, 12.2%; Government, 32.7%; Self-Employed, 0.6%.

Considerations for Job Outlook: Job prospects should be excellent for pharmacy technicians, particularly those with formal training and those with experience in retail settings.

Prepare medications under the direction of a pharmacist. Receive written prescription or refill requests, and verify that information is complete and accurate. Maintain proper storage and security conditions for drugs. Answer telephones, responding to questions or requests. Fill bottles with prescribed medications, and type and affix labels. Assist customers by answering simple questions, locating items, or referring them to the pharmacist for medication information. Price and file prescriptions that have been filled. Clean and help maintain equipment and work areas, and sterilize glassware according to prescribed methods. Establish and maintain patient profiles, including lists of medications taken by individual patients. Order, label, and count stock of medications, chemicals, and supplies, and enter inventory data into computer. Receive and store incoming supplies, verify quantities against invoices, and inform supervisors of stock needs and shortages. Transfer medication from vials to the appropriate number of sterile disposable syringes, using aseptic techniques. Under pharmacist supervision, add measured drugs or nutrients to intravenous solutions under sterile conditions to prepare intravenous (IV) packs. Supply and monitor robotic machines that dispense medicine into containers, and label the containers. Prepare and process medical insurance claim forms and records. Mix pharmaceutical preparations according to written prescriptions. Operate cash registers to accept payment from customers.

Related Military Specializations: Pharmacy Specialist; Pharmacy Technician. **Average Educational Level of Vets:** One or more years of college, no degree. **Usual Educational Requirement:** High school diploma or equivalent. **Relevant Educational Program:** Pharmacy Technician/Assistant Training. **Related Knowledge/Courses:** Medicine and Dentistry; Clerical Practices; Computers and Electronics; Customer and Personal Service; Chemistry; Mathematics. **Work Experience Needed:** None. **On-the-Job Training Needed:** Moderate-term on-the-job training. **Certification/Licensure:** Registration in most states; voluntary certification by association in others.

Personality Types: Conventional-Realistic. **Key Career Cluster:** 08 Health Science. **Key Career Pathway:** 8.1 Therapeutic Services. **Top**

Industries for Vets: Hospitals; Pharmacies and Drug Stores; National Security and International Affairs; Veterinary Services; Other Health Care Services.

Skills: Management of Financial Resources; Service Orientation; Science; Mathematics; Programming; Active Listening.

Work Environment: Indoors; standing; walking and running; using hands; repetitive motions; exposed to disease or infections.

Pile-Driver Operators

- ❋ Average Annual Earnings (All): $45,500
- ❋ Average Annual Earnings (Recent Veterans): $32,740
- ❋ Earnings Growth Potential: High (41.3%)
- ❋ Growth: 36.0%
- ❋ Annual Job Openings: 230
- ❋ Veteran Employment by Sector: For-Profit, 57.0%; Nonprofit, 1.3%; Government, 37.8%; Self-Employed, 3.9%.

Considerations for Job Outlook: Workers with the ability to operate multiple types of equipment should have the best job opportunities. As with many other construction workers, employment of construction equipment operators is sensitive to fluctuations of the economy. Workers may experience periods of unemployment when the overall level of construction falls. However, shortages of workers may occur in some areas during peak periods of building activity. Employment opportunities should be best in metropolitan areas, where most large commercial and multifamily buildings are constructed, and in states that are undertaking large transportation-related projects. In addition, the need to replace workers who leave the occupation should result in some job opportunities.

Operate pile drivers mounted on skids, barges, crawler treads, or locomotive cranes to drive pilings for retaining walls, bulkheads, and foundations of structures. Move levers and turn valves to activate power hammers, or to raise and lower drophammers that drive piles to required depths. Clean, lubricate, and refill equipment. Conduct pre-operational checks on equipment to ensure proper functioning. Drive pilings to provide support for buildings or other structures, using heavy equipment with a pile driver head. Move hand and foot levers of hoisting equipment to position piling leads, hoist piling into leads, and position hammers over pilings.

Related Military Specialization: General Construction Equipment Operator. **Average Educational Level of Vets:** High school diploma or equivalent. **Usual Educational Requirement:** High school diploma or equivalent. **Relevant Educational Program:** Construction/Heavy Equipment/Earthmoving Equipment Operation. **Related Knowledge/Courses:** Building and Construction; Mechanical Devices; Transportation; Physics; Design; Engineering and Technology. **Work Experience Needed:** None. **On-the-Job Training Needed:** Moderate-term on-the-job training. **Certification/Licensure:** Licensure in some states.

Personality Types: Realistic-Conventional-Investigative. **Key Career Cluster:** 02 Architecture and Construction. **Key Career Pathway:** 2.2 Construction. **Top Industries for Vets:** Construction; National Security and International Affairs; Executive Offices and Legislative Bodies; Support Activities For Mining; Electric Power Generation, Transmission and Distribution.

Skills: Equipment Maintenance; Operation and Control; Repairing; Operation Monitoring;

Troubleshooting; Quality Control Analysis; Equipment Selection.

Work Environment: Outdoors; standing; using hands; bending or twisting the body; repetitive motions; noise; very hot or cold; bright or inadequate lighting; contaminants; cramped work space; whole-body vibration; high places; hazardous conditions; hazardous equipment; minor burns, cuts, bites, or stings.

Pipelayers

- ❋ Average Annual Earnings (All): $35,900
- ❋ Average Annual Earnings (Recent Veterans): $32,090
- ❋ Earnings Growth Potential: Medium (35.5%)
- ❋ Growth: 25.3%
- ❋ Annual Job Openings: 2,880
- ❋ Veteran Employment by Sector: For-Profit, 78.7%; Nonprofit, 2.7%; Government, 14.3%; Self-Employed, 4.3%.

Considerations for Job Outlook: A moderate increase is expected as demand for public utility construction fell significantly during the recent recession, employment of pipelayers experienced much larger declines than the construction industry as a whole. As the public utility construction industry recovers and large-scale pipeline projects progress, employment of these workers will rebound faster than the overall industry in the next decade.

Lay pipe for storm or sanitation sewers, drains, and water mains. Check slopes for conformance to requirements, using levels or lasers. Cover pipes with earth or other materials. Cut pipes to required lengths. Connect pipe pieces and seal joints, using welding equipment, cement, or glue. Install and repair sanitary and stormwater sewer structures and pipe systems. Install and use instruments such as lasers, grade rods, and transit levels. Grade and level trench bases, using tamping machines and hand tools. Lay out pipe routes, following written instructions or blueprints, and coordinating layouts with supervisors. Dig trenches to desired or required depths, by hand or using trenching tools. Align and position pipes to prepare them for welding or sealing. Operate mechanized equipment such as pickup trucks, rollers, tandem dump trucks, front-end loaders, and backhoes. Train others in pipe-laying, and provide supervision. Tap and drill holes into pipes to introduce auxiliary lines or devices. Locate existing pipes needing repair or replacement, using magnetic or radio indicators.

Related Military Specialization: Utilitiesman—Water and Sanitation. **Average Educational Level of Vets:** High school diploma or equivalent. **Usual Educational Requirement:** High school diploma or equivalent. **Relevant Educational Programs:** Pipefitting/Pipefitter and Sprinkler Fitter; Plumbing Technology/Plumber. **Related Knowledge/Courses:** Building and Construction; Mechanical Devices. **Work Experience Needed:** None. **On-the-Job Training Needed:** Short-term on-the-job training. **Certification/Licensure:** None.

Personality Types: Realistic. **Key Career Cluster:** 02 Architecture and Construction. **Key Career Pathway:** 2.2 Construction. **Top Industries for Vets:** Construction; National Security and International Affairs; Water, Steam, Air Conditioning, and Irrigation Systems; Natural Gas Distribution; Pipeline Transportation.

Skills: Repairing; Operation and Control; Equipment Maintenance; Troubleshooting; Equipment Selection; Installation; Quality Control Analysis; Operation Monitoring.

Work Environment: Outdoors; standing; walking and running; using hands; bending or twisting the body; repetitive motions; noise; very hot or cold; bright or inadequate lighting; contaminants; cramped work space; whole-body vibration; hazardous equipment; minor burns, cuts, bites or stings.

Plumbers, Pipefitters, and Steamfitters

* Average Annual Earnings (All): $47,750
* Average Annual Earnings (Recent Veterans): $32,090
* Earnings Growth Potential: High (40.7%)
* Growth: 25.6%
* Annual Job Openings: 22,880
* Veteran Employment by Sector: For-Profit, 78.7%; Nonprofit, 2.7%; Government, 14.3%; Self-Employed, 4.3%.

Considerations for Job Outlook: Job opportunities are expected to be good as some employers continue to report difficulty finding qualified professionals. In addition, many workers are expected to retire over the next 10 years, which will result in more job openings. Workers with welding experience may have the best opportunities. Like that of many other types of construction work, employment of plumbers, pipefitters, and steamfitters is sensitive to fluctuations of the economy. On the one hand, workers may experience periods of unemployment when the overall level of construction falls. On the other hand, shortages of workers may occur in some areas during peak periods of building activity. However, maintenance and repair of plumbing and pipe systems must continue even during economic downturns, so plumbers and fitters outside of construction,

especially those in manufacturing, tend to have more stable employment.

Assemble, install, alter, and repair pipelines or pipe systems that carry water, steam, air, or other liquids or gases. For task data, see Job Specializations.

Related Military Specializations: Hull Maintenance Technician; NAMTS Pipefitter; Plumber; Shipfitter—Pipefitter; Utilitiesman; Utilitiesman—Plumber; Water Support Technician. **Average Educational Level of Vets:** High school diploma or equivalent. **Usual Educational Requirement:** High school diploma or equivalent. **Relevant Educational Programs:** Pipefitting/Pipefitter and Sprinkler Fitter; Plumbing and Related Water Supply Services, Other; Plumbing Technology/Plumber. **Work Experience Needed:** None. **On-the-Job Training Needed:** Apprenticeship. **Certification/Licensure:** Licensure.

Key Career Cluster: 02 Architecture and Construction. **Key Career Pathway:** 2.2 Construction. **Top Industries for Vets:** Construction; National Security and International Affairs; Water, Steam, Air Conditioning, and Irrigation Systems; Natural Gas Distribution; Pipeline Transportation.

Job Specialization: Pipe Fitters and Steamfitters

Lay out, assemble, install, and maintain pipe systems, pipe supports, and related hydraulic and pneumatic equipment for steam, hot water, heating, cooling, lubricating, sprinkling, and industrial production and processing systems. Cut, thread, and hammer pipe to specifications, using tools such as saws, cutting torches, and pipe threaders and benders. Assemble and secure pipes, tubes, fittings, and related equipment according to specifications by welding, brazing, cementing, soldering, and threading joints. Attach pipes to walls, structures, and fixtures, such as radiators or tanks, using brackets, clamps, tools, or welding equipment. Inspect, examine, and test installed systems and pipelines, using pressure gauge, hydrostatic testing, observation, or other methods. Measure and mark pipes for cutting and threading. Lay out full-scale drawings of pipe systems, supports, and related equipment, following blueprints. Plan pipe-system layout, installation, or repair according to specifications. Select pipe sizes and types and related materials, such as supports, hangers, and hydraulic cylinders, according to specifications. Cut and bore holes in structures such as bulkheads, decks, walls, and mains prior to pipe installation, using hand and power tools. Modify, clean, and maintain pipe systems, units, fittings, and related machines and equipment, following specifications and using hand and power tools. Install automatic controls used to regulate pipe systems. Turn valves to shut off steam, water, or other gases or liquids from pipe sections, using valve keys or wrenches. Remove and replace worn components. Prepare cost estimates for clients.

Related Knowledge/Courses: Building and Construction; Mechanical Devices; Physics; Design; Engineering and Technology; Chemistry.

Personality Types: Realistic-Conventional.

Skills: Repairing; Equipment Maintenance; Installation; Troubleshooting; Operation and Control; Quality Control Analysis; Operation Monitoring; Equipment Selection.

Work Environment: More often outdoors than indoors; standing; using hands; bending or twisting the body; repetitive motions; noise; very hot or cold; bright or inadequate lighting; contaminants; cramped work space; high places; hazardous conditions; hazardous equipment; minor burns, cuts, bites, or stings.

Job Specialization: Plumbers

Assemble, install, and repair pipes, fittings, and fixtures of heating, water, and drainage systems according to specifications and plumbing codes. Measure, cut, thread, and bend pipe to required angles, using hand and power tools or machines such as pipe cutters, pipe-threading machines, and pipe-bending machines. Study building plans and inspect structures to assess material and equipment needs to establish the sequence of pipe installations and to plan installation around obstructions such as electrical wiring. Locate and mark the position of pipe installations, connections, passage holes, and fixtures in structures, using measuring instruments such as rulers and levels. Assemble pipe sections, tubing, and fittings, using couplings, clamps, screws, bolts, cement, plastic solvent, caulking, or soldering, brazing, and welding equipment. Fill pipes or plumbing fixtures with water or air and observe pressure gauges to detect and locate leaks. Install pipe assemblies, fittings, valves, appliances such as dishwashers and water heaters, and fixtures such as sinks and toilets, using hand and power tools. Direct workers engaged in pipe cutting and preassembly and installation of plumbing systems and components. Cut openings in structures to accommodate pipes and pipe fittings, using hand and power tools. Review blueprints as well as building codes and specifications to determine work details and procedures. Install underground storm, sanitary, and water piping systems, and extend piping to connect fixtures and plumbing to these systems.

Related Knowledge/Courses: Building and Construction; Mechanical Devices; Physics; Design; Engineering and Technology; Customer and Personal Service.

Personality Types: Realistic-Conventional-Investigative.

Skills: Repairing; Equipment Maintenance; Installation; Troubleshooting; Equipment Selection; Operation and Control; Operation Monitoring; Quality Control Analysis.

Work Environment: More often outdoors than indoors; standing; walking and running; kneeling, crouching, stooping, or crawling; using hands; bending or twisting the body; repetitive motions; noise; very hot or cold; bright or inadequate lighting; contaminants; cramped work space; whole-body vibration; hazardous equipment; minor burns, cuts, bites, or stings.

Police and Sheriff's Patrol Officers

- ❋ Average Annual Earnings (All): $54,230
- ❋ Average Annual Earnings (Recent Veterans): $48,670
- ❋ Earnings Growth Potential: High (40.8%)
- ❋ Growth: 8.2%
- ❋ Annual Job Openings: 24,940
- ❋ Veteran Employment by Sector: For-Profit, 0.1%; Nonprofit, 0.0%; Government, 99.9%; Self-Employed, 0.0%.

Considerations for Job Outlook: Continued demand for public safety will lead to new openings for officers in local departments; however, both state and federal jobs may be more competitive. Because they typically offer low salaries, many local departments face high turnover rates, making opportunities more plentiful for qualified applicants. However, some smaller departments may have fewer opportunities as budgets limit the ability to hire additional officers. Jobs in state and federal agencies will remain more competitive as they often offer high pay and more opportunities

for both promotions and interagency transfers. Bilingual applicants with a bachelor's degree and law enforcement or military experience, especially investigative experience, should have the best opportunities in federal agencies.

Maintain order and protect life and property by enforcing local, tribal, state, or federal laws and ordinances. For task data, see Job Specializations.

Related Military Specializations: Accident Investigator; Basic Military Police and Corrections Marine; Dog Handler; GWOT IA/ILO Detainee Operations Interrogator; GWOT Support Assignment-Military Police (Law and Order Specialist; Kennel Master; Master-At-Arms; Military Police; Military Police Investigator (MPI); Military Working Dog Handler; Navy Law Enforcement Specialist; Physical Security Specialist; Port Security Specialist; Protective Service Specialist; Security Forces Apprentice; Security Forces Apprentice, Combat Arms; others. **Average Educational Level of Vets:** One or more years of college, no degree. **Usual Educational Requirement:** High school diploma or equivalent. **Relevant Educational Programs:** Criminal Justice/Police Science; Criminalistics and Criminal Science; Critical Incident Response/Special Police Operations; Law Enforcement Investigation and Interviewing; Law Enforcement Record-Keeping and Evidence Management; Maritime Law Enforcement; Natural Resources Law Enforcement and Protective Services; Protective Services Operations. **Work Experience Needed:** None. **On-the-Job Training Needed:** Moderate-term on-the-job training. **Certification/Licensure:** Licensure in some states.

Key Career Cluster: 12 Law, Public Safety, Corrections, and Security. **Key Career Pathway:** 12.4 Law Enforcement Services. **Top Industries for Vets:** Justice, Public Order, and Safety

Activities; National Security and International Affairs; Executive Offices and Legislative Bodies; Administration of Environmental Quality and Housing Programs; Public Finance Activities.

Job Specialization: Police Patrol Officers

Patrol assigned areas to enforce laws and ordinances, regulate traffic, control crowds, prevent crime, and arrest violators. Provide for public safety by maintaining order, responding to emergencies, protecting people and property, enforcing motor vehicle and criminal laws, and promoting good community relations. Monitor, note, report, and investigate suspicious persons and situations, safety hazards, and unusual or illegal activity in patrol area. Record facts to prepare reports that document incidents and activities. Identify, pursue, and arrest suspects and perpetrators of criminal acts. Patrol specific areas on foot, horseback, or motorized conveyance, responding promptly to calls for assistance. Review facts of incidents to determine whether criminal acts or statute violations were involved. Investigate traffic accidents and other accidents to determine causes and to determine whether crimes have been committed. Render aid to accident victims and other persons requiring first aid for physical injuries. Testify in court to present evidence or act as witness in traffic and criminal cases. Photograph or draw diagrams of crime or accident scenes, and interview principals and eyewitnesses. Relay complaint and emergency-request information to appropriate agency dispatchers. Evaluate complaint and emergency-request information to determine response requirements. Process prisoners, and prepare and maintain records of prisoner bookings and prisoner statuses during booking and pretrial processes. Monitor traffic to ensure motorists observe traffic regulations and exhibit safe driving procedures.

Related Knowledge/Courses: Psychology; Public Safety and Security; Law and Government; Customer and Personal Service; Therapy and Counseling; Sociology and Anthropology.

Personality Types:
Realistic-Enterprising-Conventional.

Skills: Negotiation; Persuasion; Service Orientation; Operation and Control; Social Perceptiveness; Active Listening; Critical Thinking; Coordination.

Work Environment: More often outdoors than indoors; sitting; using hands; noise; very hot or cold; bright or inadequate lighting; contaminants; exposed to disease or infections; hazardous equipment; minor burns, cuts, bites, or stings.

Job Specialization: Sheriffs and Deputy Sheriffs

Enforce law and order in rural or unincorporated districts, or serve legal processes of courts. May patrol courthouse, guard court or grand jury, or escort defendants. Drive vehicles or patrol specific areas to detect law violators, issue citations, and make arrests. Investigate illegal or suspicious activities. Verify that the proper legal charges have been made against law offenders. Execute arrest warrants, locating and taking persons into custody. Record daily activities, and submit logs and other related reports and paperwork to appropriate authorities. Patrol and guard courthouses, grand jury rooms, or assigned areas to provide security, enforce laws, maintain order, and arrest violators. Notify patrol units to take violators into custody or to provide needed assistance or medical aid. Place people in protective custody. Serve statements of claims, subpoenas, summonses, jury summonses, orders to pay alimony, and other court orders. Take control of accident scenes to maintain traffic flow, to assist accident victims, and to investigate causes.

Question individuals entering secured areas to determine their business, directing and rerouting individuals as necessary. Transport or escort prisoners and defendants en route to courtrooms, prisons or jails, attorneys' offices, or medical facilities. Locate and confiscate real or personal property, as directed by court order. Manage jail operations, and tend to jail inmates.

Related Knowledge/Courses: Public Safety and Security; Law and Government; Telecommunications; Psychology; Therapy and Counseling; Philosophy and Theology.

Personality Types: Enterprising-Realistic-Social.

Skills: Negotiation; Social Perceptiveness; Persuasion; Service Orientation; Management of Personnel Resources; Critical Thinking; Time Management; Reading Comprehension.

Work Environment: More often outdoors than indoors; sitting; using hands; repetitive motions; noise; very hot or cold; bright or inadequate lighting; contaminants; cramped work space; exposed to disease or infections; hazardous equipment.

Postal Service Mail Carriers

- ❋ Average Annual Earnings (All): $55,160
- ❋ Average Annual Earnings (Recent Veterans): $50,200
- ❋ Earnings Growth Potential: Low (26.6%)
- ❋ Growth: −12.0%
- ❋ Annual Job Openings: 10,340
- ❋ Veteran Employment by Sector: For-Profit, 0.0%; Nonprofit, 0.0%; Government, 100.0%; Self-Employed, 0.0%.

Considerations for Job Outlook: Very strong competition is expected for all jobs, as the number of applicants typically is greater than the number of available positions.

Sort mail for delivery. Deliver mail on established route by vehicle or on foot. Obtain signed receipts for registered, certified, and insured mail; collect associated charges; and complete any necessary paperwork. Sort mail for delivery, arranging it in delivery sequence. Deliver mail to residences and business establishments along specified routes by walking and/or driving, using a combination of satchels, carts, cars, and small trucks. Return to the post office with mail collected from homes, businesses, and public mailboxes. Turn in money and receipts collected along mail routes. Sign for cash-on-delivery and registered mail before leaving post offices. Record address changes, and redirect mail for those addresses. Hold mail for customers who are away from delivery locations. Bundle mail in preparation for delivery or transportation to relay boxes. Leave notices telling patrons where to collect mail that could not be delivered. Meet schedules for the collection and return of mail. Return incorrectly addressed mail to senders. Maintain accurate records of deliveries. Answer customers' questions about postal services and regulations. Provide customers with change-of-address cards and other forms. Report any unusual circumstances concerning mail delivery, including the condition of street letter boxes. Register, certify, and insure parcels and letters. Travel to post offices to pick up the mail for routes and/or pick up mail from postal relay boxes. Enter change of address orders into computers that process forwarding address stickers.

Related Military Specializations: None. **Average Educational Level of Vets:** High school diploma or equivalent. **Usual Educational Requirement:** High school diploma or equivalent. **Relevant Educational Program:** General Office Occupations and Clerical Services. **Related Knowledge/Courses:** Transportation; Public

Safety and Security. **Work Experience Needed:** None. **On-the-Job Training Needed:** Short-term on-the-job training. **Certification/Licensure:** None.

Personality Types: Conventional-Realistic. **Key Career Cluster:** 07 Government and Public Administration. **Key Career Pathway:** 7.7 Public Management and Administration. **Top Industries for Vets:** Postal Service.

Skills: Operation and Control.

Work Environment: More often outdoors than indoors; standing; walking and running; using hands; bending or twisting the body; repetitive motions; noise; very hot or cold; bright or inadequate lighting; contaminants; minor burns, cuts, bites, or stings.

Private Detectives and Investigators

- Average Annual Earnings (All): $43,710
- Average Annual Earnings (Recent Veterans): $64,390
- Earnings Growth Potential: High (40.7%)
- Growth: 20.5%
- Annual Job Openings: 1,490
- Veteran Employment by Sector: For-Profit, 39.3%; Nonprofit, 1.1%; Government, 56.9%; Self-Employed, 2.8%.

Considerations for Job Outlook: Competition is expected for most jobs, because private detective and investigator careers attract many qualified people, including relatively young retirees from law enforcement or military careers. The best opportunities for job seekers will be in entry-level jobs in detective agencies. People with related work experience, as well as those with interviewing and computer skills, may find more opportunities.

Gather, analyze, compile, and report information regarding individuals or organizations to clients, or detect occurrences of unlawful acts or infractions of rules in private establishment. Provide testimony as witnesses in court. Secure deceased bodies, and obtain evidence from them, preventing bystanders from tampering with bodies prior to medical examiners' arrival. Examine crime scenes to obtain clues and evidence such as loose hairs, fibers, clothing, or weapons. Obtain evidence from suspects. Record progress of investigations, maintain informational files on suspects, and submit reports to commanding officers or magistrates to authorize warrants. Check victims for signs of life such as breathing and pulse. Prepare charges or responses to charges, or information for court cases, according to formalized procedures. Obtain facts or statements from complainants, witnesses, and accused persons, and record interviews, using recording devices. Prepare and serve search and arrest warrants. Note, mark, and photograph locations of objects found such as footprints, tire tracks, bullets, and bloodstains, and take measurements of each scene. Question individuals or observe persons and establishments to confirm information given to patrol officers. Preserve, process, and analyze items of evidence obtained from crime scenes and suspects, placing them in proper containers and destroying evidence no longer needed. Secure persons at scenes, keeping witnesses from conversing or leaving scenes before investigators arrive. Take photographs from all angles of relevant parts of crime scenes, including entrance and exit routes and streets and intersections.

Related Military Specializations: CID Special Agent; Forensic Psycho-physiologist (Polygraph Examiner); GWOT IA/ILO Detainee Operations

Interrogator; Investigator; Law Enforcement and Security Officer; Military Investigator; Military Police Investigator (MPI); Special Investigations Craftsman; Special Investigations Helper; Special Investigations Journeyman. **Average Educational Level of Vets:** Bachelor's degree. **Usual Educational Requirement:** Some college, no degree. **Relevant Educational Programs:** Criminal Justice/Police Science; Cultural/Archaeological Resources Protection; Cyber/Computer Forensics and Counterterrorism; Financial Forensics and Fraud Investigation; Law Enforcement Record-Keeping and Evidence Management; Maritime Law Enforcement; Protective Services Operations. **Related Knowledge/Courses:** Clerical Practices; Law and Government; Customer and Personal Service; Computers and Electronics; Sales and Marketing; Mathematics. **Work Experience Needed:** 1 to 5 years. **On-the-Job Training Needed:** Moderate-term on-the-job training. **Certification/Licensure:** Licensure.

Personality Types: Enterprising-Conventional. **Key Career Cluster:** 12 Law, Public Safety, Corrections, and Security. **Key Career Pathway:** 12.3 Security and Protective Services. **Top Industries for Vets:** National Security and International Affairs; Investigation and Security Services; Management, Scientific and Technical Consulting Services; Justice, Public Order, and Safety Activities; Architectural, Engineering, and Related Services.

Skills: Service Orientation; Active Listening; Negotiation; Writing; Speaking; Critical Thinking; Persuasion; Social Perceptiveness.

Work Environment: More often outdoors than indoors; sitting; using hands; repetitive motions; noise; very hot or cold; bright or inadequate lighting; contaminants.

Probation Officers and Correctional Treatment Specialists

- ❋ Average Annual Earnings (All): $47,840
- ❋ Average Annual Earnings (Recent Veterans): $37,110
- ❋ Earnings Growth Potential: Low (34.8%)
- ❋ Growth: 18.4%
- ❋ Annual Job Openings: 3,730
- ❋ Veteran Employment by Sector: For-Profit, 5.0%; Nonprofit, 18.3%; Government, 76.7%; Self-Employed, 0.0%.

Considerations for Job Outlook: In addition to openings resulting from growth, many openings will be created by the need to replace large numbers of these workers expected to retire in the coming years. This occupation is not attractive to some potential entrants because of relatively low earnings, heavy workloads, and high stress. For these reasons, job opportunities should be excellent for those who qualify.

Provide social services to assist in rehabilitation of law offenders in custody or on probation or parole. Prepare and maintain case folder for each assigned inmate or offender. Write reports describing offenders' progress. Inform offenders or inmates of requirements of conditional release, such as office visits, restitution payments, or educational and employment stipulations. Discuss with offenders how such issues as drug and alcohol abuse and anger management problems might have played roles in their criminal behavior. Gather information about offenders' backgrounds by talking to offenders, their families and friends, and other people who have relevant information. Develop rehabilitation

P

programs for assigned offenders or inmates, establishing rules of conduct, goals, and objectives. Develop liaisons and networks with other parole officers; community agencies; and staff in correctional institutions, psychiatric facilities, and after-care agencies to make plans for helping offenders with life adjustments. Arrange for medical, mental health, or substance abuse treatment services according to individual needs and court orders. Provide offenders or inmates with assistance in matters concerning detainers, sentences in other jurisdictions, writs, and applications for social assistance. Arrange for post-release services such as employment, housing, counseling, education, and social activities. Recommend remedial action or initiate court action when terms of probation or parole are not complied with.

Related Military Specialization: Correctional Counselor. **Average Educational Level of Vets:** Bachelor's degree. **Usual Educational Requirement:** Bachelor's degree. **Relevant Educational Program:** Social Work. **Related Knowledge/Courses:** Therapy and Counseling; Sociology and Anthropology; Psychology; Law and Government; Public Safety and Security; Philosophy and Theology. **Work Experience Needed:** None. **On-the-Job Training Needed:** Short-term on-the-job training. **Certification/Licensure:** None.

Personality Types: Social-Enterprising-Conventional. **Key Career Cluster:** 12 Law, Public Safety, Corrections, and Security. **Key Career Pathway:** 12.1 Correction Services. **Top Industries for Vets:** Justice, Public Order, and Safety Activities; Administration of Human Resource Programs; National Security and International Affairs; Civic, Social, Advocacy Organizations, and Grantmaking and Giving Services; Individual and Family Services.

Skills: Social Perceptiveness; Service Orientation; Persuasion; Negotiation; Monitoring; Active Listening; Speaking; Reading Comprehension.

Work Environment: Indoors; sitting; exposed to disease or infections.

Production, Planning, and Expediting Clerks

- ❋ Average Annual Earnings (All): $43,100
- ❋ Average Annual Earnings (Recent Veterans): $44,530
- ❋ Earnings Growth Potential: High (40.6%)
- ❋ Growth: 6.6%
- ❋ Annual Job Openings: 8,880
- ❋ Veteran Employment by Sector: For-Profit, 49.4%; Nonprofit, 2.0%; Government, 48.6%; Self-Employed, 0.0%.

Considerations for Job Outlook: There should be favorable job opportunities for material recording clerks because of the need to replace workers who leave the occupation. The increase in RFID and other sensors will enable clerks who are more comfortable with computers to have better job prospects.

Coordinate and expedite the flow of work and materials within or between departments of an establishment according to production schedule. Examine documents, materials, and products, and monitor work processes to assess completeness, accuracy, and conformance to standards and specifications. Review documents such as production schedules, work orders, and staffing tables to determine personnel and materials requirements, and material priorities. Revise production schedules when required due to design changes, labor or material shortages, backlogs, or other interruptions, collaborating with management, marketing, sales, production, and engineering. Confer with department supervisors and other personnel to assess progress and discuss needed changes. Confer with establishment personnel, vendors, and customers to coordinate production and shipping activities, and to resolve complaints or eliminate delays. Record production data, including volume produced, consumption of raw materials, and quality control measures. Requisition and maintain inventories of materials and supplies necessary to meet production demands. Calculate figures such as required amounts of labor and materials, manufacturing costs, and wages, using pricing schedules, adding machines, calculators, or computers. Distribute production schedules and work orders to departments. Compile information such as production rates and progress, materials inventories, materials used, and customer information, so that status reports can be completed.

Related Military Specializations: 3-M System Coordinator; Aircraft Maintenance Administration Specialist; Aircraft Maintenance Data Analyst/Administrator; Aviation Maintenance Administrationman; Aviation Maintenance Controller/Production Controller; Aviation Quality Assurance Representative (QAR)/Inspector; Basic Logistics Marine; Communications—Computer Systems Operations Craftsman; Logistics/Embarkation Specialist; Maintenance Management Analysis Apprentice; Maintenance Management Analysis Helper; others. **Average Educational Level of Vets:** One or more years of college, no degree. **Usual Educational Requirement:** High school diploma or equivalent. **Relevant Educational Program:** Parts, Warehousing, and Inventory Management Operations. **Related Knowledge/Courses:** Production and Processing; Clerical Practices; Computers and Electronics; Administration and Management;

Mathematics; Customer and Personal Service. **Work Experience Needed:** None. **On-the-Job Training Needed:** Moderate-term on-the-job training. **Certification/Licensure:** None.

Personality Types: Conventional-Enterprising. **Key Career Cluster:** 13 Manufacturing. **Key Career Pathway:** 13.3 Maintenance, Installation and Repair. **Top Industries for Vets:** National Security and International Affairs; Justice, Public Order, and Safety Activities; Architectural, Engineering, and Related Services; Aircraft and Parts; Machinery, Not Elsewhere Classified.

Skills: Management of Material Resources; Negotiation; Management of Financial Resources; Reading Comprehension; Persuasion; Time Management; Speaking.

Work Environment: Indoors; sitting; noise; contaminants.

Property, Real Estate, and Community Association Managers

* Average Annual Earnings (All): $52,510
* Average Annual Earnings (Recent Veterans): $38,420
* Earnings Growth Potential: High (50.8%)
* Growth: 6.0%
* Annual Job Openings: 8,230
* Veteran Employment by Sector: For-Profit, 62.7%; Nonprofit, 3.5%; Government, 14.7%; Self-Employed, 19.0%.

Considerations for Job Outlook: Job opportunities should be best for those with a college degree in business administration, real estate, or a related field and for those who get a professional certification. Because of the projected increase in the elderly population, particularly good job opportunities are expected for those with experience managing housing for older people and with experience managing health-care facilities.

Plan, direct, or coordinate the selling, buying, leasing, or governance activities of commercial, industrial, or residential real estate properties. Meet with prospective tenants to show properties, explain terms of occupancy, and provide information about local areas. Direct collection of monthly assessments; rental fees; and deposits and payment of insurance premiums, mortgage, taxes, and incurred operating expenses. Inspect grounds, facilities, and equipment routinely to determine necessity of repairs or maintenance. Investigate complaints, disturbances, and violations, and resolve problems, following management rules and regulations. Manage and oversee operations, maintenance, administration, and improvement of commercial, industrial, or residential properties. Plan, schedule, and coordinate general maintenance, major repairs, and remodeling or construction projects for commercial or residential properties. Negotiate the sale, lease, or development of property, and complete or review appropriate documents and forms. Maintain records of sales, rental or usage activity, special permits issued, maintenance and operating costs, or property availability. Determine and certify the eligibility of prospective tenants, following government regulations. Prepare detailed budgets and financial reports for properties. Direct and coordinate the activities of staff and contract personnel, and evaluate their performance. Maintain contact with insurance carriers, fire and police departments, and other agencies to ensure protection and compliance with codes and regulations.

Related Military Specializations: None. **Average Educational Level of Vets:** Bachelor's degree. **Usual Educational Requirement:** High school diploma or equivalent. **Relevant**

Educational Programs: Real Estate; Real Estate Development. **Related Knowledge/ Courses:** Sales and Marketing; Clerical Practices; Economics and Accounting; Building and Construction; Administration and Management; Customer and Personal Service. **Work Experience Needed:** 1 to 5 years. **On-the-Job Training Needed:** None. **Certification/ Licensure:** Licensure for some specializations; voluntary certification by association.

Personality Types: Enterprising-Conventional. **Key Career Cluster:** 10 Human Services. **Key Career Pathway:** 10.5 Consumer Services. **Top Industries for Vets:** Real Estate; National Security and International Affairs; Warehousing and Storage; Management, Scientific and Technical Consulting Services; Support Activities For Mining.

Skills: Management of Financial Resources; Negotiation; Management of Personnel Resources; Operations Analysis; Persuasion; Management of Material Resources; Service Orientation; Writing.

Work Environment: More often indoors than outdoors; sitting.

Public Relations Specialists

- ❋ Average Annual Earnings (All): $53,190
- ❋ Average Annual Earnings (Recent Veterans): $43,650
- ❋ Earnings Growth Potential: High (42.0%)
- ❋ Growth: 22.5%
- ❋ Annual Job Openings: 12,720
- ❋ Veteran Employment by Sector: For-Profit, 31.5%; Nonprofit, 19.7%; Government, 47.9%; Self-Employed, 0.9%.

Considerations for Job Outlook: In addition to job growth for other reasons, opportunities should come from the need to replace public relations managers and specialists who retire or leave the occupation. Competition for entry-level jobs will likely be strong.

Engage in promoting or creating an intended public image for individuals, groups, or organizations. Prepare or edit organizational publications for internal and external audiences, including employee newsletters and stockholders' reports. Respond to requests for information from the media, or designate another appropriate spokesperson or information source. Establish and maintain cooperative relationships with representatives of community, consumer, employee, and public interest groups. Plan and direct development and communication of informational programs to maintain favorable public and stockholder perceptions of an organization's accomplishments and agenda. Confer with production and support personnel to produce or coordinate production of advertisements and promotions. Arrange public appearances, lectures, contests, or exhibits for clients to increase product and service awareness and to promote goodwill. Study the objectives, promotional policies, and needs of organizations to develop public relations strategies that will influence public opinion or promote ideas, products, and services. Consult with advertising agencies or staff to arrange promotional campaigns in all types of media for products, organizations, or individuals. Confer with other managers to identify trends and key group interests and concerns or to provide advice on business decisions. Coach client representatives in effective communication with the public and with employees. Prepare and deliver speeches to further public relations objectives.

Related Military Specializations: Basic Combat Correspondent; Broadcast Journalist; Broadcaster; Chief Public Affairs NCO; Combat Correspondent; Mass Communications; Mass Communications Specialist; Public Affairs Apprentice; Public Affairs Craftsman; Public Affairs Helper; Public Affairs Journeyman; Public Affairs Manager; Public Affairs Officer (Enlisted); Public Affairs Specialist; Public Affairs Superintendent; Public Affairs Supervisor. **Average Educational Level of Vets:** Bachelor's degree. **Usual Educational Requirement:** Bachelor's degree. **Relevant Educational Programs:** Communication, General; Family and Consumer Sciences/Human Sciences Communication; Health Communication; International and Intercultural Communication; Political Communication; Public Relations, Advertising, and Applied Communication; Public Relations/Image Management; Speech Communication and Rhetoric; Sports Communication. **Related Knowledge/ Courses:** Communications and Media; Sales and Marketing; English Language; Geography; Computers and Electronics; Customer and Personal Service. **Work Experience Needed:** None. **On-the-Job Training Needed:** Moderate-term on-the-job training. **Certification/ Licensure:** Voluntary certification by association.

Personality Types: Enterprising-Artistic-Social. **Key Career Cluster:** 04 Business, Management, and Administration. **Key Career Pathway:** 4.6 Administrative and Information Support. **Top Industries for Vets:** National Security and International Affairs; Independent Artists, Performing Arts, Spectator Sports and Related Industries; Management, Scientific and Technical Consulting Services; Advertising and Related Services; Computer Systems Design and Related Services.

Skills: Operations Analysis; Social Perceptiveness; Negotiation; Writing; Systems Evaluation; Speaking; Persuasion; Time Management.

Work Environment: Indoors; sitting.

Purchasing Agents, Except Wholesale, Retail, and Farm Products

❋ Average Annual Earnings (All): $57,580

❋ Average Annual Earnings (Recent Veterans): $54,570

❋ Earnings Growth Potential: Medium (38.1%)

❋ Growth: 5.3%

❋ Annual Job Openings: 9,120

❋ Veteran Employment by Sector: For-Profit, 51.2%; Nonprofit, 2.3%; Government, 46.0%; Self-Employed, 0.6%.

Considerations for Job Outlook: Growth will be driven largely by the performance of the wholesale and retail industries. Continued employment decreases in manufacturing, as well as decreases in federal government, which includes defense purchasing, are expected. However, growth is expected for this occupation in firms that provide health-care and computer systems design and related services.

Purchase machinery, equipment, tools, parts, supplies, or services necessary for the operation of an establishment. Purchase the highest-quality merchandise at the lowest possible price and in correct amounts. Prepare purchase orders, solicit bid proposals, and review requisitions for goods and services. Research and evaluate suppliers based on price, quality, selection, service, support, availability, reliability, production and distribution capabilities, and the supplier's reputation and history. Analyze price proposals, financial reports, and other data and information to determine reasonable prices. Monitor and follow applicable laws and regulations. Negotiate,

or renegotiate, and administer contracts with suppliers, vendors, and other representatives. Monitor shipments to ensure that goods come in on time, and trace shipments and follow up on undelivered goods in the event of problems. Confer with staff, users, and vendors to discuss defective or unacceptable goods or services and determine corrective action. Evaluate and monitor contract performance to ensure compliance with contractual obligations and to determine need for changes. Maintain and review computerized or manual records of items purchased, costs, delivery, product performance, and inventories. Review catalogs, industry periodicals, directories, trade journals, and Internet sites and consult with other department personnel to locate necessary goods and services. Study sales records and inventory levels of current stock to develop strategic purchasing programs that facilitate employee access to supplies.

Related Military Specializations: Acquisition Specialist; Advanced Contingency Contract Specialist; Basic Contingency Contract Specialist; Contracting Craftsman; Contracting Manager; Contracting Superintendent; Intermediate Contingency Contract Specialist. **Average Educational Level of Vets:** One or more years of college, no degree. **Usual Educational Requirement:** High school diploma or equivalent. **Relevant Educational Programs:** General Merchandising, Sales, and Related Marketing Operations, Other; Sales, Distribution, and Marketing Operations, General. **Related Knowledge/Courses:** Economics and Accounting; Transportation; Law and Government; Production and Processing; Clerical Practices; Administration and Management. **Work Experience Needed:** None. **On-the-Job Training Needed:** Long-term on-the-job training. **Certification/Licensure:** Voluntary certification by association.

Personality Types: Conventional-Enterprising.
Key Career Cluster: 13 Manufacturing.
Key Career Pathway: 13.1 Production. **Top Industries for Vets:** National Security and International Affairs; Hospitals; Computer Systems Design and Related Services; Construction; Architectural, Engineering, and Related Services.

Skills: Management of Financial Resources; Management of Material Resources; Negotiation; Persuasion; Active Learning; Operations Analysis; Judgment and Decision Making; Complex Problem Solving.

Work Environment: Sitting.

Radio, Cellular, and Tower Equipment Installers and Repairers

- ❀ Average Annual Earnings (All): $42,160

- ❀ Average Annual Earnings (Recent Veterans): $43,650

- ❀ Earnings Growth Potential: Medium (37.9%)

- ❀ Growth: 29.4%

- ❀ Annual Job Openings: 450

- ❀ Veteran Employment by Sector: For-Profit, 54.3%; Nonprofit, 1.1%; Government, 44.4%; Self-Employed, 0.1%.

Considerations for Job Outlook: Telecommunications companies providing many new services, such as faster Internet connections and video on demand, are expected to result in employment growth for these workers. But better equipment will require less maintenance work, slowing employment growth.

Repair, install, or maintain mobile or stationary radio transmitting, broadcasting, and receiving equipment, and two-way radio communications systems. Assemble or erect communications towers, using construction or rigging equipment. Bolt equipment into place, using hand or power tools. Check antenna positioning to ensure specified azimuths or mechanical tilts and adjust as necessary. Climb communication towers to install, replace, or repair antennas or auxiliary equipment used to transmit and receive radio waves. Inspect completed work to ensure all hardware is tight, antennas are level, hangers are properly fastened, proper support is in place, or adequate weather proofing has been installed. Install all necessary transmission equipment components, including antennas or antenna mounts, surge arrestors, transmission lines, connectors, or tower-mounted amplifiers (TMAs). Install or repair tower lighting components, including strobes, beacons, or lighting controllers. Install, connect, or test underground or aboveground grounding systems. Lift equipment into position, using cranes and rigging tools or equipment such as gin poles. Perform maintenance or repair work on existing tower equipment, using hand or power tools. Read work orders, blueprints, plans, datasheets, or site drawings to determine work to be done. Replace existing antennas with new antennas as directed. Run appropriate power, ground, or coaxial cables. Test operation of tower transmission components, using sweep testing tools or software. Climb towers to access components, using safety equipment, such as full-body harnesses. Complete reports related to project status, progress, or other work details, using computer software. Locate tower sites where work is to be performed, using mapping software. Take site survey photos or photos of work performed, using digital cameras. Transport equipment to work sites, using utility trucks and equipment trailers.

R

Related Military Specializations: Aircraft Command Control Communications and Navigation Systems Journeyman; Aircraft Communication and Navigation Systems Journeyman; AN/SRC-55(V) HYDRA Technician; AN/SSC-12 Shipboard Air Traffic Control Communications (SATCC) Technician; AN/TRC-170 Technician; AN/TSC-120 Radio Technician; AN/WSC-6(V)5 Super High Frequency (SHF) Satellite Communications (SATCOM) Maintenance; AN/WSC-6(V)7 Combatant Super High Frequency (SHF) Satellite Communications (SATCOM) Maintenance; others. **Average Educational Level of Vets:** High school diploma or equivalent. **Usual Educational Requirement:** Associate degree. **Relevant Educational Program:** Communications Systems Installation and Repair Technology. **Work Experience Needed:** None. **On-the-Job Training Needed:** Moderate-term on-the-job training. **Certification/Licensure:** Voluntary certification by association.

Key Career Cluster: 03 Arts, Audiovisual Technology, and Communications. **Key Career Pathway:** 3.6 Telecommunications Technologies. **Top Industries for Vets:** National Security and International Affairs; Wired Telecommunications Carriers; Other Telecommunication Services; Construction; Radio, TV, and Computer Stores.

Skills: Repairing; Equipment Maintenance; Installation; Troubleshooting; Equipment Selection; Quality Control Analysis; Operation and Control; Operation Monitoring.

Work Environment: Indoors; sitting; using hands; noise.

Radiologic Technologists

* Average Annual Earnings (All): $55,120
* Average Annual Earnings (Recent Veterans): $43,650
* Earnings Growth Potential: Low (32.2%)
* Growth: 27.8%
* Annual Job Openings: 9,510
* Veteran Employment by Sector: For-Profit, 48.2%; Nonprofit, 18.5%; Government, 32.5%; Self-Employed, 0.8%.

Considerations for Job Outlook: As the population grows and ages, demand for diagnostic imaging is expected to increase. Job seekers who have knowledge of multiple technologies should have the best prospects.

Take X-rays and CAT scans or administer nonradioactive materials into patient's blood stream for diagnostic purposes. Review and evaluate developed X-rays, videotape, or computer-generated information to determine whether images are satisfactory for diagnostic purposes. Use radiation safety measures and protection devices to comply with government regulations and to ensure safety of patients and staff. Explain procedures and observe patients to ensure safety and comfort during scan. Operate or oversee operation of radiologic and magnetic imaging equipment to produce images of the body for diagnostic purposes. Position and immobilize patient on examining table. Position imaging equipment, and adjust controls to set exposure time and distance, according to specification of examination. Key commands and data into computer to document and specify scan sequences, adjust transmitters and receivers, or photograph certain images. Monitor video display of area being scanned, and adjust density or contrast to improve picture quality. Monitor patients' conditions and reactions, reporting abnormal signs to physician. Set up examination rooms, ensuring that all necessary equipment is ready. Prepare and administer oral or injected contrast media to patients. Take thorough and accurate patient medical histories. Remove and process film. Record, process, and maintain patient data and treatment records, and prepare reports. Coordinate work with clerical personnel or other technologists. Demonstrate new equipment, procedures, and techniques to staff members, and provide technical assistance.

Related Military Specializations: Advanced X-Ray Technician; Basic X-Ray Technician; Diagnostic Imaging Apprentice; Diagnostic Imaging Apprentice, Nuclear Medicine; Diagnostic Imaging Craftsman; Diagnostic Imaging Craftsman, Nuclear Medicine; Diagnostic Imaging Helper; Diagnostic Imaging Helper, Nuclear Medicine; Diagnostic Imaging Journeyman; Diagnostic Imaging Journeyman, Nuclear Medicine; Diagnostic Imaging Manager; Diagnostic Imaging Superintendent; Radiology Specialist. **Average Educational Level of Vets:** Associate degree. **Usual Educational Requirement:** Associate degree. **Relevant Educational Programs:** Mammography Technician/Technology; Medical Radiologic Technology/Science—Radiation Therapist; Radiologic Technology/Science—Radiographer. **Related Knowledge/Courses:** Medicine and Dentistry; Physics; Customer and Personal Service; Biology; Psychology; Chemistry. **Work Experience Needed:** None. **On-the-Job Training Needed:** None. **Certification/Licensure:** Licensure or certification in most states.

Personality Types: Realistic-Social. **Key Career Cluster:** 08 Health Science. **Key Career Pathway:** 8.2 Diagnostics Services. **Top Industries for Vets:** Hospitals; National Security and International Affairs; Other Health Care Services; Offices of Physicians; Outpatient Care Centers.

Skills: Science; Operation and Control; Service Orientation; Quality Control Analysis; Operation Monitoring; Programming; Instructing; Social Perceptiveness.

Work Environment: Indoors; standing; walking and running; using hands; bending or twisting the body; repetitive motions; contaminants; exposed to radiation; exposed to disease or infections.

Rail Car Repairers

- ✳ Average Annual Earnings (All): $47,740
- ✳ Average Annual Earnings (Recent Veterans): $40,380
- ✳ Earnings Growth Potential: High (41.2%)
- ✳ Growth: 16.9%
- ✳ Annual Job Openings: 930
- ✳ Veteran Employment by Sector: For-Profit, 68.6%; Nonprofit, 1.8%; Government, 28.3%; Self-Employed, 1.3%.

Considerations for Job Outlook: Most job opportunities will come from the need to replace workers who retire or leave the occupation. Those with certificates from vocational schools or 2-year degrees from community colleges should have very good job opportunities as employers strongly prefer these candidates. Those without formal training will have difficulty finding jobs. The majority of job openings are expected to be in sectors that sell, rent, or lease heavy vehicles and mobile equipment, where a large proportion of service technicians are employed. The construction and mining industries, which use

R

large numbers of heavy equipment, are sensitive to fluctuations in the economy. As a result, job opportunities for service technicians in these sectors will vary with overall economic conditions. Job opportunities for farm equipment mechanics are seasonal and are generally best during warmer months.

Diagnose, adjust, repair, or overhaul railroad rolling stock, mine cars, or mass transit rail cars. Repair or replace defective or worn parts such as bearings, pistons, and gears, using hand tools, torque wrenches, power tools, and welding equipment. Test units for operability before and after repairs. Record conditions of cars, and repair and maintenance work performed or to be performed. Remove locomotives, car mechanical units, or other components, using pneumatic hoists and jacks, pinch bars, hand tools, and cutting torches. Inspect components such as bearings, seals, gaskets, wheels, and coupler assemblies to determine if repairs are needed. Inspect the interior and exterior of rail cars coming into rail yards in order to identify defects and to determine the extent of wear and damage. Adjust repaired or replaced units as needed to ensure proper operation. Perform scheduled maintenance, and clean units and components. Repair, fabricate, and install steel or wood fittings, using blueprints, shop sketches, and instruction manuals. Repair and maintain electrical and electronic controls for propulsion and braking systems. Disassemble units such as water pumps, control valves, and compressors so that repairs can be made. Measure diameters of axle wheel seats, using micrometers, and mark dimensions on axles so that wheels can be bored to specified dimensions. Align car sides for installation of car ends and crossties, using width gauges, turnbuckles, and wrenches. Replace defective wiring and insulation, and tighten electrical connections, using hand tools. Test electrical systems of cars by operating systems and using testing equipment such as ammeters. Install and repair interior flooring, fixtures, walls, plumbing, steps, and platforms. Examine car roofs for wear and damage, and repair defective sections, using roofing material, cement, nails, and waterproof paint. Paint car exteriors, interiors, and fixtures. Repair car upholstery. Repair window sash frames, attach weather stripping and channels to frames, and replace window glass, using hand tools.

Related Military Specializations: Railway Car Repairer (RC); Railway Equipment Repairer (RC). **Average Educational Level of Vets:** High school diploma or equivalent. **Usual Educational Requirement:** High school diploma or equivalent. **Relevant Educational Program:** Heavy Equipment Maintenance Technology/Technician. **Related Knowledge/Courses:** Mechanical Devices; Public Safety and Security; Production and Processing. **Work Experience Needed:** None. **On-the-Job Training Needed:** Long-term on-the-job training. **Certification/Licensure:** Voluntary certification by manufacturer.

Personality Types: Realistic-Conventional-Investigative. **Key Career Cluster:** 16 Transportation, Distribution, and Logistics. **Key Career Pathway:** 16.4 Facility and Mobile Equipment Maintenance. **Top Industries for Vets:** Construction; National Security and International Affairs; Machinery, Equipment, and Supplies Merchant Wholesalers; Rail Transportation; Machinery, Not Elsewhere Classified.

Skills: Repairing; Equipment Maintenance; Troubleshooting; Installation; Operation and Control; Equipment Selection; Quality Control Analysis; Operation Monitoring.

Work Environment: Outdoors; standing; climbing; walking and running; kneeling, crouching, stooping, or crawling; using hands; bending or twisting the body; repetitive motions; noise; very hot or cold; bright or inadequate lighting; contaminants; cramped work space; high places;

hazardous equipment; minor burns, cuts, bites, or stings.

Real Estate Brokers

- ❀ Average Annual Earnings (All): $59,340
- ❀ Average Annual Earnings (Recent Veterans): $27,280
- ❀ Earnings Growth Potential: Very high (55.9%)
- ❀ Growth: 7.6%
- ❀ Annual Job Openings: 2,970
- ❀ Veteran Employment by Sector: For-Profit, 48.5%; Nonprofit, 1.1%; Government, 1.7%; Self-Employed, 48.7%.

Considerations for Job Outlook: Although the real estate market depends on economic conditions, it is relatively easy to enter the occupation. In times of economic growth, brokers and sales agents will have good job opportunities. In an economic downturn, there tend to be fewer job opportunities, and brokers and agents often have a lower income due to fewer sales and purchases.

Operate real estate office, or work for commercial real estate firm, overseeing real estate transactions. Sell, for a fee, real estate owned by others. Obtain agreements from property owners to place properties for sale with real estate firms. Monitor fulfillment of purchase contract terms to ensure that they are handled in a timely manner. Compare a property with similar properties that have recently sold, in order to determine its competitive market price. Act as an intermediary in negotiations between buyers and sellers over property prices and settlement details, and during the closing of sales. Generate lists of properties for sale, their locations and descriptions, and available financing options, using computers.

Maintain knowledge of real estate law, local economies, fair housing laws, and types of available mortgages, financing options, and government programs. Check work completed by loan officers, attorneys, and other professionals to ensure that it is performed properly. Arrange for financing of property purchases. Appraise property values, assessing income potential when relevant. Maintain awareness of current income tax regulations, local zoning, building and tax laws, and growth possibilities of the area where a property is located. Manage and operate real estate offices, handling associated business details. Supervise agents who handle real estate transactions. Rent properties or manage rental properties. Arrange for title searches of properties being sold. Give buyers virtual tours of properties in which they are interested, using computers. Review property details to ensure that environmental regulations are met. Develop, sell, or lease property used for industry or manufacturing. Maintain working knowledge of various factors that determine a farm's capacity to produce, including agricultural variables and proximity to market centers and transportation facilities.

Related Military Specializations: None. **Average Educational Level of Vets:** One or more years of college, no degree. **Usual Educational Requirement:** High school diploma or equivalent. **Relevant Educational Programs:** Real Estate; Real Estate Development. **Related Knowledge/Courses:** Sales and Marketing; Building and Construction; Law and Government; Customer and Personal Service; Personnel and Human Resources; Economics and Accounting. **Work Experience Needed:** 1 to 5 years. **On-the-Job Training Needed:** None. **Certification/Licensure:** Licensure.

Personality Types: Enterprising-Conventional. **Key Career Cluster:** 14 Marketing, Sales, and Service. **Key Career Pathway:** 14.2 Professional Sales and Marketing. **Top Industries for**

R

Vets: Real Estate; Nondepository Credit and Related Activities; Construction; Securities, Commodities, Funds, Trusts, and Other Financial Investments; Petroleum Refining.

Skills: Negotiation; Persuasion; Judgment and Decision Making; Active Learning; Speaking; Management of Financial Resources; Service Orientation; Reading Comprehension.

Work Environment: More often indoors than outdoors; sitting.

Real Estate Sales Agents

- ✸ Average Annual Earnings (All): $39,070
- ✸ Average Annual Earnings (Recent Veterans): $27,280
- ✸ Earnings Growth Potential: High (48.3%)
- ✸ Growth: 12.2%
- ✸ Annual Job Openings: 12,760
- ✸ Veteran Employment by Sector: For-Profit, 48.5%; Nonprofit, 1.1%; Government, 1.7%; Self-Employed, 48.7%.

Considerations for Job Outlook: Although the real estate market depends on economic conditions, it is relatively easy to enter the occupation. In times of economic growth, brokers and sales agents will have good job opportunities. In an economic downturn, there tend to be fewer job opportunities, and brokers and agents often have a lower income due to fewer sales and purchases.

Rent, buy, or sell property for clients. Present purchase offers to sellers for consideration. Confer with escrow companies, lenders, home inspectors, and pest control operators to ensure that terms and conditions of purchase agreements are met before closing dates. Interview clients to determine what kinds of properties they are

seeking. Prepare documents such as representation contracts, purchase agreements, closing statements, deeds, and leases. Coordinate property closings, overseeing signing of documents and disbursement of funds. Act as an intermediary in negotiations between buyers and sellers, generally representing one or the other. Promote sales of properties through advertisements, open houses, and participation in multiple listing services. Compare a property with similar properties that have recently sold to determine its competitive market price. Coordinate appointments to show homes to prospective buyers. Generate lists of properties that are compatible with buyers' needs and financial resources. Display commercial, industrial, agricultural, and residential properties to clients, and explain their features. Arrange for title searches to determine whether clients have clear property titles. Review plans for new construction with clients, enumerating and recommending available options and features. Answer clients' questions regarding construction work, financing, maintenance, repairs, and appraisals.

Related Military Specializations: None. **Average Educational Level of Vets:** One or more years of college, no degree. **Usual Educational Requirement:** High school diploma or equivalent. **Relevant Educational Programs:** Real Estate; Real Estate Development. **Related Knowledge/ Courses:** Sales and Marketing; Customer and Personal Service; Law and Government; Building and Construction; Economics and Accounting; Computers and Electronics. **Work Experience Needed:** None. **On-the-Job Training Needed:** Long-term on-the-job training. **Certification/ Licensure:** Licensure.

Personality Types: Enterprising-Conventional. **Key Career Cluster:** 14 Marketing, Sales, and Service. **Key Career Pathway:** 14.2 Professional Sales and Marketing. **Top Industries for Vets:** Real Estate; Nondepository Credit and Related Activities; Construction; Securities,

Commodities, Funds, Trusts, and Other Financial Investments; Petroleum Refining.

Skills: Negotiation; Persuasion; Service Orientation; Systems Evaluation; Judgment and Decision Making; Mathematics; Speaking; Coordination.

Work Environment: More often indoors than outdoors; sitting.

Receptionists and Information Clerks

- Average Annual Earnings (All): $25,690
- Average Annual Earnings (Recent Veterans): $18,330
- Earnings Growth Potential: Low (30.3%)
- Growth: 23.7%
- Annual Job Openings: 56,560
- Veteran Employment by Sector: For-Profit, 67.9%; Nonprofit, 7.5%; Government, 24.4%; Self-Employed, 0.3%.

Considerations for Job Outlook: Job opportunities are expected to be very good. Many job openings will arise from the need to replace those who transfer to other occupations. Those with related work experience and good computer skills should have the best job opportunities.

Answer inquiries and provide information to the general public, customers, visitors, and other interested parties. Operate telephone switchboard to answer, screen, and forward calls, providing information, taking messages, and scheduling appointments. Receive payments, and record receipts for services. Perform administrative support tasks such as proofreading, transcribing handwritten information, and operating calculators or computers to work with pay records, invoices, balance sheets, and other documents. Greet persons entering establishment, determine nature and purpose of visit, and direct or escort them to specific destinations. Hear and resolve complaints from customers and public. File and maintain records. Transmit information or documents to customers, using computer, mail, or facsimile machine. Schedule appointments, and maintain and update appointment calendars. Analyze data to determine answers to questions from customers or members of the public. Provide information about establishment such as location of departments or offices, employees within the organization, or services provided. Keep a current record of staff members' whereabouts and availability. Collect, sort, distribute, and prepare mail, messages, and courier deliveries. Calculate and quote rates for tours, stocks, insurance policies, or other products and services. Take orders for merchandise or materials, and send them to the proper departments to be filled. Process and prepare memos, correspondence, travel vouchers, or other documents.

Related Military Specializations: None. **Average Educational Level of Vets:** High school diploma or equivalent. **Usual Educational Requirement:** High school diploma or equivalent. **Relevant Educational Program:** Receptionist Training. **Related Knowledge/ Courses:** Clerical Practices; Customer and Personal Service; Computers and Electronics; Communications and Media. **Work Experience Needed:** None. **On-the-Job Training Needed:** Short-term on-the-job training. **Certification/ Licensure:** None.

Personality Types: Conventional-Enterprising-Social. **Key Career Cluster:** 04 Business, Management, and Administration. **Key Career Pathway:** 4.6 Administrative and Information Support. **Top Industries for Vets:** National Security and International Affairs; Outpatient Care Centers; Hospitals; Business Support

R

Services; Colleges and Universities, Including Junior Colleges.

Skills: Service Orientation; Speaking; Active Listening.

Work Environment: Indoors; sitting; using hands; repetitive motions.

Registered Nurses

* Average Annual Earnings (All): $65,950
* Average Annual Earnings (Recent Veterans): $62,210
* Earnings Growth Potential: Low (31.8%)
* Growth: 26.0%
* Annual Job Openings: 120,740
* Veteran Employment by Sector: For-Profit, 41.1%; Nonprofit, 18.6%; Government, 38.8%; Self-Employed, 1.4%.

Considerations for Job Outlook: Overall, job opportunities for registered nurses are expected to be excellent. Employers in some parts of the country and in some employment settings report difficulty in attracting and keeping enough registered nurses. Job opportunities should be excellent, even in hospitals, because of the relatively high turnover of hospital nurses. To attract and keep qualified nurses, hospitals may offer signing bonuses, family-friendly work schedules, or subsidized training. In physicians' offices and outpatient care centers, registered nurses may face greater competition for positions because these jobs generally offer regular working hours and provide more comfortable working conditions than hospitals. Generally, registered nurses with at least a bachelor's degree in nursing (BSN) will have better job prospects than those without one.

Assess patient health problems and needs, develop and implement nursing care plans, and maintain medical records. Maintain accurate, detailed reports and records. Monitor, record, and report symptoms and changes in patients' conditions. Record patients' medical information and vital signs. Modify patient treatment plans as indicated by patients' responses and conditions. Consult and coordinate with health-care team members to assess, plan, implement, and evaluate patient care plans. Order, interpret, and evaluate diagnostic tests to identify and assess patient's condition. Monitor all aspects of patient care, including diet and physical activity. Direct and supervise less-skilled nursing or health-care personnel, or supervise a particular unit. Prepare patients for, and assist with, examinations and treatments. Observe nurses and visit patients to ensure proper nursing care. Assess the needs of individuals, families, or communities, including assessment of individuals' home or work environments, to identify potential health or safety problems. Instruct individuals, families, and other groups on topics such as health education, disease prevention, and childbirth, and develop health improvement programs. Prepare rooms, sterile instruments, equipment, and supplies, and ensure that stock of supplies is maintained. Inform physician of patient's condition during anesthesia. Administer local, inhalation, intravenous, and other anesthetics. Provide health care, first aid, immunizations, and assistance in convalescence and rehabilitation in locations such as schools, hospitals, and industry.

Related Military Specialization: Practical Nurse. **Average Educational Level of Vets:** Bachelor's degree. **Usual Educational Requirement:** Associate degree. **Relevant Educational Programs:** Adult Health Nurse/Nursing; Clinical Nurse Leader; Clinical Nurse Specialist Training; Critical Care Nursing; Emergency Room/Trauma Nursing; Family

Practice Nurse/Nursing; Geriatric Nurse/Nursing; Maternal/Child Health and Neonatal Nurse/Nursing; Nursing Administration; Nursing Practice; Nursing Science; Occupational and Environmental Health Nursing; Palliative Care Nursing; Pediatric Nurse/Nursing; Perioperative/Operating Room and Surgical Nurse/Nursing; Psychiatric/Mental Health Nurse/Nursing; Public Health/Community Nurse/Nursing; Registered Nursing, Nursing Administration, Nursing Research; Registered Nursing/Registered Nurse Training; Women's Health Nurse/Nursing. **Related Knowledge/Courses:** Psychology; Medicine and Dentistry; Therapy and Counseling; Biology; Philosophy and Theology; Sociology and Anthropology. **Work Experience Needed:** None. **On-the-Job Training Needed:** None. **Certification/Licensure:** Licensure.

Personality Types: Social-Investigative-Conventional. **Key Career Cluster:** 08 Health Science. **Key Career Pathway:** 8.1 Therapeutic Services. **Top Industries for Vets:** Hospitals; National Security and International Affairs; Other Health Care Services; Outpatient Care Centers; Offices of Physicians.

Skills: Science; Social Perceptiveness; Quality Control Analysis; Service Orientation; Learning Strategies; Coordination; Management of Material Resources; Instructing.

Work Environment: Indoors; standing; walking and running; using hands; exposed to disease or infections.

Job Specialization: Acute Care Nurses

Provide advanced nursing care for patients with acute conditions such as heart attacks, respiratory distress syndrome, or shock. May care for pre- and postoperative patients or perform advanced, invasive diagnostic, or therapeutic procedures. Analyze the indications, contraindications, risk complications, and cost-benefit tradeoffs of therapeutic interventions. Diagnose acute or chronic conditions that could result in rapid physiological deterioration or life-threatening instability. Distinguish between normal and abnormal developmental and age-related physiological and behavioral changes in acute, critical, and chronic illness. Manage patients' pain relief and sedation by providing pharmacologic and nonpharmacologic interventions, monitoring patients' responses, and changing care plans accordingly. Interpret information obtained from electrocardiograms (EKGs) or radiographs (X-rays). Perform emergency medical procedures, such as basic cardiac life support (BLS), advanced cardiac life support (ACLS), and other condition-stabilizing interventions. Assess urgent and emergent health conditions using both physiologically and technologically derived data. Adjust settings on patients' assistive devices such as temporary pacemakers. Assess the impact of illnesses or injuries on patients' health, function, growth, development, nutrition, sleep, rest, quality of life, or family, social, and educational relationships. Collaborate with members of multidisciplinary health-care teams to plan, manage, or assess patient treatments. Discuss illnesses and treatments with patients and family members.

Related Knowledge/Courses: Therapy and Counseling; Medicine and Dentistry; Psychology; Biology; Sociology and Anthropology; Philosophy and Theology.

Personality Types: Social-Investigative-Realistic.

Skills: Science; Social Perceptiveness; Reading Comprehension; Operation Monitoring; Service Orientation; Systems Evaluation; Operation and Control; Active Learning.

Work Environment: Indoors; standing; walking and running; using hands; noise; contaminants; cramped work space; exposed to radiation; exposed to disease or infections.

R

Job Specialization: Advanced Practice Psychiatric Nurses

Provide advanced nursing care for patients with psychiatric disorders. May provide psychotherapy under the direction of a psychiatrist. Teach classes in mental health topics such as stress reduction. Participate in activities aimed at professional growth and development including conferences or continuing education activities. Direct or provide home health services. Monitor the use and status of medical and pharmaceutical supplies. Develop practice protocols for mental health problems based on review and evaluation of published research. Develop, implement, or evaluate programs such as outreach activities, community mental health programs, and crisis situation response activities. Treat patients for routine physical health problems. Write prescriptions for psychotropic medications as allowed by state regulations and collaborative practice agreements. Refer patients requiring more specialized or complex treatment to psychiatrists, primary care physicians, or other medical specialists. Provide routine physical health screenings to detect or monitor problems such as heart disease and diabetes. Participate in treatment team conferences regarding diagnosis or treatment of difficult cases. Interpret diagnostic or laboratory tests such as electrocardiograms (EKGs) and renal functioning tests. Evaluate patients' behavior to formulate diagnoses or assess treatments. Develop and implement treatment plans. Monitor patients' medication usage and results. Educate patients and family members about mental health and medical conditions, preventive health measures, medications, or treatment plans.

Related Knowledge/Courses: Therapy and Counseling; Psychology; Medicine and Dentistry; Sociology and Anthropology; Philosophy and Theology; Biology.

Personality Types: Social-Investigative.

Skills: Social Perceptiveness; Science; Negotiation; Service Orientation; Systems Evaluation; Persuasion; Learning Strategies; Reading Comprehension.

Work Environment: Indoors; sitting; exposed to disease or infections.

Job Specialization: Clinical Nurse Specialists

Plan, direct, or coordinate daily patient care activities in a clinical practice. Ensure adherence to established clinical policies, protocols, regulations, and standards. Coordinate or conduct educational programs or in-service training sessions on topics such as clinical procedures. Observe, interview, and assess patients to identify care needs. Evaluate the quality and effectiveness of nursing practice or organizational systems. Provide direct care by performing comprehensive health assessments, developing differential diagnoses, conducting specialized tests, or prescribing medications or treatments. Provide specialized direct and indirect care to inpatients and outpatients within a designated specialty such as obstetrics, neurology, oncology, or neonatal care. Maintain departmental policies, procedures, objectives, or infection control standards. Collaborate with other health-care professionals and service providers to ensure optimal patient care. Develop nursing service philosophies, goals, policies, priorities, or procedures. Develop, implement, or evaluate standards of nursing practice in specialty area such as pediatrics, acute care, and geriatrics. Develop or assist others in development of care and treatment plans. Make clinical recommendations to physicians, other health-care providers, insurance companies, patients, or health-care organizations. Plan, evaluate, or modify treatment programs based on information gathered by observing and interviewing patients, or by analyzing patient records. Present clients with information required to make informed health-care and treatment decisions.

Related Knowledge/Courses: Medicine and Dentistry; Biology; Therapy and Counseling; Psychology; Sociology and Anthropology; Philosophy and Theology.

Personality Types: Enterprising-Social-Conventional.

Skills: Science; Operations Analysis; Instructing; Service Orientation; Negotiation; Persuasion; Judgment and Decision Making; Active Learning.

Work Environment: Indoors; standing; using hands; noise; contaminants; exposed to radiation; exposed to disease or infections.

Job Specialization: Critical Care Nurses

Provide advanced nursing care for patients in critical or coronary care units. Identify patients' age-specific needs, and alter care plans as necessary to meet those needs. Provide post-mortem care. Evaluate patients' vital signs and laboratory data to determine emergency intervention needs. Perform approved therapeutic or diagnostic procedures based upon patients' clinical status. Administer blood and blood products, monitoring patients for signs and symptoms related to transfusion reactions. Administer medications intravenously, by injection, orally, through gastric tubes, or by other methods. Advocate for patients' and families' needs, or provide emotional support for patients and their families. Set up and monitor medical equipment and devices such as cardiac monitors, mechanical ventilators and alarms, oxygen delivery devices, transducers, and pressure lines. Monitor patients' fluid intake and output to detect emerging problems such as fluid and electrolyte imbalances. Monitor patients for changes in status and indications of conditions such as sepsis or shock, and institute appropriate interventions. Assess patients' pain levels and

sedation requirements. Assess patients' psychosocial status and needs including areas such as sleep patterns, anxiety, grief, anger, and support systems. Collaborate with other health-care professionals to develop and revise treatment plans based on identified needs and assessment data. Collect specimens for laboratory tests. Compile and analyze data obtained from monitoring or diagnostic tests.

Related Knowledge/Courses: Medicine and Dentistry; Biology; Psychology; Therapy and Counseling; Sociology and Anthropology; Philosophy and Theology.

Personality Types: Social-Investigative-Realistic.

Skills: Science; Social Perceptiveness; Operation and Control; Quality Control Analysis; Operation Monitoring; Service Orientation; Monitoring; Active Learning.

Work Environment: Indoors; standing; walking and running; using hands; bending or twisting the body; noise; contaminants; cramped work space; exposed to radiation; exposed to disease or infections.

Roofers

⊛ **Average Annual Earnings (All): $35,280**

⊛ **Average Annual Earnings (Recent Veterans): $19,640**

⊛ **Earnings Growth Potential: Medium (36.4%)**

⊛ **Growth: 17.8%**

⊛ **Annual Job Openings: 5,250**

⊛ **Veteran Employment by Sector: For-Profit, 86.8%; Nonprofit, 0.0%; Government, 3.7%; Self-Employed, 9.5%.**

R

Considerations for Job Outlook: Job opportunities for roofers will occur primarily because of the need to replace workers who leave the occupation. The proportion of roofers who leave the occupation each year is higher than in most construction trades—roofing work is hot, strenuous, and dirty, and a considerable number of workers treat roofing as a temporary job until they find other work. Some roofers leave the occupation to go into other construction trades. Jobs are generally easier to find during spring and summer. As in many other construction occupations, employment of roofers is somewhat sensitive to fluctuations in the economy. Demand for roofers is less vulnerable to downturns than demand for other construction trades because much roofing work consists of repair and reroofing, in addition to new construction.

Cover roofs of structures with shingles, slate, asphalt, aluminum, wood, or related materials. Install, repair, or replace single-ply roofing systems, using waterproof sheet materials such as modified plastics, elastomeric, or other asphaltic compositions. Apply alternate layers of hot asphalt or tar and roofing paper to roofs, according to specification. Apply gravel or pebbles over top layers of roofs, using rakes or stiff-bristled brooms. Cement or nail flashing-strips of metal or shingle over joints to make them watertight. Punch holes in slate, tile, terra cotta, or wooden shingles, using punches and hammers. Hammer and chisel away rough spots or remove them with rubbing bricks to prepare surfaces for waterproofing. Align roofing materials with edges of roofs. Mop or pour hot asphalt or tar onto roof bases. Apply plastic coatings and membranes, fiberglass, or felt over sloped roofs before applying shingles. Install vapor barriers and/or layers of insulation on the roof decks of flat roofs, and seal the seams. Install partially overlapping layers of material over roof insulation surfaces, determining distance of roofing material overlap using chalk lines, gauges on shingling hatchets, or lines on shingles. Inspect problem roofs to determine the best procedures for repairing them. Glaze top layers to make a smooth finish, or embed gravel in the bitumen for rough surfaces. Cut roofing paper to size using knives; and nail or staple roofing paper to roofs in overlapping strips to form bases for other materials. Cut felt, shingles, and strips of flashing; and fit them into angles formed by walls, vents, and intersecting roof surfaces. Cover roofs and exterior walls of structures with slate, asphalt, aluminum, wood, gravel, gypsum, and/or related materials, using brushes, knives, punches, hammers and other tools. Clean and maintain equipment. Cover exposed nailheads with roofing cement or caulking to prevent water leakage and rust.

Related Military Specializations: None. **Average Educational Level of Vets:** High school diploma or equivalent. **Usual Educational Requirement:** Less than high school diploma or equivalent. **Relevant Educational Program:** Roofer Training. **Related Knowledge/Courses:** Building and Construction; Design; Engineering and Technology; Transportation. **Work Experience Needed:** None. **On-the-Job Training Needed:** Moderate-term on-the-job training. **Certification/Licensure:** None.

Personality Types: Realistic-Conventional. **Key Career Cluster:** 02 Architecture and Construction. **Key Career Pathway:** 2.2 Construction. **Top Industries for Vets:** Construction; National Security and International Affairs.

Skills: Operation and Control; Operation Monitoring; Coordination; Installation.

Work Environment: Outdoors; standing; climbing; walking and running; kneeling, crouching, stooping, or crawling; using hands; bending or twisting the body; repetitive motions; noise; very hot or cold; bright or inadequate lighting; contaminants; cramped work space; high places;

hazardous conditions; hazardous equipment; minor burns, cuts, bites, or stings.

Sailors and Marine Oilers

- ✸ Average Annual Earnings (All): $36,800
- ✸ Average Annual Earnings (Recent Veterans): $36,010
- ✸ Earnings Growth Potential: High (40.4%)
- ✸ Growth: 21.3%
- ✸ Annual Job Openings: 2,150
- ✸ Veteran Employment by Sector: For-Profit, 43.6%; Nonprofit, 1.9%; Government, 54.3%; Self-Employed, 0.2%.

Considerations for Job Outlook: Job prospects should be favorable. Many workers leave water transportation occupations, especially sailors and marine oilers, because recently hired workers often decide they do not enjoy spending a lot of time away at sea. In addition, a number of officers and engineers are approaching retirement, creating job openings. The number of applicants for all types of jobs may be limited by high regulatory and security requirements.

Stand watch to look for obstructions in path of vessel, measure water depth, turn wheel on bridge, or use emergency equipment as directed by captain, mate, or pilot. Provide engineers with assistance in repairing and adjusting machinery. Attach hoses and operate pumps in order to transfer substances to and from liquid cargo tanks. Give directions to crew members engaged in cleaning wheelhouses and quarterdecks. Load or unload materials from vessels. Lower and man lifeboats when emergencies occur. Participate in shore patrols. Read pressure and temperature gauges or displays, and record data in engineering logs. Record in ships' logs data

such as weather conditions and distances traveled. Stand by wheels when ships are on automatic pilot, and verify accuracy of courses, using magnetic compasses. Steer ships under the direction of commanders or navigating officers, or direct helmsmen to steer, following designated courses. Chip and clean rust spots on decks, superstructures, and sides of ships, using wire brushes and hand or air chipping machines. Relay specified signals to other ships, using visual signaling devices such as blinker lights and semaphores. Splice and repair ropes, wire cables, and cordage, using marlinespikes, wirecutters, twine, and hand tools. Paint or varnish decks, superstructures, lifeboats, or sides of ships. Overhaul lifeboats and lifeboat gear, and lower or raise lifeboats with winches or falls. Operate, maintain, and repair ship equipment such as winches, cranes, derricks, and weapons system. Measure depth of water in shallow or unfamiliar waters, using leadlines, and telephone or shout depth information to vessel bridges. Maintain a ship's engines under the direction of the ship's engineering officers. Lubricate machinery, equipment, and engine parts such as gears, shafts, and bearings. Handle lines to moor vessels to wharfs, to tie up vessels to other vessels, or to rig towing lines. Examine machinery to verify specified pressures and lubricant flows. Clean and polish wood trim, brass, and other metal parts. Break out, rig, and stow cargo-handling gear, stationary rigging, and running gear.

Related Military Specializations: Seaman; Seaman Apprentice; Seaman Recruit. **Average Educational Level of Vets:** High school diploma or equivalent. **Usual Educational Requirement:** Less than high school diploma or equivalent. **Relevant Educational Program:** Marine Transportation Services, Other. **Related Knowledge/Courses:** Mechanical Devices; Transportation; Public Safety and Security; Engineering and Technology; Geography;

Production and Processing. **Work Experience Needed:** None. **On-the-Job Training Needed:** Short-term on-the-job training. **Certification/Licensure:** Licensure.

Personality Types: Realistic-Conventional. **Key Career Cluster:** 16 Transportation, Distribution, and Logistics. **Key Career Pathway:** 16.1 Transportation Operations. **Top Industries for Vets:** National Security and International Affairs; Water Transportation; Services Incidental to Transportation; Administration of Economic Programs and Space Research; Construction.

Skills: Repairing; Equipment Maintenance; Operation and Control; Troubleshooting; Equipment Selection; Operation Monitoring; Quality Control Analysis; Technology Design.

Work Environment: More often outdoors than indoors; standing; walking and running; balancing; using hands; bending or twisting the body; noise; very hot or cold; bright or inadequate lighting; contaminants; cramped work space; whole-body vibration; high places; hazardous conditions; hazardous equipment.

Sales Representatives, Services, All Other

- ❋ Average Annual Earnings (All): $50,630

- ❋ Average Annual Earnings (Recent Veterans): $32,740

- ❋ Earnings Growth Potential: High (49.9%)

- ❋ Growth: 18.8%

- ❋ Annual Job Openings: 27,010

- ❋ Veteran Employment by Sector: For-Profit, 83.5%; Nonprofit, 2.3%; Government, 9.7%; Self-Employed, 4.5%.

Considerations for Job Outlook: Faster than average employment growth is projected.

All services sales representatives not listed separately. For task data, see Job Specializations.

Related Military Specializations: None. **Average Educational Level of Vets:** One or more years of college, no degree. **Usual Educational Requirement:** High school diploma or equivalent. **Relevant Educational Programs:** Retailing and Retail Operations; Selling Skills and Sales Operations. **Work Experience Needed:** None. **On-the-Job Training Needed:** Short-term on-the-job training. **Certification/Licensure:** Licensure for some specializations.

Key Career Cluster: 14 Marketing, Sales, and Service. **Key Career Pathway:** 14.2 Professional Sales and Marketing. **Top Industries for Vets:** Construction; Other Telecommunication Services; Wired Telecommunications Carriers; Business Support Services; Computer Systems Design and Related Services.

Job Specialization: Energy Brokers

Purchase or sell energy for customers. Contact prospective buyers or sellers of power to arrange transactions. Create product packages based on assessment of customers' or potential customers' needs. Educate customers, and answer customer questions related to the buying or selling of energy, energy markets, or alternative energy sources. Explain contracts and related documents to customers. Forecast energy supply and demand to minimize the cost of meeting load demands and to maximize the value of supply resources. Negotiate prices and contracts for energy sales or purchases. Price energy based on market conditions. Analyze customer bills and utility rate structures to select optimal rate structures for customers. Develop and deliver proposals or presentations on topics such as the purchase and sale of energy. Facilitate the delivery or receipt of wholesale power or retail load scheduling. Monitor the flow of energy in response to changes in consumer demand.

Related Knowledge/Courses: No data available.

Personality Types: Enterprising-Conventional.

Skills: No data available.

Work Environment: No data available.

Sales Representatives, Wholesale and Manufacturing, Except Technical and Scientific Products

- ❋ Average Annual Earnings (All): $53,540
- ❋ Average Annual Earnings (Recent Veterans): $51,290
- ❋ Earnings Growth Potential: High (49.1%)
- ❋ Growth: 15.6%
- ❋ Annual Job Openings: 55,990
- ❋ Veteran Employment by Sector: For-Profit, 92.4%; Nonprofit, 0.1%; Government, 2.0%; Self-Employed, 5.5%.

Considerations for Job Outlook: Job candidates should see very good opportunities. Because workers frequently leave this occupation, there are usually a relatively large number of openings.

Sell goods for wholesalers or manufacturers to businesses or groups of individuals. Work requires substantial knowledge of items sold. Answer customers' questions about products, prices, availability, product uses, and credit terms. Recommend products to customers based on customers' needs and interests. Contact regular and prospective customers to demonstrate

products, explain product features, and solicit orders. Estimate or quote prices, credit or contract terms, warranties, and delivery dates. Consult with clients after sales or contract signings to resolve problems and to provide ongoing support. Prepare drawings, estimates, and bids that meet specific customer needs. Provide customers with product samples and catalogs. Identify prospective customers by using business directories, following leads from existing clients, participating in organizations and clubs, and attending trade shows and conferences. Arrange and direct delivery and installation of products and equipment. Monitor market conditions; product innovations; and competitors' products, prices, and sales. Negotiate details of contracts and payments, and prepare sales contracts and order forms. Perform administrative duties, such as preparing sales budgets and reports, keeping sales records, and filing expense account reports. Obtain credit information about prospective customers. Forward orders to manufacturers. Check stock levels, and reorder merchandise as necessary. Plan, assemble, and stock product displays in retail stores, or make recommendations to retailers regarding product displays, promotional programs, and advertising.

Related Military Specializations: None. **Average Educational Level of Vets:** Bachelor's degree. **Usual Educational Requirement:** High school diploma or equivalent. **Relevant Educational Programs:** Apparel and Accessories Marketing Operations; Fashion Merchandising; General Merchandising, Sales, and Related Marketing Operations, Other; Sales, Distribution, and Marketing Operations, General; Special Products Marketing Operations. **Related Knowledge/Courses:** Sales and Marketing; Economics and Accounting; Customer and Personal Service; Transportation; Mathematics; Production and Processing. **Work Experience Needed:** None. **On-the-Job Training Needed:** Moderate-term on-the-job training. **Certification/Licensure:** Licensure for some specializations; voluntary certification by association.

Personality Types: Conventional-Enterprising. **Key Career Cluster:** 14 Marketing, Sales, and Service. **Key Career Pathway:** 14.2 Professional Sales and Marketing. **Top Industries for Vets:** Drugs, Sundries, and Chemical and Allied Products Merchant Wholesalers; Groceries and Related Products Merchant Wholesalers; Machinery, Equipment, and Supplies Merchant Wholesalers; Electrical and Electronic Goods Merchant Wholesalers; Professional and Commercial Equipment and Supplies Merchant Wholesalers.

Skills: Negotiation; Persuasion; Service Orientation; Operations Analysis; Critical Thinking; Social Perceptiveness; Active Listening; Speaking.

Work Environment: Outdoors; more often sitting than standing; walking and running; noise; contaminants.

Sales Representatives, Wholesale and Manufacturing, Technical and Scientific Products

* Average Annual Earnings (All): $74,750

* Average Annual Earnings (Recent Veterans): $51,290

* Earnings Growth Potential: High (48.5%)

* Growth: 16.4%

* Annual Job Openings: 15,970

* Veteran Employment by Sector: For-Profit, 92.4%; Nonprofit, 0.1%; Government, 2.0%; Self-Employed, 5.5%.

Considerations for Job Outlook: Job candidates should see very good opportunities. Because workers frequently leave this occupation, there are usually a relatively large number of openings.

Sell goods for wholesalers or manufacturers where technical or scientific knowledge is required. Contact new and existing customers to discuss their needs and to explain how these needs could be met by specific products and services. Answer customers' questions about products, prices, availability, product uses, and credit terms. Quote prices, credit terms, and other bid specifications. Emphasize product features based on analyses of customers' needs and on technical knowledge of product capabilities and limitations. Negotiate prices and terms of sales and service agreements. Maintain customer records, using automated systems. Identify prospective customers by using business directories, following leads from existing clients, participating in organizations and clubs, and attending trade shows and conferences. Prepare sales contracts for orders obtained, and submit orders for processing. Select the correct products, or assist customers in making product selections based on customers' needs, product specifications, and applicable regulations. Collaborate with colleagues to exchange information such as selling strategies and marketing information. Prepare sales presentations and proposals that explain product specifications and applications. Provide customers with ongoing technical support. Demonstrate and explain the operation and use of products. Inform customers of estimated delivery schedules, service contracts, warranties, or other information pertaining to purchased products.

Related Military Specializations: None. **Average Educational Level of Vets:** Bachelor's degree. **Usual Educational Requirement:** Bachelor's degree. **Relevant Educational Program:** Selling Skills and Sales Operations. **Related Knowledge/Courses:** Sales and

Marketing; Customer and Personal Service; Production and Processing; Administration and Management; Transportation; Computers and Electronics. **Work Experience Needed:** None. **On-the-Job Training Needed:** Moderate-term on-the-job training. **Certification/Licensure:** Licensure for some specializations; voluntary certification by association.

Personality Types: Enterprising-Conventional. **Key Career Cluster:** 14 Marketing, Sales, and Service. **Key Career Pathway:** 14.2 Professional Sales and Marketing. **Top Industries for Vets:** Drugs, Sundries, and Chemical and Allied Products Merchant Wholesalers; Groceries and Related Products Merchant Wholesalers; Machinery, Equipment, and Supplies Merchant Wholesalers; Electrical and Electronic Goods Merchant Wholesalers; Professional and Commercial Equipment and Supplies Merchant Wholesalers.

Skills: Persuasion; Negotiation; Management of Financial Resources; Management of Material Resources; Active Listening; Speaking; Reading Comprehension; Operations Analysis.

Work Environment: Indoors; sitting.

Job Specialization: Solar Sales Representatives and Assessors

Contact new or existing customers to determine their solar equipment needs, suggest systems or equipment, or estimate costs. Generate solar energy customer leads to develop new accounts. Prepare proposals, quotes, contracts, or presentations for potential solar customers. Select solar energy products, systems, or services for customers based on electrical energy requirements, site conditions, price, or other factors. Assess sites to determine suitability for solar equipment, using equipment such as tape measures, compasses, and computer software. Calculate potential solar resources or solar-array production for a particular site, considering issues such as climate, shading, and roof orientation. Create customized energy-management packages to satisfy customer needs. Develop marketing or strategic plans for sales territories. Gather information from prospective customers to identify their solar energy needs. Prepare or review detailed design drawings, specifications, or lists related to solar installations. Provide customers with information such as quotes, orders, sales, shipping, warranties, credit, funding options, incentives, or tax rebates. Provide technical information about solar power, solar systems, equipment, and services to potential customers or dealers. Take quote requests or orders from dealers or customers. Demonstrate use of solar and related equipment to customers or dealers.

Related Knowledge/Courses: No data available.

Personality Types: No data available.

Skills: No data available.

Work Environment: No data available.

Securities, Commodities, and Financial Services Sales Agents

- ❈ Average Annual Earnings (All): $72,060
- ❈ Average Annual Earnings (Recent Veterans): $43,650
- ❈ Earnings Growth Potential: Very high (55.4%)
- ❈ Growth: 15.2%
- ❈ Annual Job Openings: 13,370
- ❈ Veteran Employment by Sector: For-Profit, 86.4%; Nonprofit, 0.0%; Government, 0.5%; Self-Employed, 13.1%.

Considerations for Job Outlook: The high pay associated with securities, commodities, and financial services sales agents draws many more applicants than there are openings. Therefore, competition for jobs is intense. Certification and a graduate degree, such as a Chartered Financial Analyst (CFA) certification and a master's degree in business or finance, can significantly improve an applicant's prospects. For entry-level jobs, having an excellent grade-point average (GPA) in college is important.

Buy and sell securities or commodities in investment and trading firms, or provide financial services to businesses and individuals. For task data, see Job Specializations.

Related Military Specializations: None. **Average Educational Level of Vets:** Bachelor's degree. **Usual Educational Requirement:** Bachelor's degree. **Relevant Educational Programs:** Business and Personal/Financial Services Marketing Operations; Financial Planning and Services; Investments and Securities. **Work Experience Needed:** None. **On-the-Job Training Needed:** Moderate-term on-the-job training. **Certification/Licensure:** Licensure; voluntary certification by association.

Key Career Cluster: 06 Finance. **Key Career Pathway:** 6.1 Financial and Investment Planning. **Top Industries for Vets:** Securities, Commodities, Funds, Trusts, and Other Financial Investments; Nondepository Credit and Related Activities; Banking and Related Activities; Savings Institutions, Including Credit Unions.

Job Specialization: Sales Agents, Financial Services

Sell financial services such as loan, tax, and securities counseling to customers of financial institutions and business establishments. Determine customers' financial-services needs, and prepare proposals to sell services that address these needs. Contact prospective customers to present information and explain available services. Sell services and equipment, such as trusts, investments, and check-processing services. Prepare forms or agreements to complete sales. Develop prospects from current commercial customers, referral leads, and sales and trade meetings. Review business trends in order to advise customers regarding expected fluctuations. Make presentations on financial services to groups to attract new clients. Evaluate costs and revenue of agreements to determine continued profitability.

Related Knowledge/Courses: Sales and Marketing; Economics and Accounting; Customer and Personal Service; Law and Government; Mathematics; Personnel and Human Resources.

Personality Types: Enterprising-Conventional.

Skills: Persuasion; Systems Evaluation; Negotiation; Service Orientation; Mathematics; Active Learning; Speaking; Systems Analysis.

Work Environment: Indoors; sitting.

Job Specialization: Sales Agents, Securities and Commodities

Buy and sell securities in investment and trading firms and develop and implement financial plans for individuals, businesses, and organizations. Complete sales order tickets, and submit for processing of client-requested transactions. Interview clients to determine clients' assets, liabilities, cash flow, insurance coverage, tax status, and financial objectives. Record transactions accurately, and keep clients informed about transactions. Develop financial plans based on analysis of clients' financial status, and discuss financial options with clients. Review all securities transactions to ensure accuracy of information, and ensure that trades conform to regulations of governing agencies. Offer advice on the purchase or sale of particular securities. Relay buy-or-sell orders to securities exchanges or to firm trading departments. Identify potential clients, using advertising campaigns, mailing lists, and personal contacts. Review financial periodicals, stock and bond reports, business publications, and other material to identify potential investments for clients and to keep abreast of trends affecting market conditions. Contact prospective customers to determine customer needs, present information, and explain available services. Prepare documents needed to implement plans selected by clients. Analyze market conditions to determine optimum times to execute securities transactions. Explain stock market terms and trading practices to clients. Inform and advise concerned parties regarding fluctuations and securities transactions affecting plans or accounts. Calculate costs for billings and commissions purposes.

Related Knowledge/Courses: Economics and Accounting; Customer and Personal Service; Sales and Marketing; Clerical Practices; Law and Government; Mathematics.

Personality Types: Enterprising-Conventional.

Skills: Systems Analysis; Persuasion; Systems Evaluation; Management of Financial Resources; Reading Comprehension; Judgment and Decision Making; Negotiation; Service Orientation.

Work Environment: Indoors; sitting.

Job Specialization: Securities and Commodities Traders

Buy and sell securities and commodities to transfer debt, capital, or risk. Establish and negotiate unit prices and terms of sale. Buy or sell stocks, bonds, commodity futures, foreign currencies, or other securities at stock exchanges on behalf of investment dealers. Agree on buying

or selling prices at optimal levels for clients. Make bids and offers to buy or sell securities. Analyze target companies and investment opportunities to inform investment decisions. Develop and maintain supplier and customer relationships. Devise trading, option, and hedge strategies. Identify opportunities, and develop channels for purchase or sale of securities or commodities. Inform other traders, managers, or customers of market conditions, including volume, price, competition, and dynamics. Monitor markets and positions. Process paperwork for special orders, including margin and option purchases. Receive sales order tickets, and inspect forms to determine accuracy of information. Report all positions or trading results. Review securities transactions to ensure conformance to regulations. Track and analyze factors that affect price movement, such as trade policies, weather conditions, political developments, and supply-and-demand changes. Write and sign sales order confirmation forms to record and approve security transactions. Audit accounts, and correct errors. Make transportation arrangements for sold or purchased commodities. Prepare financial reports, such as reviews of portfolio positions. Reconcile account-related statements, such as quarterly and annual statements and confirmations.

Related Knowledge/Courses: No data available.

Personality Types: Enterprising-Conventional.

Skills: No data available.

Work Environment: No data available.

Security and Fire Alarm Systems Installers

- ❋ Average Annual Earnings (All): $39,540

- ❋ Average Annual Earnings (Recent Veterans): $26,190

- ❋ Earnings Growth Potential: Medium (35.9%)

- ❋ Growth: 33.0%

- ❋ Annual Job Openings: 3,670

- ❋ Veteran Employment by Sector: For-Profit, 92.3%; Nonprofit, 1.1%; Government, 2.6%; Self-Employed, 4.0%.

Considerations for Job Outlook: Rapid employment growth is projected.

Install, program, maintain, and repair security and fire alarm wiring and equipment. Ensure that work is in accordance with relevant codes. Examine systems to locate problems such as loose connections or broken insulation. Test backup batteries, keypad programming, sirens, and all security features in order to ensure proper functioning, and to diagnose malfunctions. Mount and fasten control panels, door and window contacts, sensors, and video cameras, and attach electrical and telephone wiring in order to connect components. Install, maintain, or repair security systems, alarm devices, and related equipment, following blueprints of electrical layouts and building plans. Inspect installation sites and study work orders, building plans, and installation manuals in order to determine materials requirements and installation procedures. Feed cables through access holes, roof spaces, and cavity walls to reach fixture outlets; then position and terminate cables, wires, and strapping. Adjust sensitivity of units based on room structures and manufacturers' recommendations, using programming keypads.

Test and repair circuits and sensors, following wiring and system specifications. Drill holes for wiring in wall studs, joists, ceilings, and floors. Demonstrate systems for customers, and explain details such as the causes and consequences of false alarms. Consult with clients to assess risks and to determine security requirements. Keep informed of new products and developments. Mount raceways and conduits, and fasten wires to wood framing, using staplers. Prepare documents such as invoices and warranties.

Related Military Specializations: Interior Communications Electrician; Uninterruptible Power Supply (UPS) Maintenance Technician. **Average Educational Level of Vets:** High school diploma or equivalent. **Usual Educational Requirement:** High school diploma or equivalent. **Relevant Educational Programs:** Electrician; Security System Installation, Repair, and Inspection Technology/Technician. **Related Knowledge/Courses:** Telecommunications; Building and Construction; Mechanical Devices; Computers and Electronics; Public Safety and Security; Design. **Work Experience Needed:** None. **On-the-Job Training Needed:** Moderate-term on-the-job training. **Certification/Licensure:** Licensure.

Personality Types: Realistic-Conventional. **Key Career Cluster:** 13 Manufacturing. **Key Career Pathway:** 13.3 Maintenance, Installation and Repair. **Top Industries for Vets:** Investigation and Security Services; Construction; Electrical and Electronic Goods Merchant Wholesalers; Building Material and Supplies Dealers; National Security and International Affairs.

Skills: Installation; Repairing; Equipment Maintenance; Troubleshooting; Operation and Control; Equipment Selection; Quality Control Analysis; Operation Monitoring.

Work Environment: More often indoors than outdoors; standing; climbing; using hands;

repetitive motions; noise; very hot or cold; bright or inadequate lighting; contaminants; cramped work space; high places.

Security Guards

- ❀ Average Annual Earnings (All): $23,900
- ❀ Average Annual Earnings (Recent Veterans): $31,650
- ❀ Earnings Growth Potential: Low (27.8%)
- ❀ Growth: 18.8%
- ❀ Annual Job Openings: 35,950
- ❀ Veteran Employment by Sector: For-Profit, 62.2%; Nonprofit, 4.2%; Government, 32.7%; Self-Employed, 0.9%.

Considerations for Job Outlook: Job opportunities for security guards will stem from growing demand for various forms of security. Additional opportunities will be due to turnover. Although many people are attracted to part-time positions because of the limited training requirements, there will be more competition for higher-paying positions that require more training. Those with related work experience, such as a background in law enforcement, and those with computer and technology skills should find the best job prospects.

Guard, patrol, or monitor premises to prevent theft, violence, or infractions of rules. Patrol industrial or commercial premises to prevent and detect signs of intrusion and ensure security of doors, windows, and gates. Answer alarms and investigate disturbances. Monitor and authorize entrance and departure of employees, visitors, and other persons to guard against theft and maintain security of premises. Write reports of daily activities and irregularities such as equipment or property damage, theft, presence of unauthorized persons, or unusual occurrences. Call police or fire departments in cases of emergency, such as fire or presence of unauthorized persons. Circulate among visitors, patrons, or employees to preserve order and protect property. Answer telephone calls to take messages, answer questions, and provide information during nonbusiness hours or when switchboard is closed. Warn persons of rule infractions or violations, and apprehend or evict violators from premises, using force when necessary. Operate detecting devices to screen individuals and prevent passage of prohibited articles into restricted areas. Escort or drive motor vehicle to transport individuals to specified locations or to provide personal protection. Inspect and adjust security systems, equipment, or machinery to ensure operational use and to detect evidence of tampering. Drive or guard armored vehicle to transport money and valuables to prevent theft and ensure safe delivery. Monitor and adjust controls that regulate building systems, such as air conditioning, furnace, or boiler.

Related Military Specializations: Guard; Honor Guard; Marine Basic Combat Skills Specialist; Marine Corps Security Force (MCSF) Close Quarters Battle (CQB) Team Member; Marine Corps Security Force (MCSF) Guard; Marine Security Guard (MSG). **Average Educational Level of Vets:** One or more years of college, no degree. **Usual Educational Requirement:** High school diploma or equivalent. **Relevant Educational Programs:** Securities Services Administration/Management; Security and Loss Prevention Services. **Related Knowledge/ Courses:** Public Safety and Security. **Work Experience Needed:** None. **On-the-Job Training Needed:** Short-term on-the-job training. **Certification/Licensure:** Licensure in most states; voluntary certification by association in others.

Personality Types: Realistic-Conventional-Enterprising. **Key Career Cluster:** 12 Law, Public Safety, Corrections, and Security.

Key Career Pathway: 12.3 Security and Protective Services. **Top Industries for Vets:** Investigation and Security Services; National Security and International Affairs; Hospitals; Other Amusement, Gambling, and Recreation Industries; Department and Discount Stores.

Skills: Operation and Control.

Work Environment: More often indoors than outdoors; standing; walking and running; using hands; noise; contaminants.

Self-Enrichment Education Teachers

- ❋ Average Annual Earnings (All): $36,100
- ❋ Average Annual Earnings (Recent Veterans): $52,170
- ❋ Earnings Growth Potential: High (48.4%)
- ❋ Growth: 20.9%
- ❋ Annual Job Openings: 9,150
- ❋ Veteran Employment by Sector: For-Profit, 31.3%; Nonprofit, 3.9%; Government, 63.4%; Self-Employed, 1.4%.

Considerations for Job Outlook: Growth is expected as more people want to learn new hobbies and gain marketable skills. From 2010 to 2020, adults and children are expected to continue seeking new hobbies and pastimes and will take classes to learn these skills. Self-enrichment teachers will be needed to teach these classes. In addition, more people will seek to gain skills to make themselves more attractive to prospective employers.

Teach or instruct courses other than those that normally lead to an occupational objective or degree. Adapt teaching methods and instructional materials to meet students' varying needs and interests. Conduct classes, workshops, and demonstrations, and provide individual instruction to teach topics and skills such as cooking, dancing, writing, physical fitness, photography, personal finance, and flying. Monitor students' performance to make suggestions for improvement and to ensure that they satisfy course standards, training requirements, and objectives. Observe students to determine qualifications, limitations, abilities, interests, and other individual characteristics. Instruct students individually and in groups, using various teaching methods such as lectures, discussions, and demonstrations. Establish clear objectives for all lessons, units, and projects, and communicate those objectives to students. Instruct and monitor students in use and care of equipment and materials to prevent injury and damage. Prepare students for further development by encouraging them to explore learning opportunities and to persevere with challenging tasks. Prepare materials and classrooms for class activities. Enforce policies and rules governing students. Plan and conduct activities for a balanced program of instruction, demonstration, and work time that provides students with opportunities to observe, question, and investigate. Prepare instructional program objectives, outlines, and lesson plans. Maintain accurate and complete student records as required by administrative policy.

Related Military Specializations: 2M Instructor/Master Inspector; Anti-Terrorism Training Supervisor Instructor; Aviation Water Survival Instructor; Basic Swimming and Water Survival Instructor; Crew Served Weapons (CSW) Instructor; Drill Instructor; Expeditionary Security Force Advisor/Trainer; GWOT IA/ILO Combat Training (NIACT); Indoctrination Training Officer; Instructor, General; Instructor, Technical; Marine Combat Instructor; Marine Corps Security Force (MCSF)

Cadre Trainer; Marksmanship Coach; Martial Arts Instructor; others. **Average Educational Level of Vets:** One or more years of college, no degree. **Usual Educational Requirement:** High school diploma or equivalent. **Relevant Educational Program:** Adult and Continuing Education and Teaching. **Related Knowledge/ Courses:** Education and Training; Fine Arts; Communications and Media; Customer and Personal Service; Sales and Marketing; English Language. **Work Experience Needed:** 1 to 5 years. **On-the-Job Training Needed:** None. **Certification/Licensure:** Voluntary certification for some specializations.

Personality Types: Social-Artistic-Enterprising. **Key Career Cluster:** 09 Hospitality and Tourism. **Key Career Pathway:** 9.4 Recreation, Amusements and Attractions. **Top Industries for Vets:** National Security and International Affairs; Other Schools and Instruction, and Educational Support Services; Colleges and Universities, Including Junior Colleges; Architectural, Engineering, and Related Services; Computer Systems Design and Related Services.

Skills: Learning Strategies; Operations Analysis; Instructing; Writing; Speaking; Service Orientation; Reading Comprehension; Monitoring.

Work Environment: Indoors; standing; repetitive motions.

Sheet Metal Workers

- Average Annual Earnings (All): $42,730
- Average Annual Earnings (Recent Veterans): $32,740
- Earnings Growth Potential: High (40.1%)
- Growth: 17.5%
- Annual Job Openings: 4,700
- Veteran Employment by Sector: For-Profit, 84.6%; Nonprofit, 0.0%; Government, 13.3%; Self-Employed, 2.1%.

Considerations for Job Outlook: Job opportunities should be particularly good for sheet metal workers who complete apprenticeship training or who are certified welders. Some manufacturing companies report having difficulty finding qualified applicants. Workers who have programming skills, possess multiple welding skills, and show commitment to their work will have the best job opportunities. Employment of sheet metal workers, like that of many other construction workers, is sensitive to fluctuations in the economy.

Fabricate, assemble, install, and repair sheet metal products and equipment, such as ducts, control boxes, drainpipes, and furnace casings. Determine project requirements, including scope, assembly sequences, and required methods and materials, according to blueprints, drawings, and written or verbal instructions. Lay out, measure, and mark dimensions and reference lines on material, such as roofing panels, according to drawings or templates, using calculators, scribes, dividers, squares, and rulers. Maneuver completed units into position for installation, and anchor the units. Convert blueprints into shop drawings to be followed in the construction and assembly of sheet metal products. Install assemblies, such as flashing, pipes, tubes, heating and air conditioning ducts, furnace casings, rain gutters, and downspouts, in supportive frameworks. Select gauges and types of sheet metal or non-metallic material, according to product specifications. Drill and punch holes in metal, for screws, bolts, and rivets.

Related Military Specializations: NAMTS Sheetmetal Worker; Shipfitter—Metalsmith. **Average Educational Level of Vets:** High school diploma or equivalent. **Usual Educational Requirement:** High school diploma or equivalent. **Relevant Educational Program:** Sheet Metal Technology/Sheetworking. **Related Knowledge/Courses:** Building and Construction; Mechanical Devices; Design; Engineering and Technology; Production and Processing; Mathematics. **Work Experience Needed:** None. **On-the-Job Training Needed:** Apprenticeship. **Certification/Licensure:** Voluntary certification for some specializations.

Personality Types: Realistic. **Key Career Cluster:** 02 Architecture and Construction. **Key Career Pathway:** 2.2 Construction. **Top Industries for Vets:** Construction; Structural Metals, and Boiler, Tank, and Shipping Containers; Aircraft and Parts; National Security and International Affairs; Rail Transportation.

Skills: Repairing; Equipment Maintenance; Installation; Equipment Selection; Quality Control Analysis; Technology Design; Mathematics; Troubleshooting.

Work Environment: Outdoors; standing; walking and running; using hands; bending or twisting the body; repetitive motions; noise; very hot or cold; bright or inadequate lighting; contaminants; cramped work space; high places; hazardous equipment; minor burns, cuts, bites, or stings.

Ship Engineers

* Average Annual Earnings (All): $70,840
* Average Annual Earnings (Recent Veterans): $36,010
* Earnings Growth Potential: High (43.0%)
* Growth: 18.0%
* Annual Job Openings: 620
* Veteran Employment by Sector: For-Profit, 43.6%; Nonprofit, 1.9%; Government, 54.3%; Self-Employed, 0.2%.

Considerations for Job Outlook: Job prospects should be favorable. Many workers leave water transportation occupations, especially sailors and marine oilers, because recently hired workers often decide they do not enjoy spending a lot of time away at sea. In addition, a number of officers and engineers are approaching retirement, creating job openings. The number of applicants for all types of jobs may be limited by high regulatory and security requirements.

Supervise and coordinate activities of crew engaged in operating and maintaining engines, boilers, deck machinery, and electrical, sanitary, and refrigeration equipment aboard ship. Record orders for changes in ship speed and direction, and note gauge readings and test data, such as revolutions per minute and voltage output, in engineering logs and bellbooks. Install engine controls, propeller shafts, and propellers. Perform and participate in emergency drills as required. Fabricate engine replacement parts such as valves, stay rods, and bolts, using metalworking machinery. Operate and maintain off-loading liquid pumps and valves. Maintain and repair engines, electric motors, pumps, winches, and other mechanical and electrical equipment, or assist other crew members with maintenance and repair duties. Maintain electrical power, heating, ventilation, refrigeration, water, and sewerage. Monitor and test operations of engines and other equipment so that malfunctions and their causes can be identified. Monitor engine, machinery, and equipment indicators when vessels are underway, and report abnormalities to appropriate shipboard staff. Start engines to propel ships, and regulate engines and power transmissions to control speeds of ships, according to directions from captains or bridge computers. Order and receive engine rooms' stores such as oil and spare parts; maintain inventories and record usage of supplies. Act as liaison between ships' captains and shore personnel to ensure that schedules and budgets are maintained and that ships are operated safely and efficiently. Clean engine parts, and keep engine rooms clean.

Related Military Specializations: Auxiliary Machinery Officer; Boiler Officer (1200 psi Steam System); Boiler Officer (General); Causeway Lighterage Engineer; Engineering Afloat; Engineman; Engineman Basic; Gas Turbine System Technician; Gas Turbine Systems Technician Basic; Machinery Technician; Machinist's Mate; Machinist's Mate (Nuclear); Machinist's Mate (Submarine); Machinist's Mate (Surface); Machinist's Mate Basic; Main Propulsion Assistant (1200 psi Steam System); Main Propulsion Assistant (Diesel); others. **Average Educational Level of Vets:** High school diploma or equivalent. **Usual Educational Requirement:** Bachelor's degree. **Relevant Educational Program:** Marine Science/Merchant Marine Officer. **Related Knowledge/Courses:** Mechanical Devices; Building and Construction; Engineering and Technology; Transportation; Chemistry; Public Safety and Security. **Work Experience Needed:** None. **On-the-Job Training Needed:** None. **Certification/Licensure:** Licensure.

Personality Types: Realistic-Conventional-Enterprising. **Key Career Cluster:** 16 Transportation, Distribution, and Logistics. **Key Career Pathway:** 16.1 Transportation Operations. **Top Industries for Vets:** National Security and International Affairs; Water Transportation; Services Incidental to Transportation; Administration of Economic Programs and Space Research; Construction.

Skills: Repairing; Equipment Maintenance; Troubleshooting; Equipment Selection; Operation and Control; Operation Monitoring; Quality Control Analysis; Science.

Work Environment: Outdoors; standing; using hands; noise; very hot or cold; bright or inadequate lighting; contaminants; cramped work space; whole-body vibration; high places; hazardous conditions; hazardous equipment; minor burns, cuts, bites, or stings.

Social and Community Service Managers

- ❈ Average Annual Earnings (All): $58,660
- ❈ Average Annual Earnings (Recent Veterans): $43,650
- ❈ Earnings Growth Potential: High (40.3%)
- ❈ Growth: 26.7%
- ❈ Annual Job Openings: 6,480
- ❈ Veteran Employment by Sector: For-Profit, 15.9%; Nonprofit, 71.6%; Government, 12.5%; Self-Employed, 0.0%.

Considerations for Job Outlook: Growth is due to the needs of an aging population. An increase in the number of older adults will result in growth in demand for social services. Elderly people often need services, such as adult day care and meal delivery. Social and community service managers, who administer programs that provide these services, will likely be needed to meet this increased demand. As a result, employment of social and community service managers is expected to grow fastest in industries serving the elderly, such as home health-care services and services for the elderly and persons with disabilities. Services for the elderly and persons with disabilities are included in the individual and family services industry.

Plan, direct, or coordinate the activities of a social service program or community outreach organization. Establish and maintain relationships with other agencies and organizations in the community to meet community needs and to ensure that services are not duplicated. Prepare and maintain records and reports, such as budgets, personnel records, or training manuals. Direct activities of professional and technical staff members and volunteers. Evaluate the work of staff and volunteers to ensure that programs are of appropriate quality and that resources are used effectively. Establish and oversee administrative procedures to meet objectives set by boards of directors or senior management. Participate in the determination of organizational policies regarding such issues as participant eligibility, program requirements, and program benefits. Research and analyze member or community needs to determine program directions and goals. Speak to community groups to explain and interpret agency purposes, programs, and policies. Recruit, interview, and hire or sign up volunteers and staff. Represent organizations in relations with governmental and media institutions. Plan and administer budgets for programs, equipment, and support services. Analyze proposed legislation, regulations, or rule changes to determine how agency services could be impacted. Act as consultants to agency staff and other community programs regarding the interpretation of program-related federal, state, and county regulations and policies. Implement and evaluate staff training programs.

Related Military Specialization: Community Services Management. **Average Educational Level of Vets:** Bachelor's degree. **Usual Educational Requirement:** Bachelor's degree. **Relevant Educational Programs:** Business Administration and Management, General; Business/Commerce, General; Community Organization and Advocacy; Human Services, General; Non-Profit/Public/Organizational Management; Public Administration; Social Work; Social Work, Other; Youth Services/Administration. **Related Knowledge/Courses:** Therapy and Counseling; Psychology; Sociology and Anthropology; Philosophy and Theology; Personnel and Human Resources; Customer and Personal Service. **Work Experience Needed:** 1 to 5 years. **On-the-Job Training Needed:** None. **Certification/Licensure:** None.

Personality Types: Enterprising-Social. **Key Career Cluster:** 10 Human Services. **Key Career Pathway:** 10.2 Counseling and Mental Health Services. **Top Industries for Vets:** Civic, Social, Advocacy Organizations, and Grantmaking and Giving Services; Individual and Family Services; Business, Professional, Political and Similar Organizations; Residential Care Facilities, Without Nursing; Administration of Human Resource Programs.

Skills: Management of Financial Resources; Management of Personnel Resources; Management of Material Resources; Systems Evaluation; Operations Analysis; Social Perceptiveness; Systems Analysis; Learning Strategies.

Work Environment: Indoors; sitting.

Social and Human Service Assistants

* Average Annual Earnings (All): $28,740

* Average Annual Earnings (Recent Veterans): $37,110

* Earnings Growth Potential: Low (33.3%)

* Growth: 27.6%

* Annual Job Openings: 18,910

* Veteran Employment by Sector: For-Profit, 5.0%; Nonprofit, 18.3%; Government, 76.7%; Self-Employed, 0.0%.

Considerations for Job Outlook: Low pay and heavy workloads cause many workers to leave this occupation, which creates good opportunities for new workers entering the field.

Assist in providing client services in a wide variety of fields, such as psychology, rehabilitation, or social work, including support for families. Keep records and prepare reports for owner or management concerning visits with clients. Submit reports, and review reports or problems with superior. Interview individuals and family members to compile information on social, educational, criminal, institutional, or drug histories. Provide information and refer individuals to public or private agencies or community services for assistance. Consult with supervisors concerning programs for individual families. Advise clients regarding food stamps, child care, food, money management, sanitation, or housekeeping. Oversee day-to-day group activities of residents in institution. Visit individuals in homes or attend group meetings to provide information on agency services, requirements, and procedures. Monitor free, supplementary meal program to ensure cleanliness of facility and that eligibility guidelines are met for persons receiving meals. Meet with youth groups to acquaint them with consequences of delinquent acts. Assist in planning of food budgets, using charts and sample budgets. Transport and accompany clients to shopping areas or to appointments, using automobiles. Assist in locating housing for displaced individuals. Observe and discuss meal preparation, and suggest alternate methods of food preparation. Observe clients' food selections, and recommend alternative economical and nutritional food choices. Explain rules established by owner or management, such as sanitation and maintenance requirements or parking regulations.

Related Military Specialization: Airman and Family Readiness Center Readiness NCO. **Average Educational Level of Vets:** Bachelor's degree. **Usual Educational Requirement:** High school diploma or equivalent. **Relevant Educational Programs:** Developmental Services Worker; Human Services, General. **Related Knowledge/Courses:** Therapy and Counseling; Philosophy and Theology; Psychology; Customer and Personal Service; Sociology and Anthropology; Clerical Practices. **Work Experience Needed:** None. **On-the-Job Training Needed:** Short-term on-the-job training. **Certification/Licensure:** None.

Personality Types: Conventional-Social-Enterprising. **Key Career Cluster:** 10 Human Services. **Key Career Pathway:** 10.3 Family and Community Services. **Top Industries for Vets:** Justice, Public Order, and Safety Activities; Administration of Human Resource Programs; National Security and International Affairs; Civic, Social, Advocacy Organizations, and Grantmaking and Giving Services; Individual and Family Services.

Skills: Social Perceptiveness; Service Orientation; Active Listening; Science; Speaking; Learning Strategies; Systems Analysis; Persuasion.

Work Environment: Indoors; sitting.

Software Developers, Systems Software

* Average Annual Earnings (All): $96,600
* Average Annual Earnings (Recent Veterans): $78,580
* Earnings Growth Potential: Medium (35.3%)
* Growth: 32.4%
* Annual Job Openings: 16,800
* Veteran Employment by Sector: For-Profit, 75.0%; Nonprofit, 3.2%; Government, 20.8%; Self-Employed, 1.0%.

Considerations for Job Outlook: Job prospects will be best for applicants with knowledge of the most up-to-date programming tools and languages. Consulting opportunities for software developers also should be good as businesses seek help to manage, upgrade, and customize their increasingly complicated computer systems.

Research, design, develop, and test operating systems-level software, compilers, and network distribution software. Modify existing software to correct errors, adapt it to new hardware, or upgrade interfaces and improve performance. Design and develop software systems, using scientific analysis and mathematical models to predict and measure outcome and consequences of design. Consult with engineering staff to evaluate the interface between hardware and software, develop specifications and performance requirements, and resolve customer problems. Analyze information to determine, recommend, and plan installation of a new system or modification of an existing system. Develop and direct software system testing and validation procedures. Direct software programming and development of documentation. Consult with customers or other departments on project status, proposals, and technical issues such as software system design and maintenance. Advise customer about, or perform, maintenance of software system. Coordinate installation of software system. Monitor functioning of equipment to ensure system operates in conformance with specifications. Store, retrieve, and manipulate data for analysis of system capabilities and requirements. Confer with data processing and project managers to obtain information on limitations and capabilities for data processing projects. Prepare reports and correspondence concerning project specifications, activities, and status. Evaluate factors such as reporting formats required, cost constraints, and need for security restrictions to determine hardware configuration.

Related Military Specializations: Classic Wizard Configuration Maintenance Analyst; Software Analyst. **Average Educational Level of Vets:** Bachelor's degree. **Usual Educational Requirement:** Bachelor's degree. **Relevant Educational Programs:** Artificial Intelligence; Computer Engineering, General; Computer Programming, Specific Applications; Computer Programming/Programmer, General; Computer Science; Computer Software Engineering; Computer Software Technology/Technician; Informatics; Information Science/Studies; Information Technology. **Related Knowledge/Courses:** Computers and Electronics; Engineering and Technology; Design; Telecommunications; Mathematics; Communications and Media. **Work Experience Needed:** None. **On-the-Job Training Needed:** None. **Certification/Licensure:** Voluntary certification by vendor or association.

Personality Types: Investigative-Conventional-Realistic. **Key Career Cluster:** 11 Information Technology. **Key Career Pathway:** 11.4

Programming and Software Development. **Top Industries for Vets:** Computer Systems Design and Related Services; Architectural, Engineering, and Related Services; National Security and International Affairs; Aircraft and Parts; Management, Scientific and Technical Consulting Services.

Skills: Programming; Technology Design; Operations Analysis; Science; Equipment Selection; Quality Control Analysis; Systems Evaluation; Mathematics.

Work Environment: Indoors; sitting; repetitive motions.

Structural Iron and Steel Workers

- ❋ Average Annual Earnings (All): $45,690
- ❋ Average Annual Earnings (Recent Veterans): $32,740
- ❋ Earnings Growth Potential: High (42.0%)
- ❋ Growth: 21.9%
- ❋ Annual Job Openings: 2,540
- ❋ Veteran Employment by Sector: For-Profit, 90.0%; Nonprofit, 0.0%; Government, 7.0%; Self-Employed, 3.0%.

Considerations for Job Outlook: Those who are certified in welding and rigging should have the best job opportunities. Those with prior military service are also viewed favorably during initial hiring. As with many other construction workers, employment of iron workers is sensitive to the fluctuations of the economy.

Raise, place, and unite iron or steel girders, columns, and other structural members to form completed structures or structural

frameworks. Read specifications and blueprints to determine the locations, quantities, and sizes of materials required. Verify vertical and horizontal alignment of structural-steel members, using plumb bobs, laser equipment, transits, and/or levels. Connect columns, beams, and girders with bolts, following blueprints and instructions from supervisors. Hoist steel beams, girders, and columns into place, using cranes, or signal hoisting equipment operators to lift and position structural-steel members. Bolt aligned structural-steel members in position for permanent riveting, bolting, or welding into place. Ride on girders or other structural-steel members to position them, or use rope to guide them into position. Fabricate metal parts such as steel frames, columns, beams, and girders, according to blueprints or instructions from supervisors. Pull, push, or pry structural-steel members into approximate positions for bolting into place. Cut, bend, and weld steel pieces, using metal shears, torches, and welding equipment. Fasten structural-steel members to hoist cables, using chains, cables, or rope. Assemble hoisting equipment and rigging, such as cables, pulleys, and hooks, to move heavy equipment and materials. Force structural-steel members into final positions, using turnbuckles, crowbars, jacks, and hand tools. Erect metal and precast concrete components for structures such as buildings, bridges, dams, towers, storage tanks, fences, and highway guard rails. Unload and position prefabricated steel units for hoisting as needed. Drive drift pins through rivet holes in order to align rivet holes in structural-steel members with corresponding holes in previously placed members. Dismantle structures and equipment. Insert sealing strips, wiring, insulating material, ladders, flanges, gauges, and valves, depending on types of structures being assembled. Catch hot rivets in buckets, and insert rivets in holes, using tongs. Place blocks under reinforcing bars used to reinforce floors.

Related Military Specializations: Advanced Steelworker; Carpentry and Masonry Specialist; Steelworker; Steelworker—Erector; Steelworker—Fabricator; Structural Apprentice; Structural Helper; Structural Journeyman. **Average Educational Level of Vets:** High school diploma or equivalent. **Usual Educational Requirement:** High school diploma or equivalent. **Relevant Educational Program:** Metal Building Assembly/Assembler. **Related Knowledge/Courses:** Building and Construction; Engineering and Technology; Mechanical Devices; Production and Processing; Design; Physics. **Work Experience Needed:** None. **On-the-Job Training Needed:** Apprenticeship. **Certification/Licensure:** Voluntary certification by association.

Personality Types: Realistic-Investigative-Conventional. **Key Career Cluster:** 02 Architecture and Construction. **Key Career Pathway:** 2.2 Construction. **Top Industries for Vets:** Construction; Advertising and Related Services; Support Activities For Mining; Miscellaneous Manufacturing, Not Elsewhere Classified; National Security and International Affairs.

Skills: Equipment Selection; Operation and Control; Repairing; Equipment Maintenance; Quality Control Analysis; Installation; Troubleshooting; Operation Monitoring.

Work Environment: Outdoors; standing; climbing; walking and running; balancing; using hands; bending or twisting the body; repetitive motions; noise; very hot or cold; bright or inadequate lighting; contaminants; cramped work space; whole-body vibration; high places; hazardous conditions; hazardous equipment; minor burns, cuts, bites, or stings.

Substance Abuse and Behavioral Disorder Counselors

* Average Annual Earnings (All): $38,560
* Average Annual Earnings (Recent Veterans): $35,800
* Earnings Growth Potential: Low (34.4%)
* Growth: 27.3%
* Annual Job Openings: 4,170
* Veteran Employment by Sector: For-Profit, 23.1%; Nonprofit, 17.6%; Government, 58.6%; Self-Employed, 0.7%.

Considerations for Job Outlook: Job prospects are excellent for substance abuse and behavioral disorder counselors, particularly for those with specialized training or education. Employers often have difficulty recruiting workers with the proper educational requirements and experience in working with addiction. In addition, many workers leave the field after a few years and need to be replaced. As result, those interested in entering this field should find favorable prospects.

Counsel and advise individuals with alcohol, tobacco, drug, or other problems, such as gambling and eating disorders. Counsel clients and patients individually and in group sessions to assist in overcoming dependencies, adjusting to life, and making changes. Complete and maintain accurate records and reports regarding the patients' histories and progress, services provided, and other required information. Develop client treatment plans based on research, clinical experience, and client histories. Review and evaluate clients' progress in relation to measurable goals described in treatment and care plans. Interview clients, review records, and confer with other professionals to evaluate individuals' mental and physical condition and to determine their suitability for participation in a specific program. Intervene as advocate for clients or patients to resolve emergency problems in crisis situations. Provide clients or family members with information about addiction issues and about available services and programs, making appropriate referrals when necessary. Modify treatment plans to comply with changes in client status. Coordinate counseling efforts with mental health professionals and other health professionals such as doctors, nurses, and social workers. Attend training sessions to increase knowledge and skills. Plan and implement follow-up and aftercare programs for clients to be discharged from treatment programs. Conduct chemical-dependency program orientation sessions. Counsel family members to assist them in understanding, dealing with, and supporting clients or patients.

Related Military Specializations: None. **Average Educational Level of Vets:** Bachelor's degree. **Usual Educational Requirement:** High school diploma or equivalent. **Relevant Educational Programs:** Clinical Pastoral Counseling/Patient Counseling; Clinical/Medical Social Work; Substance Abuse/Addiction Counseling. **Related Knowledge/Courses:** Therapy and Counseling; Psychology; Sociology and Anthropology; Philosophy and Theology; Education and Training; Clerical Practices. **Work Experience Needed:** None. **On-the-Job Training Needed:** Moderate-term on-the-job training. **Certification/Licensure:** Licensure in many states; voluntary certification by association in others.

Personality Types: Social-Artistic-Investigative. **Key Career Cluster:** 10 Human Services. **Key Career Pathway:** 10.2 Counseling and Mental Health Services. **Top Industries for Vets:** National Security and International Affairs; Colleges and Universities, Including Junior

Colleges; Justice, Public Order, and Safety Activities; Individual and Family Services; Elementary and Secondary Schools.

Skills: Social Perceptiveness; Service Orientation; Persuasion; Learning Strategies; Active Listening; Negotiation; Monitoring; Systems Analysis.

Work Environment: Indoors; sitting.

Supervisors of Construction and Extraction Workers

- ❋ Average Annual Earnings (All): $59,150
- ❋ Average Annual Earnings (Recent Veterans): $41,470
- ❋ Earnings Growth Potential: Medium (37.7%)
- ❋ Growth: 23.5%
- ❋ Annual Job Openings: 25,970
- ❋ Veteran Employment by Sector: For-Profit, 67.6%; Nonprofit, 0.4%; Government, 15.5%; Self-Employed, 16.5%.

Considerations for Job Outlook: A small increase is expected as the streamlining of employment, such as reducing administrative staff, will reduce these noncraft workers relative to supervisors.

Directly supervise and coordinate activities of construction or extraction workers. Examine and inspect work progress, equipment, and construction sites to verify safety and to ensure that specifications are met. Read specifications such as blueprints to determine construction requirements and to plan procedures. Estimate material and worker requirements to complete jobs. Supervise, coordinate, and schedule the activities of construction or extractive workers. Confer with managerial and technical personnel, other departments, and contractors in order to resolve problems and to coordinate activities. Coordinate work activities with other construction project activities. Locate, measure, and mark site locations and placement of structures and equipment, using measuring and marking equipment. Order or requisition materials and supplies. Record information such as personnel, production, and operational data on specified forms and reports. Assign work to employees based on material and worker requirements of specific jobs. Provide assistance to workers engaged in construction or extraction activities, using hand tools and equipment. Train workers in construction methods, operation of equipment, safety procedures, and company policies. Analyze worker and production problems, and recommend solutions such as improving production methods or implementing motivational plans. Arrange for repairs of equipment and machinery. Suggest or initiate personnel actions such as promotions, transfers, and hires.

Related Military Specializations: Civil Engineer Manager; Combat Engineering Senior Sergeant; Construction Engineering Supervisor; Construction Equipment Supervisor; Emergency Management Manager; Engineer Equipment Chief; Explosive Ordnance Disposal Manager; General Engineering Supervisor; Heavy Repair Superintendent; Horizontal Construction Engineer; IMA Rigging and Weight Testing Shop Journeyman; Master Chief Constructionman; Master Chief Equipmentman; Master Chief Utilitiesman; Pavements and Construction Equipment Craftsman; others. **Average Educational Level of Vets:** High school diploma or equivalent. **Usual Educational Requirement:** High school diploma or equivalent. **Relevant Educational Programs:** Blasting/Blaster; Building Construction Technology; Building/Construction Site Management/Manager; Building/Home/Construction

Inspection/Inspector; Building/Property Maintenance; Carpentry/Carpenter; Carpet, Floor, and Tile Worker; Concrete Finishing/Concrete Finisher; Construction Trades, General; Drywall Installation/Drywaller; Electrician; Glazier Training; Insulator Training; Masonry/Mason Training; Painting/Painter and Wall Coverer Training; Pipefitting/Pipefitter and Sprinkler Fitter; Plumbing Technology/Plumber; Roofer Training; Well Drilling/Driller. **Related Knowledge/Courses:** Building and Construction; Mechanical Devices; Design; Engineering and Technology; Production and Processing; Public Safety and Security. **Work Experience Needed:** More than 5 years. **On-the-Job Training Needed:** None. **Certification/Licensure:** None.

Personality Types: Enterprising-Realistic-Conventional. **Key Career Cluster:** 02 Architecture and Construction. **Key Career Pathway:** 2.2 Construction. **Top Industries for Vets:** Construction; National Security and International Affairs; Support Activities For Mining; Building Material and Supplies Dealers; Cement, Concrete, Lime, and Gypsum Products.

Skills: Equipment Selection; Management of Personnel Resources; Equipment Maintenance; Operation and Control; Quality Control Analysis; Operations Analysis; Management of Material Resources; Troubleshooting.

Work Environment: Outdoors; standing; using hands; noise; very hot or cold; bright or inadequate lighting; contaminants; hazardous equipment.

Job Specialization: Solar Energy Installation Managers

Direct work crews installing residential or commercial solar photovoltaic or thermal systems. Plan and coordinate installations of photovoltaic (PV) solar and solar thermal systems to ensure conformance to codes. Supervise solar installers, technicians, and subcontractors for solar installation projects to ensure compliance with safety standards. Assess potential solar installation sites to determine feasibility and design requirements. Assess system performance or functionality at the system, subsystem, and component levels. Coordinate or schedule building inspections for solar installation projects. Monitor work of contractors and subcontractors to ensure projects conform to plans, specifications, schedules, or budgets. Perform start-up of systems for testing or customer implementation. Provide technical assistance to installers, technicians, or other solar professionals in areas such as solar electric systems, solar thermal systems, electrical systems, and mechanical systems. Visit customer sites to determine solar system needs, requirements, or specifications. Develop and maintain system architecture, including all piping, instrumentation, or process flow diagrams. Estimate materials, equipment, and personnel needed for residential or commercial solar installation projects. Evaluate subcontractors or subcontractor bids for quality, cost, and reliability. Identify means to reduce costs, minimize risks, or increase efficiency of solar installation projects. Prepare solar installation project proposals, quotes, budgets, or schedules.

Related Knowledge/Courses: No data available.

Personality Types: No data available.

Skills: No data available.

Work Environment: No data available.

Surgical Technologists

* Average Annual Earnings (All): $40,950
* Average Annual Earnings (Recent Veterans): $30,560
* Earnings Growth Potential: Low (29.5%)
* Growth: 18.9%
* Annual Job Openings: 3,390
* Veteran Employment by Sector: For-Profit, 54.5%; Nonprofit, 12.2%; Government, 32.7%; Self-Employed, 0.6%.

Considerations for Job Outlook: Job prospects should be best for surgical technologists who have completed an accredited education program and who maintain their professional certification.

Assist in operations, under the supervision of surgeons, registered nurses, or other surgical personnel. Count sponges, needles, and instruments before and after operations. Maintain a proper sterile field during surgical procedures. Hand instruments and supplies to surgeons and surgeons' assistants, hold retractors, cut sutures, and perform other tasks as directed by surgeons during operations. Prepare patients for surgery, including positioning patients on operating tables and covering them with sterile surgical drapes to prevent exposure. Scrub arms and hands, and assist surgical teams to scrub and put on gloves, masks, and surgical clothing. Wash and sterilize equipment, using germicides and sterilizers. Monitor and continually assess operating room conditions, including needs of the patient and the surgical team. Prepare dressings or bandages, and apply or assist with their application following surgeries. Clean and restock operating rooms, gathering and placing equipment and supplies and arranging instruments according to instructions such as those found on a preference card.

Operate, assemble, adjust, or monitor sterilizers, lights, suction machines, and diagnostic equipment to ensure proper operation. Prepare, care for, and dispose of tissue specimens taken for laboratory analysis. Provide technical assistance to surgeons, surgical nurses, and anesthesiologists. Maintain supply of fluids such as plasma, saline, blood, and glucose for use during operations. Maintain files and records of surgical procedures. Observe patients' vital signs to assess physical condition.

Related Military Specializations: Dental Surgical Technologist; Operating Room Specialist; Ophthalmic Surgical Technician; Surgical Technologist; Surgical Service Apprentice; Surgical Service Apprentice, Orthopedics; Surgical Service Apprentice, Otorhinolaryngology; Surgical Service Apprentice, Urology; Surgical Service Craftsman; Surgical Service Craftsman, Orthopedics; Surgical Service Craftsman, Otorhinolaryngology; Surgical Service Craftsman, Urology; Surgical Service Helper; Surgical Service Helper, Orthopedics; others. **Average Educational Level of Vets:** One or more years of college, no degree. **Usual Educational Requirement:** Postsecondary vocational training. **Relevant Educational Programs:** Pathology/Pathologist Assistant Training; Sterile Processing Technology/Technician Training; Surgical Technology/Technologist. **Related Knowledge/Courses:** Medicine and Dentistry; Biology; Psychology; Chemistry; Therapy and Counseling; Customer and Personal Service. **Work Experience Needed:** None. **On-the-Job Training Needed:** None. **Certification/Licensure:** Voluntary certification by association.

Personality Types: Realistic-Social-Conventional. **Key Career Cluster:** 08 Health Science. **Key Career Pathway:** 8.1 Therapeutic Services. **Top Industries for Vets:** Hospitals; Pharmacies and Drug Stores; National Security and International Affairs; Veterinary Services; Other Health Care Services.

Skills: Equipment Maintenance; Equipment Selection; Operation Monitoring; Repairing; Quality Control Analysis; Operation and Control; Management of Material Resources; Coordination.

Work Environment: Indoors; standing; using hands; bending or twisting the body; repetitive motions; contaminants; exposed to radiation; exposed to disease or infections; hazardous conditions; hazardous equipment; minor burns, cuts, bites, or stings.

Surveying and Mapping Technicians

* Average Annual Earnings (All): $39,350

* Average Annual Earnings (Recent Veterans): $37,110

* Earnings Growth Potential: Medium (37.9%)

* Growth: 15.9%

* Annual Job Openings: 2,000

* Veteran Employment by Sector: For-Profit, 92.4%; Nonprofit, 0.0%; Government, 6.9%; Self-Employed, 0.7%.

Considerations for Job Outlook: Recent advancements in mapping technology have led to new uses for maps and a need for more of the data used to build maps. As a result, surveying and mapping technicians should have more work.

Perform surveying and mapping duties, usually under the direction of an engineer, surveyor, cartographer, or photogrammetrist. For task data, see Job Specializations.

Related Military Specializations: Construction Surveyor; Engineering Aide; Engineering Aide—Surveyor; Field Artillery Surveyor; Field Artillery Surveyor/Meteorological Crewmember; Geographic Intelligence Specialist; Imagery Analysis Specialist; Intelligence Specialist; Terrain Analyst; Topographic Analyst; Topographic Engineering Supervisor; Topographic Surveyor. **Average Educational Level of Vets:** High school diploma or equivalent. **Usual Educational Requirement:** High school diploma or equivalent. **Relevant Educational Program:** Surveying Technology/Surveying. **Work Experience Needed:** None. **On-the-Job Training Needed:** Moderate-term on-the-job training. **Certification/Licensure:** Voluntary certification by association.

Key Career Cluster: 15 Science, Technology, Engineering, and Mathematics. **Key Career Pathway:** 15.1 Engineering and Technology. **Top Industries for Vets:** Architectural, Engineering, and Related Services; Construction; Other Administrative, and Other Support Services; Wired Telecommunications Carriers; Other Professional, Scientific and Technical Services.

Job Specialization: Mapping Technicians

Calculate mapmaking information from field notes and draw and verify accuracy of topographical maps. Check all layers of maps to ensure accuracy, identifying and marking errors and making corrections. Determine scales, line sizes, and colors to be used for hard copies of computerized maps, using plotters. Monitor mapping work and the updating of maps to ensure accuracy, the inclusion of new and/or changed information, and compliance with rules and regulations. Identify and compile database information to create maps in response to requests. Produce and update overlay maps to show information boundaries, water locations, and

topographic features on various base maps and at different scales. Trace contours and topographic details to generate maps that denote specific land and property locations and geographic attributes. Lay out and match aerial photographs in sequences in which they were taken, and identify any areas missing from photographs. Compare topographical features and contour lines with images from aerial photographs, old maps, and other reference materials to verify the accuracy of their identification. Compute and measure scaled distances between reference points to establish relative positions of adjoining prints and enable the creation of photographic mosaics. Research resources such as survey maps and legal descriptions to verify property lines and to obtain information needed for mapping. Form three-dimensional images of aerial photographs taken from different locations, using mathematical techniques and plotting instruments.

Related Knowledge/Courses: Geography; Design; Computers and Electronics; Engineering and Technology; Mathematics; Clerical Practices.

Personality Types: Conventional-Realistic.

Skills: Programming; Mathematics; Quality Control Analysis; Management of Personnel Resources; Learning Strategies; Instructing; Operation and Control; Writing.

Work Environment: Indoors; sitting; using hands; repetitive motions.

Job Specialization: Surveying Technicians

Adjust and operate surveying instruments such as theodolite and electronic distance-measuring equipment and compile notes, make sketches, and enter data into computers. Perform calculations to determine Earth curvature corrections, atmospheric impacts on measurements, traverse closures and adjustments, azimuths, level runs, and placement of markers. Record survey measurements and descriptive data using notes, drawings, sketches, and inked tracings. Search for section corners, property irons, and survey points. Position and hold the vertical rods, or targets, that theodolite operators use for sighting to measure angles, distances, and elevations. Lay out grids, and determine horizontal and vertical controls. Compare survey computations with applicable standards to determine adequacy of data. Set out and recover stakes, marks, and other monumentation. Conduct surveys to ascertain the locations of natural features and man-made structures on Earth's surface, underground, and underwater, using electronic distance-measuring equipment and other surveying instruments. Direct and supervise work of subordinate members of surveying parties. Compile information necessary to stake projects for construction, using engineering plans. Prepare topographic and contour maps of land surveyed, including site features and other relevant information, such as charts, drawings, and survey notes. Place and hold measuring tapes when electronic distance-measuring equipment is not used. Collect information needed to carry out new surveys using source maps, previous survey data, photographs, computer records, and other relevant information.

Related Knowledge/Courses: Geography; Design; Building and Construction; Mathematics; Law and Government; Engineering and Technology.

Personality Types: Realistic-Conventional.

Skills: Equipment Maintenance; Operation and Control; Repairing; Science; Equipment Selection; Mathematics; Troubleshooting; Operation Monitoring.

Work Environment: More often outdoors than indoors; standing; walking and running; using hands; noise; very hot or cold; contaminants; hazardous equipment; minor burns, cuts, bites, or stings.

Teacher Assistants

- ❀ Average Annual Earnings (All): $23,580
- ❀ Average Annual Earnings (Recent Veterans): $15,280
- ❀ Earnings Growth Potential: Low (27.5%)
- ❀ Growth: 14.8%
- ❀ Annual Job Openings: 48,160
- ❀ Veteran Employment by Sector: For-Profit, 10.9%; Nonprofit, 10.7%; Government, 78.4%; Self-Employed, 0.0%.

Considerations for Job Outlook: In addition to job openings from employment growth, numerous openings will arise as assistants leave the job and must be replaced. Because this occupation requires limited formal education and has low pay, many workers transfer to other occupations or leave the labor force because of family responsibilities, to return to school, or for other reasons. Job opportunities for teacher assistants vary significantly by geography. Opportunities should be better in the South and West, which are expected to have rapid increases in enrollment, and in urban schools, which often have difficulty recruiting and keeping teacher assistants.

Perform duties that are instructional in nature or deliver direct services to students or parents. Provide extra assistance to students with special needs, such as non-English-speaking students or those with physical and mental disabilities. Tutor and assist children individually or in small groups to help them master assignments and to reinforce learning concepts presented by teachers. Supervise students in classrooms, halls, cafeterias, school yards, and gymnasiums, or on field trips.

Enforce administration policies and rules governing students. Observe students' performance, and record relevant data to assess progress. Discuss assigned duties with classroom teachers to coordinate instructional efforts. Instruct and monitor students in the use and care of equipment and materials to prevent injuries and damage. Present subject matter to students under the direction and guidance of teachers, using lectures, discussions, or supervised role-playing methods. Organize and label materials and display students' work in a manner appropriate for their eye levels and perceptual skills. Type, file, and duplicate materials. Distribute teaching materials such as textbooks, workbooks, papers, and pencils to students. Use computers, audio-visual aids, and other equipment and materials to supplement presentations. Attend staff meetings and serve on committees, as required. Prepare lesson materials, bulletin board displays, exhibits, equipment, and demonstrations. Organize and supervise games and other recreational activities to promote physical, mental, and social development. Laminate teaching materials to increase their durability under repeated use. Distribute tests and homework assignments and collect them when they are completed. Carry out therapeutic regimens such as behavior modification and personal development programs, under the supervision of special education instructors, psychologists, or speech-language pathologists. Provide disabled students with assistive devices, supportive technology, and assistance accessing facilities such as restrooms.

Related Military Specializations: None. **Average Educational Level of Vets:** One or more years of college, no degree. **Usual Educational Requirement:** High school diploma or equivalent. **Relevant Educational Program:** Teacher Assistant/Aide Training. **Related Knowledge/ Courses:** Therapy and Counseling; Psychology; Sociology and Anthropology. **Work Experience Needed:** None. **On-the-Job Training Needed:**

Short-term on-the-job training. **Certification/ Licensure:** Licensure in some states.

Personality Types: Social-Conventional. **Key Career Cluster:** 05 Education and Training. **Key Career Pathway:** 5.3 Teaching/Training. **Top Industries for Vets:** Elementary and Secondary Schools; Child Day Care Services; Other Schools and Instruction, and Educational Support Services; Colleges and Universities, Including Junior Colleges; Architectural, Engineering, and Related Services.

Skills: Learning Strategies; Instructing; Technology Design; Service Orientation; Social Perceptiveness.

Work Environment: Indoors; standing.

Technical Writers

- ❋ Average Annual Earnings (All): $64,610
- ❋ Average Annual Earnings (Recent Veterans): $62,210
- ❋ Earnings Growth Potential: High (41.2%)
- ❋ Growth: 17.2%
- ❋ Annual Job Openings: 1,830
- ❋ Veteran Employment by Sector: For-Profit, 83.6%; Nonprofit, 0.0%; Government, 16.4%; Self-Employed, 0.0%.

Considerations for Job Outlook: Job opportunities, especially for applicants with technical skills, are expected to be good. The growing reliance on technologically sophisticated products in the home and the workplace and the increasing complexity of medical and scientific information needed for daily living will create many new job opportunities for technical writers. In addition to job openings stemming from employment growth, some openings will arise as experienced workers retire, transfer to other occupations, or leave the labor force. However, there will be competition among freelance technical writers.

Write technical materials, such as equipment manuals, appendices, or operating and maintenance instructions. Organize material and complete writing assignment according to set standards regarding order, clarity, conciseness, style, and terminology. Maintain records and files of work and revisions. Edit, standardize, or make changes to material prepared by other writers or establishment personnel. Confer with customer representatives, vendors, plant executives, or publisher to establish technical specifications and to determine subject material to be developed for publication. Review published materials, and recommend revisions or changes in scope, format, content, and methods of reproduction and binding. Select photographs, drawings, sketches, diagrams, and charts to illustrate material. Study drawings, specifications, mockups, and product samples to integrate and delineate technology, operating procedure, and production sequence and detail. Interview production and engineering personnel and read journals and other material to become familiar with product technologies and production methods. Observe production, developmental, and experimental activities to determine operating procedure and detail. Arrange for typing, duplication, and distribution of material. Assist in laying out material for publication. Analyze developments in specific field to determine need for revisions in previously published materials and development of new material. Review manufacturer's and trade catalogs, drawings, and other data relative to operation, maintenance, and service of equipment.

Related Military Specializations: Journalist; Journalist Tracking NEC. **Average Educational Level of Vets:** One or more years of college, no degree. **Usual Educational Requirement:** Bachelor's degree. **Relevant Educational**

Programs: Business/Corporate Communications; Family and Consumer Sciences/Human Sciences Communication; Professional, Technical, Business, and Scientific Writing; Technical and Scientific Communication; Writing, General. **Related Knowledge/Courses:** Communications and Media; Clerical Practices; English Language; Computers and Electronics; Education and Training; Engineering and Technology. **Work Experience Needed:** 1 to 5 years. **On-the-Job Training Needed:** Short-term on-the-job training. **Certification/Licensure:** None.

Personality Types: Artistic-Investigative-Conventional. **Key Career Cluster:** 15 Science, Technology, Engineering, and Mathematics. **Key Career Pathway:** 15.1 Engineering and Technology. **Top Industries for Vets:** Architectural, Engineering, and Related Services; National Security and International Affairs; Scientific Research and Development Services; Computer Systems Design and Related Services; Aircraft and Parts.

Skills: Writing; Reading Comprehension; Active Learning; Speaking; Operations Analysis; Critical Thinking; Active Listening; Complex Problem Solving.

Work Environment: Indoors; sitting; using hands; repetitive motions.

Telecommunications Line Installers and Repairers

❀ Average Annual Earnings (All): $51,720

❀ Average Annual Earnings (Recent Veterans): $39,290

❀ Earnings Growth Potential: High (46.9%)

❀ Growth: 13.6%

❀ Annual Job Openings: 5,140

❀ Veteran Employment by Sector: For-Profit, 89.3%; Nonprofit, 0.0%; Government, 7.5%; Self-Employed, 3.2%.

Considerations for Job Outlook: Good job opportunities are expected overall. Highly skilled workers with apprenticeship training or a 2-year associate degree in telecommunications, electronics, or electricity should have the best job opportunities.

Install and repair telecommunications cable, including fiber optics. Travel to customers' premises to install, maintain, and repair audio and visual electronic reception equipment and accessories. Inspect and test lines and cables, recording and analyzing test results, to assess transmission characteristics and locate faults and malfunctions. Splice cables, using hand tools, epoxy, or mechanical equipment. Set up service for customers, installing, connecting, testing, and adjusting equipment. Measure signal strength at utility poles, using electronic test equipment. Place insulation over conductors, and seal splices with moisture-proof covering. Access specific areas to string lines and install terminal boxes, auxiliary equipment, and appliances, using bucket trucks, or by climbing poles and ladders or entering tunnels, trenches, or crawl spaces. String cables between structures and lines from poles, towers, or trenches and pull lines to proper tension. Install equipment such as amplifiers and repeaters in order to maintain the strength of communications transmissions. Lay underground cable directly in trenches, or string it through conduits running through trenches. Pull up cable by hand from large reels mounted on trucks; then pull lines through ducts by hand or with winches. Clean and maintain tools and test equipment. Explain cable service to subscribers after installation, and collect any installation fees that are due. Compute impedance of wires from poles to houses in order to determine additional resistance needed for reducing signals to desired levels. Use a variety of construction equipment to complete installations, including digger derricks, trenchers, and cable plows. Dig trenches for underground wires and cables. Dig holes for power poles, using power augers or shovels, set poles in place with cranes, and hoist poles upright, using winches. Fill and tamp holes, using cement, earth, and tamping devices. Participate in the construction and removal of telecommunication towers and associated support structures.

Related Military Specializations: Basic Communications Marine; Cable and Antenna Systems Apprentice; Cable and Antenna Systems Craftsman; Cable and Antenna Systems Helper; Cable and Antenna Systems Journeyman; Cable Systems Installer-Maintainer; Cable Systems Technician; Construction Wireman; Signal Support Systems Specialist; Tactical Switching Operator; Telephone Technician—Outside; Wire Systems Installer. **Average Educational Level of Vets:** High school diploma or equivalent. **Usual Educational Requirement:** High school diploma or equivalent. **Relevant Educational Program:** Communications Systems Installation and Repair Technology. **Related Knowledge/Courses:** Telecommunications; Building and Construction; Engineering and Technology; Customer and Personal Service; Design; Mechanical Devices.

Work Experience Needed: None. **On-the-Job Training Needed:** Long-term on-the-job training. **Certification/Licensure:** Voluntary certification by association.

Personality Types: Realistic-Enterprising. **Key Career Cluster:** 03 Arts, Audiovisual Technology, and Communications. **Key Career Pathway:** 3.6 Telecommunications Technologies. **Top Industries for Vets:** Broadcasting, Including Internet Publishing and Web Search Portals; Wired Telecommunications Carriers; Construction; National Security and International Affairs; Other Telecommunication Services.

Skills: Troubleshooting; Equipment Maintenance; Repairing; Operation and Control; Equipment Selection; Quality Control Analysis; Operation Monitoring; Installation.

Work Environment: Outdoors; standing; walking and running; kneeling, crouching, stooping, or crawling; using hands; bending or twisting the body; repetitive motions; noise; very hot or cold; bright or inadequate lighting; contaminants; cramped work space; high places; hazardous equipment; minor burns, cuts, bites, or stings.

Tile and Marble Setters

- Average Annual Earnings (All): $37,080
- Average Annual Earnings (Recent Veterans): $24,120
- Earnings Growth Potential: High (42.7%)
- Growth: 25.4%
- Annual Job Openings: 2,770
- Veteran Employment by Sector: For-Profit, 77.7%; Nonprofit, 0.0%; Government, 2.7%; Self-Employed, 19.5%.

Considerations for Job Outlook: Overall job prospects should improve over the coming decade as construction activity rebounds from the recent recession. As with many other construction workers, employment of tile and marble setters is sensitive to the fluctuations of the economy. On the one hand, workers may experience periods of unemployment when the overall level of construction falls. On the other hand, shortages of workers may occur in some areas during peak periods of building activity. Highly skilled workers with a good job history and work experience in construction will have the best opportunities.

Apply hard tile, marble, and wood tile to walls, floors, ceilings, and roof decks. Align and straighten tile, using levels, squares, and straightedges. Determine and implement the best layout to achieve a desired pattern. Cut and shape tile to fit around obstacles and into odd spaces and corners, using hand- and power-cutting tools. Finish and dress the joints and wipe excess grout from between tiles, using damp sponge. Apply mortar to tile back, position the tile, and press or tap with trowel handle to affix tile to base. Mix, apply, and spread plaster, concrete, mortar, cement, mastic, glue, or other adhesives to form a bed for the tiles, using brush, trowel, and screed. Prepare cost and labor estimates based on calculations of time and materials needed for project. Measure and mark surfaces to be tiled, following blueprints. Level concrete, and allow to dry. Build underbeds, and install anchor bolts, wires, and brackets. Prepare surfaces for tiling by attaching lath or waterproof paper or by applying a cement mortar coat onto a metal screen. Study blueprints and examine surface to be covered to determine amount of material needed. Cut, surface, polish, and install marble and granite or install precast terrazzo, granite, or marble units. Install and anchor fixtures in designated positions, using hand tools. Cut tile backing to required size, using shears. Remove any old tile, grout, and adhesive, using chisels and scrapers, and clean the surface carefully. Lay and set mosaic tiles to create decorative wall, mural, and floor designs.

Related Military Specializations: None. **Average Educational Level of Vets:** High school diploma or equivalent. **Usual Educational Requirement:** Less than high school diploma or equivalent. **Relevant Educational Programs:** Carpet, Floor, and Tile Worker; Masonry/Mason Training. **Related Knowledge/Courses:** Building and Construction; Design; Mechanical Devices. **Work Experience Needed:** None. **On-the-Job Training Needed:** Long-term on-the-job training. **Certification/Licensure:** None.

Personality Types: Realistic-Conventional-Artistic. **Key Career Cluster:** 02 Architecture and Construction. **Key Career Pathway:** 2.2 Construction. **Top Industries for Vets:** Construction; Furniture and Home Furnishings Stores; Building Material and Supplies Dealers; Prefabricated Wood Buildings and Mobile Homes; Hospitals.

Skills: Equipment Maintenance; Equipment Selection; Repairing; Troubleshooting; Operation and Control; Mathematics; Operation Monitoring; Quality Control Analysis.

Work Environment: Standing; kneeling, crouching, stooping, or crawling; using hands; bending or twisting the body; repetitive motions; noise; very hot or cold; bright or inadequate lighting; contaminants; cramped work space; hazardous equipment; minor burns, cuts, bites, or stings.

Training and Development Specialists

- ❋ Average Annual Earnings (All): $55,150
- ❋ Average Annual Earnings (Recent Veterans): $56,750
- ❋ Earnings Growth Potential: High (42.4%)
- ❋ Growth: 28.3%
- ❋ Annual Job Openings: 9,830
- ❋ Veteran Employment by Sector: For-Profit, 38.1%; Nonprofit, 3.5%; Government, 57.2%; Self-Employed, 1.1%.

Considerations for Job Outlook: Much faster than average employment growth is projected.

Design and conduct training and development programs to improve individual and organizational performance. Keep up with developments in area of expertise by reading current journals, books, and magazine articles. Present information, using a variety of instructional techniques and formats such as role playing, simulations, team exercises, group discussions, videos, and lectures. Schedule classes based on availability of classrooms, equipment, and instructors. Organize and develop, or obtain, training procedure manuals and guides and course materials such as handouts and visual materials. Offer specific training programs to help workers maintain or improve job skills. Monitor, evaluate, and record training activities and program effectiveness. Attend meetings and seminars to obtain information for use in training programs, or to inform management of training program status. Coordinate recruitment and placement of training program participants. Evaluate training materials prepared by instructors, such as outlines, text, and handouts. Develop alternative training methods if expected improvements are not seen. Assess training needs through surveys, interviews with employees, focus groups, or consultation with managers, instructors or customer representatives. Screen, hire, and assign workers to positions based on qualifications. Select and assign instructors to conduct training. Devise programs to develop executive potential among employees in lower-level positions. Design, plan, organize, and direct orientation and training for employees or customers of industrial or commercial establishment. Negotiate contracts with clients, including desired training outcomes, fees, and expenses. Supervise instructors, evaluate instructor performance, and refer instructors to classes for skill development. Monitor training costs to ensure budget is not exceeded, and prepare budget reports to justify expenditures. Refer trainees to employer relations representatives, to locations offering job placement assistance, or to appropriate social services agencies if warranted.

Related Military Specializations: Academy Military Training NCO; Education and Training Apprentice; Education and Training Craftsman; Education and Training Helper; Education and Training Journeyman; Education and Training Manager; Education and Training Superintendent; First Term Airmen Center (FTAC) NCOIC; Instructor; Military Training Instructor; Military Training Leader; Professional Development Instructor; Professional Military Education Instructor. **Average Educational Level of Vets:** Bachelor's degree. **Usual Educational Requirement:** Bachelor's degree. **Relevant Educational Programs:** Human Resources Development; Human Resources Management/Personnel Administration, General. **Related Knowledge/Courses:** Education and Training; Sociology and Anthropology; Sales and Marketing; Clerical Practices; Personnel and Human Resources; Psychology. **Work Experience Needed:** None. **On-the-Job Training Needed:**

None. **Certification/Licensure:** Voluntary certification by association.

Personality Types: Social-Artistic-Conventional. **Key Career Cluster:** 04 Business, Management, and Administration. **Key Career Pathway:** 4.3 Human Resources. **Top Industries for Vets:** National Security and International Affairs; Architectural, Engineering, and Related Services; Administration of Human Resource Programs; Management, Scientific and Technical Consulting Services; Construction.

Skills: Operations Analysis; Learning Strategies; Science; Instructing; Systems Evaluation; Management of Material Resources; Writing; Management of Financial Resources.

Work Environment: Indoors; sitting.

Transportation Inspectors

* Average Annual Earnings (All): $62,230
* Average Annual Earnings (Recent Veterans): $48,020
* Earnings Growth Potential: High (47.1%)
* Growth: 14.4%
* Annual Job Openings: 1,070
* Veteran Employment by Sector: For-Profit, 36.2%; Nonprofit, 3.7%; Government, 60.1%; Self-Employed, 0.0%.

Considerations for Job Outlook: About average employment growth is projected.

Inspect equipment or goods in connection with the safe transport of cargo or people. For task data, see Job Specializations.

Related Military Specializations: Marine Gas Turbine Inspector; Observation Airplane Technical Inspector; Tactical Transport

Helicopter Technical Inspector. **Average Educational Level of Vets:** Associate degree. **Usual Educational Requirement:** Some college, no degree. **Relevant Educational Program:** No related CIP programs; this job is learned through work experience in a related occupation. **Work Experience Needed:** None. **On-the-Job Training Needed:** Short-term on-the-job training. **Certification/Licensure:** Voluntary certification for some specializations.

Key Career Cluster: 07 Government and Public Administration. **Key Career Pathway:** 7.6 Regulation. **Top Industries for Vets:** National Security and International Affairs; Administration of Economic Programs and Space Research; Services Incidental to Transportation; Air Transportation; Justice, Public Order, and Safety Activities.

Job Specialization: Aviation Inspectors

Inspect aircraft, maintenance procedures, air navigational aids, air traffic controls, and communications equipment to ensure conformance with federal safety regulations. Inspect work of aircraft mechanics performing maintenance, modification, or repair and overhaul of aircraft and aircraft mechanical systems to ensure adherence to standards and procedures. Start aircraft and observe gauges, meters, and other instruments to detect evidence of malfunctions. Examine aircraft access plates and doors for security. Examine landing gear, tires, and exteriors of fuselage, wings, and engines for evidence of damage or corrosion and to determine whether repairs are needed. Prepare and maintain detailed repair, inspection, investigation, and certification records and reports. Inspect new, repaired, or modified aircraft to identify damage or defects and to assess airworthiness and conformance to standards, using checklists, hand tools, and test instruments. Examine maintenance records and flight logs to determine if service and maintenance checks and overhauls were performed at prescribed intervals. Recommend replacement, repair, or modification of aircraft equipment. Recommend changes in rules, policies, standards, and regulations based on knowledge of operating conditions, aircraft improvements, and other factors. Issue pilots' licenses to individuals meeting standards. Investigate air accidents and complaints to determine causes. Observe flight activities of pilots to assess flying skills and to ensure conformance to flight and safety regulations.

Related Knowledge/Courses: Mechanical Devices; Physics; Transportation; Chemistry; Design; Law and Government.

Personality Types: Realistic-Conventional-Investigative.

Skills: Science; Equipment Maintenance; Troubleshooting; Repairing; Operation and Control; Equipment Selection; Quality Control Analysis; Operation Monitoring.

Work Environment: More often indoors than outdoors; sitting; noise.

Job Specialization: Freight and Cargo Inspectors

Inspect the handling, storage, and stowing of freight and cargoes. Prepare and submit reports after completion of freight shipments. Inspect shipments to ensure that freight is securely braced and blocked. Record details about freight conditions, handling of freight, and any problems encountered. Advise crews in techniques of stowing dangerous and heavy cargo. Observe loading of freight to ensure that crews comply with procedures. Recommend remedial procedures to correct any violations found during inspections. Inspect loaded cargo, cargo lashed to decks or in storage facilities, and cargo-handling devices to determine compliance with health and safety regulations and need for maintenance. Measure ships' holds and depths of fuel and water in tanks, using sounding lines and tape measures. Notify workers of any special treatment required for shipments. Direct crews to reload freight or to insert additional bracing or packing as necessary. Check temperatures and humidities of shipping and storage areas to ensure that they are at appropriate levels to protect cargo. Determine cargo transportation capabilities by reading documents that set forth cargo-loading and securing procedures, capacities, and stability factors. Read draft markings to determine depths of vessels in water. Issue certificates of compliance for vessels without violations. Write certificates of admeasurement that list details such as designs, lengths, depths, and breadths of vessels, and methods of propulsion.

Related Knowledge/Courses: Transportation; Engineering and Technology; Public Safety and Security; Physics; Geography; Mechanical Devices.

Personality Types: Realistic-Conventional.

Skills: Operation and Control; Quality Control Analysis; Operation Monitoring; Science; Management of Personnel Resources; Troubleshooting; Writing; Judgment and Decision Making.

Work Environment: More often outdoors than indoors; standing; noise; very hot or cold; bright or inadequate lighting; contaminants; cramped work space; high places; hazardous equipment.

Job Specialization: Transportation Vehicle, Equipment, and Systems Inspectors, Except Aviation

Inspect and monitor transportation equipment, vehicles, or systems to ensure compliance with regulations and safety standards. Conduct vehicle or transportation equipment tests, using diagnostic equipment. Investigate

and make recommendations on carrier requests for waiver of federal standards. Prepare reports on investigations or inspections and actions taken. Issue notices and recommend corrective actions when infractions or problems are found. Investigate incidents or violations such as delays, accidents, and equipment failures. Investigate complaints regarding safety violations. Inspect repairs to transportation vehicles and equipment to ensure that repair work was performed properly. Examine transportation vehicles, equipment, or systems to detect damage, wear, or malfunction. Inspect vehicles and other equipment for evidence of abuse, damage, or mechanical malfunction. Examine carrier operating rules, employee qualification guidelines, and carrier training and testing programs for compliance with regulations or safety standards. Inspect vehicles or equipment to ensure compliance with rules, standards, or regulations.

Related Knowledge/Courses: Mechanical Devices; Transportation; Public Safety and Security; Engineering and Technology; Administration and Management; Physics.

Personality Types: Realistic-Conventional-Investigative.

Skills: Equipment Maintenance; Repairing; Troubleshooting; Science; Operation and Control; Quality Control Analysis; Operation Monitoring; Equipment Selection.

Work Environment: Outdoors; standing; walking and running; using hands; bending or twisting the body; repetitive motions; noise; very hot or cold; bright or inadequate lighting; contaminants; cramped work space; hazardous equipment; minor burns, cuts, bites, or stings.

Transportation, Storage, and Distribution Managers

❋ Average Annual Earnings (All): $80,860

❋ Average Annual Earnings (Recent Veterans): $48,020

❋ Earnings Growth Potential: High (40.9%)

❋ Growth: 10.0%

❋ Annual Job Openings: 3,370

❋ Veteran Employment by Sector: For-Profit, 44.2%; Nonprofit, 2.2%; Government, 53.1%; Self-Employed, 0.5%.

Considerations for Job Outlook: In courier services, a small decrease is expected as better technology and routing increase efficiency and decrease the demand for transportation workers and managers in this industry.

Plan, direct, or coordinate transportation, storage, or distribution activities in accordance with organizational policies and applicable government laws or regulations. For task data, see Job Specializations.

Related Military Specialization: Aircraft Loadmaster Manager. **Average Educational Level of Vets:** High school diploma or equivalent. **Usual Educational Requirement:** High school diploma or equivalent. **Relevant Educational Programs:** Aeronautics/Aviation/Aerospace Science and Technology, General; Aviation/Airway Management and Operations; Business Administration and Management, General; Business/Commerce, General; Logistics, Materials, and Supply Chain Management; Public Administration; Transportation/Mobility Management. **Work Experience Needed:** More than 5 years. **On-the-Job Training Needed:** None. **Certification/Licensure:** None.

Key Career Cluster: 04 Business, Management, and Administration. **Key Career Pathway:** 4.1 Management. **Top Industries for Vets:** National Security and International Affairs; Hardware, Plumbing and Heating Equipment, and Supplies Merchant Wholesalers; Furniture and Home Furnishings Stores; Warehousing and Storage; Truck Transportation.

Job Specialization: Logistics Managers

Plan, direct, or coordinate purchasing, warehousing, distribution, forecasting, customer service, or planning services. Manage logistics personnel and logistics systems and direct daily operations. Train shipping department personnel in roles or responsibilities regarding global logistics strategies. Maintain metrics, reports, process documentation, customer service logs, or training or safety records. Implement specific customer requirements, such as internal reporting or customized transportation metrics. Resolve problems concerning transportation, logistics systems, imports or exports, or customer issues. Develop risk management programs to ensure continuity of supply in emergency scenarios. Plan or implement improvements to internal or external logistics systems or processes. Recommend optimal transportation modes, routing, equipment, or frequency. Participate in carrier management processes, such as selection, qualification, or performance evaluation. Negotiate transportation rates or services. Monitor product import or export processes to ensure compliance with regulatory or legal requirements. Establish or monitor specific supply chain-based performance measurement systems. Ensure carrier compliance with company policies or procedures for product transit or delivery. Direct distribution center operation to ensure achievement of cost, productivity, accuracy, or timeliness objectives. Create policies or procedures for logistics activities. Collaborate with other departments to integrate logistics with business systems or processes, such as customer sales, order management, accounting, or shipping. Analyze the financial impact of proposed logistics changes, such as routing, shipping modes, product volumes or mixes, or carriers. Supervise the work of logistics specialists, planners, or schedulers. Plan or implement material flow management systems to meet production requirements. Direct inbound or outbound logistics operations, such as transportation or warehouse activities, safety performance, or logistics quality management.

Related Knowledge/Courses: Transportation; Production and Processing; Geography; Administration and Management; Economics and Accounting; Personnel and Human Resources.

Personality Types: Enterprising-Conventional.

Skills: Management of Financial Resources; Management of Material Resources; Management of Personnel Resources; Negotiation; Systems Evaluation; Time Management; Monitoring; Active Learning.

Work Environment: Indoors; sitting.

Job Specialization: Storage and Distribution Managers

Plan, direct, and coordinate the storage and distribution operations within organizations or the activities of organizations that are engaged in storing and distributing materials and products. Supervise the activities of workers engaged in receiving, storing, testing, and shipping products or materials. Plan, develop, and implement warehouse safety and security programs and activities. Review invoices, work orders, consumption reports, and demand forecasts to estimate peak delivery periods and to issue work assignments. Schedule and monitor air or surface pickup, delivery, or distribution of products or materials. Interview, select, and train warehouse and supervisory personnel. Confer with department heads to coordinate warehouse activities, such as production, sales, records control, and purchasing. Respond to customers' or shippers' questions and complaints regarding storage and distribution services. Inspect physical conditions of warehouses, vehicle fleets and equipment, and order testing, maintenance, repair, or replacement as necessary. Develop and document standard and emergency operating procedures for receiving, handling, storing, shipping, or salvaging products or materials. Examine products or materials to estimate quantities or weight and type of container required for storage or transport. Issue shipping instructions and provide routing information to ensure that delivery times and locations are coordinated. Negotiate with carriers, warehouse operators and insurance company representatives for services and preferential rates. Examine invoices and shipping manifests for conformity to tariff and customs regulations. Prepare and manage departmental budgets. Prepare or direct preparation of correspondence, reports, and operations, maintenance, and safety manuals. Arrange for necessary shipping documentation, and contact customs officials to effect release of shipments. Advise sales and billing departments of transportation charges for customers' accounts. Evaluate freight costs and the inventory costs associated with transit times to ensure that costs are appropriate. Participate in setting transportation and service rates.

Related Knowledge/Courses: Transportation; Personnel and Human Resources; Production and Processing; Administration and Management; Economics and Accounting; Psychology.

Personality Types: Enterprising-Conventional.

Skills: Management of Financial Resources; Management of Material Resources; Operations Analysis; Management of Personnel Resources; Negotiation; Coordination; Operation and Control; Systems Evaluation.

Work Environment: Indoors; standing.

Job Specialization: Transportation Managers

Plan, direct, and coordinate the transportation operations within an organization or the activities of organizations that provide transportation services. Analyze expenditures and other financial information to develop plans, policies, and budgets for increasing profits and improving services. Set operations policies and standards, including determination of safety procedures for the handling of dangerous goods. Plan, organize, and manage the work of subordinate staff to ensure that the work is accomplished in a manner consistent with organizational requirements. Negotiate and authorize contracts with equipment and materials suppliers, and monitor contract fulfillment. Collaborate with other managers and staff members to formulate and implement policies, procedures, goals, and objectives. Monitor spending to ensure that expenses are consistent with approved budgets. Supervise workers assigning tariff classifications and preparing billing. Promote safe work activities by conducting safety audits, attending company safety meetings, and meeting with individual staff members. Direct investigations to verify and resolve customer or shipper complaints. Direct procurement processes including equipment research and testing, vendor contracts, and requisitions approval. Recommend or authorize capital expenditures for acquisition of new equipment or property to increase efficiency and services of operations department. Monitor operations to ensure that staff members comply with administrative policies and procedures, safety rules, union contracts, and government regulations. Direct activities related to dispatching, routing, and tracking transportation vehicles such as aircraft and railroad cars. Direct and coordinate, through subordinates, activities of operations department to obtain use of equipment, facilities, and human resources. Conduct employee training sessions on subjects such as hazardous material handling, employee orientation, quality improvement, and computer use. Prepare management recommendations, such as proposed fee and tariff increases or schedule changes. Implement schedule and policy changes.

Related Knowledge/Courses: Transportation; Geography; Production and Processing; Personnel and Human Resources; Administration and Management; Economics and Accounting.

Personality Types: Enterprising-Conventional.

Skills: Management of Financial Resources; Systems Evaluation; Negotiation; Systems Analysis; Social Perceptiveness; Management of Material Resources; Management of Personnel Resources; Operations Analysis.

Work Environment: Indoors; sitting.

Veterinary Technologists and Technicians

* Average Annual Earnings (All): $30,140

* Average Annual Earnings (Recent Veterans): $30,560

* Earnings Growth Potential: Low (30.7%)

* Growth: 52.0%

* Annual Job Openings: 5,570

* Veteran Employment by Sector: For-Profit, 54.5%; Nonprofit, 12.2%; Government, 32.7%; Self-Employed, 0.6%.

Considerations for Job Outlook: Overall job opportunities for veterinary technologists and technicians are expected to be excellent, particularly in rural areas. The number of veterinary technology programs has been growing, but rapid employment growth means that the number of positions available will continue to outpace the number of new graduates. Workers leaving the occupation will also result in job openings.

Perform medical tests in a laboratory environment for use in the treatment and diagnosis of diseases in animals. Observe the behavior and condition of animals, and monitor their clinical symptoms. Maintain controlled drug inventory and related log books. Administer anesthesia to animals, under the direction of a veterinarian, and monitor animals' responses to anesthetics so that dosages can be adjusted. Care for and monitor the condition of animals recovering from surgery. Perform laboratory tests on blood, urine, and feces, such as urinalyses and blood counts, to assist in the diagnosis and treatment of animal health problems. Administer emergency first aid, such as performing emergency resuscitation or other life-saving procedures. Prepare and administer medications, vaccines, serums, and treatments, as prescribed by veterinarians. Fill prescriptions, measuring medications and labeling containers. Collect, prepare, and label samples for laboratory testing, culture, or microscopic examination. Prepare treatment rooms for surgery. Take and develop diagnostic radiographs, using X-ray equipment. Clean kennels, animal holding areas, surgery suites, examination rooms, and animal loading/unloading facilities to control the spread of disease. Take animals into treatment areas, and assist with physical examinations by performing such duties as obtaining temperature, pulse, and respiration data. Provide veterinarians with the correct equipment and instruments, as needed. Clean and sterilize instruments, equipment, and materials. Maintain laboratory, research, and treatment records, as well as inventories of pharmaceuticals, equipment, and supplies. Prepare animals for surgery, performing such tasks as shaving surgical areas. Give enemas and perform catheterizations, ear flushes, intravenous feedings, and gavages. Maintain instruments, equipment, and machinery to ensure proper working condition. Provide assistance with animal euthanasia and the disposal of remains. Supervise and train veterinary students and other staff members.

Related Military Specialization: Animal Care Specialist. **Average Educational Level of Vets:** One or more years of college, no degree. **Usual Educational Requirement:** Associate degree. **Relevant Educational Program:** Veterinary/Animal Health Technology/Technician and Veterinary Assistant. **Related Knowledge/Courses:** Biology; Medicine and Dentistry; Chemistry; Customer and Personal Service; Mathematics; Psychology. **Work Experience Needed:** None. **On-the-Job Training Needed:** None. **Certification/Licensure:** Licensure, registration, or certification in most states.

Personality Types: Realistic-Investigative. **Key Career Cluster:** 01 Agriculture, Food, and Natural Resources. **Key Career Pathway:** 1.3 Animal Systems. **Top Industries for Vets:** Hospitals; Pharmacies and Drug Stores; National Security and International Affairs; Veterinary Services; Other Health Care Services.

Skills: Science; Equipment Maintenance; Operation and Control; Equipment Selection; Quality Control Analysis; Service Orientation; Troubleshooting; Critical Thinking.

Work Environment: Indoors; standing; walking and running; using hands; bending or twisting the body; repetitive motions; noise; contaminants; exposed to radiation; exposed to disease or infections; minor burns, cuts, bites, or stings.

Water and Wastewater Treatment Plant and System Operators

* ❀ Average Annual Earnings (All): $41,780

* ❀ Average Annual Earnings (Recent Veterans): $37,540

* ❀ Earnings Growth Potential: Medium (39.2%)

* ❀ Growth: 11.6%

* ❀ Annual Job Openings: 4,150

* ❀ Veteran Employment by Sector: For-Profit, 21.4%; Nonprofit, 1.8%; Government, 76.8%; Self-Employed, 0.0%.

Considerations for Job Outlook: Job prospects for water and wastewater treatment plant and system operators should be excellent. New jobs will be created when existing plants expand and new plants are built. Applicants will also have many job opportunities because many current operators are expected to retire. In addition, the number of applicants for these positions is normally low, primarily because of the physically demanding and unappealing nature of some of the work. Job prospects will be best for those with training or education in water or wastewater systems and good mechanical skills.

Operate or control an entire process or system of machines, often through the use of control boards, to transfer or treat water or wastewater. Add chemicals such as ammonia, chlorine, or lime to disinfect and deodorize water and other liquids. Operate and adjust controls on equipment to purify and clarify water, process or dispose of sewage, and generate power. Inspect equipment or monitor operating conditions, meters, and gauges to determine load requirements and detect malfunctions. Collect and test water and sewage samples, using test equipment and color-analysis standards. Record operational data, personnel attendance, or meter and gauge readings on specified forms. Maintain, repair, and lubricate equipment, using hand tools and power tools. Clean and maintain tanks and filter beds, using hand tools and power tools. Direct and coordinate plant workers engaged in routine operations and maintenance activities.

Related Military Specializations: Utilitiesman; Water and Fuel Systems Maintenance Apprentice; Water and Fuel Systems Maintenance Helper; Water and Fuel Systems Maintenance Journeyman; Water Support Technician; Water Treatment and Plumbing Systems Specialist; Water Treatment Specialist. **Average Educational Level of Vets:** High school diploma or equivalent. **Usual Educational Requirement:** High school diploma or equivalent. **Relevant Educational Program:** Water Quality and Wastewater Treatment Management and Recycling Technology/Technician. **Related Knowledge/Courses:** Physics; Building and Construction; Mechanical Devices; Biology; Chemistry; Engineering and Technology. **Work Experience Needed:** None. **On-the-Job Training Needed:** Long-term on-the-job training. **Certification/Licensure:** Licensure.

Personality Types: Realistic-Conventional. **Key Career Cluster:** 01 Agriculture, Food, and Natural Resources. **Key Career Pathway:** 1.6 Environmental Service Systems. **Top Industries for Vets:** Sewage Treatment Facilities; Water, Steam, Air Conditioning, and Irrigation Systems; National Security and International Affairs; Waste Management and Remediation Services; Coating, Engraving, Heat Treating and Allied Activities.

Skills: Repairing; Equipment Maintenance; Operation and Control; Troubleshooting;

Equipment Selection; Operation Monitoring; Quality Control Analysis; Systems Evaluation.

Work Environment: Outdoors; standing; climbing; walking and running; kneeling, crouching, stooping, or crawling; using hands; bending or twisting the body; repetitive motions; noise; very hot or cold; bright or inadequate lighting; contaminants; cramped work space; exposed to disease or infections; hazardous conditions; hazardous equipment; minor burns, cuts, bites, or stings.

Welders, Cutters, Solderers, and Brazers

- ❈ Average Annual Earnings (All): $35,920

- ❈ Average Annual Earnings (Recent Veterans): $32,190

- ❈ Earnings Growth Potential: Low (31.8%)

- ❈ Growth: 15.0%

- ❈ Annual Job Openings: 14,070

- ❈ Veteran Employment by Sector: For-Profit, 82.9%; Nonprofit, 0.7%; Government, 14.2%; Self-Employed, 2.2%.

Considerations for Job Outlook: Overall job prospects will vary by skill level. Job prospects should be good for welders trained in the latest technologies. Welding schools report that graduates have little difficulty finding work, and many welding employers report difficulty finding properly skilled welders. However, welders who do not have up-to-date training may face competition for jobs. For all welders, job prospects should be better for those willing to relocate.

Use hand-welding, flame-cutting, hand soldering, or brazing equipment to weld or join metal components or to fill holes, indentations, or seams of fabricated metal products. For task data, see Job Specializations.

Related Military Specializations: Advanced Welder; Aeronautical Welder; Aircraft Metals Technology Apprentice; Aircraft Metals Technology Craftsman; Aircraft Metals Technology Helper; Aircraft Metals Technology Journeyman; Aircraft Welder; General Maintenance Welder; Metal Worker; Metalworking Apprentice; Nuclear Power Plant Components Welder; Submarine Nuclear Propulsion Plant Emergency Welder. **Average Educational Level of Vets:** High school diploma or equivalent. **Usual Educational Requirement:** High school diploma or equivalent. **Relevant Educational Programs:** Welding Engineering Technology/Technician; Welding Technology/Welder. **Work Experience Needed:** Less than 1 year. **On-the-Job Training Needed:** Moderate-term on-the-job training. **Certification/Licensure:** Voluntary certification for some specializations.

Key Career Cluster: 13 Manufacturing. **Key Career Pathway:** 13.1 Production. **Top Industries for Vets:** Construction; National Security and International Affairs; Commercial and Industrial Machinery and Equipment Repair and Maintenance; Structural Metals, and Boiler, Tank, and Shipping Containers; Machinery, Not Elsewhere Classified.

Job Specialization: Solderers and Brazers

Braze or solder together components to assemble fabricated metal parts with soldering iron, torch, or welding machine and flux. Melt and apply solder along adjoining edges of workpieces to solder joints, using soldering irons, gas torches, or electric-ultrasonic equipment. Heat soldering irons or workpieces to specified temperatures for soldering, using gas flames or electric current. Examine seams for defects, and rework defective joints or broken parts. Melt and separate brazed or soldered joints to remove and straighten damaged or misaligned components, using hand torches, irons, or furnaces. Melt and apply solder to fill holes, indentations, and seams of fabricated metal products, using soldering equipment. Clean workpieces to remove dirt and excess acid, using chemical solutions, files, wire brushes, or grinders. Guide torches and rods along joints of workpieces to heat them to brazing temperature, melt braze alloys, and bond workpieces together. Adjust electric current and timing cycles of resistance welding machines to heat metals to bonding temperature. Turn valves to start flow of gases, and light flames and adjust valves to obtain desired colors and sizes of flames. Clean equipment parts, such as tips of soldering irons, using chemical solutions or cleaning compounds. Brush flux onto joints of workpieces or dip braze rods into flux, to prevent oxidation of metal. Remove workpieces from fixtures, using tongs, and cool workpieces, using air or water. Align and clamp workpieces together, using rules, squares, or hand tools, or position items in fixtures, jigs, or vises. Sweat together workpieces coated with solder. Smooth soldered areas with alternate strokes of paddles and torches, leaving soldered sections slightly higher than surrounding areas for later filing. Remove workpieces from molten solder and hold parts together until color indicates that solder has set. Select torch tips, flux, and brazing alloys from data charts or work orders. Turn dials to set intensity and duration of ultrasonic impulses, according to work order specifications.

Related Knowledge/Courses: Production and Processing; Mechanical Devices.

Personality Types: Realistic.

Skills: Equipment Maintenance; Repairing; Equipment Selection; Troubleshooting; Quality Control Analysis; Operation Monitoring.

Work Environment: Indoors; more often sitting than standing; using hands; repetitive motions;

noise; contaminants; minor burns, cuts, bites, or stings.

Job Specialization: Welders, Cutters, and Welder Fitters

Use hand-welding or flame-cutting equipment to weld or join metal components or to fill holes, indentations, or seams of fabricated metal products. Operate safety equipment, and use safe work habits. Weld components in flat, vertical, or overhead positions. Ignite torches or start power supplies and strike arcs by touching electrodes to metals being welded, completing electrical circuits. Clamp, hold, tack-weld, heat-bend, grind, and/or bolt component parts to obtain required configurations and positions for welding. Detect faulty operation of equipment and/or defective materials, and notify supervisors. Operate manual or semi-automatic welding equipment to fuse metal segments, using processes such as gas tungsten arc, gas metal arc, flux-cored arc, plasma arc, shielded metal arc, resistance welding, and submerged arc welding. Monitor the fitting, burning, and welding processes to avoid overheating of parts or warping, shrinking, distortion, or expansion of material. Examine workpieces for defects, and measure workpieces with straightedges or templates to ensure conformance with specifications. Recognize, set up, and operate hand and power tools common to the welding trade, such as shielded metal arc and gas metal arc welding equipment. Lay out, position, align, and secure parts and assemblies prior to assembly, using straightedges, combination squares, calipers, and rulers. Chip or grind off excess weld, slag, or spatter, using hand scrapers or power chippers, portable grinders, or arc-cutting equipment. Analyze engineering drawings, blueprints, specifications, sketches, work orders, and material safety data sheets to plan layout, assembly, and welding operations. Connect and turn regulator valves to activate and adjust gas flow and pressure so that desired flames are obtained. Weld separately or in combination, using aluminum, stainless steel, cast iron, and other alloys. Mark and/or tag material with proper job number, piece marks, and other identifying marks as required. Determine required equipment and welding methods, applying knowledge of metallurgy, geometry, and welding techniques.

Related Knowledge/Courses: Building and Construction; Mechanical Devices; Design; Engineering and Technology.

Personality Types: Realistic-Conventional.

Skills: Repairing; Operation and Control; Troubleshooting; Equipment Maintenance; Equipment Selection; Operation Monitoring; Quality Control Analysis; Installation.

Work Environment: Standing; using hands; bending or twisting the body; repetitive motions; noise; very hot or cold; bright or inadequate lighting; contaminants; hazardous equipment; minor burns, cuts, bites, or stings.

Wholesale and Retail Buyers, Except Farm Products

- ✷ Average Annual Earnings (All): $50,490
- ✷ Average Annual Earnings (Recent Veterans): $38,200
- ✷ Earnings Growth Potential: High (41.4%)
- ✷ Growth: 9.0%
- ✷ Annual Job Openings: 4,170
- ✷ Veteran Employment by Sector: For-Profit, 94.7%; Nonprofit, 2.2%; Government, 0.8%; Self-Employed, 2.3%.

Considerations for Job Outlook: Growth will be driven largely by the performance of the wholesale and retail industries. Continued employment decreases in manufacturing, as well as decreases in federal government, which includes defense purchasing, are expected. However, growth is expected for this occupation in firms that offer health-care and computer systems design and related services.

Buy merchandise or commodities, other than farm products, for resale to consumers at the wholesale or retail level, including both durable and nondurable goods. Use computers to organize and locate inventory, and operate spreadsheet and word processing software. Negotiate prices, discount terms, and transportation arrangements for merchandise. Manage the department for which they buy. Confer with sales and purchasing personnel to obtain information about customer needs and preferences. Examine, select, order, and purchase at the most favorable price merchandise consistent with quality, quantity, specification requirements, and other factors. Analyze and monitor sales records, trends, and economic conditions to anticipate consumer buying patterns and determine what the company will sell and how much inventory is needed. Set or recommend mark-up rates, mark-down rates, and selling prices for merchandise. Authorize payment of invoices or return of merchandise. Interview and work closely with vendors to obtain and develop desired products. Conduct staff meetings with sales personnel to introduce new merchandise. Inspect merchandise or products to determine value or yield. Monitor competitors' sales activities by following their advertisements in newspapers and other media. Train and supervise sales and clerical staff. Consult with store or merchandise managers about budget and goods to be purchased. Provide clerks with information to print on price tags, such as price, mark-ups or mark-downs, manufacturer number, season code, and style number. Determine which products should be featured in advertising, the advertising medium to be used, and when the ads should be run.

Related Military Specializations: None. **Average Educational Level of Vets:** One or more years of college, no degree. **Usual Educational Requirement:** High school diploma or equivalent. **Relevant Educational Programs:** Apparel and Accessories Marketing Operations; Apparel and Textile Marketing Management; Fashion Merchandising; General Merchandising, Sales, and Related Marketing Operations, Other; Merchandising and Buying Operations; Sales, Distribution, and Marketing Operations, General; Wine Steward/Sommelier. **Related Knowledge/Courses:** Production and Processing; Sales and Marketing; Economics and Accounting; Administration and Management; Building and Construction; Customer and Personal Service. **Work Experience Needed:** None. **On-the-Job Training Needed:** Long-term on-the-job training. **Certification/Licensure:** Licensure for some specializations.

Personality Types: Enterprising-Conventional. **Key Career Cluster:** 14 Marketing, Sales, and Service. **Key Career Pathway:** 14.2 Professional Sales and Marketing. **Top Industries for Vets:** Groceries and Related Products Merchant Wholesalers; Automobile Dealers; Department and Discount Stores; Motor Vehicles, Parts and Supplies Merchant Wholesalers; Shoe Stores.

Skills: Management of Financial Resources; Management of Material Resources; Negotiation; Persuasion; Systems Evaluation; Mathematics; Operations Analysis; Monitoring.

Work Environment: Indoors; sitting.

APPENDIX

Definitions of Skills and Knowledge/ Courses

In the Part III job descriptions, you may be unfamiliar with some of the terms that are used for skills and for related knowledge/courses. They are derived from the O*NET database. Rather than define these terms repeatedly in Part III, I put the definitions here in the appendix.

Definitions of Skills in Job Descriptions	
Skill Name	Definition
Active Learning	Working with new material or information to grasp its implications.
Active Listening	Listening to what other people are saying and asking questions as appropriate.
Complex Problem Solving	Identifying complex problems, reviewing the options, and implementing solutions.
Coordination	Adjusting actions in relation to others' actions.
Critical Thinking	Using logic and analysis to identify the strengths and weaknesses of different approaches.
Equipment Maintenance	Performing routine maintenance and determining when and what kind of maintenance is needed.
Equipment Selection	Determining the kind of tools and equipment needed to do a job.
Installation	Installing equipment, machines, wiring, or programs to meet specifications.

(continued)

(continued)

Definitions of Skills in Job Descriptions

Skill Name	Definition
Instructing	Teaching others how to do something.
Judgment and Decision Making	Weighing the relative costs and benefits of a potential action.
Learning Strategies	Using multiple approaches when learning or teaching new things.
Management of Financial Resources	Determining how money will be spent to get the work done and accounting for these expenditures.
Management of Material Resources	Obtaining and seeing to the appropriate use of equipment, facilities, and materials needed to do certain work.
Management of Personnel Resources	Motivating, developing, and directing people as they work; identifying the best people for the job.
Mathematics	Using mathematics to solve problems.
Monitoring	Assessing how well one is doing when learning or doing something.
Negotiation	Bringing others together and trying to reconcile differences.
Operation and Control	Controlling operations of equipment or systems.
Operation Monitoring	Watching gauges, dials, or other indicators to make sure a machine is working properly.
Operations Analysis	Analyzing needs and product requirements to create a design.
Persuasion	Persuading others to approach things differently.
Programming	Writing computer programs for various purposes.
Quality Control Analysis	Evaluating the quality or performance of products, services, or processes.
Reading Comprehension	Understanding written sentences and paragraphs in work-related documents.
Repairing	Repairing machines or systems, using the needed tools.
Science	Using scientific methods to solve problems.
Service Orientation	Actively looking for ways to help people.

Definitions of Skills in Job Descriptions

Skill Name	Definition
Social Perceptiveness	Being aware of others' reactions and understanding why they react the way they do.
Speaking	Talking to others to effectively convey information.
Systems Analysis	Determining how a system should work and how changes will affect outcomes.
Systems Evaluation	Looking at many indicators of system performance and taking into account their accuracy.
Technology Design	Generating or adapting equipment and technology to serve user needs.
Time Management	Managing one's own time and the time of others.
Troubleshooting	Determining what is causing an operating error and deciding what to do about it.
Writing	Communicating effectively with others in writing as indicated by the needs of the audience.

Definitions of Knowledge/Courses in Job Descriptions

Knowledge/Course Name	Definition
Administration and Management	Knowledge of principles and processes involved in business and organizational planning, coordination, and execution. This includes strategic planning, resource allocation, manpower modeling, leadership techniques, and production methods.
Biology	Knowledge of plant and animal living tissue, cells, organisms, and entities, including their functions, interdependencies, and interactions with each other and the environment.
Building and Construction	Knowledge of materials, methods, and the appropriate tools to construct objects, structures, and buildings.
Chemistry	Knowledge of the composition, structure, and properties of substances and of the chemical processes and transformations that they undergo. This includes uses of chemicals and their interactions, danger signs, production techniques, and disposal methods.

(continued)

(continued)

Definitions of Knowledge/Courses in Job Descriptions

Knowledge/Course Name	Definition
Clerical Studies	Knowledge of administrative and clerical procedures and systems such as word-processing systems, filing and records management systems, stenography and transcription, forms, design principles, and other office procedures and terminology.
Communications and Media	Knowledge of media production, communication, and dissemination techniques and methods, including alternative ways to inform and entertain via written, oral, and visual media.
Computers and Electronics	Knowledge of electric circuit boards, processors, chips, and computer hardware and software, including applications and programming.
Customer and Personal Service	Knowledge of principles and processes for providing customer and personal services, including needs assessment techniques, quality service standards, alternative delivery systems, and customer satisfaction evaluation techniques.
Design	Knowledge of design techniques, principles, tools, and instruments involved in the production and use of precision technical plans, blueprints, drawings, and models.
Economics and Accounting	Knowledge of economic and accounting principles and practices, the financial markets, banking, and the analysis and reporting of financial data.
Education and Training	Knowledge of instructional methods and training techniques, including curriculum design principles, learning theory, group and individual teaching techniques, design of individual development plans, and test design principles.
Engineering and Technology	Knowledge of equipment, tools, and mechanical devices and their uses to produce motion, light, power, technology, and other applications.
English Language	Knowledge of the structure and content of the English language, including the meaning and spelling of words, rules of composition, and grammar.
Fine Arts	Knowledge of theory and techniques required to produce, compose, and perform works of music, dance, visual arts, drama, and sculpture.

Definitions of Knowledge/Courses in Job Descriptions

Knowledge/Course Name	Definition
Food Production	Knowledge of techniques and equipment for planting, growing, and harvesting of food for consumption, including crop rotation methods, animal husbandry, and food storage/handling techniques.
Foreign Language	Knowledge of the structure and content of a foreign (non-English) language, including the meaning and spelling of words, rules of composition and grammar, and pronunciation.
Geography	Knowledge of various methods for describing the location and distribution of land, sea, and air masses, including their physical locations, relationships, and characteristics.
History and Archeology	Knowledge of past historical events and their causes, indicators, and impact on particular civilizations and cultures.
Law and Government	Knowledge of laws, legal codes, court procedures, precedents, government regulations, executive orders, agency rules, and the democratic political process.
Mathematics	Knowledge of numbers and their operations and interrelationships, including arithmetic, algebra, geometry, calculus, and statistics and their applications.
Mechanical Devices	Knowledge of machines and tools, including their designs, uses, benefits, repair, and maintenance.
Medicine and Dentistry	Knowledge of the information and techniques needed to diagnose and treat injuries, diseases, and deformities. This includes symptoms, treatment alternatives, drug properties and interactions, and preventive health-care measures.
Personnel and Human Resources	Knowledge of policies and practices involved in personnel/human resource functions. This includes recruitment, selection, training, and promotion regulations and procedures; compensation and benefits packages; labor relations and negotiation strategies; and personnel information systems.
Philosophy and Theology	Knowledge of different philosophical systems and religions, including their basic principles, values, ethics, ways of thinking, customs, and practices and their impact on human culture.

(continued)

(continued)

Definitions of Knowledge/Courses in Job Descriptions

Knowledge/Course Name	Definition
Physics	Knowledge and prediction of physical principles, laws, and applications, including air, water, material dynamics, light, atomic principles, heat, electric theory, earth formations, and meteorological and related natural phenomena.
Production and Processing	Knowledge of inputs, outputs, raw materials, waste, quality control, costs, and techniques for maximizing the manufacture and distribution of goods.
Psychology	Knowledge of human behavior and performance, mental processes, psychological research methods, and the assessment and treatment of behavioral and affective disorders.
Public Safety and Security	Knowledge of weaponry; public safety; security operations, rules, regulations, precautions, and prevention; and the protection of people, data, and property.
Sales and Marketing	Knowledge of principles and methods involved in showing, promoting, and selling products or services. This includes marketing strategies and tactics, product demonstration and sales techniques, and sales control systems.
Sociology and Anthropology	Knowledge of group behavior and dynamics; societal trends and influences; and cultures and their history, migrations, ethnicity, and origins.
Telecommunications	Knowledge of transmission, broadcasting, switching, control, and operation of telecommunications systems.
Therapy and Counseling	Knowledge of information and techniques needed to rehabilitate physical and mental ailments and to provide career guidance, including alternative treatments, rehabilitation equipment and its proper use, and methods to evaluate treatment effects.
Transportation	Knowledge of principles and methods for moving people or goods by air, rail, sea, or road, including their relative costs, advantages, and limitations.

Index

D

J